Contents

3 *The Study of School Administration*   **50**

Contemporary School Administration

An Introduction

SECOND EDITION

Theodore J. Kowalski
University of Dayton

Boston • New York • San Francisco
Mexico City • Montreal • Toronto • London • Madrid • Munich • Paris
Hong Kong • Singapore • Tokyo • Cape Town • Sydney

Series Editor: *Arnis E. Burvikovs*
Editorial Assistant: *Matthew Forster*
Marketing Manager: *Tara Whorf*
Editorial-Production Administrator: *Annette Joseph*
Editorial-Production Coordinator: *Holly Crawford*
Editorial-Production Service: *Lynda Griffiths, TKM Productions*
Composition Buyer: *Linda Cox*
Electronic Composition: *Publishers' Design and Production Services, Inc.*
Manufacturing Buyer: *JoAnne Sweeney*
Cover Administrator: *Kristina Mose-Libon*
Cover Designer: *Jenny Hart*

For related titles and support materials, visit our online catalog at www.ablongman.com

Between the time Website information is gathered and then published, it is not unusual for some sites to have closed. Also, the transcription of URLs can result in unintended typographical errors. The publisher would appreciate notification where these occur so that they may be corrected in subsequent editions.

Library of Congress Cataloging-in-Publication Data

Kowalski, Theodore J.
    Contemporary school administration : an introduction / Theodore J. Kowalski.—
2nd ed.
      p. cm.
    Includes bibliographical references and indexes.
    ISBN 0-205-34792-4
    1. School management and organization—United States.   2. Educational leadership—United States.   3. Education—Social aspects—United States.   I. Title.

LB2805 .K635 2003
371.2'00973—dc21
                                            2002019621

Printed in the United States of America

10 9 8 7 6 5 4 3 2 1   07 06 05 04 03 02

6   *Social, Political, and Historical Context of Private Education*   **123**

7   *Organizational Dimensions of Schools*   **142**

8   *The Roles of School in Society*   **165**

9   *Administrative Strategies and Styles*   **181**

11   *Important Aspects of Practice*   **224**

12   *Demands for School Reform*   **247**

Preface

Since the first edition of this book was published, many changes have occurred in education and school administration. Both state deregulation and district decentralization have become primary reform strategies. Faculties at dozens of universities have implemented programmatic changes, many parts of the country have experienced critical shortages of administrative applicants, and most states have taken action to strengthen licensing requirements. In addition, the quest for meaningful school reform continues.

The primary goal of this second edition is to place the study and practice of school administration in a contemporary context. One of the book's unique features is the attention given to career considerations. For example, the first four chapters focus largely on career-related questions commonly asked by students in introductory courses or by students contemplating a career in school administration. The final chapter in the book provides a rationale and framework for developing an individual career plan.

Another special feature is a chapter on private schools. Three conditions suggest that this topic deserves more attention in administrator preparation programs. First, enrollments in private schools are increasing, and the prospect of vouchers and tax credits creates an environment in which these increases could accelerate dramatically. Second, collaboration between public and private schools is becoming more common. Thus, public school administrators benefit from a greater understanding of private education. Last, a growing number of school administration students intend to work in private schools.

Contemporary School Administration also emphasizes the contextual nature of practice in school administration. More specifically, trends affecting contemporary practice are identified and analyzed. Examples of these trends include population changes, the need for women and minorities to enter administration, and the changing nature of school reform initiatives.

Last, this current edition contains a considerable amount of new material. For example, Chapter 10 includes a major section on decision making and Chapter 11 contains a comprehensive section on communication. Other expanded material is found in Chapters 12, 13, and 14, which discuss school reform and school change.

Material found at the end of each chapter is designed to encourage introspection—that is, to help you consider how the chapter content relates to contemporary practice and to your personal needs and interests. This reflective process requires you to identify your personal frame of reference—your values, beliefs, needs, experiences, motivations, wants, and knowledge—and to interface them with the material you have read. By relating your personal frame of reference to the book's content, you will learn how to integrate new information and experiences into your evolving professional knowledge base.

I am especially grateful to four colleagues at the University of Dayton for their assistance and support. Two of them, Elizabeth Ann Pearn, my office assistant, and Father Charles Kanai, my doctoral assistant, helped me with the technical aspects of preparing the manuscript. The other two, Thomas J. Lasley, Dean of the School of Education, and Father Joseph D. Massucci, Chair of the Department of Educational Leadership, provided encouragement and a supportive environment. Thank you also to the following reviewers of this second edition: Jay A. Heath, University of South Dakota; Susan J. Rippberger, University of Texas at El Paso; and Helen C. Sobehart, Duquesne University.

Introduction

Purposes of the Book

- This book addresses career-related questions commonly asked by students who are beginning the study of school administration. These questions pertain to various specializations within administration, the career patterns of administrators, academic requirements for entering practice, state licensing, and conditions of practice.
- Material is provided to help you understand how districts and schools are controlled, governed, and organized. This knowledge provides an essential foundation for your subsequent courses and clinical experiences.
- As an introductory text, this book gives you a broad overview of school administration as a specialized field of study and as an applied field of professional practice. You are introduced to basic concepts and subject matter that you will study in greater depth as you advance in your graduate studies.
- Special attention is given to describing the social, political, and economic contexts of contemporary practice. This information is intended to help you understand the similarities and differences between practice in school administration and practice in other professions.

Special Features

- **A Broad Perspective of Administration**
  Administration is a process that entails both leadership and management. Each of these areas is deemed critical to effective practice, and each function is described in detail.

- **Career Planning**
  Special attention is given to integrating personal and professional knowledge in relation to career planning. The first four chapters include essential information about careers, and the entire last chapter is devoted to career planning.

- **Reflective Practice**
  Practitioners in all professions utilize reflection as a means of professional growth. The process entails the integration of knowledge with experience. A section called *Implications for Practice* found after the content of each chapter encourages you to consider how the material relates to contemporary condi-

tions in education. In addition, the process of reflection is described in detail in Chapter 10.

- **Discussion Questions**

  The questions provided at the end of each chapter may be used to test your comprehension of the content. Often, instructors use them to guide in-class discussion or as the basis for out-of-class assignments. You also can review them as a means of self-assessment.

- **Suggested Activities**

  Learning often is enhanced by application. Therefore, each chapter contains several suggested activities intended to apply chapter content. Typically, both group and individual activities are included.

- **Diversity**

  Issues of social, economic, and political diversity are central to contemporary practice. These topics are addressed from two perspectives: the effects on communities and schools as well as the effects on the school administration profession. Special consideration is given to the need to increase the representation of women and minorities in the profession.

- **Attention to Private Schools**

  There are at least two important reasons why all school administrators need to have a basic understanding of private schools. First, current reform initiatives are serving to increase interaction between public and private schools. Second, the number of school administration graduates entering practice in private schools is increasing. Chapter 6 is devoted to this topic.

1

Perspective of Educational Administration

Chapter Content

Defining Leadership, Management, and Administration
Evolution of School Administration
Contemporary Conditions
Implications for Practice

> *The greatest mistake you can make in life is to be continually fearing you will make one.*
>
> —Elbert Hubbard

Transitions to an age of information and global economy in the last quarter of the twentieth century revealed a basic truth about organizations: They either adapt effectively to changing needs and wants or they risk extinction. Increasingly, educational administrators are realizing that this fact pertains to all organizations, including the institutions in which they work. Political debates over vouchers, tuition tax credits, and charter schools, for example, exhibit that many people no longer accept the premise that schools are sufficiently effective to serve the real needs of society. Consequently, most policymakers continue to seek meaningful educational reform and effective administrators who are capable and willing to lead the process.

This first chapter addresses several foundational issues. The topics include distinctions between leadership and management, the organizational nature of districts and schools, the history of the profession of educational administration, and current societal conditions. Collectively, these issues provide a framework for further exploration into the profession of school administration.

Defining Leadership, Management, and Administration

Unfortunately, the literature on school administration does not contain uniform definitions of three key concepts: *administration*, *management*, and *leadership*. As a result, disparate meanings have contributed to two common problems: treating these terms as if they were synonymous (Yukl, 1989) and using the terms without actually defining them (Shields & Newton, 1994). In the context of school reform, for example, many educators have recently characterized leadership as a positive role and management as a negative role. This is indeed unfortunate, because an effective administrator usually must be both a leader and a manager. Historically, most principals and superintendents have been prepared to be good managers, but not necessarily prepared to be productive leaders. This condition became more troublesome in the 1980s as efforts to reform public education intensified. The popularity of school restructuring and cultural change strategies in particular brought to light the fact that many superintendents and principals had limited leadership skills.

In large measure, graduate students in educational administration find it difficult to separate management and leadership because they often self-define both roles. One professor, for instance, asked his students over a three-year period to define leadership; he received about 50 definitions that either focused on administrative practice, administrative theory, or historical perspectives (Glasman & Glasman, 1997). One way to distinguish between these two roles is to compare them on the basis of six criteria:

1. *Nature of the activities:* What do leaders and managers do?
2. *Purposes associated with influencing others:* Why do leaders and managers attempt to influence people?
3. *Creativity and innovation:* To what extent are leaders and managers expected to think independently?
4. *Administrative strategy:* To what extent do leaders and managers use different strategies?
5. *Attention to external forces:* How do leaders and managers view forces outside of their organizations?
6. *Flexibility:* To what extent are leaders and managers encouraged to adapt to changing conditions?

An important difference between management and leadership is the nature of the work. Management concentrates on making decisions about *how* things should be done; that is, work is directed toward controlling and using resources (Hanson, 1996). The primary activities of managers include worker supervision, material resource supervision, and conflict resolution—actions intended to sustain organizational efficiency (Orlosky, McCleary, Shapiro, & Webb, 1984). Leadership, on the other hand, focuses on making decisions about *what* should be done to improve an organization. Thus, responsibilities such as visioning, planning, and consensus building are central to this role. Both leadership and management functions are intended to influence people, but the purposes and methods for doing so differ. Consider the following definitions of leadership:

> Leadership is influencing people to follow in the achievement of a common goal. (Koontz & O'Donnell, 1959, p. 435)

> Leadership is the activity of influencing people to strive willingly for group objectives. (Terry, 1960, p. 493)

Although both definitions state that leadership involves influencing people, this objective does not separate this role from management. Rather, the key words are *common goals* and *group objectives*. Whereas management seeks to influence people so that they will achieve predetermined organizational objectives, leadership strives to influence people to create shared objectives and then attain them.

Expectations regarding creativity and innovation are not the same for managers and leaders. Managers are trained to apply standard procedures to ensure uniformity and efficiency; leaders are educated to think independently. In school reform, for example, principal-managers carry out ideas that have been developed by others and formalized as laws, policies, or regulations. For instance, the principal supervises teachers to ensure that the new language arts curriculum is being implemented. By comparison, principal-leaders generate new insights and innovative solutions, articulate them to others, and build consensus and support for them. Their behavior is both symbolic (reinforcing values and norms) and political (building coalitions to compete for scarce resources necessary for implementing key ideas) (Bolman & Deal, 1994).

Management is oriented toward failure-avoidance strategies. These strategies generally rely on using simple values, goals, and methods to achieve organizational efficiency. Leadership, by comparison, is oriented toward success-seeking strategies—a problem-solving and risk-taking orientation to administration (Bassett, 1970). School administrators often find it extremely difficult to use success-seeking strategies for two reasons: (1) their socialization as educators has influenced them to use failure-avoidance strategies and (2) the political and economic dimensions of their work provide little or no incentives for taking risks (Kowalski, 1999). Thus, functioning as a manager has been a more natural role for educators who become administrators.

Another distinction between leadership and management involves work orientation. Managers usually have internal orientations to work; that is, they concentrate on what goes on within the boundaries of districts and schools. Some superintendents and principals, for instance, rarely leave their offices or the buildings in which their offices are located. Leaders, by comparison, have both internal and external orientations. External orientations relate to keeping up to date on evolving societal circumstances that affect the mission and operations of schools. Such circumstances may include new laws, economic developments, political realignments, demographic changes, and social trends. Consequently, leaders are better prepared than managers to ascertain the need for change and to select appropriate change initiatives (Kowalski, 1999).

Management is skewed toward organizational uniformity and stability; consequently, managers tend not to be very flexible in making decisions. Rather, they are inclined to make consistent and highly predictable decisions, especially in the area of policy enforcement. Leaders have a different disposition; they are open to change and new information. They commonly adapt their behavior and work methods in response to new information, changing conditions, and unexpected obstacles. As a result, leaders are more willing and better prepared to deal with organizational change.

Although it is easy to characterize administration as including both management and leadership, actually being able to perform both functions is quite difficult. One reason is that fundamental values push administrators toward career orientations as either managers or leaders. Career-oriented managers and leaders, for example, have quite different views of the world and people. Abraham Zaleznik (1989) explained these differences: "Career-oriented managers are more likely to exhibit the effects of narcissism than leaders. While busily adapting to their environment, managers are narrowly engaged in maintaining their identity and self-esteem through others, whereas leaders have self-confidence growing out of the awareness of who they are and the visions that drive them to achieve" (p. 6). In addition, school administrators historically have functioned primarily as managers, and pressures to engage in leadership activities have threatened many superintendents and principals.

In summary, management and leadership are defined as separate functions in this book. And although they are separate, both roles are viewed as being integral to contemporary practice in administration. James Guthrie and Rodney Reed (1991) summarized this perspective: "School administrators must be both managers and leaders. As managers they must ensure that fiscal and human resources are used effectively in accomplishing organizational goals. As leaders they must display the vision and skills necessary to create and maintain a suitable teaching and learning environment, to develop school goals, and to inspire others to achieve these goals" (pp. 231–232). Thus, *administration* is defined here as a process that encompasses both management and leadership responsibilities.

Evolution of School Administration

One-room schoolhouses were the norm in colonial America, and these unadorned structures mirrored the values and resources of those times. A single teacher operated the school and provided instruction for students of all ages; there were no administrators. Teachers in these simple schools were employed by and reported to township trustees. But by the latter stages of the nineteenth century, many communities had to build larger and more sophisticated schoolhouses to accommodate growing numbers of students. Multiple teachers staffed these new buildings, and commonly one of them was designated to be the head teacher. This was a quasi-administrative position; the head teacher functioned as a teacher but had some authority to enforce policy. As schools became larger and even more complex, the position of principal was created. Persons who held this job became the first educators with full-time administrative and supervisory duties (Brubaker, 1947). Prior to the twentieth century, most principals had no special training in management and supervision. Therefore, they had to rely on common sense, innate abilities, and political insights to perform largely management-related tasks (Callahan, 1962).

Most of the elementary schools and high schools in the early 1900s were small and offered only a limited curriculum. Tasks now commonly performed by principals—such as curriculum coordination and staff development—had not yet evolved. Principals basically functioned as managers, supervising the work of teachers and making physical resource decisions. They were teachers who had been reassigned to administrative duties. Some were made administrators simply because the school trustees thought they possessed the necessary qualities—attributes such as a willingness to enforce rules. Others were chosen because they were effective teachers and it was assumed that effective teachers would be effective principals. Some were made principals largely because they were males who possessed traits commonly associated with management (e.g., being tall). And some were appointed to administrative positions purely for political reasons (e.g., they were friends of the school trustees). Their work was challenging, because they were expected to keep schools operating with limited resources. For instance, principals often had to enlist the assistance of community volunteers to do repairs and improvements to the school building (Grieder, Pierce, & Jordan, 1969).

Corresponding with the development of cities was the creation of local school districts. These larger, more complex organizational structures required coordination to ensure that schools were implementing a common curriculum, and they required a new layer of management. Thus, the position of local district superintendent was created to meet these evolving needs (Kowalski, 1999). Advocates of creating local school districts pointed out that this new structure provided several advantages over operating schools as separate entities. Examples of these purported advantages include the following:

- Greater levels of efficiency were achieved by serving more students in a single organization. For example, paper and materials were purchased in bulk quantities by the district and then distributed to individual schools.
- Serving larger numbers of students permitted a division of students by age. Separate elementary schools (then called grammar schools) and high schools were created.
- Basic management tasks, such as budgeting and payroll, were consolidated into a single district administrative office.

• School districts had a greater concentration of economic and cultural resources than did single schools, and this advantage resulted in more material support for program development.

The concept of forming local school districts was also advanced by the successes of the earliest districts in large cities such as Boston, New York, and Chicago. These school systems were the lighthouses for public education in the late 1800s and early 1900s, and their superintendents were admired and emulated by administrators across the United States (Callahan, 1962).

As local districts became more common and larger, other specialized positions were created. One of the first was the business manager. This individual was assigned the responsibility of overseeing the district's fiscal resources. Other positions that became relatively common in larger districts were assistant superintendents and curriculum directors. Typically, former principals occupied these new district-level positions.

Over the past 100 years, the education and licensing standards for school administrators have increased. Prior to World War II, it was rare for a district superintendent or principal to have earned a doctorate degree. Those who did usually were employed in large, affluent districts. Today, as many as 75 percent of the superintendents in some states now hold either the Doctor of Education (Ed.D.) or the Doctor of Philosophy (Ph.D.) degree. Three interacting issues help explain why and how school administration has evolved over the past 100 years. These elements are academic study, certification, and practice.

Academic Study

In the first two decades of the twentieth century, considerable pressure was placed on school officials to adopt management practices that were evolving in business and industry. During this period, several education professors who were interested in the emerging roles of superintendents and principals sought to establish school administration as a truly separate profession. They did so for three reasons (Callahan, 1962):

1. They were responding to a perceived need to provide management training for educators who occupied these positions. Many influential policymakers and industrial leaders were advocating that the science of management be applied to schools.
2. They were acting out of conviction. They essentially accepted the argument that the principles of scientific management would produce more functional schools, lower-cost schools, and improved public perceptions of education.
3. They believed that by improving the efficiency and reputation of schools, administrators would separate themselves from teachers. Administrators would have higher status and salaries—an outcome that also would benefit the professors who prepared these administrators.

Prior to 1900, there were very few administration courses offered in schools and departments of education. Columbia University awarded the first two doctorates in this specialization in 1905 (Cooper & Boyd, 1987). Yet, six years after conferring these inaugural degrees, the Teachers College of Columbia University offered only two courses in school administration: a practicum and a seminar. Starting in 1914, however, the pressures to utilize management techniques to broaden the education of school executives resulted in Teachers College giving more attention to business methods, finance, and efficiency techniques. By 1917, the offerings in educational administration at Columbia increased to eight courses. By 1927, the catalogue of this institution described the superintendent of schools as the general manager of the entire school system and claimed that the job compared with the best of older professions in business and industry (Callahan, 1962).

In the 1920s, discussions of educational administration as a field of practice became common in textbooks and journal articles. Elwood Cubberly (1922), a professor who was one of the pioneers in this specialization, enthusiastically described the opportunities that awaited educators who pursued careers in this emerging field of practice:

> School supervision represents a new profession, and one which in time will play a very important part in the development of American life. The opportunities offered in this new profession to men of strong character, broad sympathies, high purpose, fine culture, courage, exact training, and executive skill, and who are willing to take the time and spend the energy necessary to prepare themselves for large service, are today not excelled in any of the professions, learned or otherwise. (pp. 130–131)

The establishment of school administration as a separate specialization in education had both positive and negative repercussions. Individuals aspiring to become administrators could now take courses specifically designed to prepare them for this responsibility and professional organizations were formed, allowing practitioners to share their knowledge. At the same time, however, administration and teaching were cast as separate occupations. Principals, for example, usually treated teachers as subordinates rather than as peers.

By the 1930s, graduate school degrees and professional degrees in educational administration became more prominent. Although the graduate schools of established universities had offered the Master of Arts (M.A.) and Ph.D. degrees, such degrees were intended to prepare a select number of educators to be professors and researchers. The establishment of schools of education changed the focus of graduate study in education. These new entities created professional degrees intended to meet the needs of teachers and administrators who were practicing in elementary and secondary schools. Examples included the Master of Education (M.Ed.), Education Specialist (Ed.S.), and Ed.D. degrees.

During the 1940s, an increasing number of universities started offering graduate courses and degrees in school administration in response to a growing need for more administrators. The number of school-age children was increasing and new schools were being built. Leaders in the development of school administration urged university presidents to provide graduate education for all educators who aspired to work in this specialization. They also promoted the idea of broadening academic study in administration to include theoretical content. The latter initiative was particularly cogent because a preoccupation with management roles and skills prior to 1940 prompted most professors to treat research and theory as relatively unimportant (Grieder et al., 1969).

Today, the knowledge base for school administration includes both theoretical content and artistry (see Figure 1.1). The latter component, often referred to as *craft knowledge,* has been developed incrementally by practicing administrators through their actual experiences. All professions have struggled with striking appropriate balances between teaching theory and addressing practice-based problems. Until the 1970s, for example, medical schools were often criticized for placing too much emphasis on scientific research while providing students with insufficient practical knowledge that they could apply after graduating (Schön, 1987). Today, medical schools commonly immerse even first-year students in problems of practice by having them do clinical work in teaching hospitals. The history of professional preparation in school administration since the 1940s also reveals tensions between theory and practice. Professors recognized the value of both research and practical knowledge, and they attempted to bridge the two components of the knowledge base (Miklos, 1983).

The study of school administration varies markedly across the approximately 500 institutions offering courses in this specialization. Differences are based on resources, mission, and philosophy. Some programs have as many as 12 to 15 professors; others operate with only 1 full-time faculty member. Some programs focus almost entirely on preparing professors; most programs focus largely on preparing practitioners at the master's degree level. Philosophically, programs differ with respect to expressing values and beliefs about what knowledge is of most worth and about the processes for teaching students. For example, some programs include early and continuing clinical experiences; others require no clinical experiences. Many experts in school administration (e.g., Bridges & Hallinger, 1997;

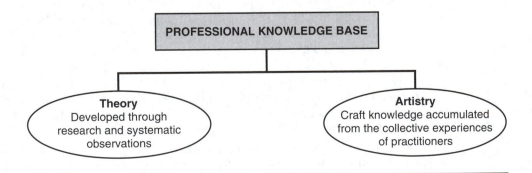

FIGURE 1.1   *Components of the Professional Knowledge Base*

Daresh, 1997) believe that students are not served well either by studying only theory or by studying only the accumulated wisdom of practitioners. Rather, the most effective professional preparation occurs when these two elements are squarely joined. However, this goal is quite difficult to accomplish. Many universities have not been willing to sacrifice academic study in order to expose students to greater practical and experiential training (Alllson, 1989). In addition, clinical education can be quite expensive, time consuming, and difficult to schedule—especially in school administration because the typical student works full time and pursues graduate degrees on a part-time basis (Milstein & Krueger, 1997).

Opinions and evidence regarding the effectiveness of professional preparation remain mixed. Some advocates for reform (e.g., Murphy & Hallinger, 1987) have argued that practitioners are usually disillusioned by the failure of their professors to "ground training procedures in the realities of the workplace and by their reluctance to treat content viewed useful by administrators" (p. 252). Yet, studies of administrators frequently reveal that practitioners believe that their academic preparation adequately prepared them for practice (e.g., Glass, Björk, & Brunner, 2000; Kowalski, 1995). Different perspectives about the effectiveness of administrator preparation are largely explained by the fact that the quality of programs differs markedly across the country and by the fact that adequacy is not a precisely defined criterion. For example, many students in professional programs and practitioners (and some professors) have argued that preparation should remain focused on management-related problems. By comparison, persons calling for reform have emphasized the need for broadening the curriculum to include courses and clinical experiences in areas such as instructional leadership (e.g., Murphy, 1992; Murphy & Hallinger, 1987) and program evaluation (e.g., Gerritz, Koppich, & Guthrie, 1984).

Suggestions for improving the preparation of school administrators have ranged from making programs much more rigorous (e.g., raising admission standards and increasing degree requirements) to eliminating university-based programs in favor of practitioner-operated programs. The range of options for studying school administration has become broader as even more universities and alternative education providers have entered the arena. In addition, technology in the form of the World Wide Web and satellite television has made it increasingly possible for educators to pursue study in school administration.

Certification and Licensure

Certification of school administrators played a pivotal role in the evolution of preparation programs. During the 1920s, the certification of administrators was advocated for two primary reasons: (1) many superintendents of that period had not taken a single college course in school administration and (2) certification was perceived as essential to professionalizing school administration. Individual states, usually through state departments of education, controlled certification. By 1932, nearly half of the states had adopted certification standards for administrators (Callahan, 1962).

As states promulgated certification requirements, they relied on universities to prepare educators to meet the prescribed standards. Such standards usually were quite specific, specifying both minimum degree requirements and exact courses. By establishing academic requirements that could be met only through university study, state certification of school administration played a key role in establishing school administration as a specialized area of study. State certification also ensured departments of educational administration a steady stream of graduate students (Kowalski, 2000).

In the 1980s, the certification of educators became a reform target for state policymakers. By 1985, 28 states had revised portions of professional certification and another 16 states were considering such modifications (Stellar, 1985). The changes, however, were not uniform across states. While some states increased requirements, others lessened them by allowing alternative paths to certification. By 1993, 12 states had adopted alternative certification for administrators (Gooden & Leary, 1995). Such policy, although widely opposed by educators who saw the action as yet another affirmation of society's indifference toward their profession, was typically defended on the following grounds:

- In some states (especially in areas with rapid population growth), the supply of licensed professionals was inadequate to meet the demand. Proponents of alternative certification (e.g., Penning, 1990) argued that their remedy provided a quick and inexpensive solution to this problem.
- Some proponents (e.g., Jacobson, 1990) advocated a realignment of administrative work to emphasize quality management. This action would cast administration as management and allow individuals with degrees outside of education (e.g., graduates of M.B.A. programs) to assume school administration jobs.
- Some proponents (e.g., Cooperman, 1988) concluded that highly talented managers were willing to work in district and school settings but unwilling to waste time getting degrees in education.

At the same time that policymakers in about 20 percent of the states were promulgating new certification standards that permitted noneducators to become school administrators, reformers elsewhere were trying to improve the quality of educational leaders by treating education as a true profession. For example, professional standards boards composed entirely or primarily of educators have been created in several states (e.g., Connecticut and Indiana). These boards, analogous to those used to regulate practice in professions such as law and medicine, were given the authority to grant, regulate, and rescind licenses for teachers and administrators. Proponents (e.g., Wise, 1994) argued that treating education as a licensed profession and raising accountability was preferable to "quick fixes" that deregulate requirements for entering practice.

Debate over licensing standards for administrators continues to this present day. In large measure, positions on administrator licensing are molded by philosophical dispositions concerning what people believe should be the ideal roles of superintendents and principals. Those who want administrators to be managers tend to view professionalism and licensing as political ploys to protect educators; those who want administrators to be both educational leaders and managers view professionalism and licensing as essential. Clearly, licensing and certification standards have indirectly determined the nature of practice in school administration, because such standards convey direct and symbolic messages regarding what is considered to be important (Peterson & Finn, 1988). In this vein, state policies regarding entry into school administration have played and continue to play a central role in the evolution of practice.

Practice

School administrators in the early 1900s were expected to be effective managers and individuals of unquestionable character. Elwood Cubberly (1922) developed a lengthy list of characteristics that represented popular thought of what was necessary to become a superintendent in his day. He noted that this chief executive must

- be clean and temperate
- be able to look others straight in the eye
- possess a sense of honor
- possess good manners
- not be prone to bragging
- avoid oracularism
- possess the solemnity and dignity of an owl
- possess a sense of humor
- be alert
- understand common human nature
- know when to keep silent
- be able to accept success without vainglory
- possess political skills
- be clever
- avoid being a "grouch"
- possess a level head
- know when to take the public into his confidence
- avoid falling victim to political tricks and the discoveries of wild-eyed reformers
- know how to accept defeat without being embittered

Early role expectations such as these were critically important, because they helped frame the norms for practice. Especially in the last half of the nineteenth century and the first half of the twentieth century, school administrators were cast as a curious hybrid of a caring and meek minister and a stern and ruthless industrial manager.

Education historians (e.g., Butts & Cremin, 1953) noted that establishing a professional orientation to the superintendency was not an easy task. Circa 1900, the public typically viewed state superintendents as "political hacks." Persons appointed to this position typically served relatively short terms and received low salaries in comparison to other state officials. Citizens often viewed local district superintendents in the same way. Big-city mayors often tried to control public education, fearing that superintendents could accumulate considerable power if they were allowed to raise and spend tax money without controls (Callahan, 1962). Despite attempts to relegate school administration to the status of a low-level civil servant, influential professors and superintendents during that era were able to move school administration toward professionalism. Both graduate education and certification were pivotal in this regard. School boards in large-city systems, for example, often took pride in being able to lure educators with a doctorate to serve as their chief executive officers. Many of these highly educated leaders became father figures in their communities; they were respected and able to wield considerable power (Kowalski, 1999).

Following World War II, two significant demographic changes occurred in the United States. People began moving to newly developed suburbs and birth rates began rising rapidly. These changes resulted in the realignment of public education into larger local districts. State legislators were encouraged to pass school reorganization laws that would require small rural schools to consolidate into modern districts. One of the primary advocates for district reorganization was Stephan Knezevich, a highly respected school administration professor. He wrote:

> Only in extreme cases can districts with fewer than 1,000 enrolled pupils be justified. There is evidence to show that effective district structure is an important step toward the improvement of quality in education; there is a definite relationship between pupil achievement and school size; and there is considerable variability in the size of enrollments and geographic area of school districts in the United States. (Knezevich, 1962, p. 149)

The district consolidation movement was extremely controversial in the late 1950s and early 1960s because it pitted two cherished American values against each other. On one side were advocates of liberty who argued that local control should be preserved; on the other side were advocates of equality who argued that all public schools in a state should provide students with reasonably equal educational opportunities. In the period between 1930 to 1980, approximately 90 percent of the local school districts in the United States were eliminated at a time when school enrollments almost doubled and the number of teachers increased by 250 percent (Knezevich, 1984).

As school districts became larger, an increasing number of them found it necessary to create centralized administrative positions to serve on the superintendent's staff. An organizational model for district administration already existed in large urban school systems, and it became the prototype for newly formed districts. Central to this model were the concepts of efficiency, centralization, and specialization. Implementation of these concepts was fashioned by emulating practices being used in business and industry during the Industrial Revolution (Callahan,

1962). Eventually, small school districts adopted the same organizational principles and bureaucratic ideals (Campbell, Cunningham, Nystrand, & Usdan, 1990). The standard organizational model for district administration was the appointment of several assistant superintendents who were designated to supervise major functions such as business, curriculum, and student services.

Individual schools, especially secondary schools, also began increasing in size following World War II. James Conant (1959) declared that any high school with fewer than 100 students in the graduating class was too small to provide a sufficiently diverse curriculum. The movement to larger high schools took place at the same time that school reorganization laws were being passed. The two actions were intertwined, because district consolidation almost always resulted in merging high schools. As high schools became larger, the position of assistant principal became more common.

The creation of larger districts and schools strengthened notions that administrators must be good managers. In many communities, the superintendent was responsible for the largest bus and food service in the community. In addition, millions of dollars were being spent annually on facilities and employees. In the last half of the twentieth century, the conceptualizations of administrators as politicians and social scientists also took hold. These roles were predicated on the need for administrators to compete for scarce resources, to resolve conflict, and to address mounting social concerns such as poverty and racism. Principals and superintendents were expected to be spokespersons for children and public education. These broadened roles made the practice of school administration more difficult and stressful (Hess, 1983).

Contemporary Conditions

Public education has been subjected to repeated reform proposals for more than two decades. Currently, efforts to improve schooling are focused on developing new organizational structures for districts and schools. At the core of these efforts is the realization that meaningful and lasting improvement is unlikely unless the primary values and beliefs guiding the behavior of educators are changed (Sarason, 1996). Efforts to impose change on schools through state mandates have been only moderately successful; therefore, both state deregulation and district decentralization have become more acceptable reform strategies. The former entails state government allowing local districts to have greater latitude in determining policy and priorities; the latter entails districts allowing individual schools the same privilege. Collectively, these two strategies require administrators to provide much more leadership than they have in the past.

Expectations for leadership revolve around the need to produce effective organizational adaptations. Traditionally, public schools have not been flexible institutions because they had cultures that protected centralization and avoided external interventions (i.e., attempts by persons, groups, or agencies outside the district to influence school operations) (Diggins, 1997). In today's world, needs and wants are constantly changing. Ensuring that their organizations are adaptive means that administrators must personally support change and inspire others to become change agents (Bennis & Nanus, 1985). For many administrators who were prepared only to be managers, these are uncommon and threatening expectations. Empowering teachers, for example, is contrary to their belief that they must control others; and site-based management is contrary to their belief that managers should protect their power and authority. As such, they must change long-standing values and norms if they are to lead others successfully to create visions, plans, and new programs.

The profession of school administration is faced with many challenges beyond balancing leadership and management. Among the more important tasks are the following:

- Women, who comprise approximately two-thirds of the nation's teaching force, are still underrepresented in highly visible positions such as district superintendent (Glass et al., 2000) and high school principal (Scollay & Logan, 1999).
- The fastest growing segments of school-age population in the United States are among minority children. Despite this reality, recruiting and retaining racial minorities to education careers remains a serious problem (Gonzalez, 1997).
- Questions regarding the future relationships between administrators and teachers remain unanswered. For example, will principals treat teachers as professional peers or as subordinates? Teacher autonomy—giving teachers greater authority and responsibility over what occurs in the classroom (Conley, 1990)—requires a reconsideration of how schools are organized and how administrators exercise power.
- Questions regarding the academic preparation of school administrators remain unanswered. Reforms in departments of educational administration are often attenuated by the lack of a national curriculum for preparing principals and superintendents (Kowalski, 2000).
- Large numbers of administrators are retiring, and there are growing concerns about the ability of the current system of administrator preparation to attract and properly educate the retirees' replacements.
- In a world that is rapidly changing technologically, socially, economically, and politically, the future structure of schools and the delivery of instruction have become somewhat uncertain. Consequently, many facets of school administration over the next few decades are yet to be determined.

These unsettled matters help explain why the practice of school administration is more demanding now than it was three or four decades ago.

Although school administration is a challenging career, it is also a very rewarding career. Few leaders in public life have as great an opportunity to affect the lives of so many people. Education is a cornerstone of American society, and the country's welfare depends on an effective system of elementary and secondary schools. In today's context of deregulation and decentralization, forward-thinking superintendents and principals are playing pivotal roles in building a new generation of educational institutions.

Implications for Practice

Both leadership and management are considered essential components of school administration in this book. Why is this important for you to remember? Two common errors are still made in defining the scope of contemporary practice. The first is that administrators are only managers; the second is that leadership has replaced management. In truth, leadership expectations have broadened the scope of administrative work and increased the need for professional knowledge. Although the foci of leadership and management are different, competent administrators are able to fulfill both roles.

Your understanding of current practice is enhanced by studying the evolution of school administration as an area of academic study and an area of practice. Historically, academic study, state certification requirements, and actual practices skewed administration toward management activities. Recent reform efforts, however, have created a demand for a new type of administrator. Today's superintendents and principals are expected to be visionaries, planners, consensus builders, policy specialists, and change agents. They are also expected to assume these relatively new responsibilities while continuing to provide effective management for large complex organizations.

A host of factors are converging to create new expectations and demands on administrative roles. These include not only reform efforts but also factors such as changing demographics, technology development and applications, philosophies of education, and social conditions. Many policymakers have concluded that effective school reform is most likely to occur at the district and individual school levels. Consequently, greater leeway is being given to local educational officials to pursue meaningful improvements. In this context, administration has become more challenging and more exciting.

As you think about the content of this chapter, try to visualize an ideal administrator. Also try to visualize yourself as an administrator. Would you be comfortable leading and managing? Which role will require you to make the most adaptations? These types of questions encourage you to reflect on your motivations and to determine whether you truly want to be an administrator.

For Further Discussion

1. What factors created the need for districts and schools to have administrators?

2. How did management science affect the development of school administration during and immediately following the Industrial Revolution?

3. What are basic differences between leadership and management?

4. Why has leadership been emphasized so much in the past few decades?

5. Why did universities start offering courses and degree programs in school administration?

6. How did state certification contribute to the evolution of school administration as a specialization within the education profession?

7. Both leaders and managers seek to influence people. Do they have different motives in doing so? Discuss.

8. How did school reorganization laws affect practice in school administration?

9. What are the arguments for and against alternative certification for school administrators?

10. There is compelling evidence that women are underrepresented in highly visible administrative positions such as the superintendency and the high school principalship. What does this mean? Why is this condition considered a problem?

11. What are professional standards boards? How might these boards affect school administration as a profession?

Other Suggested Activities

1. Obtain a job description for a school principal. Determine whether the job description addresses both management and leadership.

2. Describe an ideal administrator. What is the basis for your description?

3. Discuss why some veteran administrators may feel threatened by expectations that they function as leaders.

4. Discuss the reasons why educators decide to become administrators. Evaluate the reasons and classify them as being positive or negative.

5. Identify the requirements for becoming a principal in your state and determine whether the requirements address both leadership and management.

6. Imagine that your state legislature is contemplating a new law that would permit individuals to receive an alternative license as principal if they have a master's degree in business management or if they complete a series of 10 workshops provided by the state principals' association. Develop a position for or against the proposed legislation.

References

Allison, D. J. (1989). *Toward the fifth age: The continuing evolution of academic educational administration.* (ERIC Document Reproduction Service No. ED 306 662)

Bassett, G . (1970). Leadership style and strategy. In L. Netzer, G. Eye, R. Krey, & J. F. Overman (Eds.), *Interdisciplinary foundations of supervision* (pp. 221–231). Boston: Allyn and Bacon.

Bennis, W. G., & Nanus, B. (1985). *Leaders: The strategies for taking charge.* New York: Harper and Row.

Bolman, L. G., & Deal, T. E. (1994). Looking for leadership: Another search party's report. *Educational Administration Quarterly, 30*(1), 77–96.

Bridges, E., & Hallinger, P. (1997). Problem-based leadership development: Preparing educational leaders for changing times. *Journal of School Leadership, 7*(6), 592–608.

Brubaker, J. S. (1947). *A history of the problems of education.* New York: McGraw-Hill.

Butts, R. F., & Cremin, L. A. (1953). *A history of education in American culture.* New York: Henry Holt and Company.

Callahan, R. F. (1962). *Education and the cult of efficiency.* Chicago: University of Chicago Press.

Campbell, R. F., Cunningham, L. L., Nystrand, R. O., & Usdan, M. D. (1990). *The organization and control of American schools* (6th ed.). Columbus, OH: Merrill.

Conant, J. B. (1959). *The American high school today.* New York: McGraw-Hill.

Conley, S. C. (1990). A metaphor for teaching: Beyond the bureaucratic-professional dichotomy. In S. Bacharach (Ed.), *Education reform: Making sense of it all* (pp. 313–324). Boston: Allyn and Bacon.

Cooper, B. S., & Boyd, W. L. (1987). The evolution of training for school administrators. In J. Murphy & P. Hallinger (Eds.), *Approaches to administrative training in education* (pp. 3–27). Albany: State University of New York Press.

Cooperman, S. (1988). We can't afford closed-shop principalships. *Executive Educator, 10*(11), 44.

Cubberly, E. P. (1922). *Public school administration.* Boston: Houghton Mifflin.

Daresh, J. C. (1997). Improving principal preparation: A review of common strategies. *NASSP Bulletin, 81*(585), 3–8.

Diggins, P. B. (1997). Reflections on leadership characteristics necessary to develop and sustain learning school communities. *School Leadership and Management, 17*(3), 413–425.

Gerritz, W., Koppich, J., & Guthrie, J. (1984). *Preparing California school leaders: An analysis of supply, demand, and training.* Berkeley: University of California.

Glasman, N., & Glasman, L. (1997). Connecting the preparation of school leaders to the practice of school leadership. *Peabody Journal of Education, 72*(2), 3–20.

Glass, T., Björk, L., & Brunner, C. (2000). *The study of the American school superintendent 2000: A look at the superintendent of education in the new millennium.* Arlington, VA: American Association of School Administrators.

Gonzalez, J. M. (1997). Recruiting and training minority teachers: Student views of the preservice program. *Equity and Excellence in Education, 30*(1), 56–64.

Gooden, J. S., & Leary, P. A. (1995). The status of alternative certification for school administrators: A national study. *Journal of School Leadership, 5*(4), 316–333.

Goodlad, J. I. (1990). *Teachers for our nation's schools.* San Francisco: Jossey-Bass.

Grieder, C., Pierce, T. M., & Jordan, K. F. (1969). *Public school administration* (3rd ed.). New York: Ronald Press.

Guthrie, J. W., & Reed, R. J. (1991). *Educational administration and policy* (2nd ed.). Englewood Cliffs, NJ: Prentice-Hall.

Hanson, E. M. (1996). *Educational administration and organizational behavior* (4th ed.). Boston: Allyn and Bacon.

Hess, F. (1983). Evolution in practice. *Educational Administration Quarterly, 19*(3), 223–248.

Hitt, W. D. (1988). *The leader-manager.* Columbus, OH: Battelle Press.

Jacobson, S. L. (1990). Future educational leaders: From where will they come? In S. Jacobson & J. Conway (Eds.), *Educational leadership in an age of reform* (pp. 160–180). New York: Longman.

Knezevich, S. J. (1962). *Administration of public education.* New York: Harper and Row.

Knezevich, S. J. (1984). *Administration of public education* (4th ed.). New York: Harper and Row.

Koontz, H., & O'Donnell, C. (1959). *Principles of management* (2nd ed.). New York: McGraw-Hill.

Kowalski, T. J. (1995). *Keepers of the flame: Contemporary urban superintendents.* Thousand Oaks, CA: Corwin.

Kowalski, T. J. (1999). *The school superintendent: Theory, practice, and cases.* Upper Saddle River, NJ: Merrill, Prentice-Hall.

Kowalski, T. J. (2000, August). *Preparing superintendents in the 21st century.* Paper presented at the annual meeting of National Council of Professors of Educational Administration. Ypsilanti, MI.

Miklos, E. (1983). Evolution in administrator preparation programs. *Educational Administration Quarterly, 19*(3), 153–177.

Milstein, M. M., & Krueger, J. A. (1997). Improving educational administration preparation programs: What we have learned over the past decade. *Peabody Journal of Education, 72*(2), 100–116.

Murphy, J. (1992). *The landscape of leadership preparation: Reframing the education of school administrators.* Newbury Park, CA: Corwin.

Murphy, J., & Hallinger, P. (1987). New directions in the professional development of school administrators: A synthesis and suggestions for improvement. In J. Murphy & P. Hallinger (Eds.), *Approaches to administrative training in education* (pp. 245–283). Albany: State University of New York Press.

Orlosky, D. E., McCleary, L. E., Shapiro, A., & Webb, L. D. (1984). *Educational administration today.* Columbus, OH: Merrill.

Penning, N. (1990). The alternate route to teaching. *School Administrator, 47*(4), 34, 36.

Peterson, K., & Finn, C. (1988). Principals, superintendents, and the administrator's art. In D. Griffiths, R. Stout, & P. Forsyth (Eds.), *Leaders for America's schools: Final report and papers of the National Commission on Excellence in Educational Administration* (pp. 89–107). Berkeley, CA: McCutchan.

Sarason, S. (1996). *Revisiting "The culture of school and the problem of change."* New York: Teachers College Press.

Schön, D. A. (1987). *Educating the reflective practitioner.* San Francisco: Jossey-Bass.

Scollay, S., & Logan, J. P. (1999). The gender equity role of educational administration: Where are we? Where do we want to go? *Journal of School Leadership, 9*(2), 97–124.

Shields, C., & Newton, E. (1994). Empowered leadership: Realizing the good news. *Journal of School Leadership, 4*(2), 171–196.

Stellar, A. W. (1985). Implications for programmatic excellence and equity. In V. Mueller & M. McKeown (Eds.), *The fiscal, legal, and political aspects of state reform of elementary and secondary education* (pp. 65–120). Cambridge, MA: Ballinger.

Terry, G. (1960). *Principles of management* (3rd ed.). Homewood, IL: Irwin.

Wise, A. E. (1994). Choosing between professionalism and amateurism. *Educational Forum, 58*(2), 139–146.

Yukl, G. A. (1989). *Leadership in organizations* (2nd ed.). Englewood Cliffs, NJ: Prentice-Hall.

Zaleznik, A. (1989). *The managerial mystique.* New York: Harper and Row.

2

Administration Roles in Professional Education

Chapter Content

Much like other professions, education contains distinguishable specializations. For example, counselors, speech therapists, reading specialists, and psychologists as well as teachers and administrators work in elementary and secondary schools. School administration, a field of study as well as an area of practice, is considered a specialization within the education profession. As a field of study, common components include research, theory, and craft knowledge developed in schools of education and practice as well as subject matter in disciplines typically housed in arts and sciences and professional schools of business. Examples include management science, public administration, and the behavioral sciences. As an area of professional practice, there are numerous subdivisions of school administration relating either to the locus of work (e.g., school building level or district level) or the nature of work assignments (e.g., business manager or curriculum director).

As you begin your study of school administration, it is important to build a solid foundation of accurate information. This includes answering the following three important questions:

1. Is school administration a profession?
2. What exactly do school administrators do?
3. What are the various jobs available in school administration?

This chapter contains information that addresses each of these queries.

School Administration as a Profession

What is a profession? Does school administration meet the same standards as other professions (e.g., law, medicine, etc.)? Some argue that education, and more specifically school administration, is not a profession. Consider the following conditions that suggest that education may not be a true profession:

- Administrators do not control specific practices, salaries, or working conditions. Rather, governmental agencies or officials determine these issues (e.g., state legislatures, local school boards, etc.).
- Historically, administrators have not controlled who gets admitted to practice. In more established professions, licensure is controlled either directly or indirectly by those who practice in the profession. For example, states maintain medical boards composed of licensed physicians and law boards composed of licensed lawyers, and these agencies determine the standards for practice and make judgments on license applications. Historically, state legislatures or state departments of education—agencies that are more political than professional—have made decisions about entry into education.
- Casting educators as professionals is reductionist because this classification generally distorts the moral dimensions and democratic character of education (Coulter & Orme, 2000).

There are considerations, however, that provide a different perspective to this question.

Justification of Professional Status

Judgments about teachers as professionals often are extended to include school administrators. Writing about teachers, Joel Spring (1990) noted that certain conditions justify their being classified as professionals:

- They are required to possess specialized knowledge.
- A college degree is required to enter practice.
- States require a license or certificate to practice.

- States increasingly require some form of examination as a condition of licensure.

In addition, educators are considered professionals for the following reasons:

- Teachers and administrators are expected to engage in lifelong learning to ensure currency in their practice.
- Teachers and administrators are expected to rely on a professional knowledge base to guide their practice.
- Research is conducted to construct theory and to solve problems of practice.

Examining linkages between standards and effective practice is another approach that may be used to validate a profession. If administrators who utilize professional knowledge and skills consistently excel in performing their responsibilities, whereas those who rely on intuition do not, then one may conclude that the necessity of certain knowledge and skills makes school administration a profession. Research conducted for the American Association of School Administrators by the University of Texas–Austin revealed two significant findings fortifying the existence of such a linkage among school administrators. In observing school superintendents, it was found that the most effective practitioners complete more graduate work and hold more and advanced certification than their peers, and the most effective superintendents are more likely to be involved in professional activities such as conferences and workshops (Burnham, 1989).

James Guthrie and Rodney Reed (1991) noted that administrators must possess knowledge in two domains if they are to earn professional integrity. The first is an understanding of pedagogy and curriculum; the second is an understanding of the institution of education. Accordingly, they argue that successful business executives or retired military officers should not serve as professional school administrators. Although these individuals may have proven themselves in different organizational climates, they usually lack credibility in the eyes of the educators they must lead. This fundamental argument about professional integrity is central to the future of school administration.

Professional Organizations

Professions are also marked by the existence of state and national organizations supporting the needs and interests of practitioners. There are multiple organizations that perform this service for school administrators. In fact, many administrators hold memberships in several professional organizations simultaneously. Usually, individuals join professional organizations in education on the basis of their jobs, their interests, or the urgings of their employers. Table 2.1 displays information about some of the major administrative organizations and lists the types of administrators (by position classification) most likely to hold membership.

The diversity of administrative work is one reason why there are multiple national organizations serving administrators. Having more than one professional

TABLE 2.1 *Examples of Major National Organizations for Administrators*

Organization	Most Likely Members*
American Association of School Administrators (AASA)	Superintendents, central office administrators, professors
National Association of Secondary School Principals (NASSP)	High school principals, junior high/middle school principals assistant principals, directors of secondary education
National Association of Elementary School Principals (NAESP)	Elementary school principals, assistant principals, directors of elementary education
Association of School Business Officials International (ASBO)	Business managers, directors of facility management
Association for Supervision and Curriculum Development (ASCD)	Curriculum directors, principals, college professors, subject area coordinators

*This is not intended to be an inclusive list of members. For instance, there are principals who belong to AASA and superintendents who belong to NASSP or NAESP.

association, however, often attenuates the political power of administrators. Because no single organization consistently speaks for all school administrators, there have been occasions when administrative organizations actually have taken divergent positions on critical issues. Historically, most professional associations serving administrators were affiliated with the National Education Association (NEA). During the late 1960s and early 1970s, virtually all specialized divisions of the NEA, especially those serving school administrators, disaffiliated due to growing tensions stemming from the increased popularity of collective bargaining (Hessong & Weeks, 1991). Unionization separated administrators and teachers, and those organizations catering to the needs and interests of administrators became independent of NEA. Although many of the administrator associations collaborate on key policy issues, they often compete for members. For example, high school principals may join the National Association of Secondary School Principals (NASSP), the Association for Supervision and Curriculum Development (ASCD), and the American Association of School Administrators (AASA); both principal associations welcome middle school principals as members. Because most practitioners cannot afford to join three or four national associations, they are forced to pick and choose those that best meet their needs. In the past three decades, national professional associations and their state affiliates have worked to advance the professional stature of school administration.

Lingering Doubts

Many Americans continue to view school administration as a quasi-profession. Educators, in general, are perceived as being of high value to society, but they are also viewed as having low status—a dubious distinction shared with the clergy (Elam, 1990). Laws, policies, and regulations generally control the work of all educators. Any time an occupation is subjected to considerable governmental control, the public tends to view the occupation as a semi-profession. In this vein, education is frequently compared to nursing and social work—other occupations in which practitioners have somewhat limited freedom to apply their knowledge and skills.

Existing doubts about education as a true profession were deepened in the 1960s and 1970s as teachers embraced unionism. The movement toward unionism and collective bargaining further eroded public perceptions of educators as professionals (Judge, 1988). An advocate for public employee unions during the 1960s and 1970s, Myron Lieberman (1988) later reversed his position, arguing that education could never be a true profession if teachers engaged in collective bargaining. He pointed out that formulating and enforcing a code of ethics, actions central to a profession, would be blocked so long as collective bargaining remained the dominant employment relations process in education. In some large school districts, even principals have unionized in order to negotiate master contracts with boards of education. Although the development of teachers' unions is understandable,* these organizations are a factor that encourages the public to view educators as nonprofessionals.

School Reform and Professionalism

At least in the eyes of the public, a profession's status is largely determined by quantitative and qualitative standards for being admitted to practice. The more difficult it is to be accepted to professional study and the more rigorous the examinations for licensure, the higher the status accorded by society. Lamenting the fact that applicant pools for administrative positions are dwindling, some observers believe that higher standards are responsible for this condition. In truth, more individuals are earning degrees and certificates in school administration now than in the past, but fewer of them are actually applying for positions (McAdams, 1998). Reluctance on the part of licensed administrators to pursue jobs in this specialization may reflect perceptions that principalships and superintendencies have become high-risk, low-status positions.

Reacting to concerns about the quality of administrator professional preparation, some reformers (e.g., Clark, 1989) have argued that the number of graduate programs in school administration and the number of students admitted to them should be dramatically reduced. Thomas Sergiovanni (1991), however, challenged the wisdom of pursuing professionalization by simply increasing academic

---

*Teachers often were treated poorly by school board members and administrators. Unionization provides a source of political power.

standards and by raising degree requirements to obtain a license. He feared that such actions would circuitously lead to an even greater emphasis on management science and drive a wedge deeper between administrators and teachers. Sharing the belief that administrator preparation needed to be reformed, he suggested "that we build a more limited and hierarchically flattering profession of educational administration, one based on shared educational expertise with teachers, limited specialized knowledge in management and organization, and blurred role distinctions that open rather than restrict access to the profession" (Sergiovanni, 1991, p. 526).

For Sergiovanni, and others who embrace his views, the core of professional knowledge in school administration consists of knowledge and skills possessed and embraced by all educators. The collective wisdom of organizational managers, although important, should not be sole justification for giving principals and superintendents greater authority and higher salaries. This perspective of professionalism is congruous with the idea that the study of teaching and the study of education foundations (e.g., history and philosophy of education) are essential to professional integrity.

The treatment of teachers as true professionals also serves to redefine administrative work. Writing about professionalism in education, Gary Sykes (1999) noted that major reform initiatives were casting a new light on traditional functions such as direct supervision and control. Substitutes to these hallmarks of the bureaucratic organization are being encouraged "so that the staff of the organization has the capacity, the resources, and the autonomy to optimally fulfill the organization's mission" (p. 244).

Last, reformers have identified lifelong learning as a responsibility in true professions. Administrators certainly qualify since they need to experience intellectual growth by engaging in continuing education, staff development, and reflective practice once they have entered practice (Hallinger & Murphy, 1991). Connections between professional identity and lifelong learning are becoming more apparent as studies (e.g., Boris-Schacter & Merrifield, 2000) probe the characteristics of effective principals. Not surprisingly, most states have moved away from issuing life licenses and have adopted continuing education requirements for both teachers and administrators.

Nature of Administrative Work

Popular images of the work performed by teachers and administrators are often narrow—and at times inaccurate. These perceptions, frequently drawn from personal experiences and images portrayed by the entertainment industry, tend to be stereotypical and unflattering (Glanz, 1998). In reality, administrators have different personalities and dispositions toward working with people. Their work is multifaceted, and individual traits, contextual variables, and leadership style interact to shape their behavior. Thus, your overall understanding of administrators is enhanced by knowing the purposes of administration and by examining their work lives.

Purposes of Administration

In the preceding chapter, management and leadership were identified as essential components of administration. Within any organization, including districts and schools, those who assume responsibility for providing direction are expected to make decisions about what should be done and about how to do things appropriately. The former involves leadership; the latter focuses on management (Bennis & Nanus, 1985). These two responsibilities are quite different, and most individuals are inclined to make one or the other their dominant role. Administrator work behavior can be placed on a continuum, as exhibited in Figure 2.1.

In contemporary practice, ideal administrative roles are framed primarily by the need for districts and schools to adapt to changing societal and world conditions. This is because "in a changing world, the only constant is change" (Carnall, 1990, p. 1). Therefore, superintendents and principals are expected to provide leadership for change and to manage initiatives once they are adopted. These responsibilities are extremely important because organizations do not always move in planned or desired directions. Some districts and schools, for instance, simply react

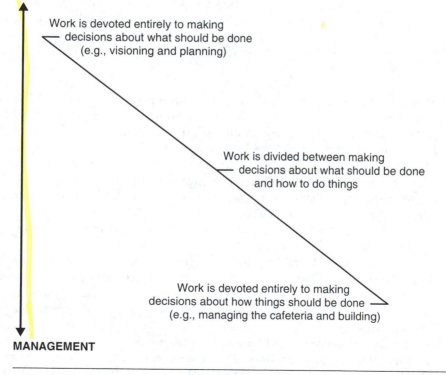

LEADERSHIP

Work is devoted entirely to making decisions about what should be done (e.g., visioning and planning)

Work is divided between making decisions about what should be done and how to do things

Work is devoted entirely to making decisions about how things should be done (e.g., managing the cafeteria and building)

MANAGEMENT

FIGURE 2.1 *Leaders and Managers: Continuum of Administrative Behavior*

to prevailing circumstances randomly; and in these unfortunate situations, decisions to embrace or not embrace a given idea are often spontaneous and intuitive.

Research on organizational behavior reveals that there are multiple inducements that influence how leaders and organizations deal with change. James March (1984) identified six models that provide a framework for understanding and studying the routine adaptations of organizations:

1. *Evolutionary selection:* Action created by the application of standard operating procedures or rules to appropriate situations (e.g., collection of textbook rental fees is relaxed because of a strike at a local factory)
2. *Intended rational choice:* Action created by attempts to solve problems (e.g., a new daily schedule is adopted to alleviate space problems caused by an unanticipated enrollment increase)
3. *Trial and error:* Action created by past learning (e.g., the length of lunch periods is altered by five minutes in each of three successive months in an effort to determine the most effective time frame for cafeteria operations)
4. *Politics and bargaining:* Action created by conflict and conflict resolution (e.g., rules for evaluating teaching are altered as a condition of reaching a contractual settlement with the teachers' union)
5. *Diffusion:* Action that spreads from one organization to another (e.g., adopting block scheduling solely because other local schools are using it)
6. *Regeneration:* Action caused by a mix of intentions and competencies among humans in the organization (e.g., teachers are given a greater role in decision making both because they have a great deal to offer and because the principal wants them to be cooperative)

The impetus for change may emanate from within a district or school or it may come from external forces. In the case of public education, pressures to pursue adaptations almost always fall into the latter category.

Since change is inevitable, administrators face the ongoing challenge of ensuring that the districts and schools in which they work remain effective. This responsibility entails moving the organization from its present state to a desired state (Hitt, 1988). Planning, implementing, and coping with change are the three primary functions involved (Carnall, 1990). The extent to which an administrator is able to meet this challenge depends on the selection and deployment of an appropriate change strategy.

School administration, however, is not limited to dealing with change. There are other responsibilities that relate to supporting operations and augmenting the work of those who perform the primary tasks of producing services. These duties are broadly divided between instructional leadership and general management. In the former category, administrators work collaboratively with teachers and others to make decisions about the scope of the curriculum and effective instruction. In the latter category, administrators control support functions such as budgets, facilities, and food service programs. Thus, the purposes of administration are twofold: to provide direction and support for organizational change and to provide direction and support for essential operations.

Work Lives of Administrators

What is the work of superintendents and principals really like? This is another basic question asked by students in introductory courses, and it can be answered in several ways. One perspective is nested in the social nature of administrative activity. For example, some writers describe the work of principals in relation to interactions they have with teachers, students, parents, and others during the school day (e.g., Fraze & Hetzel, 1990; Walton, 1973). These descriptions have been particularly useful with respect to exhibiting why human relations and communication are important to effective practice.

Another approach to describing the work of administrators involves an analysis of role expectations. The all-inclusive tasks of providing direction and support to organizational activity can be separated into nine general areas (discussed next) of responsibilities pervasive in administrative work. Although all nine functions are relevant, their order of importance varies from one work assignment to another. This variance is attributable to an intricate mix of organizational, contextual, and individual circumstances.

Representing.   Administrators are the visible heads of their organizations. For example, superintendents serve as the official representatives of their organizations to the community and external agencies. Likewise, principals function as official representatives of their individual schools. The representative role has both formal and informal elements (Blumberg, 1985). For instance, a superintendent represents his or her school district formally with appearances before state agencies or regulatory commissions. Informally, he or she provides visibility for the school district at social functions and other community-based events. The role of official representative is especially important, because administrators are usually expected to maintain a high level of public visibility and to be active in civic functions.

School boards want their administrators to project an image that is congruous with community standards. Thus, they pay particular attention to personal appearance, communication skills, tact, personality, and warmth when interviewing superintendent candidates. The manner in which an administrator represents his or her employer is symbolically important, because the image projected is viewed as being indicative of the school's philosophy and culture.

Planning.   A myriad of factors contribute to an increased emphasis on formal organizational planning. One is a demand for increased accountability. During the past two decades, governors and legislators, responding to public pressures, have required schools to be more answerable for resources at their disposal. Movement to a global economy, the rapid deployment of technology, and the advancement of knowledge in many fields of study exemplify additional factors raising the need for more precise organizational planning. Other elements creating a demand for greater planning at the local level include the following:

- *Public dissatisfaction:* Growing sentiments that schools are not as effective as they should be
- *Uncertainty:* Doubts about the nature and configuration of schooling in coming decades
- *State deregulation:* Movement toward emphasizing outputs and allowing local districts greater freedom to set policy
- *District decentralization:* Movement toward providing individual schools greater autonomy to address the specific needs of students being served

Planning consists of two essential activities: (1) setting goals and objectives and (2) developing blueprints and strategies for implementation (Sergiovanni, 2001). These processes can be executed either at the district or the individual school levels; however, the trend has been to do both. In systems where both tasks are addressed, individual school plans are developed as extensions of district plans. The value of building-level planning is supported by effective schools research that has identified two notable outcomes (Purkey & Smith, 1983):

1. Effective schools frequently engage in building-level collaborative planning.
2. Effective schools develop and use clearly stated goals that are produced through a planning process.

Movement toward decentralized planning increases expectations that principals possess knowledge and skills in two critical areas: (1) knowledge and skills related to planning as an administrative process and (2) knowledge and skills related to collaborative decision making. The latter expectation is increasingly essential because concepts such as teacher empowerment and site-based management have grown in popularity.

Organizing.   Although related, planning and organizing are different administrative functions. Organization includes the arrangement of people, materials, and other resources to ensure proper operations. At the building level, for example, principals provide organizational structure by developing and administering a daily class schedule and an extracurricular events schedule. Superintendents organize by integrating the various elements of the system in an effort to provide adequate and equal educational opportunities. Organization is essential to achieving favorable cost-benefit ratios for human and material resources; and in the eyes of taxpayers, this is often one of the most important tasks of school administration.

   Although administrators make many different organizational decisions, perhaps the most important relate to instructional programs. Yet, it is in this area that the greatest gaps between ideal and real roles are often found. Although there is widespread agreement that instruction is the most important function in schools, research indicates that principals typically devote little of their workday to organizational responsibilities in this area (Wimpleberg, 1987).

Leading.   Historically, schools have been agencies of stability (Spring, 1990), and administrators have been expected to protect that status. This is one reason why managerial functions have been dominant in school administration. More recently, however, reformers have challenged administrators to provide leadership for school improvement. Many veteran administrators view this expectation as being laden with risk, because there are a myriad of environmental and organizational barriers that may prevent administrators from functioning as leaders. These barriers range from societal expectations to school cultures to personal knowledge. Nevertheless, research indicates that the most effective practitioners have been able to overcome the obstacles that otherwise prevent leadership and management responsibilities from being balanced (Burlingame, 1987).

Leading requires a broad range of knowledge and skills, not the least of which are human relations and communication. Consequently, administrators must not only understand how organizations function but they must also know how their own interactions either contribute to or hinder efforts to build common visions and to produce change (Kowalski, 1998). This is especially true in the areas of curriculum and instruction, because actions to improve teaching and learning need to occur in whole systems rather than in isolated classrooms (Elmore, 1999–2000). Therefore, reformers are paying much greater attention to how administrators are prepared. In particular, they are calling for broader professional preparation to ensure that practitioners are capable of both instructional and organizational leadership (Clark & Clark, 1996a).

Managing.   Managing is a process that involves a preoccupation with the here-and-now aspects of goal attainment (Bryman, 1986). It is a process focusing on the efficient utilization of resources to achieve the purposes of the organization. The professional manager is less concerned with determining major intentions and directions and more concerned with finding out what consumers want from the schools and delivering services accordingly (Sergiovanni, Burlingame, Coombs, & Thurston, 1987). In essence, management focuses on immediate and specific problems (Yukl, 1989). Table 2.2 contains common management tasks performed by principals. Often, principals find themselves devoting nearly all of their time to management responsibilities, because many of issues demanding their time are unanticipated. This is another reason why it is difficult to balance leadership and management.

In the past few years, demands for educational improvement have circuitously devalued the importance of management in school administration. In part, this has occurred because management and instructional leadership are viewed as mutually exclusive responsibilities. This is most unfortunate, because both are essential. Public schools represent massive financial investments, and as such, the public demands efficiency. Although calls for leadership are pervasive in the literature and reform reports, real practice suggests that time constraints and

TABLE 2.2 *Examples of Common Management Tasks Performed by Principals*

Task	Examples of Management Activities
Operating support services	School lunch programs; transportation programs
Operating financial services	Controlling the school budget; requisitioning and purchasing materials
Maintaining the physical plant	Supervising custodial staff; requesting repairs
Managing personnel	Creating and maintaining personnel files; conducting performance evaluations
Scheduling	Determining dates for special events; setting a daily schedule
Maintaining health and safety	Conducting fire drills; developing rules to ensure that employees and students are safe
Controlling student behavior	Establishing discipline rules as extensions of district policy; making decisions about suspensions and expulsions
Extracurricular activities	Scheduling athletic events; assigning teachers to supervise activities

external priorities still require principals to spend most of their time managing (Portin, Shen, & Williams, 1998).

Facilitating.   Although the task of educating students falls most directly on the shoulders of classroom teachers, administrators are expected to facilitate this essential process. How do administrators fulfill this function? They simply make it easier for teachers to teach. More precisely, they provide human and material assistance, permitting teachers to function more effectively. Facilitation in school administration may be direct or indirect. A principal helping a teacher obtain software is an example of direct assistance; a superintendent recommending a policy on the acquisition of instructional materials exemplifies indirect assistance.

Communication is central to the facilitating role. Administrators are information links between teachers and other parties, such as parents, central office administrators, and state agency personnel. The ability of teachers to access and use data rapidly has become essential to their practice. Examples of how principals and other administrators can keep teachers informed include policy analysis, the dissemination of applied research, new product analysis, and staff development.

Collegiality also is integral to the facilitator role. Initiatives such as site-based management and teacher empowerment have raised awareness to this issue. Roland Barth (1987) noted that in far too many schools, the work of administrators and teachers mirrored "parallel play"—a term used to describe children who play in opposite ends of a sandbox while largely ignoring each other. He argued that with proper leadership, adversarial and competitive relationships among adults could be transformed into cooperative, collegial ones. Ideas such as teacher empowerment directly challenge the long-standing bureaucratic tenet that administrators will lose power if they treat teachers as professional peers. Through effective facilitation, a principal can actually gain the respect and admiration of teachers; and in so doing, he or she can actually experience an increase of power (Nyberg, 1990).

Mediating. Conflict is inevitable in all organizations (Owens, 2001). Disputes between and among groups (e.g., the custodians' union and the school board disagree over whether employees should be paid for holidays when they do not work) or between and among individuals (e.g., two teachers disagree over how to use a shared piece of equipment) occur with regularity in public education. In part, the inevitability of conflict is attributable to the fact that individuals and groups bring varying beliefs, values, knowledge, and experiences to the organization. For instance, elementary teachers might disagree on the amount of homework that should be assigned to students in the various grade levels, or middle school teachers might disagree with each other about grading policies.

For many years, school officials viewed conflict as an undesirable element of organizational life; they went to great lengths to avoid it or to eradicate it quickly. Both actions appear to conserve energy and time, but they actually are nonmanagement choices that almost always produce unforeseen problems (Hanson, 1996). Administrator reactions to collective bargaining with teachers' unions during the 1970s and early 1980s provided numerous examples of how administrators attempted to avoid conflict by either quickly agreeing to demands or by refusing to negotiate them (Kowalski, 1982).

Unfortunately, some continue to define mediation as simply choosing sides in a dispute. Effectively executed, this administrative function requires much more. Mediators should understand the human and political dimensions of schools and they should possess knowledge and skills that allow them to resolve conflict. Effectiveness in this role is properly judged by the degree to which the leader is able to build harmony and cooperation among individuals and groups (Yukl, 1989).

Evaluating. Administrators are expected to evaluate both individuals and programs. The two responsibilities, however, are quite different. For example, determining whether a teacher is performing adequately is not the same thing as determining whether a social studies curriculum is producing its intended results. Confusion between personnel evaluation and program evaluation exists primarily because it is generally impossible to completely separate the two tasks. Both processes can serve three primary functions: (1) providing a guide for decisions, (2) maintaining accountability, and (3) fostering understandings about organizational behavior (Stufflebeam & Webster, 1988).

Typically, performance evaluation is used to determine whether an employee is meeting job expectations so that a retention or dismissal decision can be made—a process referred to as *summative evaluation*. The ability of principals to effectively evaluate teachers has been a long-standing argument in education. In the after-math of collective bargaining, for example, teacher unions formally challenged whether principals could perform this critical task without bias (Medley, Coker, & Soar, 1984). Despite recurring criticisms of performance evaluation in schools, the practice has been sustained, largely because of convictions that the process is essential school improvement (Iwanicki, 1990). When performance evaluation also is used to help employees improve their performance, the process is referred to as *formative evaluation*. In contemporary practice, greater emphasis has been placed on balancing the formative and summative functions (Natriello, 1990). Some principals have attempted to do this by blending praise, affirmation, suggestions, and constructive criticism (Marshall, 1996).

Evaluation has both descriptive and judgmental components but it is the latter that is most difficult to complete. This is because describing behavior is usually much easier than assessing its worth. Not surprisingly, skepticism about the utility of evaluation is most often directed at the judgmental aspects of the process. Partly for this reason, teachers and administrators do not always agree on the necessity of evaluation. Studies (e.g., Kowalski, Reitzug, McDaniel, & Otto, 1992) often reveal that principals place far more value on formal evaluations than do teachers. In part, this outcome is explained by two conditions:

1. Administrators typically must make summative judgments about employees —a duty that may require painful and legally risky decisions.
2. Many administrators continue to use evaluation as a means for exercising power over employees. That is, they are able to influence employee behavior because of the formal judgments they make about the employees.

Performance evaluation continues to be a demanding responsibility of school administrators, and if not conducted properly, the act of judging other professionals can also be frustrating and destructive (Kimbrough & Burkett, 1990).

Communicating.   Historically, communication was treated as a routine function in school administration. School districts commonly relied on one-way channels that permitted administrators to share information on a "need-to-know" basis. This process, modeled after the bureaucratic organization, typically served five purposes: (1) providing job instructions; (2) providing job rationale; (3) explaining established policy, procedures, and practices; (4) providing performance feedback; and (5) informing people about mission and objectives (Katz & Kahn, 1978).

Emerging ideas about organizational adaptations and movement into the Information Age, however, generated new expectations for communication. Administrators are now expected to

- Construct and use two-way channels of communication that allowed them to receive as well as transmit information
- Access and use information rapidly to identify and solve problems
- Utilize modern technologies to facilitate communication

- Manage change predicated on the shifting needs and wants of the populations being served (Kowalski, 1999)
- Provide information to employees so that they may be empowered to perform their work more effectively (Laud, 1998)

In the past, many administrators with poor communication skills were able to survive by isolating themselves and communicating only when absolutely essential. Today, administrators find it nearly impossible to hide problems such as poor listening skills, poor writing skills, and a lack of credibility. This is because principals and superintendents are constantly in the public eye. Their continuous exposure to the media, including television in many larger districts, has made communication a central function of their work.

Noted change expert, Michael Fullan (1998) observed that administrators need good communication skills if they are to learn from their critics. He believes that real change in schools must be internally driven, and this task requires principals to collaborate with a wide range of people who have a vested interest in schools. In addition, administrators are increasingly expected to shape school reform initiatives and to convince the public to support them. Both of these essential tasks depend on communication.

School-Level Administration

Positions in school administration can be broadly classified as either school based or central office. In the former category, one's assignment is primarily or entirely at an individual school. Central office administration, by contrast, involves districtwide responsibilities and authority. Distinctions between school-based and central office roles in very small districts are often difficult to make because the superintendent's office may be located in one of the schools or a principal may be assigned to some districtwide duties. But in the vast majority of school systems, distinctions between central office or school-based administrators are rather clear.

Elementary School Administration

Over the years, the structure of elementary schools has been altered in several ways. At one time, many elementary schools included kindergarten through grade 8. With the emergence of junior high schools, circa 1910, many school districts reduced the scope of elementary schools by removing grades 7 and 8 from them. More recently, the popularity of the middle school concept has resulted in the removal of the sixth grade, and in some instances also the fourth and fifth grades, from the elementary school. At the other end of the grade continuum, many elementary schools now provide pre-kindergarten programs (e.g., for special needs students) and there is mounting support nationally for public schools to expand programming in kindergarten from a half day to a full day. The net result of these changes is that the modern elementary school has many different grade configurations based on needs, interests, policy, and financial resources.

The position of elementary school principal has also evolved over time. Initially, "head" or "lead" teachers were assigned to perform necessary management functions such as ensuring that the building was maintained and secure. As schools became larger and facilities more complex, this practice became impractical, and assigning full-time administrators (i.e., principals) became the modal practice. Today, the range of enrollment in elementary schools varies considerably; some enroll over 1,200 pupils, and others have fewer than 100 pupils. The average elementary school has three or four classes (or sections) at each grade level—an organizational arrangement that typically serves between 300 and 400 pupils.

Program complexity has also played a part in creating the need for more supervision and management in elementary schools. Table 2.3 contains several examples of conditions that made the role of elementary school principal more demanding. You should note that some of these conditions apply to both elementary and secondary school principals, and some are unique to elementary schools.

Elementary school administrators almost always receive employment contracts that extend beyond the customary nine-month school year. The length of the extension, however, may vary among and within local districts. As an example, elementary principals may have annual employment contracts that are between 10 and 12 months. The size of the school, past practices, and philosophy typically determine the degree to which a principal's contract is extended beyond nine months. During the summer recess, elementary school principals may supervise summer school programs, engage in planning activities, make schedules for the coming school year, participate in the employment of new teachers and staff, enroll new students, meet with parents, and oversee maintenance activities. In some instances, elementary principals also manage summer recreational programs.

What principals really do is a product of an intricate combination of public perceptions, organizational expectations, socialization, past practices, and reform initiatives. Some continue to function primarily as managers; however, most have now assumed some leadership responsibilities. Reform ideas, such as site-based management, are primarily responsible for altering both the ideal and actual roles of principals (Laud, 1998; Tanner & Stone, 1998).

Assistant principals are often employed in elementary schools with more than 400 pupils. These positions may be full-time or part-time administrative assignments (e.g., a person may be employed as a teacher half time and as an assistant principal half time), and they provide an entry into school administration. At one time, most educators considered the assistant principalship as a stepping-stone to becoming a principal. Although that is still generally true, there are a growing number of individuals who view the assistant principalship as their ultimate career goal. Elementary school assistant principals almost always have general responsibilities instead of being relegated to specific functions. However, assistant principals may be assigned to primarily management functions in situations where the principal seeks to devote more time being an instructional leader. Assistant principals who aspire to become principals should seek to gain experience in both management and leadership.

TABLE 2.3 *Examples of Factors Influencing the Complexity of Elementary School Administration*

Factor	Examples of Possible Effects
School consolidation	When small districts were consolidated to achieve operational efficiency, it was possible for districts to build larger elementary schools. This development increased the scope of the principal's role.
Curricular expansion	The scope of subjects offered in elementary schools has gradually expanded; some schools, for example, now offer foreign languages. The broader curriculum requires the principal to supervise and evaluate more programs.
Teacher specialization	Initially, elementary teachers taught every subject in a self-contained classroom; however, specialized teachers are now employed in subjects such as art, music, and physical education. The greater diversification of staffing requires the principal to have broader knowledge of curriculum and instruction.
Technology	Computers and other modern technologies have changed both instructional methods and communication in schools. Elementary school principals are now expected to create two-way channels of communication with various stakeholders to ensure that information flows freely.
Accountability and reform	State deregulation and district decentralization require principals to spend more time visioning, planning, and evaluating.
Changing philosophy	Many districts have taken initiatives to pursue democratic approaches to decision making; today's principal often shares power and authority with teachers and others.
Expanding knowledge base	Principals are expected to know a great deal about teaching and administration; keeping current requires a commitment to lifelong professional growth.
Legal and legislative interventions	Both the courts and state legislatures have had a profound effect on schools; principals are required to enforce a variety of laws and policies (e.g., discrimination laws, special education laws, etc.).
Accountability and student testing	Many states now require proficiency tests, and principals play a key role in preparing staff to deal with these mandates as well as disseminating information about tests and test outcomes to parents and the general public.

Middle/Junior High School Administration

The junior high school emerged as a result of studies regarding the vertical organization of public schools; the Commission on the Reorganization of Secondary Education conducted one of the most influential pieces of research in 1918. This study concluded that U.S. schools should adopt an organization structure that placed kindergarten and grades 1 through 6 in elementary schools and the remaining six grades in secondary schools (Anderson & Van Dyke, 1963). School districts that embraced this conclusion either created junior/senior high schools (grades 7 through 12) or separate junior high schools (grades 7 through 9) and senior high schools (grades 10 through 12). By 1920, only 55 separate junior high schools existed in the United States, but that figure increased to nearly 8,000 by 1970 (Wood, Nicholson, & Findley, 1985). The primary purposes of the junior high school were to provide a transition from the self-contained instructional format of the elementary school to the departmentalized organization of the secondary school, and to provide an appropriate social setting for children reaching puberty and undergoing a difficult growth period. Over time, however, concerns emerged regarding the effectiveness of the junior high school as the appropriate format for meeting these missions: "There is a growing belief that the junior high school is no longer serving its original purpose and is taking on more and more characteristics of a senior high school. Some also believe that American children today are reaching adolescence much earlier than children of many years ago" (Wood et al., 1985, p. 6).

Continuing questions as to whether the junior high school was accomplishing its original mission led to the exploration of alternatives for middle grades education. The middle school, typically containing grades 6 through 8 or 5 through 8, emerged in the 1960s and 1970s as an alternative to the junior high school. Grade span, however, was not the sole distinguishing factor between these two concepts. The middle school provided a different philosophy and espoused different practices that were believed to be more conducive for accommodating the needs of early adolescents (Epstein, 1990).

Virtually all junior high school principals were former secondary school teachers. This was because both junior high schools and high schools were departmentalized and teachers were required to have licenses or certificates that permitted them to teach specific subjects at these grade levels. Middle school principals, by comparison, included both former elementary and former secondary teachers, largely because many states allowed individuals with teaching experience at either level to obtain a middle school principal's license. Even today, both elementary and secondary school principal associations recruit middle school principals as members.

Most middle schools attempt to address both the academic and social needs of students. In addition, the schools are intended to provide a transition experience between the self-contained environment of an elementary school and the departmentalized environment of the high school. Instructional teaming and block scheduling are popular strategies for achieving these goals. Both depend heavily on collaboration. Middle school principals play a key role, both directly and symbolically, in determining whether collaboration is achieved. They do this by valuing and recognizing contributions of others (Clark & Clark, 1996b; Rottier, 1996). Hence, the ability to work closely with teachers, parents, and students is an important attribute for this position.

Historically, the demands facing middle-level principals resulted in them being more reactive than proactive (Kron, 1990). Principals have had to spend considerable time with student discipline issues and other managerial responsibilities associated with operating a school—a condition that prevented them from functioning as instructional leaders. In an effort to alleviate this problem, most districts now assign one or more assistant principals to middle schools. In some instances, assistant principals at this level may be assigned almost exclusively to handling discipline problems—an assignment that may not prepare them well for the principalship (Porter, 1996). Thus, you should carefully weigh your career goals if you are considering applying for a middle-level assistant principalship. You need to ask yourself if a particular position will provide you with the experiences that will enhance your ultimate career goals.

Larger middle schools (those with more than 400 students) also may employ persons in the following positions that may be classified as administrative or quasi-administrative:

- Dean of students (a person typically assigned to oversee student discipline)
- Director of counseling or student services
- Athletic director
- Department chairs

Conditions specified in collective bargaining agreements usually determine whether these positions are treated as administrative assignments. Such designation precludes persons in these jobs from being in the teachers' bargaining unit, but it does allow them to perform supervisory (e.g., evaluation) and managerial (e.g., budget management) functions.

Middle school principals typically are compensated at a level between elementary and high school principals, although there are exceptions based on experience and performance. Employment contracts for these positions almost always cover 11 or 12 months. You also should recognize that superintendents and school board members often seek to employ principals for middle schools who are devoted to working at this level.

High School Administration

High schools are organized with various grade configurations ranging from grades 7 through 12 (combined junior and senior high schools) to grades 9 through 12 or grades 10 through 12 (commonly called senior high schools). The growing popularity of the middle school has caused a resurgence of the grades 9 through 12 organizational format. High schools tend to be larger in enrollment than either elementary or middle grade schools, and they provide a broader curriculum and expanded extracurricular programs—conditions that make administration even more complex. Although conditions vary across schools, high school principals generally have opportunities to make decisions that will influence the climate and productivity of the schools in which they work (Myers & Murphy, 1993).

In many communities, the high school principal is a highly visible person. The public role of this position is an important personal consideration for those who aspire to occupy this post. "The behaviors of principals, as authority figures, communicate what is really valued to both teachers and students. Teachers and students tend to imitate the actions, attitudes, and beliefs of those in authority, such as the principal" (Rossow, 1990, p. 34). Although the behavior of principals at all levels is symbolically important, high school principals typically receive the most attention from the public. On the other hand, high school principals usually receive higher salaries and longer employment contracts than their peers working in lower-level schools. A less-recognized benefit involves career development. Studies on career paths of administrators have exhibited that high school principals usually find it easier to move to the superintendency than either elementary school or middle school principals (Miklos, 1988).

The scope of programs in a high school requires principals to devote considerable time to their jobs. For example, high schools typically provide a diverse program of athletic and other extracurricular programs. Even in smaller high schools, it is not uncommon for a high school principal to spend two to three evenings a week and approximately 15 to 20 nonschool days (e.g., Saturdays or days during scheduled breaks) at school-related functions.

Assistant principals generally have had less prestige and less power than that of principals (Hartzell, 1993); nevertheless, experience in this role has been viewed as nearly essential for becoming a principal. Two developments are noteworthy with regard to the high school assistant principalship. First, a growing number of educators appear to be making this job their ultimate career goal—that is, they do not view this position as a stepping-stone to the principalship. Second, women have been more likely to bypass this position and move directly from the classroom to the principalship (Spencer & Kochan, 2000). Interests in employing female assistant principals in high schools, however, appear to be rising. A recent study of employment decisions related to selecting assistant principals, for example, found that hypothetical female candidates were evaluated more highly than male applicants and were more likely to be selected for interviews (Reis, Young, & Jury, 1999).

Other positions in a high school that may be classified as administrative (e.g., student deans and department heads) were described in the previous section on middle school principals. And as noted there, administrative classifications typically connote two conditions: (1) persons in these jobs have supervisory responsibility for other professional personnel and (2) persons in these jobs are excluded from the teachers' collective bargaining unit.

District-Level Administration

Larger-city school districts created the position of district superintendent. By most accounts, the very first persons were appointed to this position in 1837 in the cities of Buffalo (New York) and Louisville (Kentucky) (Grieder, Pierce, & Jordan, 1969). As urban systems grew in enrollment, programming and services expanded. Superintendents created their own support staffs by adding positions with titles such as assistant superintendent and director of instruction. Thus, the structure of central administrative services was created. The need for such districtwide leadership and management was the product of a number of environmental and educational considerations. Several of these factors are listed in Table 2.4.

TABLE 2.4   *Examples of Factors Promoting Growth in School District Administration*

Factor	Consequences
District consolidation	The creation of fewer, but larger, school districts required coordination and management from a central agency in areas such as funding and transportation.
Expanded curriculum	Broader programming created the need for more curriculum and instructional specialists to provide services to principals and teachers.
Education legislation	New laws required administrators to maintain records and ensure compliance; often these duties were assigned to district administrators.
Legal interventions	Major court decisions in areas such as civil rights and special education also required administrators to maintain records and ensure compliance; often these duties were assigned to district administrators.
Improved facilities	More sophisticated and larger buildings created a need for specialized maintenance.
Instructional leadership	The goal of having superintendents and principals function as true instructional leaders created a need for more support staff.
Accountability	Demands for increased accountability required administrators to devote more time to visioning, planning, and evaluation; most of these tasks were assigned to "specialists" in the central office.
Pursuit of efficiency	Some primary functions, such as budgeting and personnel administration, could be performed more efficiently at the district level than at the individual school level.

Today, every school district has some level of centralized administration—even if it is the superintendent alone. In smaller districts, the centralized staff may include only a superintendent and a handful of secretaries and bookkeepers. In the very largest districts, there are as many as several hundred licensed administrators in central administration.

Local District Superintendent

The most visible position in school administration is that of chief school district administrator: the superintendent of schools. The position is analogous to a company president in the private sector. In its formative years, the superintendency, like the principalship, was viewed largely as a managerial position. Characteristics deemed appropriate for industrial managers often guided school boards as they selected someone to fill this key post. For example, they pursued applicants who looked and acted like a manager—individuals who could be stern and use authority to control employees. Over the past few decades, this narrow perception has dissipated. "As power and knowledge become more dispersed, as multiple constituencies demand attention, as schooling becomes more decentralized and professionalized, and as mistrust of government grows, the Terminator approach simply will not work. The image of the steely-eyed, top-down manager who has all the vision and all the answers must be coupled with a gentler, less heroic image" (Murphy, 1991, p. 512). Compared to 20 or 30 years ago, today's superintendent is apt to spend more time building consensus, developing and analyzing policy, and executing strategic planning—responsibilities that require analytical and human relations skills (Kowalski, 1999).

Although most superintendents are former principals, recent research has revealed that the actual roles of superintendents and principals are becoming increasingly dissimilar (Glass, Björk, & Brunner, 2000). Unlike a principal, the superintendent is not bound to a single school, and this fact results in greater freedom to develop one's personal schedule and to exercise personal judgment in making decisions (Blumberg, 1985; Kowalski, 1995). Whereas principals spend most of their time on site working with teachers, staff, and students, superintendents spend a considerable amount of time away from their offices working with government officials, business leaders, and other superintendents.

Noted historian Raymond Callahan (1966) observed that local district superintendents are expected to fill four distinct roles:

1. *Teacher of teachers*: Being a professional educator and instructional leader
2. *Manager*: Providing supervisions and control over human and material resources
3. *Statesman*: Reflecting the reality that schools in a democratic society are subjected to political decisions.
4. *Social scientist*: Dealing with behavioral and social problems through the use of research and theory

More recently, a fifth role—*effective communicator*—has been added to this list. This role relates to the expectation that superintendents are able to use information to identify and solve problems rapidly (Kowalski, 1999). Although superintendents often are required to emphasize one role over the others (usually depending on national trends and local philosophy), none of the roles is inconsequential.

Superintendents are almost always employed on 12-month contracts and some states mandate that initial employment contracts span two to four years. The superintendent usually receives the highest salary in a school district; however, the gap between the superintendent's compensation and the next highest-paid employee varies markedly among districts. In one school system, this gap may be as high as $25,000 to $30,000, whereas in another district, it may be as low as $2,000. Actual salaries for this position vary significantly depending on the size of the district, geographic location, existing problems, economic status of local taxpayers, and similar conditions. Some superintendents in larger school systems earn salaries exceeding $200,000 a year.

Other District-Level Positions

The most common titles used for central office personnel other than *superintendent* are *assistant superintendent, director,* and *coordinator*. Although these titles have no universal meaning, persons holding assistant superintendent positions are usually *line* administrators (i.e., they have other professional staff reporting to them), whereas those holding the title of coordinator are often *staff* administrators (i.e., individuals primarily serving a support function in the organization). In many states, one must hold a superintendent's license to have a position as an assistant superintendent. Table 2.5 shows a variety of titles that may be used for central office positions. As the examples in Table 2.5 reveal, not all central office administrators may be professional educators. Today, many school business managers are persons who have academic degrees in accounting.

The duties of central office administrators are typically divided into divisions. Moderately sized districts may have only two: instruction and business affairs. As districts become larger, functions tend to get placed in divisions and responsibilities get compartmentalized. Table 2.6 contains examples of common functions in central administration. The scope of these functions sheds light on just how complex school administration has become. Many times, taxpayers fail to comprehend the magnitude of operations carried out in a school district. For example, the fact that local districts must provide large food and transportation programs often is ignored.

Positions in central administration vary in levels of compensation and contract length. Salaries for assistant, associate, and deputy superintendents typically are higher than for building-level principals in the same school system. Positions not occupied by professional educators tend to have the lowest central office salaries (this is particularly the case if the persons in these jobs do not have a college degree).

TABLE 2.5 *Common Titles for Central Office Personnel*

Title	Description of Authority
Deputy superintendent	Typically a title used in larger districts when there is a desire to designate one person as being "second in command"—the highest-ranking administrator serving under the superintendent.
Associate superintendent	Typically a title used for high-ranking positions to designate that the officeholders have more authority than assistant superintendents.
Assistant superintendent	Typically a title assigned to administrators who report directly to the superintendent and who have general responsibility for a division of the district (e.g., finance or curriculum).
Assistant to the superintendent	Typically a title assigned to an individual who either is in a staff position or who does not hold the proper credentials or license to be called an assistant superintendent.
Administrative assistant	Typically a title assigned to a person who is not a professional administrator (e.g., an office manager) but who provides general assistance directly to the superintendent.
Director	Typically a title used to connote a staff position in the education domain (e.g., director of curriculum or director of instruction) or a management position in other domains (e.g., director of facilities or director of transportation); in almost all instances, directors have no line authority over licensed professional educators.
Business manager	Typically a title used to designate the district's chief financial officer when a higher title (e.g., assistant superintendent) is not used.
Coordinator	Typically a title used to connote a staff position in the education domain (e.g., coordinator of reading or coordinator of science)

TABLE 2.6 *Common Functions in District-Level Administration*

Area of Administration	Examples of Functions
Instructional services	Curriculum development, instructional support, textbook selection, program evaluation, instructional coordination
Business services	Budgeting, purchasing, debt management, payroll, risk management
Personnel services	Employment, personnel record keeping, fringe benefit analysis, collective bargaining
Pupil personnel services	Testing programs, health programs, guidance/counseling, social work
Public relations	Newsletters, press releases, media coordination, public opinion polling
Governmental relations	Legal issues, state and federal programs, grants, relationships with other governmental units
Special services	Special education, gifted and talented education
Food services	Menu planning, food purchasing, cafeteria record keeping
Transportation services	Bus routing, bus purchasing, bus maintenance
Maintenance services	Maintenance and custodial services, purchase of custodial supplies, work coordination

Other Careers in Administration

Although most persons who specialize in school administration work for public school districts, a number of other job opportunities exist. Table 2.7 contains information that outlines these opportunities. You should note that the level of education and experience required for these positions varies considerably.

Many states have implemented early retirement programs that allow administrators and other educators to receive full benefits from state retirement programs between the ages of 50 and 60. School administrators who have taken advantage of this benefit have often found their services are in demand by businesses and other governmental agencies (Kowalski & Sweetland, 2001). Consequently, many administrators now experience dual careers because their knowledge and skills are transferable to other types of organizational settings.

TABLE 2.7   *Other Career Opportunities for School Administration Specialists*

Sector	Position Descriptions
State government	Many of the employees in a state department of education hold degrees in education administration or closely related fields. This is especially true in higher-level positions. In addition, some other state agencies may employ persons who have degrees in education administration (e.g., policy analysts working with the state legislature).
Federal government	The U.S. Department of Education employs many individuals who have degrees in education administration; typically, persons with doctoral degrees and considerable experience are recruited for many of these positions.
Higher education	Persons with doctorates in education administration are employed in higher education to be professors, researchers, and administrators.
Private consulting	Although anyone can self-identify as a consultant, most persons who are successful in providing such services for school administration possess a doctorate and extensive experience in administration.
Commercial	Some persons with degrees in school administration work for profit-seeking companies that provide goods or services to schools and districts. The most common are book companies, software companies, and instructional program companies.

Implications for Practice

The discussion of professionalism presented here serves two purposes: to create an awareness of similarities and differences between education administration and other professions and to create an understanding of the relationship between professionalism and practice. Pronouncements that administrators are professionals have not automatically resulted in public acceptance of the claim. Those engaged in the study and practice of school administration must give meaning to this classification, because the concept entails more than income and status. For school administrators, professionalism also involves factors such as a knowledge base, academic preparation for practice, moral and ethical decision making, and an intricate balance of management and leadership roles.

As you contemplate a career as a school administrator, you should establish a foundation of information that permits you to make enlightened choices. You need to know that school administration encompasses many jobs, that each job includes a variety of responsibilities, and that practice occurs in many different types of environments. You should have valid information about the quality of life afforded by a career in school administration, and this includes both extrinsic and intrinsic rewards. In essence, good choices are made possible by complete information about preparation, licensure, and practice. Most important, you should know that the nature of work performed by school administrators continues to change as teachers become closer to true professionals.

This chapter has provided information about the general functions of administration as well as the application of these functions in various jobs. Too often, educators allow random circumstances in life to determine their career paths. You can avoid this pitfall if you honestly look at yourself with regard to *what you like to do* and *what you are capable of doing.*

For Further Discussion _____

1. Is school administration a real profession? Why or why not?

2. What are the advantages and disadvantages of being a school principal?

3. Why do schools have principals?

4. What are some reasons why an elementary school might have an assistant principal?

5. What are the differences between a junior high school and a middle school? How do these differences influence the roles of principals?

6. What is meant by an extended contract? Why do principals almost always have extended contracts?

7. Do you believe that high school principals, middle school principals, and elementary school principals require the same qualities to be successful? Why or why not?

8. What is the difference between the titles of deputy superintendent, associate superintendent, and assistant superintendent?

9. What is the typical difference between the roles of assistant superintendent for curriculum and director of curriculum?

10. Over the past 100 years, superintendents have been expected to assume several different roles. What are they?

11. To what extent are the principalship and superintendency dissimilar roles?

Other Suggested Activities _____

1. Discuss the possible reasons why persons in your class want to become an administrator.

2. Divide the class into three groups: elementary school educators, middle school educators, and high school educators. Compare and contrast what you have observed in principal behavior.

3. Discuss the advantages and disadvantages of requiring principals to have at least three years of successful teaching experience.

4. Determine the scope of district-level administration in your local school system. Compare and contrast the outcomes in class.

5. Develop a list of goals you would like to accomplish during your study of school administration. What are your expectations of professional preparation?

References

Anderson, L., & Van Dyke, L. (1963). *Secondary school administration*. Boston: Houghton Mifflin.

Barth, R. S. (1987). The principal and the profession of teaching. In W. Greenfield (Ed.), *Instructional leadership* (pp. 249–270). Boston: Allyn and Bacon.

Bennis, W., & Nanus, B. (1985). *Leaders: The strategies for taking charge*. New York: Harper and Row.

Blumberg, A. (1985). *The school superintendent: Living with conflict*. New York: Teachers College Press.

Blumberg, A., & Greenfield, W. (1980). *The effective principal: Perspectives on school leadership*. Boston: Allyn and Bacon.

Boris-Schacter, S., & Merrifield, S. (2000). Why "particularly good" principals don't quit. *Journal of School Leadership, 10*(1), 84–98.

Bryman, A. (1986). *Leadership and organizations*. Boston: Routledge & Kegan Paul.

Burlingame, M. (1987). Images of leadership in effective school literature. In W. Greenfield (Ed.), *Instructional leadership* (pp. 3–16). Boston: Allyn and Bacon.

Burnham, J. B. (1989). Superintendents on the fast track. *The School Administrator, 9*(46), 18–19.

Callahan, R. E. (1966). *The superintendent of schools: An historical analysis*. (ERIC Document Reproduction Service No. ED 0104 410)

Carnall, C. A. (1990). *Managing change in organizations*. London: Prentice-Hall International.

Clark, D. C., & Clark, S. N. (1996a). Better preparation of educational leaders. *Educational Researcher, 25*(9), 18–20.

Clark, D. C., & Clark, S. N. (1996b). Building collaborative environments for successful middle level school restructuring. NA*SSP Bulletin, 80*(578), 1–16.

Clark, D. L. (1989). Time to say enough! *Agenda* (Newsletter of the National Policy Board for Education Administration), *1*(1), 1, 4–5.

Coulter, D., & Orme, L. (2000). Teacher professionalism: The wrong conversation. *Education Canada, 40*(1), 4–7.

Elam, S. M. (1990). The 22nd annual Gallup Poll of the public's attitudes toward the public schools. *Phi Delta Kappan, 72*(1), 41–55.

Elmore, R. F. (1999–2000). Building a new structure for school leadership. *American Educator, 23*(4), 6–13.

Epstein, J. L. (1990). What matters in the middle grades—Grade span or practices? *Phi Delta Kappan, 71*(6), 438–444.

Fraze, L., & Hetzel, R. (1990). *School management by wandering around.* Lancaster, PA: Technomic.

Fullan, M. (1998). Leadership for the 21st century: Breaking the bonds of dependency. *Educational Leadership, 55*(7), 6–10.

Granz, J. (1998). Autocrats, bureaucrats and buffoons: Images of principals. *The School Administrator, 55*(9), 34–36.

Glass, T., Björk, L., & Brunner, C. (2000). *The study of the American school superintendent 2000: A look at the superintendent of education in the new millennium.* Arlington, VA: American Association of School Administrators.

Grieder, C., Pierce, T. M., & Jordan, K. F. (1969). *Public school administration* (3rd ed.). New York: Ronald Press.

Guthrie, J. W., & Reed, R. J. (1991). *Educational administration and policy: Effective leadership for American education* (2nd ed.). Englewood Cliffs, NJ: Prentice-Hall.

Hallinger, P., & Murphy, J. (1991). Developing leaders for tomorrow's schools. *Phi Delta Kappan, 72*(7), 514–520.

Hanson, E. (1996). *Educational administration and organizational beha*vior (4th ed.). Boston: Allyn and Bacon.

Hartzell, G. N. (1993). When you're not at the top. *High School Magazine, 1*(2), 16–19.

Hessong, R. F., & Weeks, T. H. (1991). *Introduction to the foundations of education* (2nd ed.). New York: Macmillan.

Hitt, W. D. (1988). *The leader-manager.* Columbus, OH: Battelle Press.

Hughes, L. W., & Ubben, G. C. (1980). *The secondary principal's handbook.* Boston: Allyn and Bacon.

Iwanicki, E. F. (1990). Teacher evaluation for school improvement. In J. Millman & L. Darling-Hammond (Eds.), *The new handbook of teacher evaluation* (pp. 158–174). Newbury Park, CA: Sage.

Judge, H. G. (1988). Cross-national perceptions of teachers. *Comparative Education Review, 32*(2), 143–158.

Katz, D., & Kahn, R. (1978). *The social psychology of organizations* (2nd ed.). New York: Wiley.

Kimbrough, R. B., & Burkett, C. W. (1990). The principalship: Concepts and practices. Englewood Cliffs, NJ: Prentice-Hall.

Kowalski, T. J. (1982). Organizational climate, conflict, and collective bargaining. *Contemporary Education, 54*(1), 27–31.

Kowalski, T. J. (1995). *Keepers of the flame: Contemporary urban superintendents.* Thousand Oaks, CA: Corwin.

Kowalski, T. J. (1998). The role of communication in providing leadership for school restructuring. *Mid-Western Educational Researcher, 11*(1), 32–40.

Kowalski, T. J. (1999). *The school superintendent: Theory, practice, and cases.* Upper Saddle River, NJ: Merrill, Prentice-Hall.

Kowalski, T., Reitzug, U., McDaniel, P., & Otto, D. (1992). Perceptions of desired skills for principals. *Journal of School Leadership, 2*(3), 299–309.

Kowalski, T. J., & Sweetland, S. R. (2001, October). *A comparative analysis of school administrator public retirement systems.* Paper presented at the Annual Meeting of the Midwest Educational Research Association, Chicago.

Kron, J. (1990). The effective middle school principal. In R. Hopstrop (Ed.), *The effective school administrator* (pp. 249–261). Palm Springs, CA: ETC Publications.

Laud, L. E. (1998). Changing the way we communicate. *Educational Leadership, 55*(7), 23–25.

Lieberman, M. (1988). Professional ethics in public education: An autopsy. *Phi Delta Kappan, 70*(2), 159–160.

March, J. G. (1984). How we talk and how we act: Administrative theory and administrative life. In T. Sergiovanni & J. Corbally (Eds.), *Leadership and organizational culture* (pp. 18–35). Urbana: University of Illinois Press.

Marshall, K. (1996). How I confronted HSPS (hyperactive superficial principal syndrome) and began to deal with the heart of the matter. *Phi Delta Kappan, 77*(5), 336–345.

McAdams, R. P. (1998). Who'll run the schools? *American School Board Journal, 185*(8), 37–39.

Medley, D. M., Coker, H., & Soar, R. S. (1984). *Measurement-based evaluation of teacher performance.* New York: Longman.

Miklos, E. (1988). Administrator selection, career patterns, succession, and socialization. In N. J. Boyan (Ed.), *Handbook of research on educational administration* (pp. 53–76). New York: Longman.

Morris, V. C., Crowson, R. L., Porter-Gehrie, C., & Hurwitz, E. (1984). *Principals in action: The realities of managing schools.* Columbus, OH: Charles E. Merrill.

Murphy, J. T. (1991). Superintendents as saviors: From the Terminator to Pogo. *Phi Delta Kappan, 72*(7), 507–513.

Myers, E., & Murphy, J. (1993). The administrative control of high school principals by superintendents: The supervisory function. *Journal of Personnel Evaluation in Education, 7*(1), 67–79.

Natriello, G. (1990). Intended and unintended consequences: Purposes and effects of teacher evaluation. In J. Millman & L. Darling-Hammond (Eds.), *The new handbook of teacher evaluation* (pp. 35–45). Newbury Park, CA: Sage.

Nyberg, D. A. (1990). Power, empowerment, and educational authority. In S. Jacobson & J. Conway (Eds.), *Educational leadership in an age of reform* (pp. 47–64). New York: Longman.

Owens, R. G. (2001). *Organizational behavior in education* (7th ed.). Boston: Allyn and Bacon.

Porter, J. J. (1996). What is the role of the middle level assistant principal, and how should it change? *NASSP Bulletin, 80*(578), 25–30.

Portin, B. S., Shen, J., & Williams, R. C. (1998). The changing principalship and its impact: Voices from principals. *NASSP Bulletin, 82*(602), 1–8.

Purkey, S., & Smith, M. (1983). Effective schools: A review. *Elementary School Journal, 83*, 427–452.

Reis, S. B., Young, I. P., & Jury, J. C. (1999). Female administrators: A crack in the glass ceiling. *Journal of Personnel Evaluation in Education, 13*(1), 71–82.

Rossow, L. F. (1990). *The principalship: Dimensions in instructional leadership.* Englewood Cliffs, NJ: Prentice-Hall.

Rottier, J. (1996). The principal and teaming: Unleashing the power of collaboration. *Schools in the Middle, 5*(4), 31–36.

Schön, D. A. (1987). *Educating the reflective practitioner.* San Francisco: Jossey-Bass.

Sergiovanni, T. J. (1991). The dark side of professionalism in educational administration. *Phi Delta Kappan, 72*(7), 521–526.

Sergiovanni, T. J. (2001). *The principalship: A reflective practice perspective* (4th ed.). Boston: Allyn and Bacon.

Sergiovanni, T. J., Burlingame, M., Coombs, F. S., & Thurston, P. W. (1987). *Educational governance and administration* (2nd ed.). Englewood Cliffs, NJ: Prentice-Hall.

Spencer, W. A., & Kochan, F. K. (2000). Gender related differences in career patterns of principals in Alabama: A statewide study. *Education Policy Analysis Archives, 8*(9).

Spring, J. (1990). *The American school: 1642–1990* (2nd ed.). New York: Longman.

Stufflebeam, D., & Webster, W. J. (1988). Evaluation as an administrative function. In N. Boyan (Ed.), *Handbook of research on educational administration* (pp. 569–602). New York: Longman.

Sykes, G. (1999). The "new professionalism" in education: An appraisal. In J. Murphy & K. Seashore Louis (Eds.), *Handbook of research on educational administration* (2nd ed.) (pp. 227–249). San Francisco: Jossey-Bass.

Tanner, C. K., & Stone, C. D. (1998). School improvement policy: Have administrative functions of principals changed in schools where site-based management is practiced? *Education Policy Analysis Archives, 6*(6), 4–7.

Task Force on Teaching as a Profession. (1986). *A nation prepared: Teachers for the 21st century.* New York: Carnegie Forum on Education and the Economy.

Walton, H. F. (1973). *The man in the principal's office: An ethnography.* New York: Holt, Rinehart and Winston.

Wimpleberg, R. K. (1987). The dilemma of instructional leadership and a central role for central office. In W. Greenfield (Ed.), *Instructional leadership* (pp. 100–117). Boston: Allyn and Bacon.

Wood, C. I., Nicholson, E. W., & Findley, D. G. (1985). *The secondary school principal* (2nd ed.). Boston: Allyn and Bacon.

Yukl, G. (1989). *Leadership in organizations* (2nd ed.). Englewood Cliffs, NJ: Prentice-Hall.

3

The Study of School Administration

Chapter Content _____

During the middle to late 1980s, as the focus of school reform shifted from students to educators, many states revised standards for teacher education and licensing. Yet, the quality of school administrator education received only slight attention during this period (Glass, 1991). One group that did question the efficacy of the preparation of principals and superintendents was the National Commission on Excellence in Educational Administration. Members of this reform coalition pointed out that among the more than 500 colleges and universities offering courses or degrees in school administration, less than 200 had the resources and commitments necessary to meet recommended standards for preparing practitioners (Leaders for America's Schools, 1988). As the focus of school reform moved toward issues of governance during the 1990s, concerns about administrator preparation began receiving much more attention. Before long, many states were revising licensing requirements and accreditation standards, literally forcing departments of school administration to reconsider their long-standing practices.

This chapter is designed to help you understand the nature and scope of school administration as a field of study. Students taking their first course in this specialization commonly ask questions about the amount and type of courses that they will need to enter practice. Although programs vary considerably across colleges and universities, the general framework of professional preparation is characterized by six categories of responsibilities, functions, and experiences:

1. Management
2. Instructional leadership
3. Organizational leadership
4. Position-specific courses
5. Research
6. Field-based experiences

The concluding portion of the chapter examines forces that are prodding school administration professors to revise their curricula.

Professional Preparation Programs

Most professions have structured their educational programs to accommodate individuals who have just graduated from college with a bachelor's degree. The typical student begins medical school at about age 22, attends only one school for at least four consecutive years on a full-time basis, and is admitted and graduates as part of a cohort. Competition for admission is fierce, even though the tuition is usually higher than graduate study in any other discipline. None of these conditions is generally true with respect to school administration. Most often, graduate study in school administration is completed sporadically, at several institutions, and over long time periods (Stout, 1989). School administration students often are mid-career educators attending school part time while working full time. Today, many of the courses they take are delivered away from the campus, either by extension, by the Internet, or by satellite television.

Degrees in School Administration

Three levels of graduate degrees are commonly granted in school administration:

1. Master's degrees (e.g., M.A., M.S., M.Ed.)
2. Specialist's degrees (Ed.S.)
3. Doctoral degrees (Ph.D. and Ed.D.)

The master's degree is the first level of graduate study and typically requires 30 to 40 semester hours of course credits. In some states, students are able to obtain a principal's license by completing a master's degree; in other states, some level of post-master's work is also necessary. A combination of institutional degree requirements and state licensing requirements results in a substantial amount of variability across institutions preparing administrators.

The specialist degree or certificate is unique to the education profession. The most common title for this degree is Education Specialist (Ed.S.). Some universities grant a formal certificate instead of a degree to designate completion of a structured sixth-year of graduate study; the most common titles for this program are the Certificate of Advanced Graduate Study (C.A.G.S.) and the Certificate of Advanced Study (C.A.S.). The continued presence of a sixth year of structured graduate study in school administration is attributable to two factors. First, some states (e.g., Arkansas, Indiana, and Iowa) require either an Ed.S. (or equivalent degrees or certificates) or a doctorate to be eligible to obtain a superintendent's license. Second, a number of nondoctoral-granting institutions offer the Ed.S. in order to provide students an opportunity to earn a second graduate degree. Completion of a sixth-year degree usually requires 30 to 45 semester hours of academic work beyond the master's degree. A practicum or internship is almost always required, and some institutions also require a thesis.

Early in the twentieth century, school administrators possessing an earned doctoral degree were rare. This was largely true because doctoral degree programs in school administration were just being developed. In addition, most school boards during that period did not believe it was necessary to employ an individual with this degree. Today, conditions are quite different. As many as 75 percent of the local district superintendents now possess earned doctorates in some states.

Two doctoral degrees are awarded in school administrators. The Doctor of Philosophy (Ph.D.) is the traditional degree awarded by graduate schools in most disciplines. The degree continues to be viewed by many as a research/scholarship degree. The Doctor of Education (Ed.D.) was established as a professional school degree oriented toward the needs of individuals who intended to become practitioners; it is similar to practitioner degrees offered in other professions (e.g., the J.D. in law, the D.D.S. in dentistry, or the M.D. in medicine). Although some still consider the Ph.D. to be primarily a research degree and the Ed.D. a practice-based degree, there are no universal standards that separate them. One university's Ed.D. may be another university's Ph.D. (Griffiths, Stout, & Forsyth, 1988). A 1987 study of 27 doctoral programs, for example, found that research and statistical course requirements for the Ed.D. and Ph.D. degrees differed only slightly, except for a somewhat higher expectation for exposure to research methods in Ph.D. programs (Norton & Levan, 1988). Some institutions offer both doctoral degrees; and it is in these universities that the greatest distinctions are likely.

Completion of a doctoral degree typically requires a total of 80 to 100 semester hours of graduate work. Requirements for the Ph.D. often include successful completion of courses and proficiency examinations for research tools, such as foreign languages, computer programming, or statistical analysis. These same requirements also may exist for the Ed.D. degree at some institutions. The completion of a residency, a period of full-time study on campus, has either been redefined or dropped at many institutions. Overall, students in both Ph.D. and Ed.D. programs are still required to pass comprehensive written and oral examinations and to successfully write and defend a dissertation (Hackman & Price, 1995).

Nondegree Programs

Typically, school administration departments offer licensure and certification programs as well as degree programs. Therefore, many students enrolled in courses are not pursuing graduate degrees. Nondegree students may be categorized as follows:

- *Licensure students:* A large number of students pursue licensure in administration after having completed a master's degree in an area other than school administration.
- *Continuing education students:* Some educators simply enroll in courses in an effort to remain current in their profession.
- *License renewal students:* Many states have discontinued issuing life licenses— a decision that requires practitioners to complete a specified number of courses in order to renew their licenses.
- *Nonschool administration students:* Some persons who have no intention of being a school administrator enroll in school administration courses. Examples include classroom teachers who want to learn more about a specific topic (e.g., learning more about public finance, leadership, or school law) and public agency officials who feel they can benefit from such classes (e.g., a YMCA director taking a course in personnel administration or public relations).

Requirements for enrolling in courses as a nondegree-seeking student vary across universities.

Studying School Administration

Some writers (e.g., Campbell, Corbally, & Nystrand, 1983) have characterized school administration as an applied field similar to engineering or medicine and not a discipline in the sense that chemistry and history are disciplines. Such descriptions can be misleading, because school administration is a legitimate discipline within academe. Study in this specialization, however, includes knowledge, information, and skills from several academic areas. Thus, the typical curriculum for studying school administration is eclectic. Amalgamating knowledge and practices from several disciplines and professions is not unique to education. Management and leadership in all types of organizations are commonly studied in the context of their application rather than as isolated topics. Examples of this format for academic study are found in university-based programs in business administration, hotel and restaurant management, public administration, and hospital administration, just to name a few.

Some critics (e.g., Haller, Brent, & McNamara, 1997) have argued that there is little or no evidence showing that completing degrees or licensing courses in school administration influences school effectiveness; however, most policymakers and university officials have rejected a broader conclusion that professional preparation is insignificant. One reason why school administration is subject to criticisms is the lack of uniformity in graduate study. Unlike most other professional schools, schools of education do not deliver a national curriculum (Kowalski, 1999). Variations in professional study are found in the number and types of courses required for specific degrees, the number and types of clinical experiences required, and the titles given to courses of study. These variations are related to differences in the following areas:

- State licensing standards
- Faculty philosophy
- Institutional history and culture
- Needs and interests of students being served

Despite the fact that preparation programs are not alike, school administration has relied on "one best model" for professional licensing (Cooper & Boyd, 1987). The connotation of a dominant model refers to common criteria embraced by both state licensing boards and departments of school administration relative to obtaining a first license (almost always a principal's license). This traditional path for initially entering practice has included a minimum of three years of teaching experience, a master's degree (usually in school administration), and the completion of specified courses (either as part of or in addition to a master's degree).

Professional Preparation Components

Although specific courses and course titles vary, the study of school administration commonly is divided into six categories. These categories and their most typical components are illustrated in Figure 3.1. You should note several issues as you study these categories:

- The components discussed here are not quantitatively equal. For example, students are likely to complete many more credits in the area of management studies than in field experiences.
- Balance among the categories varies, in some instances markedly, from one university-based program to another.
- Some courses do not fit neatly into a single category. As an example, courses in communication and technology have applicability across all categories.

Keeping these points in mind, you should acquire an understanding of the scope of academic preparation in school administration.

Management Studies

Management studies concentrate on knowledge and skills related to controlling or supervising human and material resources. There are two reasons why this component of school administration is the most readily recognized. First, many of the

Management Studies
- Financial management
- School law
- Public relations
- Facility management
- Personnel management
- Collective bargaining

Instructional Leadership Studies
- Curriculum
- Instruction
- Social foundations of education
- Staff development

Organizational Leadership Studies
- Organizational theory
- Leadership theory
- Policy analysis
- Organizational planning
- Behavioral sciences

Position-Specific Studies
- Principalship
- Superintendency

Research

Field Experiences

FIGURE 3.1   *Common Content of School Administration Programs*

actual responsibilities relegated to administrators involve management. Second, the public commonly focuses most directly on management practices when evaluating administrators. For example, taxpayers often focus most directly on budget management, personnel management, and facilities management when they demand accountability from superintendents and principals.

Financial Management.   Managing fiscal resources has obvious importance in public education. School finance studies consist of three basic functions (Guthrie, Garms, & Pierce, 1988):

1. How revenues are generated
2. How revenues are distributed
3. How revenues are managed

The study of school finance is generally divided into two courses: one focusing on the economics of education and one focusing on business management. The former includes theoretical instruction intended to provide you with a foundation for understanding economic and political decisions that determine public policies for funding education. Common topics in this course include the economic value of education, principles of taxation, federal funding, state funding concepts, equalization of resources, and the use of public funds for private schools. The second course is geared toward management applications. Typically included are units on budget planning, budget management, purchasing, insurance programs (risk management), and auditing. Usually, this course also contains subject matter related to support services such as food services, transportation, and facility maintenance—responsibilities frequently supervised by business managers.

Many students incorrectly assume that school finance courses are not relevant for principals. In reality, building-level administrators need considerable knowledge on this topic because they engage in a range of finance activities (Buchanan, 1995). For example, they make allocation and purchasing decisions that require an understanding of district budgets; they manage school-based funds (e.g., extracurricular accounts and book rental accounts); and they explain fiscal decisions to staff and parents. And more recently, the movement toward site-based management has increased the likelihood that principals will have to make a greater range of fiscal decisions (Sharp, 1994).

The need to study finance is more obvious in relation to district-level administrative positions. Superintendents as well as business managers require a solid grounding in both public-sector economics and business management. Licensing criteria for district administrators in many states reflect this fact.

School Law. Operating in the public domain, schools are subject to myriad laws and regulations. If these laws were immutable or if they stemmed from a single source, the life of the school administrator would be less complex. But such is not the case. New laws are enacted, and existing laws altered and eradicated, almost continuously. Laws originate from one of three sources (Valente, 1980):

1. Written constitutions
2. Statutes
3. Judge-made law

The first category constitutes the highest form of law. Constitutions provide the basic structure and powers of state and federal governments and their agencies. Statutes, enacted by Congress at the federal level and state legislatures at the state level, are the next highest form of law. Statutes cannot be in conflict with constitutional provisions and are subject to change over time. Judges interpret the meanings of constitutions and statutes; and in so doing, they establish precedents that have a bearing on the enforcement of laws.

Recognizing the dynamic nature of legal issues, school law courses are structured to concentrate on rights, responsibilities, and liabilities of members of the educational community (i.e., administrators, teachers, students, parents, and school board members). In a litigious society, the study of school law is essential for both school-based and central office administrators. Students in these courses commonly examine legal concepts (e.g., *in loco parentis*), discuss legal responsibilities (e.g., reporting child abuse cases) that permeate the work life of principals and superintendents, and examine case law in key areas of practice (e.g., special education placements and tort liability). One of the major aims of studying school law is to inform administrators that they cannot develop policy and regulations in an unrestricted manner. School law students learn that there are constraints placed on their rule-making prerogatives and they examine the nature of those constraints (McCarthy, Cambron-McCabe, & Thomas, 1997).

Public Relations. Schools, especially public schools, are concerned about relationships with community agencies, private businesses, and other organizations that help form public opinion. In democratic societies, public agencies are expected to maintain a reciprocal relationship with surrounding communities for the following reasons (Kowalski, 2000):

- Taxpayers provide the fiscal resources necessary for operating schools.
- Schools are central to community life in a democracy.
- Opinions, needs, and frustrations existing in the community-at-large can significantly affect the success of schools and districts.
- The ability of schools and districts to identify and solve problems depends on administrators accessing and using accurate information.

Both increasing levels of state deregulation and district decentralization have made public relations an even more important element of school administration because more and more policy decisions are being made at the local level.

The study of public relations (also referred to as school/community relations) became a part of school administration as far back as the 1920s. The main objectives were to promote awareness of the importance of schooling, to build confidence and financial support, and to encourage parents to become more involved in their children's education (Holliday, 1990). The study of public relations is designed to provide the practitioner with information necessary to provide information, to receive information, and to establish planned relationships. In the context of contemporary school administration practice, public relations is viewed as an evolving social science and leadership process relying on multimedia approaches designed to (Kowalski, 2000):

- Build goodwill
- Enhance the public's attitude toward education
- Augment interaction and two-way symmetrical communication between schools and their ecosystems
- Provide vital and useful information to the public and employees
- Serve as integral part of planning and decision making

Since America's movement into an Information Age, the study of school public relations has become even more important. Topics in this course commonly include internal and external communication, communication channels, media relationships, ethical and moral standards of practice, the use of technology for communication, and evaluation of school and district public relations programs. For many students, a course in school public relations is their only opportunity to study communication.

Facility Management.   School buildings constitute sizeable investments and they are overt symbols of a community's beliefs and values with regard to education. Seasoned practitioners attest that facilities-related issues are often among the most emotional they encounter. Arguments over the location or size of a new school or disputes regarding which elementary school to close because of declining enrollments exemplify aspects of facility management that can become quite controversial.

A number of contemporary conditions have made facility planning and management more exacting. Consider the following:

- Approximately half of the school buildings in the United States need to be renovated or replaced (General Accounting Office, 1996).
- In some states (e.g., Florida and Georgia), enrollments are growing so rapidly that some districts must build new schools every year.
- Escalating costs for school construction, without corresponding changes in funding formulas, have made the financing of facility projects more difficult in many states (Kowalski & Schmielau, 2001).
- The infusion of technology into schools and districts requires administrators to have an understanding of how these tools can be deployed.
- Concerns about energy sources and environmental pollution have increased demands for more exact planning in areas such as energy efficiency.
- Concerns for health and safety of school facilities (e.g., asbestos and radon) have caused the need to alter many existing buildings.
- Research on the effects of learning environments (e.g., colors and lighting) raises expectations that educators will play a more prominent role in specifying the needs of educational environments.
- Many communities are reluctant to provide funding for new or improved facilities; thus, administrators must play key roles in building taxpayer support (Kowalski, 2002).

Administrator responsibilities in the area of school facilities are divided into two broad categories: planning and managing. *Planning* includes using various approaches for assessing the need for facility improvements and determining how those needs should be met. *Managing* entails the day-to-day care of buildings and grounds, which includes preventive maintenance, routine maintenance, and custodial services. Many principals underestimate how much of their time is actually consumed with facility-related responsibilities and problems. The need to renovate or replace nearly half of the nation's schools stems from decades of neglect during which administrators diverted from maintenance to more politically visible problems without adequately considering the consequences (Chick, Smith, & Yeabower, 1987).

Personnel Management. Courses in personnel administration concentrate on the management and development of human resources, required tasks in every organization. Often, educators have a narrow vision of this function, thinking that it involves only employment practices (Rebore, 1997). Actually, it includes the following range of responsibilities:

- Establishing quantitative and qualitative specifications that identify the organization's needs with regard to employment
- Creating recruitment strategies and the actual recruitment of personnel
- Establishing selection parameters and the actual selection of personnel
- Planning placement and induction activities
- Planning and organizing staff development
- Conducting performance appraisals of personnel
- Fashioning a compensation program (including management of a benefits program) and administering it
- Maintaining personnel records (a task made more difficult by a host of legal considerations—for instance, privacy laws)
- Planning and organizing a program of performance evaluation

Collective bargaining often is considered a part of personnel management; however, it is addressed next as a separate topic.

Although initial employment is not the sole activity in personnel administration, it remains its most visible and critical element. This is particularly true with regard to employing professional staff (teachers and administrators). Increasingly, employment practices are being scrutinized with respect to school effectiveness and compliance with legal and ethical standards. Principals, for example, are encouraged to continuously revise teacher selection criteria as part of their overall effort to achieve school improvement (Hirsh, 1995). In addition, administrators are encouraged to remain current with existing laws governing discriminatory practices (Young & Prince, 1999).

Collective Bargaining. Since the late 1960s, administrators in virtually all school systems have had to address collective bargaining issues. By the mid-1980s, slightly over two-thirds of the states required school boards to engage in this unbidden practice (Lieberman, 1986). The magnitude of collective bargaining on the lives of school administrators is generally not visible to the public. For instance, most taxpayers do not recognize that school boards and administrators often must negotiate and subsequently manage contracts with multiple employee groups.

Many departments of school administration have separated collective bargaining from personnel administration so that distinct courses could be taught on each topic. Where this has occurred, the following issues are usually included in the collective bargaining course:

- History of unions in education
- Purposes of collective bargaining
- Strategies for the employer in negotiating contracts
- Associated procedures, such as arbitration and mediation
- Management of problems stemming from bargaining (e.g., strikes and boycotts)
- Contract management
- Alternatives to traditional bargaining (e.g., consensus bargaining)
- Evaluation of bargaining procedures

Clearly, the total process of collective bargaining requires more than management. Many of the decisions affecting policy require leadership. Superintendents and other administrators often recommend, or help forge, school board positions on delicate matters, many of which have direct implications for instructional programming. Often, administrators have a negative view of teachers' unions because they believe that collective bargaining weakens efforts to produce school reform (DeMitchell & Barton, 1996). Studying collective bargaining provides administrators an opportunity to examine their own biases and philosophy and to gain understandings regarding more effective approaches to working collaboratively with teachers and other employees.

Instructional Leadership Studies

Research on school improvement exhibits the positive role that can be played by building-level administrators (e.g., Firestone & Wilson, 1985; Hallinger & Heck, 1998) as well as superintendents and their support staffs (e.g., Pajak & Glickman, 1989) in producing desired instructional goals. In part, this research has reinforced long-standing beliefs that both building-based and central office administrators should be first and foremost instructional leaders. Realization of this goal, however, has been hampered by a multitude of obstacles. One of the most serious has been the expectation that superintendents and principals treat teachers as subordinates rather than as professional colleagues (Liftig, 1990).

The popularity of decentralization concepts such as site-based management has heightened concerns about principals who fail to be instructional leaders. Yet, many principals spend much of their workdays either isolated in their offices or away from the school campus (Frase & Hetzel, 1990). Critics ask, Is this lack of visibility in classrooms because principals are not prepared to be instructional leaders or is it because they choose not to assume this role? Graduate study can prepare a person to be an instructional leader, but the decision to assume this responsibility is often a product of individual preferences and school culture. "Although the experiential, institutional, and political forces influencing principals are often similar, the personal predilections and perceptions of individuals regarding the limits of what can be done appear to vary significantly" (Crowson & McPherson, 1987, p. 152). In districts where administrators are expected to assume purely managerial roles, a natural selection process often occurs so that only those who embrace this value survive.

In an effort to avoid the pitfall of preparing administrators to be only managers, state licensing boards and school administration departments require aspiring administrators to complete courses related to instructional leadership. These courses fall into two broad categories: curriculum and instruction. *Curriculum* commonly entails the selection and sequencing of courses of study and related learning experiences. *Instruction*, by contrast, is process oriented—it focuses on the application of teaching paradigms, the selection and use of equipment and materials, and similar functions associated with teaching.

Curriculum. The study of curriculum includes a number of domains. The most common are:

- Curriculum theory (determining what knowledge is of most worth or how knowledge can be structured for desired outcomes)
- Curriculum development (deciding what to teach and what materials to use)
- Curriculum assessment (measuring and evaluating structure and outcomes)

The primary reason why administrators study curriculum is to acquire knowledge and skill relative to planning, organizing, and evaluating learning experiences.

The number of curriculum courses required by universities varies because of inconstant state licensing criteria and differing program philosophies. Generally, students complete only the minimum number of courses despite observations that it is difficult, if not impossible, to be an effective instructional leader without a thorough grasp of curriculum (Rossow, 1990). The connection between academic study and practice is significant. As Robert Wimpelberg (1987) assessed, one common reason why principals shy away from an active involvement in instructional leadership is that they simply do not have an adequate academic grounding in curriculum and instruction.

The focus and extent of curriculum study often depends on the degree program or license being sought. For example, a person acquiring a master's degree in order to obtain certification as an elementary principal may take only one course in elementary school curriculum. A candidate seeking a Ph.D. with the intention of obtaining a school superintendent's license may take two or three different curriculum courses. Some students choose to complete a minor or cognate in curriculum, especially if they desire to work in positions requiring instructional leadership skills (e.g., principal or curriculum director).

School administrators do not work alone to develop curriculum. Parents, school board members, state legislatures, governors, teachers, students, and even textbook publishers may play critical roles in determining what is taught in schools (Schubert, 1986). District and school administrators are expected to provide leadership that facilitates the collective work of others. To fulfill this expectation, administrators must know how to plan, organize, and evaluate the content of school programs. In addition, they must have the ability to evaluate the social context of schooling, especially with regard to reflectively examining personal beliefs (Liston & Zeichner, 1990). Determining what knowledge is of most worth, organizing that knowledge into instructional segments that meet the tests of vertical and horizontal integration, and evaluating the outcomes are critical responsibilities in the realm of curriculum leadership. Increasingly, superintendents' roles in curriculum are being recognized as pivotal; these administrators commonly assume roles as visionaries, collaborators, supporters, and delegators (Bredeson, 1996).

Instruction.   Whereas curriculum focuses on what should be taught and the organizational dimensions of subject matter, instruction concentrates on delivery systems. With regard to school administration, three functions are especially cogent (Olivia & Pawlas, 2000):

1. Helping teachers plan for instruction
2. Helping teachers present instruction
3. Helping teachers evaluate instruction

The term *instructional leadership,* much like *leadership,* has multiple meanings in the literature and in practice. Wilma Smith and Richard Andrews (1989) created a list of expectations that help describe the role:

- A provider of human resources
- A provider of instructional resources
- A communicator
- A visible presence in instructional activities

Clinical supervision is a specialized element of instructional leadership. It is defined as "that phase of instructional supervision which draws its data from first-hand observations of actual teaching events, and involves face-to-face (and other associated) interaction between the supervisor and teacher in the analysis of teaching behavior and activities for instructional improvement" (Goldhammer, Anderson, & Krajewski, 1980, pp. 19–20). Clinical supervision is considered the most direct means by which a principal functions as an instructional leader (Smith & Andrews, 1987).

Supervision of instruction is a common course completed by school administration students. In addition, internships often provide students with hands-on and face-to-face activities entailing instructional leadership activities. Responsibilities in instructional supervision are the primary reason why states customarily require applicants for a principal's license to have both a teaching license and teaching experience.

Social Foundations of Education.   In Chapter 1, a notation was made that schools are complex organizations that have evolved over many decades. The effects of culture, individual learner needs, social trends, popular values and beliefs, and information about learning exemplify factors that have contributed to shaping modern schools. Students preparing to be school administrators acquire knowledge regarding these forces in courses commonly referred to as the "The Social Foundations of Education." The most common content includes history, philosophy, and sociology of education.

As mentioned, courses taken by school administration students do not fall neatly into any one category of study, and this is especially true of foundations courses. Educational psychology, for example, is considered to be part of educational foundations at some universities; others view this subject to be part of instructional theory; and still others categorize it as a totally separate area of study. Multicultural education is treated in a similar fashion. Some institutions combine the study of social foundations into a single generic course that has direct applicability to the needs and interests of aspiring administrators. Such a course may be called "The Social Foundations of School Administration."

Knowledge of history, philosophy, sociology, and educational psychology provides an administrator with insights enhancing leadership responsibilities. Take, for instance, the tasks of curriculum planning and evaluation. Not all school-based learning experiences are planned or visible in curriculum guides. In every school there is a hidden curriculum composed of unstated, implicit, and sometimes unintentional messages transmitted to students through classes, extracurricular activities, and even social relationships (Bennett & LeCompte, 1990). A solid grounding in educational foundations increases an administrator's ability to integrate the visible and invisible curriculum. In addition, this knowledge enhances an educator's ability to make decisions in all areas of responsibility and to serve as a moral agent (Pietig, 1998).

Staff Development. American industry has learned many lessons in the past 50 years, and one of the most important relates to the need to continuously improve employee performance. In a global economy, profit-seeking companies search for advancements that give them a competitive edge in manufacturing, marketing, and sales. These improvements might include the acquisition of new technologies or the enhancement of employee knowledge and skills. As a consequence, U.S. businesses now spend more money and time on staff development than they have in the past, largely because they realize that investments in human capital are critical to organizational development.

Informed school leaders also recognize that purposeful organizational change does not occur easily or naturally. Like their counterparts in business, they especially realize that planned change is a slow and difficult process for the professional staff (Guskey, 1985). But despite the realization that lasting educational change is almost always evolutionary, contemporary practitioners face mounting pressures to reshape schools immediately. Observations made in private industry indicate that organizational change is enhanced when leaders are able to identify employees who have an especially high need for change and to provide them with growth opportunities (Connor & Lake, 1988). In essence, change is best accomplished with

people who are willing to change and when these individuals are properly prepared to engage the process. Essentially, administrators must have an accurate assessment of the organization's climate and culture—knowledge that may take several
years to acquire.

The heavy reliance on people to reform education is a reality that gives staff
development both its importance and its urgency (Harris, 1980). Unlike conditions in highly mechanized factories, school improvement cannot be achieved by
merely modernizing equipment or installing robotics. Indeed, computers and other
technology can facilitate improved instruction, but it is staff development that
permits the cultivation of teacher knowledge and skills—a powerful factor in
school improvement (Boyer, 1983).

Historically, schools have invested very little in staff development. This oversight has strengthened the erroneous belief that teachers and administrators
should and do learn everything they need to know prior to entering practice. The
lack of attention to continuous learning opportunities has become especially obvious during the past two decades as districts and schools moved toward concepts
such as decentralization, shared decision making, and teacher empowerment.
One reason why administrators study staff development is to ensure that they are
prepared to facilitate this crucial process. This responsibility includes serving as a
facilitator to involve others in self-improvement activities (Glickman, 1990).

Organizational Leadership Studies

In this book, leadership functions are divided between those that are primarily
instructional and those that are primarily organizational. The demarcation
between these two responsibilities is not a bold line but more of a gray area where
one role bleeds into the other. Whereas instructional leadership is concerned with
subject matter largely unique to schools, organizational leadership deals with functions common to all institutions. Broadly, these areas include organizational theory, leadership theory, policy analysis, organizational planning, and the behavioral
sciences.

Organizational Theory.   Theory is not a dream or a wish; it is not a supposition
or speculation; nor is theory a philosophical position indicating the way things
should be (Owens, 2001). Rather, theory is briefly described as "a set of systematically related propositions specifying causal relationships among variables" (Black
& Champion, 1976, p. 56). Theory is developed through research and serves as a
guideline for understanding phenomena. Organizational theory involves the systematic ordering of knowledge within the context of organizational behavior.
Included are the study of interactions among a particular organizational structure,
individuals, groups, and the general environment.

Study in organizational theory examines several key concepts:

- Organizational climate (policies, management styles, communication techniques, and similar functions that create expectations and understandings
  commonly held by those within the organization)

- Organizational development (the conceptual framework of how organizations function; a strategy for helping organizations self-correct and self-renew)
- Organizational variance (differences in size, structure, leadership, goals, methods, and so forth among organizations)
- Organizational adaptability (how institutional change occurs to meet needs and demands)

The study of these and related concepts reveals the significant differences that exist among schools and districts. The organizational dimensions of schools are discussed in detail in Chapter 6.

Leadership Theory.   Although organizational and leadership theories are highly intertwined, they are clearly separate domains of study. Leadership in education almost always occurs in organizations; and as such, the outcome of any decision or behavior is likely to be a mixture of environmental, organizational, and personal conditions. Thus, it is often difficult to determine where one domain begins and the other ends.

Historically, researchers studied administrators by examining selected traits thought to be associated with effective leadership. Such traits included personality type, intelligence, dispositions toward people, age, and even gender. Today, however, efforts to describe leadership have combined the individual and situational variables—that is, both the leader as a person and the circumstances under which behavior occurs are studied. Two critical concepts studied by school administrators are leadership style and leadership strategies. More recently, two other topics have received increased attention in these courses: differences between male and female administrators and the ethical and moral dimensions of leadership (Campbell, 1997). Leadership theory is also discussed in considerable detail later in this book.

Policy Analysis.   Although the U.S. public often goes to great lengths to separate politics and education, the truth is that schooling has many political dimensions. This is especially the case with regard to policy formulation. Policies are broad guidelines created to give direction to organizations. In public education, policy is made by the federal government (e.g., laws governing the rights of children with disabilities), state government (e.g., mandates that certain subjects be taught), courts of law (e.g., rulings regarding employee rights and responsibilities), and local school boards (e.g., requiring students to do homework). Administrators facilitate the implementation of policy by developing rules and regulations. It should be noted, however, that distinctions between board policy and administrative regulations, especially legal distinctions, are neither crisp nor clear.

Public policy making has five distinct components (Portney, 1986):

1. Problem formation-identification
2. Policy formulation
3. Policy adoption
4. Policy implementation
5. Policy evaluation

Policy analysis is defined as "the process of determining which of various alternative public or governmental policies will most achieve a given set of goals in light of the relations between the policies and goals" (Nagel, 1988, p. 3). Accordingly, policy analysis in education is a procedure used by practitioners and scholars to weigh alternative paths to goal achievement. For example, there are various ways that local school boards can deal with discipline problems. Policy analysis provides a mechanism for weighing the advantages and disadvantages of the options. If done properly, social, political, educational, and financial issues are integrated as the analysis evolves.

The importance of studying policy analysis in schools has been elevated by several conditions:

- Public administrators have relied almost entirely on trial and error to test policy in the past. In today's world, technology, demographics, and scarce resources make this approach unacceptable.
- Public organizations are less apt than are private, profit-seeking organizations to employ policy analysis specialists (Quade, 1989); thus, the responsibility for policy issues rests with administrative staff.
- The growing popularity of decentralization and deregulation as reform strategies is nested in two beliefs: (1) school improvement is most likely if it is achieved through local policies and (2) knowing what to do and how to do it are critical skills if policy is to be successfully developed (Rubin, 1984). Consequently, deregulation and decentralization require administrators to have a good understanding of how to formulate and evaluate public policy.
- Policy development can be enhanced markedly by integrating the process into a systemwide strategic planning effort (Bell, 1989). A greater emphasis on visioning and planning at the local district level has therefore increased the amount of attention given to policy development and analysis.

Despite the critical nature of policy responsibilities, however, practitioners reflecting on their academic preparation often cite policy development and analysis as areas where they feel inadequately prepared (Stout, 1989).

Organizational Planning. Several forms of planning are used in education, but strategic planning has become the most common. Strategic planning involves proposed actions by which administrators systematically evaluate organizational opportunities and the potential impacts of environmental changes in an effort to fulfill the missions of the school district (or school) (Justis, Judd, & Stephens, 1985). The word *strategic* stems from military applications and implies that three elements must be addressed (Stone, 1987):

1. Recognition of an existing situation
2. Depiction of a desired future situation
3. A strategy for adaptation

In other words, strategic planning is a procedure by which school leaders identify gaps between what is and what is desired and develop a plan of action to eradicate those gaps. Modern strategic planning is predicated on the belief that organizations are shaped by external (e.g., communities, courts, legislatures) and internal (e.g., school district policies, needs identified by teachers and administrators) forces. Accordingly, planning is viewed as a series of linkages between a school (or district) and its community. Strengths of the school district are interfaced with needs, demands, and potential support in an effort to provide overall organizational directions (Verstegen & Wagoner, 1989).

The study of organizational planning is often integrated into several courses, but some school administration departments offer a course devoted entirely to this topic. The purpose of studying organizational planning is to enable practitioners to be analysts and assessors of their situations in terms of politics, markets, and finances. Students are expected to learn to use political, social, educational, economic, and demographic data to adjust visions, missions, and procedures (Mauriel, 1989).

Behavioral Sciences.   Emphasis on the behavioral sciences in the preparation of school administrators peaked in the 1960s and 1970s as school administration professors focused on *systems analysis*. This process serves to create understandings of how each part of an organization is interrelated with all other parts. As an example, a decision to discontinue teaching French at a high school could have repercussions for the entire school district. The advances of systems analysis models in public education were a primary, but not sole, factor leading to the inclusion of behavioral sciences in school administration study (Milstein & Belasco, 1973). Emphasizing the behavioral sciences also reflected two interrelated goals: (1) making professional preparation more theoretical and (2) preparing practitioners who could function as social scientists.

During the 1960s and 1970s, it was not uncommon to require doctoral students in school administration to complete a cognate (the equivalent of a minor) in one of the behavioral sciences. Eventually, this requirement fell into disfavor because the focus on the behavioral sciences "resulted in a glaring absence of consideration of the problems faced by practicing school administrators" (Murphy & Forsyth, 1999, p. 19). Today, students preparing to be administrators typically take one to three courses in the behavioral sciences, including courses in education psychology (e.g., learning theory).

Position-Specific Studies

School administration departments also offer courses that are designed to prepare individuals for a specific position. The two that are rather standard are the principalship and the superintendency. These position-specific courses examine the scope of responsibilities associated with a single assignment, and the emphasis is on the application of leadership and management techniques in the context of a given administrative role.

The public school system in the United States is largely organized on a three-tier pattern: elementary, middle, and high school. The latter two divisions have many commonalities, such as departmentalized teaching, extracurricular activities, and segmented instructional periods. Partly for this reason, middle schools (and junior high schools) and high schools are commonly grouped as secondary schools. The study of the principalship may be presented in separate courses (i.e., a course on elementary school administration and a course on secondary school administration) or in a generic course (e.g., the principalship).

Position-specific courses offer an excellent opportunity to bridge theory with practice. They allow students to apply knowledge to problems and to reflect on the potential consequences of their decisions. For this reason, students usually are required to complete several basic courses in school administration before taking position-specific courses. At some institutions, students complete principal or superintendent courses simultaneously with internships in these positions.

Research Methods

In professional practice, knowledge is power, especially when practitioners utilize scientific methods to address current concerns, develop alternative solutions, and evaluate the merits of each alternative. The primary process used to gain such knowledge is research. *Scientific research* has been defined as the "systematic, controlled, empirical, and critical investigation of natural phenomena guided by theory and hypotheses about the presumed relations among such phenomena" (Kerlinger, 1986, p. 10).

Some students question why they have to study research, especially if they have no intention of becoming a researcher. The reason relates to realities of decision making and problem solving in school administration. Practitioners may use research in two primary ways. The first involves addressing current problems or issues. As an example, a high school principal may collect and analyze data that give clearer focus to a pending decision regarding graduation requirements. The second way that research is used to inform practice is through the application of existing research findings (Kowalski & Place, 1998). As an example, a middle school principal who is considering regulations for social activities locates and reads studies that address this issue. To do this, the principal must be prepared to be a research consumer. All administrators can profit from keeping abreast of new knowledge reported in journals and books. Typically, students pursuing a master's degree or a principal's license will be required to complete a course in research methodology; students completing a doctorate are usually required to complete three or more research courses, including statistics and qualitative research courses.

Field-Based Experiences

Recurring criticisms that preparation programs fail to do an adequate job of bridging theory with practice have led to an increased emphasis on field-based experiences. These experiences are broadly divided between practicum experiences and internship experiences. Mark Anderson (1989) distinguished between the two by noting that the practicum is usually a significant project, at least one semester in duration, that permits the student to demonstrate a specific skill or skills and it is not typically a full-time assignment. He described the internship as an experience that is usually a full-time endeavor and more generic in orientation. Since few internships in school administration are full time, the field experiences are really of a practicum nature, although they are called internships.

The internship generally serves two purposes. First, it allows students an opportunity to apply knowledge they have acquired through course work; second, it permits students to determine if they possess the ability and desire to be administrators (Milstein, Bobroff, & Restine, 1991). Typically, universities develop partnerships with local districts and schools so that internships sites are made available. These field-based experiences typically occur toward the latter stages of a student's program.

Preparing Administrators in the Twenty-First Century

Since approximately 1990, traditional school administration programs have come under scrutiny. Critics claim that many of these programs are inadequate and should be improved or discontinued. Doubts about the need for and efficacy of university-based programs for preparing school administrators certainly are not new. School administration professors, however, were able to dismiss their detractors in the past. One reason was that the critics usually failed to support their charges of ineffectiveness with evidence—an omission that often made their motives appear more political than professional. Another reason was that school administration professors enjoyed the unfailing support of practitioner associations and key state leaders.

Current Need for Reform

More recently when reformers began looking at how schools were organized and controlled, they resurrected long-standing apprehensions to bolster their argument that preparation programs were ineffective. These presumptive imperfections included:

- Low standards for recruiting and selecting students (Griffiths, Stout, & Forsyth, 1988)
- A preoccupation with management and an insufficient attention to leadership (e.g., Sergiovanni, 1991)
- Irrelevance caused largely by rigid state licensing requirements and university norms (e.g., Hallinger & Murphy, 1991)
- Inadequate funding and staffing for professional education (e.g., Twombly & Ebmeier, 1989)
- Inadequate clinical education (e.g., Gousha & Mannan, 1991)

- An adrocentric bias in the curriculum (e.g., Shakeshaft, 1989)
- Failure to address gender-related issues affecting practitioners (e.g., Skrla, 1998)
- Abysmal admission and graduation standards (e.g., Clark, 1989)
- Overly theoretical and insufficiently practical curriculum (e.g., Goldman & Kempner, 1988; Maher, 1988)
- A fragmented and overlapping curriculum that contained some useless courses (Cooper & Boyd, 1987)

In the midst of sustained pressures for school reform, these shortcomings were no longer dismissed routinely. Instead, state policymakers cited them frequently as they revised licensure requirements and state accreditation standards.

The National Policy Board for Educational Administration (1989), a reform group composed primarily of school administration professors, recommended that elements of the professional curriculum should contain a common core of knowledge and skills grounded in real problems confronted by practitioners. Many of these real problems are in the realms of instructional and organizational leadership. The recommended core addressed the following topics:

- Societal and cultural influences on schooling
- Teaching and learning processes and school improvement
- Organizational theory
- Methodologies of organizational studies and policy analysis
- Leadership and management processes and functions
- Policy studies and politics of education
- Moral and ethical dimensions of schooling (p. 19)

Over the past two decades, national standards have been developed for licensing, program accreditation, and practice in school administration. Those developed by the Interstate School Leadership Licensure Consortium (ISLLC), for example, have already been adopted by most states. The ISLLC also has sponsored the development of a paper-and-pencil test that the Educational Testing Service designed to be used as part of the license application process. The National Council for the Accreditation of Teacher Education (NCATE) grants professional accreditation to schools of education, and their criteria address both undergraduate and graduate programs. Over the past two decades, the NCATE has strengthened many of its standards in areas such as faculty loads, professional experience, and qualifications for supervising clinical education.

School administration programs have reacted in varying ways to change pressures. Some have initiated new course delivery systems, such as Web-based courses and distance learning courses delivered via satellite television. Others have increased requirements for field-based experiences and created new positions for clinical professors (individuals who focus on practice related knowledge). In a few cases, programs have been transformed radically. The efficacy of these changes and their durability have yet to be determined (McCarthy, 1999). Variations in reforms, however, attest to the less than uniform nature of professional preparation.

Personal Commitment

Regardless of the quality of your experiences in a formal preparation program, you need to commit yourself to lifelong learning. John Goodlad (1990) noted that programs for all professional educators must be conducted in such a way that practitioners accept the responsibility for continual inquiry as a natural aspect of professional practice. In the case of administrators, this means understanding that a degree or licensure program does not constitute complete and comprehensive "training"; rather, such study provides the tools permitting you to become increasingly proficient by utilizing experience, continuing education, and reflection.

Structured learning experiences clearly are not the sole or, in some instances, the primary determinant of practitioner behavior. Philip Hallinger and Joseph Murphy (1991) claimed that although graduates of school administration programs can recite the characteristics of effective schools, many remain unconvinced of their applicability. This suggests that personal and organizational values and beliefs often trump the knowledge administrators receive in classrooms. Once they begin working in schools, practitioners are socialized to accept the prevailing institutional culture—and often that culture reinforces the belief that principals and superintendents are simply managers. Thus, personal motivations and convictions are extremely important with regard to determining how you behave as an administrator. Unless you commit to lifelong learning and to ethical and moral practice, the value of your formal education will be attenuated.

Implications for Practice

In planning your career, you should understand school administration as an applied science—and this includes understanding the academic requirements for entering practice. Often, new students in school administration ask, "How many courses will I have to take? What do I study in these courses?" Since the curriculum encompasses study in several areas, the overview in this chapter was designed to provide basic answers to these queries.

In addition to deciding whether you are willing and able to make the time commitments to becoming an administrator, you need to think about your personal motivations and convictions with regard to this profession. Why are you considering a career in school administration? What type of administrator do you want to become? Are you willing to devote yourself to lifelong learning? These are questions you should answer as early as possible. You are more apt to approach your studies with enthusiasm if you understand the nature and purposes of professional preparation. Students who see courses as senseless hurdles are likely to put forth little effort; as a result, they gain little that will serve them in their career.

Perhaps the most essential point that needs to be made is that courses and internships do not give you all the knowledge and skills you need to be an effective administrator. Rather, they provide basic knowledge and skills and a deep appreciation for what it means to be a professional. Effective practice throughout your career requires a personal commitment to enhancing this knowledge base through continuous learning.

For Further Study

1. What is the difference between a degree program and a licensure program?

2. Why do administrators study research methods?

3. Identify two areas of administrative responsibility that involve both management and leadership.

4. What is theory? Why do administrators study organizational and leadership theory?

5. Define instructional leadership. How can principals provide instructional leadership? How can superintendents provide instructional leadership?

6. Identify the differences between professional preparation in medicine and in school administration. Do you think these differences are important? Why or why not?

7. Should it be possible for persons who have no preparation and experience in teaching to receive a principal's license? Why or why not?

8. What two primary purposes are served by internships?

9. Why should administrators study school finance?

10. In what ways would the study of the philosophy of education enhance the preparation of a school administrator?

11. What forces are prompting reforms in the preparation of school administrators?

Other Suggested Activities

1. Determine the degree requirements for being a principal and superintendent in your state.

2. Obtain the course of study for your current degree program. Determine if you understand the purpose of each of the courses listed.

3. Discuss changes in the preparation of school administrators that are supported by you and others in your class.

4. Read "The Dark Side of Professionalism in Educational Administration" by Thomas Sergiovanni (see the references at the end of this chapter for a full citation). Discuss the major points Sergiovanni makes and how his arguments could affect professional education.

5. Discuss the meaning of lifelong learning and ways that administrators might engage in this process.

References

Anderson, M. E. (1989). Training and selecting school leaders. In S. Smith & P. Piele (Eds.), *School leadership: Handbook for excellence* (2nd ed.) (pp. 53–63). Eugene, OR: ERIC Clearinghouse on Educational Management.

Bell, E. D. (1989). The interaction of strategic planning, policy development, and settings in education. A case study. *Planning and Changing, 20*(4), 237–248.

Bennett, K. P., & LeCompte, M. D. (1990). *How schools work: A sociological analysis of education.* New York: Longman.

Black, J. A., & Champion, D. J. (1976). *Methods and issues in social research.* New York: Wiley.

Boyd, W. L. (1988). Policy analysis, educational policy, and management: Through a glass darkly? In N. Boyan (Ed.), *Handbook of research on educational administration* (pp. 501–522). New York: Longman.

Boyer, E. L. (1983). *High school: A report on secondary education in America.* New York: Harper and Row.

Bredeson, P. V. (1996). Superintendents' roles in curriculum development and instructional leadership: Instructional visionaries, collaborators, supporters, and delegators. *Journal of School Leadership, 6*(3), 243–264.

Buchanan, J. D. (1995). What your principals really want. *School Business Affairs, 61*(4), 20–22.

Campbell, E. (1997). Ethical school leadership: Problems of an elusive role. *Journal of School Leadership, 7*(4), 287–300.

Campbell, R. F., Corbally, J. E., & Nystrand, R. O. (1983). *Introduction to educational administration* (6th ed.). Boston: Allyn and Bacon.

Castetter, W. B. (1981). *The personnel function in educational administration* (3rd ed.). New York: Macmillan.

Chick, C., Smith, P., & Yeabower, G. (1987). Last in first out maintenance budgets. *CEPF Journal, 25*(4), 4–6.

Clark, D. L. (1989). Time to say enough! *Agenda* (Newsletter of the National Policy Board for Educational Administration), *1*(1), 1, 4–5.

Connor, P. E., & Lake, L. K. (1988). *Managing organizational change.* New York: Praeger.

Cooper, B. S., & Boyd, W. L. (1987). The evolution of training for school administrators. In J. Murphy & P. Hallinger (Eds.), *Approaches to administrative training in education* (pp. 3–27). Albany: State University of New York Press.

Crowson, R. L., & McPherson, R. B. (1987). Sources of constraints and opportunities for discretion in the principalship. In J. Lane & H. Walberg (Eds.), *Effective school leadership* (pp. 129–156). Berkeley, CA: McCutchan.

Cuban, L. (1988). *The managerial imperative and the practice of leadership in schools.* Albany: State University of New York Press.

DeMitchell, T. A., & Barton, R. M. (1996). Collective bargaining and its impact on local educational reform efforts. *Educational Policy, 10*(3), 366–378.

Firestone, W. A., & Wilson, B. L. (1985). Using bureaucratic and cultural linkages to improve instruction: The principal's contribution. *Educational Administration Quarterly, 21*(2), 17–30.

Frase, L., & Hetzel, R. (1990). *School management by wandering around.* Lancaster, PA: Technomic.

General Accounting Office. (1996). *School facilities: America's schools report differing conditions.* Washington, DC: U.S. Government Printing Office.

Glass, T. E. (1991). The slighting of administration preparation. *The School Administrator, 48*(4), 29–30.

Glickman, C. D. (1990). *Supervision of instruction: A developmental approach* (2nd ed.). Boston: Allyn and Bacon.

Goldhammer, R., Anderson, R. H., & Krajewski, R. J. (1980). *Clinical supervision* (2nd ed.). New York: Holt, Rinehart and Winston.

Goldman, P., & Kempner, K. (1988). *The administrator's view of administrative training.* (ERIC Document Reproduction Service No. ED 325 979)

Goodlad, J. I. (1990). *Teachers for our nation's schools.* San Francisco: Jossey-Bass.

Gorton, R. A. (1976). *School administration: Challenge and opportunity for leadership.* Dubuque, IA: Wm. C. Brown.

Gousha, R. P., & Mannan, G. (1991). *Analysis of selected competencies: Components, acquisition and measurement. Perceptions of three groups of stakeholders in education.* (ERIC Document Reproduction Service No. ED 336 850)

Griffiths, D. E., Stout, R. T., & Forsyth, P. B. (1988). The preparation of educational administrators. In D. Griffiths, R. Stout, & P. Forsyth (Eds.), *Leaders for America's schools* (pp. 284–304). Berkeley, CA: McCutchan.

Guskey, T. R. (1985). Staff development and teacher change. *Educational Leadership, 42*(7), 57–60.

Guthrie, J. W., Garms, W. I., & Pierce, L. C. (1988). *School finance and education policy: Enhancing educational efficiency, equality, and choice* (2nd ed.). Englewood Cliffs, NJ: Prentice-Hall.

Hackman, D. G., & Price, W. J. (1995). *Preparing school leaders for the 21st century: Results of a national survey of educational leadership doctoral programs.* (ERIC Document Reproduction Service No. ED 378 863)

Haller, E. J., Brent, B. O., & McNamara, J. H. (1997). Does graduate training in educational administration improve America's schools? *Phi Delta Kappan, 79*(3), 222–227.

Hallinger, P., & Heck, R. H. (1998). Exploring the principal's contribution to school effectiveness: 1980–1995. *School Effectiveness and School Improvement, 9*(2), 157–191.

Hallinger, P., & Murphy, J. (1991). Developing leaders for tomorrow's schools. *Phi Delta Kappan, 72*(7), 514–520.

Harris, B. M. (1980). *Improving staff performance through in-service education.* Boston: Allyn and Bacon.

Hirsh, S. (1995). Keeping your school improvement plan on track. *Journal of Staff Development, 16*(1), 2–4.

Holliday, A. E. (1990). Revise the scope of your school-community relations program to enhance student achievement. *Record in Educational Administration and Supervision, 11*(1), 54–59.

Johnson, W. L., & Snyder, K. J. (1989–90). A study on the instructional leadership training needs of school administrators. *National Forum of Educational Administration and Supervision Journal, 6*(3), 80–95.

Justis, R. T., Judd, R. J., & Stephens, D. B. (1985). *Strategic management and policy.* Englewood Cliffs, NJ: Prentice-Hall.

Kerlinger, F. N. (1986). *Foundations of behavioral research* (3rd ed.). New York: Holt, Rinehart and Winston.

Kimbrough, R. B., & Burkett, C. W. (1990). *The principalship: Concepts and practices.* Englewood Cliffs, NJ: Prentice-Hall.

Kindred, L. W., Bagin, D., & Gallagher, D. R. (1990). *The school and community relations* (4th ed.). Englewood Cliffs, NJ: Prentice-Hall.

Kowalski, T. J. (1995). Chasing the wolves from the schoolhouse door. *Phi Delta Kappan, 76*, 486–489.

Kowalski, T. J. (1999). *The school superintendent: Theory, practice, and cases.* Upper Saddle River, NJ: Merrill, Prentice-Hall.

Kowalski, T. J. (2000). School public relations: A new agenda. In T. J. Kowalski (Ed.), *Public relations in schools* (2nd ed.) (pp. 3–29). Upper Saddle River, NJ: Merrill, Prentice-Hall.

Kowalski, T. J. (2002). *Planning and managing school facilities* (2nd ed.). Westport, CT: Bergin and Garvey.

Kowalski, T. J., & Place, A. W. (1998). Reconsidering the role of research in educational administration doctoral programs. In. R. Muth & M. Martin (Eds.), *Toward the year 2000: Leadership for quality schools.* The sixth yearbook of the National Council of Professors of Educational Administration (pp. 36-48). Lancaster, PA: Technomic.

Kowalski, T. J., & Schmielau, R. E. (2001). Potential for states to provide equality in funding construction. *Equity and Excellence in Education, 34*(2), 54–61.

Leaders for America's schools: The report of the National Commission on Excellence in Educational Administration. (1988). In D. Griffiths, R. Stout, & P. Forsyth (Eds.), *Leaders for America's schools* (pp. 284–304). Berkeley, CA: McCutchan.

Lewis, A. (1989). *Wolves at the schoolhouse door: An investigation of the condition of public school buildings.* Washington, DC: Education Writers Association.

Lieberman, M. (1986). *Beyond public education.* New York: Praeger.

Liftig, R. (1990). Our dirty little secrets: Myths about teachers and administrators. *Educational Leadership, 47*(8), 67–70.

Liston, D. P., & Zeichner, K. M. (1990). Teacher education and the social context of schooling: Issues for curriculum development. *American Educational Research Journal, 27*(4), 610–636.

Maher, R. (1988). Are graduate schools preparing tomorrow's administrators? *NASSP Bulletin, 72*(508), 30–34.

Mauriel, J. J. (1989). *Strategic leadership for schools.* San Francisco: Jossey-Bass.

McCarthy, M. M. (1999). The evolution of educational leadership preparation programs. In J. Murphy & K. Seashore Louis (Eds.), *Handbook of research on educational administration* (2nd ed.) (pp. 119–140). San Francisco: Jossey-Bass.

McCarthy, M. M., Cambron-McCabe, N. H., & Thomas, S. B. (1997). *Public school law: Teachers' and students' rights* (4th ed.). Boston: Allyn and Bacon.

Milstein, M. M., & Belasco, J. A. (1973). *Educational administration and the behavioral sciences: A systems approach.* Boston: Allyn and Bacon.

Milstein, M. M., Bobroff, B. M., & Restine, L. N. (1991). *Internship programs in educational administration.* New York: Teachers College Press.

Murphy, J. T. (1991). Superintendents as saviors: From the Terminator to Pogo. *Phi Delta Kappan, 72*(7), 507–513.

Murphy, J., & Forsyth, P. B. (1999). A decade of change: An overview. In J. Murphy & P. Forsyth (Eds.), *Educational administration a decade of reform* (pp. 3–38). Thousand Oaks, CA: Corwin.

Nagel, S. S. (1988). *Policy studies: Integration and evaluation.* New York: Greenwood Press.

National Policy Board for Educational Administration. (1989). *Improving the preparation of school administrators: An agenda for reform.* Charlottesville: University of Virginia.

Norton, M. S., & Levan, F. D. (1988). Doctoral studies of students in educational administration programs in UCEA-member institutions. In D. Griffiths, R. Stout, & P. Forsyth (Eds.), *Leaders for America's schools* (pp. 351–359). Berkeley, CA: McCutchan.

Oliva, P. F., & Pawlas, G. E. (2001). *Supervision for today's schools* (6th ed.). New York: Wiley & Sons.

Owens, R. C. (2001). *Organizational behavior in education* (7th ed.). Boston: Allyn and Bacon.

Pajak, E. F., & Glickman, C. D. (1989). Dimensions of school district improvement. *Educational Leadership*, 46(8), 61–64.

Pietig, J. (1998). How educational foundations can empower tomorrow's teachers: Dewey revisited. *Teacher Education Quarterly, 25*(4), 102–106.

Pitner, N. (1982). *Training of the school administrator: State of the art*. Eugene: Center for Educational Policy and Management at the University of Oregon.

Pitner, N. (1988). School administrator preparation: The state of the art. In D. Griffiths, R. Stout, & P. Forsyth (Eds.), *Leaders for America's schools* (pp. 367–402). Berkeley, CA: McCutchan.

Popper, S. H. (1989). The instrumental value of the humanities in administrative preparation. In J. Burdin (Ed.), *School leadership* (pp. 366–389). Newbury Park, CA: Sage.

Portney, K. E. (1986). *Approaching public policy analysis*. Englewood Cliffs, NJ: Prentice-Hall.

Quade, E. S. (1989). *Analysis for public decisions* (3rd ed.) New York: North-Holland.

Rebore, R. W. (1997). *Personnel administration in education* (5th ed.). Boston: Allyn and Bacon.

Rossow, L. F. (1990). *The principalship: Dimensions in instructional leadership*. Englewood Cliffs, NJ: Prentice-Hall.

Rubin, L. (1984). Formulating education policy in the aftermath of the reports. *Educational Leadership, 42*(2), 7–10.

Schubert, W. H. (1986). *Curriculum: Perspective, paradigm, and possibility*. New York: Macmillan.

Sergiovanni, T. J. (1991). The dark side of professionalism in educational administration. *Phi Delta Kappan, 72*(7), 521–526.

Shakeshaft, C. (1989). *Women in educational administration* (updated ed.). Newbury Park, CA: Sage.

Sharp, W. L. (1994). Seven things a principal should know about school finance. *NASSP Bulletin, 78*(566), 1–5.

Skrla, L. (1998). *Women superintendents in politically problematic work situations: The role of gender in structuring conflict*. (ERIC Document Reproduction Service No. ED 425 504)

Smith, W. F., & Andrews, R. L. (1987). Clinical supervision of principals. *Educational Leadership, 45*(1), 34–37.

Smith, W. F., & Andrews, R. L. (1989). *Instructional leadership: How principals make a difference*. Alexandria, VA: Association for Supervision and Curriculum Development.

Snyder, K. J., & Anderson, R. H. (1986). *Managing productive schools*. Orlando, FL: Academic Press College Division.

Stone, S. C. (1987). *Strategic planning for independent schools*. Boston: National Association of Independent Schools.

Stout, R. T. (1989). A review of criticisms of educational administration: The state of the art. In J. Burdin (Ed.), *School leadership* (pp. 390–402). Newbury Park, CA: Sage.

Twombly, S., & Ebmeier, H. (1989). Educational administration programs: The cash cow of the university? *Notes on Reform*, Number 4, The National Policy Board for Educational Administration. Charlottesville: University of Virginia.

Valente, J. (1980). *Law and the schools*. Columbus, OH: Merrill.

Verstegen, D. A., & Wagoner, J. L. (1989). Strategic planning for policy development—An evolving model. *Planning and Changing, 20*(1), 33–49.

Wimpelberg, R. K. (1987). The dilemma of instructional leadership and a central role for central office. In W. Greenfield (Ed.), *Instructional leadership: Concepts, issues, and controversies* (pp. 100–117). Boston: Allyn and Bacon.

Young, I. P., & Prince, A. L. (1999). Legal implications for teacher selection as defined by the ADA and the ADEA. *Journal of Law and Education, 28*(4), 517–530.

Yukl, G. A. (1989). *Leadership in organizations* (2nd ed.). Englewood Cliffs, NJ: Prentice-Hall.

4

School Administration

Requirements and Opportunities

*Chapter Content*_____

Licensing and Certification
Quality-of-Life Considerations
Contemporary Opportunities
Implications for Practice

Content in the previous chapter examined the academic requirements for preparing to be a school administrator. This chapter focuses on licensing and issues related to applying for administrative positions. Since the mid-1980s, virtually all states have updated and revised licensing standards for professional educators (Gousha, LoPresti, & Jones, 1988). Unfortunately, changes across the states have not been uniform, and often the reforms adopted by universities have not been coordinated with the reforms adopted by state licensing officials. Since the decisions you make during professional preparation affect your eligibility for licensing, it is critical that you have some basic understanding of why and how states regulate practice in school administration. This knowledge allows you to make informed choices about selecting a university for graduate study and for tailoring your courses to meet your career objectives.

This chapter also provides information about school administration as a career. Often, students contemplating becoming a principal or district administrator have only limited perspectives of the real work lives of persons in these positions. In addition, they know very little about how to pursue positions once they have obtained a license.

Licensing and Certification

The terms *certification* and *licensing* are often used synonymously, but it is a mistake to do so. Although both words connote authorization to perform certain tasks, duties, and authority, there are important distinctions between them. *Licensing* is typically used in conjunction with a mandatory process; for example, one cannot practice medicine without a medical license. *Certification,* by comparison, typically refers to a voluntary procedure; for example, a person who holds a license to practice medicine may also be board certified in a specialized area of medicine (e.g., surgery). Whereas the license is required, certification is not.

Historically, many states used the term *certification* rather than *licensing* for educators. This practice, however, is changing rapidly in the United States. Three reasons are especially responsible for this change:

1. Many educators have come to realize that distinctions between licensing and certification are important. Licensing is more apt to create public perceptions that teachers and administrators are true professionals.
2. A growing number of states (e.g., Connecticut and Indiana) have established professional standards boards similar to those existing for other professions. These boards, composed primarily or entirely of professional educators, have been more prone to using the word *licensing*.
3. Efforts are being made at both the state and national levels to establish true certification for educators. A national group, a professional association, or a state standards board could issue certificates. An administrator, for example, could hold a principal's license and be certified as a school business official. Such a distinction would indicate that the person has special skills beyond those required for a basic license.

Although some states still issue certificates rather than licenses, the latter term is used generically in the remainder of this chapter.

The need for state officials to regulate entry and continued practice into teaching and administration grew out of a belief that larger and more complex schools required individuals who had specialized training (Armstrong, Henson, & Savage, 1989). Licensing was used to protect public interests—that is, to ensure that educators were competent to provide the services for which they were employed. Prior to World War II, a number of states did not even issue administrative licenses; and in states where licensing was mandatory, the requirements for specific study in educational administration and supporting areas were not extensive (Campbell, Fleming, Newell, & Bennion, 1987).

Licensing and Professional Preparation

Completing a degree program in school administration does not automatically result in a state license to be a school administrator. Colleges and universities set degree requirements; licensing standards are established by each of the 50 states (and other official territories of the United States). Historically, certificates (or licenses) were controlled through state departments of education. Since the late 1980s, as previously noted, some states have established professional standards boards similar to those used in professions such as law, dentistry, and architecture. Education standards boards may function in an autonomous regulatory capacity or as an advisory body (e.g., to the state department of education or state board of education) (Shive, 1988).

One controversy that has surrounded the establishment of professional standards boards relates to member selection. In some states, legislatures have enacted laws that place all education licenses under a single standards board composed primarily of classroom teachers. People in specialized positions (e.g., administrators and psychologists) often voice concerns about such arrangements, fearing that critical decisions regulating their practice will be influenced by standards board members who represent the interests of teacher unions. School administration professors also have been left off standards boards in some states.

Earlier in the book, it was noted that the two processes of earning a graduate degree and receiving a license to practice, although distinctively different, are related. This is because universities, and especially public universities, almost always shape degree requirements to be congruous with state licensing standards (Wise, 1994). In the past, the reverse may have been true in some states. That is, state licensing requirements were based on the decisions made at universities by education professors. During the early 1980s, the power of professors to control entry into the profession came under attack. Ernest Boyer (1983), for example, contended that "those who educate prospective teachers also control credentialing" (p. 180), and he called for the reduction of this power. Other reform leaders, however, disagreed. John Goodlad (1990) argued that professional education programs could not be self-renewing unless they were "free from curricular specifications by licensing agencies and restrained only by enlightened, professionally driven requirements for accreditation" (p. 302).

Actions during the 1990s suggest that education professors have lost some control over licensing standards. This has been especially true in states with practitioner-dominated licensing boards and states in which legislators have aggressively pursued their own political agendas. As an example, some states are proposing or approving alternative forms of professional preparation, allowing persons without university-based preparation to obtain licenses. In general, the level of friction between professional preparation and licensing standards remains rather high, and licensure decisions over the next decade clearly will determine whether universities will retain the responsibility of preparing administrators.

Legal Meaning of License

A certificate to practice as an educator, be it teacher or administrator, is not a property right. That is to say, it is not a contract between the individual practitioner and the state (Hessong & Weeks, 1991). This fact is critical because a state issuing a license retains the right to change conditions of issuance without legal concern for violating the property rights of certificate holders. Even so, state leaders traditionally have been politically sensitive about establishing new requirements that adversely affect those already in practice: "Few substantial changes in certification requirements affect those with certificates in hand. For political reasons, state legislatures find it easier to pass changes in certification requirements by exempting those already holding certificates from many, if not all, of the new requirements" (Armstrong et al., 1989, p. 307). This common practice of granting exemptions, referred to as *grandfathering*, is one way of establishing new requirements while avoiding a political battle with those already licensed.

The power of state legislatures to control state-issued licenses is well established. This includes the power to impose new requirements, to modify existing requirements, and to withhold or revoke a license for cause (Reutter, 1985). Typically, legislatures relegate their power to state boards and agencies that actually oversee the licensing process.

State Requirements

Differences in state licensing requirements exist primarily in the types of licenses issued, academic degree required for licensing, and the amount of professional experience required for licensing (e.g., classroom teaching experience). A valuable resource for reviewing exact specifications in each of the states is the *Manual on Certification and Preparation of Educational Personnel in the United States,* prepared by the National Association of State Directors of Teacher Education and Certification (NASDTEC). This manual is updated every few years and is available through certification advisors working with university-based programs. You should understand that state standards change frequently; and as such, examples cited here are subject to modification.

Types of Licenses Issued.   Not only do specific requirements for administrative licensing vary, but so do the number and types of administrative licenses issued. Some states (e.g., Georgia and New Mexico) offer only one general administrative license that permits a practitioner to occupy any leadership position ranging from assistant principal to local district superintendent. Other states (e.g., Alabama and Delaware) offer multiple licenses for specific types of positions. Michigan is rather unique in that it offers but does not require administrative certificates. Because there are so many differences among the states, you should always inquire about licensing standards in the state(s) where you may be employed.

Many states also stipulate that one must possess a first-level or probationary administrative license in order to be eligible for a higher-level or more permanent license. This concept is referred to as *layered licenses* (or *certificates*). The two most common examples of this practice are obtaining a superintendent's license after holding a principal's license, and moving from a provisional license to a professional license. Provisional licenses are usually issued for a limited time period (e.g., two to four years) and are the first licenses issued. A professional license typically is valid for a longer period of time. In the past, many states issued life licenses, but this practice has become far less common as a result of the perceived need to require continuing education.

Degrees. The vast majority of the states require the completion of at least a master's degree to obtain an administrative license. No state requires a doctorate for licensing; however, seven states do require either a specialist degree or doctoral degree to obtain a superintendent's license.

Although the major of the graduate degree may not be specified in the license requirements, many states stipulate that applicants must have completed an approved preparation program for the appropriate license. Thus, a teacher with a master's degree in English could obtain a principal's license by completing the necessary administration courses without completing another degree.

Professional Experience. Many of the states require teaching experience to obtain an administrative license. This requirement is often accompanied by a stipulation that such experience must have been gained while the individual held a valid teaching license. The modal requirement is three years of teaching experience. Some states (e.g., California) also accept experience gained in other licensed positions, such as a speech therapist or school counselor.

States with layered licensing also commonly require administrative experience to obtain higher-level licenses. For example, moving from a probationary to a professional principal's license may require two to three years of successful experience as an assistant principal or principal.

Special Requirements. In addition to standard criteria such as graduate degrees and professional experience, many states have special licensing provisions. Among the more common requirements are the following:

- Obtaining specified scores on national or state tests
- Graduating from an accredited university with an approved school administration program
- Completion of an approved internship
- Criminal background checks

Several states (e.g., Illinois) require applicants to pass examinations on the United States and respective state constitutions.

National Certification Initiatives

The tremendous diversity that exists in state licensing standards has prompted several national initiatives to reduce licensing problems. One of them is the Interstate School Leaders Licensure Consortium (ISLLC). Established in 1994, the ISLLC is a consortium of 32 education agencies and 13 administrative associations, and its purpose is to provide the means through which states can collaborate to set and implement effective licensing standards. As of 2001, 35 states had formally adopted the ISLLC standards (http://www.ccsso.org/isllc.html).

The National Board for Professional Teaching Standards (Carnegie Forum, 1987) sponsors another initiative that has had some influence on licensure. This group has promoted a trilateral agenda for improving the certification of educators:

- Rigorous assessment
- An extended course of professional study
- Well supervised practica

Although the initial focus was on teachers, the board's recommendations had a subsequent effect on recommendations for improving the preparation and licensing of school administrators (e.g., National Commission on Excellence in Educational Administration, 1987). The intent of national certification is to emulate board certification in medicine. That is, certificate holders could claim a high-level of competence in a specialization. In the case of school administration, that might include the principalship, curriculum and supervision, business management, or the superintendency. Although this initiative is now over 15 years old, it has had only limited influence on employment decisions.

A third national initiative related to licensing and certification has occurred through professional associations. The Association of School Business Officials International, for example, has been offering certificates in three categories for some time. They include:

- Registered School Business Administrator (RSBA)
- Registered School Business Official (RSBO)
- Registered School Business Specialist (RSBS)

Qualifications depend on the person's background, professional education, and experience. To date, the American Association of School Administrators—the primary association for local district superintendents—and the national principals' associations have not initiated similar certification programs.

Quality-of-Life Considerations

Although there is no one set of factors that draws educators to become administrators, quality-of-life issues are certainly important. These considerations include income, status, work requirements, life in the public's eye, and job security. Generalizations about these factors are difficult because conditions vary markedly across and within states. A summary of the more important criteria is provided here.

Income

In any given state, salaries for a given administrative position may differ considerably. For example, one high school principal may be paid $90,000 while another is paid $55,000. There are several reasons for this variance. The more prevalent and comments about their effects are shown in Table 4.1.

Providing precise statistics about salaries is of limited value because these figures change annually. Profiles, however, provide snapshots of the conditions in specific positions. In the mid-1990s, approximately 9 percent of all principals in

TABLE 4.1   *Variables Affecting Administrator Salaries*

Variable	*Most Likely Effect*
Location of the school or district	Often, the location of a district can affect the supply and demand for job applicants; urban districts, for example, must often pay higher salaries to attract qualified administrators.
Size of the school or district	Larger organizations (in terms of student enrollment) tend to pay higher salaries than do smaller organizations.
Administrator's level of experience	The level of experience in administration tends to increase salary level; the same is not necessarily true with respect to teaching experience (except for initial appointments to administrative positions).
Administrator's education level	Administrators with advanced degrees (Ed.S., Ed.D., Ph.D.) usually receive higher salaries.
Supply and demand	Salaries tend to increase when supply is low and demand is high.
Performance	Many administrators receive merit salary increases; thus, job performance often affects salary.
Length of employment contract	Not all administrators are employed to work the same number of days annually. Obviously, persons who have 12-month contracts tend to have higher annual salaries than those who have 10-month contracts.
Local philosophy	Communities differ with regard to their beliefs about compensating educators; affluent communities often pay higher salaries than other communities.

the United States had a Ph.D. or Ed.D., and another 26 percent had an Ed.S. or equivalent degree-certificate. Only about 1 percent of the nation's principals reported not having a master's degree. In addition, the average principal had approximately nine years of experience in that position (National Center for Education Statistics, 1999). In the late 1990s, only 13 percent of all local district superintendents were females and only 5 percent identified themselves as members of racial minority groups. Slightly over 80 percent of the superintendents were between the ages of 46 and 60, and the average age of superintendents has been slowly increasing since the early 1970s (Glass, Björk, & Brunner, 2000).

Administrator salaries vary among and across positions. Salaries paid to local district superintendents in 2000 ranged from approximately $50,000 to $250,000. Table 4.2 shows typical ranges in administrator salaries indexed to the local district superintendent's salary. In 1998, the middle 50 percent of all administrators earned between $43,870 and $80,030 (Bureau of Labor Statistics, 2001). The National Association of Secondary School Principals (2001) reported the following mean salaries for secondary school administrators during the 2000–01 school year:

Junior high/Middle school principals	$77,382
Junior high/Middle school assistant principals	$63,709
High school principals	$83,367
High school assistant principals	$67,593

Salaries do not provide a complete picture of actual compensation. Much like managers in the private sector, school administrators are increasingly moving toward expanded compensation programs that provide a range of fringe benefits (called *collateral benefits*). Administrators usually receive the same general employment benefits provided teachers; however, they may also receive additional ones. Superintendents, in particular, are likely to receive a special employment contract

TABLE 4.2   *Common Relationship of Administrator Salaries in a Local District*

Position	Percentage of Superintendent's Salary
Local district superintendent	100
Deputy or associate superintendent	90–95
Assistant superintendent	85–93
High school principal	78–88
Middle school principal	75–83
Business manager	70–85
Curriculum director	70–80
Elementary school principal	70–80
High school assistant principal	70–80
Middle school assistant principal	62–72
Elementary school principal	60–70

outlining a unique fringe benefits package tailored to meet individual needs. It is not uncommon for the superintendent's employment contract to include specific provisions covering annuities and defined compensation (e.g., tax-sheltered programs), vacation, medical examinations, leave provisions, disability insurance, life insurance, professional growth support, professional dues, an automobile, and liability insurance. Other possible fringe benefits include retirement programs, provisions for permitting consulting work, and severance payments.

Although some school districts write unique contracts for each administrator, this is not the rule. Often, all administrators, with the exception of the superintendent, receive the same benefits package provided to teachers. In a growing number of large school systems, administrators are forming organizations and reaching formal agreements with school boards. In some of the largest urban systems (e.g., New York City, Boston, St. Louis, and Detroit), administrative organizations have affiliated with national unions. The American Federation of School Administrators, an affiliate of the AFL-CIO, serves as an example of a national union whose membership consists of principals, assistant principals, directors, and supervisors. Since such organizations engage in collective bargaining, the exclusion of high-ranking officials (e.g., superintendents and assistant superintendents) is to be expected.

In general, administrators have higher incomes than the highest-paid teachers in the same districts; however, administrators typically have more responsibilities, work longer hours, and have less job security. Beginning in the late 1990s, the demand for administrators at all levels began to increase as applicant pools started to dwindle. A 1998 study sponsored by the Association of California School Administrators, for example, found that many high school administrative positions in that state went unfilled due to stress, salary, and shortage of qualified candidates (Yerkes & Guaglianone, 1998). Studies in New York, Pennsylvania, and California similarly indicated a shortage of qualified school business officials (Armstrong, Burkybile, Dembowski, & Guiney, 1999). There is some evidence that salary is a primary factor with regard to administrators staying in the position (e.g., Shen, Cooley, & Ruhl-Smith, 1999); thus, low salaries may well be a primary factor contributing to administrator shortages. Sustained high-market demands for administrators, however, are likely to have a positive effect on administrator salaries.

Status

Status, like salary, varies among and across administrator positions. In some areas of the country, superintendents and principals maintain relatively high levels of social respect. In rural areas where there are commonly few professionals, the superintendent's level of education alone may be sufficient to provide social status. As the United States has become a more highly educated society, however, simply being a college graduate does not ensure high status.

Both the community and the school system set standards for administrators (Kimbrough & Burkett, 1990); in so doing, they help establish public perceptions regarding the importance of administrators in society. And since communities and school systems are unique entities, the status of administrators, professionally and socially, is less than uniform. The following factors often provide clues regarding the level of importance local citizens place on education:

- Salaries paid to teachers
- Quality of educational facilities
- Community participation in education activities
- Level of collaboration between community agencies and the local schools
- Public comments made by school board members about the school system and employees

Historically, the public and the media have vacillated with respect to treating educators as true professionals. In part, this is because educators, and especially administrators, work in environments that unmeditatedly hybridize bureaucracy with professionalism. This means that the work of educators is often highly prescribed and controlled, even though teachers and administrators claim to be true professionals. Politics also serves to diminish the stature of administrators as professionals. Although administrators are licensed to practice on the basis of professional knowledge and experience, they make decisions and policy recommendations in political contexts (Wirt & Kirst, 1997). This means that their actions are often openly questioned and challenged by the public. To many observers, professionalism and politics serve discordant purposes; and when administrators apply political tactics (and especially when they are successful in doing so), the public's view of them as professionals often is diminished. Administrators have historically been perceived as having higher status than teachers (Gerritz, Koppich, & Guthrie, 1984). Also, there is evidence that esteem still influences individual decisions to enter school administration (e.g., Shen et al., 1999).

Autonomy and influence are two other variables that affect status. Often, these two factors get confused. Although many observers, including teachers, believe that administrators have considerable freedom to do as they wish, that rarely is true. Principals and superintendents are constantly in the public's eye, and there are many controls over their work activities. They do, however, have opportunities to make important decisions that affect large numbers of people. In this respect, they often can do some things (e.g., establish rules and regulations) that teachers cannot (Black & English, 1986). For many, power, even limited power, enhances status.

Public perceptions are also shaped by the degree to which professions limit entry. That is, the more difficult it is to enter a profession, the more likely the public will view its practitioners as having status. Often, the quantity and quality of preparation required determine the degree of difficulty associated with entering a profession. In this regard, Joel Spring (1985) noted "a claim to rigorous training and specialized knowledge is one of the most important ingredients in maintaining professional status" (p. 50). During the last two decades of the twentieth century, the academic preparation of both teachers and administrators was questioned and criticized by would-be reformers, and this scrutiny sustained doubt as to whether educators were true professionals.

In most professions, prestige is acquired simply by virtue of being admitted to practice. This rarely has been true in school administration, a profession in which prestige had to be earned through successful practice (Swart, 1990). Certainly some principals and superintendents have proven that high levels of status and prestige are indeed possible.

Work Requirements and Occupational Stress

One issue that receives considerable thought from prospective administrators is *time requirements*. Some administrators spend 60 or 70 hours per week on job-related functions. High school principals, for example, frequently find it necessary to be at school or school-related functions three or more evenings every week. Some studies of principals have cited time requirements as one of the least satisfying aspects of the job (e.g., Johnson, 1988), and work overload has been identified as one of the leading causes of occupational stress (Sarros, 1988).

Virtually all administrators spend more time in their jobs than the customary 40 hours per week. However, their ability to manage time is an important factor in determining whether this condition detracts either from their health or from their job satisfaction. Some administrators delegate authority and focus on work activities that they most enjoy; others do not feel comfortable unless they are doing everything personally. Opinions regarding the extent to which *burnout* is a legitimate occupational problem in school administration vary. Some writers (e.g., McAdams, 1998) cite job-related stress as a major factor in the decline of administrative applicants; selected studies, however, indicate that the extent of actual burnout among principals is less than commonly believed (e.g, Whitaker, 1994).

Despite mixed evidence about the effects of work on the lives of administrators, several general observations can be made:

- Most administrators spend more than 50 hours per week in work-related activity.
- Administrators have different levels of time-management skills. Whereas one principal may spend 70 hours a week at work, another is more productive at just 50 hours.
- The effects of work requirements are not uniform, largely because administrators have different levels of stress tolerance.
- Measuring negative effects of time requirements on job satisfaction is very difficult. Longer work hours may actually increase satisfaction for some individuals—for example, principals who derive satisfaction from completing difficult tasks and principals who derive satisfaction from social contacts.

Clearly, some administrators spend as much as 75 hours per week in their jobs and enjoy every minute of that time.

Burnout cannot be blamed entirely on work. An individual's emotional well-being, physical health, and personality are contributing factors (Raith, 1988). This explains why not all administrators react to the time requirements of their jobs in the same way. Many make healthy adjustments and go on with their professional and personal lives. Because personal variables are critical, you should know your strengths and your weaknesses, your aspirations and your fears, and your needs and your abilities. Ralph Kimbrough and Charles Burkett (1990) noted that "knowledge, acceptance, and truthfulness about yourself are prerequisites to effectiveness as a leader" (p. 32).

Life in the Public's Eye

For better or for worse, many communities have tended to treat administrators as if they were public property (Blumberg, 1985; Kowalski, 1995). In part, this means that administrators are expected to be accessible and responsive to concerns from parents and other taxpayers. It also means that most administrators cannot neatly separate their private and public lives. Many administrators, however, believe that life in a fishbowl is outweighed by several job benefits, such as:

- Compared to teachers, administrators tend to have more diversified career opportunities. That is, they can change jobs more readily and they usually have greater control of personal work.
- Administrators usually function more independently than do teachers. This is especially true of district superintendents, because they usually have latitude to determine how they will spend their work time (Kowalski, 1999).
- Administrators have many opportunities to receive intrinsic rewards. For those who genuinely like helping students, working with parents, and resolving conflict, jobs in school administration can be immensely satisfying.

Potential benefits such as these offset concerns about being treated as public property for most administrators.

Job Security

One reason many college students opt to enter teaching is job security acquired through tenure. Tenure is a product of state laws and regulations; therefore, criteria for obtaining it and the scope of protection provided are not uniform across the United States. State tenure laws, for instance, may or may not adequately protect a principal's job security (Zirkel & Gluckman, 1996). For this reason, you should never make assumptions about tenure. In many states, administrators acquire tenure as teachers but not as administrators. Where this is the case, an administrator usually has the option of returning to teaching when he or she leaves administration. Some states extend separate tenure to administrative posts, but rarely to the highest positions, (e.g., superintendents) (Valente, 1980).

Contemporary Opportunities

Early retirement programs as well as improved teacher salaries have contributed to a growing need for more qualified school administrators. The demand has become so great in some areas of the country that local districts are searching for ways to develop their own talent pools in conjunction with universities and professional associations.

Supply and Demand

Slightly less than 450,000 persons were employed as education administrators in 1998. The vast majority (90 percent) worked in elementary, secondary, or higher education. The rest worked in child day-care centers, religious organizations, job training centers, state departments of education, and businesses and other organizations that provided training for their employees (Bureau of Labor Statistics, 2001). Approximately one-half of the administrators working in education institutions work specifically in elementary/secondary school settings. During the 1990s, many experienced administrators left the profession, with most opting to retire.

Competition for assistant principal and principal jobs has lessened because many teachers no longer have strong incentives to move into administrative positions. As noted earlier, many district superintendents have reported that they found it difficult to find qualified applicants during the 1990s. During the period from 1998 to 2008, job opportunities in school administration are expected to grow as fast as the average for all occupations (Bureau of Labor Statistics, 2001).

Research on the demand for school administrators has often produced mixed results. The primary reason is that some studies have focused on the number of licensed administrators in a given state. This statistic rarely provides accurate supply-and-demand data for the following reasons:

- Persons obtaining administrative licenses may be career bound or place bound. Career-bound individuals seek positions primarily for career advancement without much regard for geographic location (or at least geographic location is a secondary consideration). By contrast, place-bound individuals are tied to a geographic area (sometimes to a single district). Therefore, they will pursue positions only in acceptable geographic areas (Miklos, 1988). Some 30 years ago, most administrators were career bound; today, that is probably not true. Dual-family incomes are a primary reason for the reduction in mobility.
- In many school systems, teachers can advance on the salary schedule by completing graduate courses in education. In such situations, teachers often opt to take administrative classes and obtain administrative license even though they have no intention of becoming an administrator. The license provides possible opportunities for career advancement rather than a planned career enhancement.
- Some license holders become discouraged after applying for one or two jobs, and they do not pursue additional opportunities in administration.
- After receiving an administrative license, teachers may realize that the salary differential between teaching and administration is not that great—especially if it is calculated on a per-diem or hourly basis.

A much better indicator of the actual supply and demand for administrators is applicant pool data recorded by school districts. When this variable is examined, the demand for administrators appears to be growing faster than the supply (e.g., Cooper, Fusarelli, & Carella, 2000; Moore, 1999; Yerkes & Guaglianone, 1998).

Selection into school administration occurs at two points: when the individual is admitted to a university program and when the individual is actually employed (Campbell, Cunningham, Nystrand, & Usdan, 1990). Both of these checkpoints are influenced by prevailing conditions. Two of the more important ones are regional influences and the need to correct the underrepresentation of women and minorities in the profession. Both conditions are affected by demographic trends. For example, rapidly growing states, such as California and Texas, have a high demand for administrative personnel; and in 2000, approximately one in every three residents of California was a Hispanic (U.S. Census Bureau, 2001). In the aftermath of licensing reforms during the 1990s, one could argue that licensing has become a third checkpoint, especially in states now requiring standardized testing of applicants.

The issue of alternative licensing needs to be considered in relation to job opportunities. Licensing was discussed in the first part of this chapter; however, a notation needs to be made here that state-level licensing decisions and the future supply of school leaders are related matters. In some states, legislators have responded to warnings about shortages of educators by making it easier for noneducators to be employed in administrative positions. This solution is purely political and economic, because it ignores the need for administrators to have a firm grounding in pedagogy and the professional knowledge base for school administration.

Overall Outlook

The outlook for jobs in school administration is favorable. The number of jobs in school administration is expected to increase about 10 to 20 percent between 1998 and 2008 (Bureau of Labor Statistics, 2001). The greatest number of jobs is expected at the more elementary school level, simply because there are more elementary schools than there are secondary schools. Current trends toward providing a greater range of services for students is likely to increase the demand for district-level administrators in areas such as testing, social services, and curriculum.

Implications for Practice

Your study of school administration is enhanced if you have a firm understanding of how one prepares for and enters practice. There are two critical assessments you should make as you plan your career. The first task is to engage in an objective self-evaluation so that you can candidly identify your strengths, interests, and career aspirations. Second, you need to evaluate conditions surrounding school administration in the geographic region where you intend to enter practice. This task includes looking at job requirements, actual work roles, compensation, and quality-of-life considerations. To ensure that you develop a balanced perspective, pay particular attention to highly successful administrators; they provide positive examples of what can be accomplished.

Although these are challenging times for elementary and secondary education, opportunities abound for dedicated educators who want to devote themselves to serving others. Applicant pools are dwindling at a time when even more new jobs in administration are being created. Many school districts are actively seeking to correct the underrepresentation of women and minorities, making opportunities for these groups especially promising.

For Further Discussion

1. Historically, the term *administrative certification* was more common than *administrative licensing* for school administrators. How do these two terms differ in meaning?

2. In what ways is school administration similar to other professions? In what ways is it different?

3. What factors contribute to and detract from the status of school administrators?

4. What factors contribute to differences in administrative salaries? Which factors are most prevalent in your local community?

5. In what ways does state licensure affect the professional preparation of school administrators?

6. What conditions associated with school administration are most appealing and least appealing to you?

7. Why do many parents and taxpayers view administrators as public property?

8. Does the political context of administrative work tend to reduce the public's perception of school administrators as professionals? Why or why not?

9. What is meant by a *property right* with regard to tenure and licensing? Why is this legal concept important?

10. What is a professional standards board? Do you believe such boards are in the best interest of school administrators? Why or why not?

Other Suggested Activities

1. Determine the tenure rights of administrators in your state.

2. Invite several local administrators to visit your class to discuss their attitudes and experiences about compensation, job security, and professional status.

3. Discuss the rate of turnover in administrative positions in your community. What factors are responsible for turnovers?

4. Contact the placement office at the university you are attending and determine whether the demand for school administrators is increasing or decreasing.

5. Determine if salary data for administrative positions in your state are available from either the state department of education or from administrative associations. Discuss the data in class.

6. Discuss possible reasons why women and racial minorities remain underrepresented in school administration.

7. Debate the merits of allowing noneducators to serve as principals and superintendents.

References

AASA Leadership News. (1991). Urban superintendent salary averages 6 figures for first time in study. American Association of School Administrators, No. 82, April 15, pp. 1–2.

American Association of School Administrators. (1990). *Talking about the superintendent's employment contract.* Arlington, VA: Author.

Armstrong, D. G., Henson, K. T., & Savage, T. V. (1989). *Education: An introduction* (3rd ed.). New York: Macmillan.

Armstrong, W. I., Burkybile, S., Dembowski, F. L., & Guiney, S. (1999). Crisis and confidence: The changing faces of the school business official. *School Business Affairs, 65*(12), 29–31.

Baptist, B. J. (1989). *State certification requirements for school superintendents.* (ERIC Document Reproduction Services No. ED 318 107)

Black, J. A., & English, F. W. (1986). *What they don't tell you in schools of education about school administration.* Lancaster, PA: Technomic.

Bliss, J. R. (1988). Public school administrators in the United States: An analysis of supply and demand. In D. Griffiths, R. Stout, & P. Forsyth (Eds.), *Leaders for America's schools* (pp. 193–199). Berkeley, CA: McCutchan.

Blumberg, A. (1985). *The school superintendent: Living with conflict.* New York: Teachers College Press.

Boyer, E. L. (1983). *High school.* New York: Harper and Row.

Bureau of Labor Statistics. (2001). *Occupational outlook handbook, 2000–01 edition.* Washington, DC: U.S. Department of Labor.

Campbell, R. F., Cunningham, L. L., Nystrand, R. O., & Usdan, M. D. (1990). *The organization and control of American schools* (6th ed.). Columbus, OH: Merrill.

Campbell, R. F., Fleming, T., Newell, L. J., & Bennion, J. W. (1987). *A history of thought and practice in educational administration.* New York: Teachers College Press.

Carnegie Forum on Education and the Economy. (1987). *The National Board for Professional Teaching Standards: A prospectus.* Washington, DC: Author.

Clark, D. L. (1989). Time to say enough! *Agenda* (Newsletter of the National Policy Board for Educational Administration), *1*(1), 1, 4–5.

Cooper, B. S., Fusarelli, L. D., & Carella, V. A. (2000). *Career crisis in the school superintendency? The results of a national survey.* Arlington, VA: American Association of School Administrators.

Doud, J. L. (1989). *The K–8 principal in 1988: A ten year study.* (ERIC Document Reproduction Services No. ED 319 134)

Edelfelt, R. A. (1988). *Careers in education.* Lincolnwood, IL: VGM Career Horizons.

Elam, S. M. (1990). The 22nd annual Gallup Poll of the public's attitudes toward the public schools. *Phi Delta Kappan, 72*(1), 41–55.

Encyclopedia of Careers and Vocational Guidance. (1990). W. E. Hopke (Ed.). Volume two: Professional careers. Chicago: J. G. Ferguson.

Gerritz, W., Koppich, J., & Guthrie, J. W. (1984). *Preparing California school leaders: An analysis of supply, demand, and training.* (ERIC Document Reproduction Services No. ED 270 872)

Glass, T., Björk, L., & Brunner, C. (2000). *The study of the American school superintendent 2000: A look at the superintendent of education in the new millennium.* Arlington, VA: American Association of School Administrators.

Goodlad, J. I. (1990). *Teachers for our nation's schools.* San Francisco: Jossey-Bass.

Gousha, R. P., LoPresti, P. L., & Jones, A. H. (1988). Report on the first annual survey of certification and employment standards for educational administrators. In D. Griffiths, R. Stout, & P. Forsyth (Eds.), *Leaders for America's schools* (pp. 200–206). Berkeley, CA: McCutchan.

Hessong, R. F., & Weeks, T. H. (1991). *Introduction to education* (2nd ed.). New York: Macmillan.

Hitt, W. D. (1988). *The leader-manager.* Columbus, OH: Battelle Press.

Johnson, N. A. (1988). *Perceptions of effectiveness and principals' job satisfaction in elementary schools.* Unpublished Ph.D. thesis, University of Alberta, Canada.

Kimbrough, R. B., & Burkett, C. W. (1990). *The principalship: Concepts and practices.* Englewood Cliffs, NJ: Prentice-Hall.

Kowalski, T. J. (1988). One case for the national certification of teachers. *The Teacher Educator, 23*(4), 2–9.

Kowalski, T. J. (1995). *Keepers of the flame: Contemporary urban superintendents.* Thousand Oaks, CA: Corwin.

Kowalski, T. J. (1999). *The school superintendent: Theory, practice, and cases.* Upper Saddle River, NJ: Merrill, Prentice-Hall.

McAdams, R. P. (1998). Who'll run the schools? *American School Board Journal, 185*(8), 37–39.

Miklos, E. (1988). Administrator selection, career patterns, succession, and socialization. In N. J. Boyan (Ed.), *Handbook of research on educational administration* (pp. 53–76). New York: Longman.

Miskel, C., & Ogawa, R. (1988). Work motivation, job satisfaction, and climate. In N. J. Boyan (Ed.), *Handbook of research on educational administration* (pp. 279–304). New York: Longman.

Moore, D. H. (1999). *Where have all the principals gone?* (ERIC Document Reproduction Service No. ED 429 368)

Murphy, J. T. (1991). Superintendents as saviors: From the Terminator to Pogo. *Phi Delta Kappan, 72*(7), 507–513.

National Association of Secondary School Principals. (2001, May). How are salaries of secondary school principals and assistant principals stacking up? *NewsLeader, 48*(9), 6–7.

National Center for Education Statistics. (1999). *Digest of education statistics, 1999.* Washington, DC: U.S. Department of Education.

National Commission on Excellence in Educational Administration. (1987). *Leaders for America's schools.* Tempe, AZ: University Council for Educational Administration.

O'Reily, R. C. (1989). *The instability of certification for educational administration.* (ERIC Document Reproduction Services No. ED 307 575)

Raith, F. D. (1988). *Reported locus-of-control and level of occupational stress of elementary principals in Georgia.* Unpublished Ed.D. thesis, University of Georgia, Athens.

Reutter, E. E. (1985). *The law of public education* (3rd ed.). Mineola, NY: Foundation Press.

Sarros, J. C. (1988). Administrator burnout: Findings and future directions. *Journal of Educational Administration, 26*(2), 184–196.

Sergiovanni, T. J. (1991). The dark side of professionalism in educational administration. *Phi Delta Kappan, 72*(7), 521–526.

Shen, J., Cooley, V. E., & Ruhl-Smith, C. D. (1999). Entering and leaving school administrative positions. *International Journal of Leadership in Education, 2*(4), 353–367.

Shive, J. J. (1988). Professional practices boards for teachers. *Journal of Teacher Education, 39*(6), 2–7.

Spring, J. (1985). *American education* (3rd ed.). New York: Longman.

Sullivan, J. R. (1989). *Study shows administrative shortage.* (ERIC Document Reproduction Services No. EJ 398 959)

Swart, E. (1990). So, you want to be a professional? *Phi Delta Kappan, 72*(4), 315–317.

United States Census Bureau. (2001). *United States census 2000.* Retrieved July 7, 2001, from the World Wide Web: http://www.census.gov.dmd.2khome.htm.

Valente, W. D. (1980). *Law in the schools.* Columbus, OH: Merrill.

Valverde, L. A., & Brown, F. (1988). Influences on leadership development among racial and ethnic minorities. In N. J. Boyan (Ed.), *Handbook of research on educational administration* (pp. 143–158). New York: Longman.

Warner, A. R. (1990). Legislative limits on certification requirements: Lessons from the Texas experience. *Journal of Teacher Education, 41*(4), 26–33.

Whitaker, K. (1994). Are principals really burned out? *Educational Research Quarterly, 17*(4), 5–23.

Wirt, F. M., & Kirst, M. W. (1997). *The political dynamics of American education.* Berkeley, CA: McCutchan.

Wise, A. (1994). The coming revolution in teacher licensure: Redefining teacher preparation. *Action in Teacher Education, 16*(2), 1–13.

Yerkes, D. M., & Guaglianone, C. (1998). Where have all the high school administrators gone? *Thrust for Educational Leadership, 28*(2), 10–14.

Zirkel, P. A., & Gluckman, I. B. (1996). Downsizing school administrators. *Principal, 75*(4), 60–61.

5

Control and Authority in Public Education

The system of public education in the United States is a unique amalgamation of values, beliefs, needs, and practices. Whereas most other countries operate federal systems of education, the United States has autonomous units in each state, the District of Columbia, and its territories (e.g., Puerto Rico). In all states, except Hawaii, the authority to operate public schools is delegated to local school systems, making the structure of education even more decentralized.

Since school leaders are expected to enforce a myriad of laws and regulations and to resolve a continuous flow of problems, their understanding of the evolution of the U.S. system of education is foundational to effective practice. The intent of this chapter is to (1) examine the government's interest of public education; (2) highlight the roles of the federal, state, and local governmental units; and (3) provide an overview of why this information is critical to practice in school administration.

Government's Interest in Education

In colonial America, citizens often struggled to create a balance between freedom and order. Their experiences with oppression and war heightened their appreciation of freedom, but their strong religious and political values led them to fear that they might create a decadent and chaotic society (Spring, 1990). It was within this context that education became an important process. Education was intended to free individuals to do virtuous acts and to create an enlightened citizenry—both critical responsibilities in an emerging democracy.

The United States Constitution, drafted in 1787, made no mention of education. This omission is often misinterpreted as reflecting an indifference toward this essential service. "Despite the lack of specific mention of public education in the federal Constitution, the critical importance of the schools in preserving its meaning and heritage has been stressed throughout American history" (Campbell, Cunningham, Nystrand, & Usdan, 1990, p. 42). Although Americans from the earliest days of the country saw the value of a free and public education, they did not necessarily agree as to what knowledge should be stressed. Even today, we confront lingering questions such as, What should be the primary goals for public education? Over time, such queries resurface in the context of school improvement debates—and there have been many recurring debates since colonial days. Should schools enable men and women to be free? Should schools be expected to develop a workforce that ensures a healthy national economy? Should schools be expected to develop an educated citizenry capable of defending and protecting the Republic?

Interests in Colonial America

A distinguishing feature of colonial America was the constant clashes between old values the settlers brought from Europe and new ideas expressed by those who sought to build a unique society. In this context, many colonial leaders discovered that traditional education outlooks were incongruent with the values stemming from novel religious, philosophic, and scientific attitudes that surfaced in the United States. This conflict gave birth to a hybrid conception of education (Butts & Cremin, 1953).

Education for Christian salvation was a theme of the earliest schools (Brubacher, 1947), but religious ideals were not the only influences shaping public education. Colonial education also had a practical theme more closely tied to governmental interests. V. T. Thayer (1965) described this condition when he wrote:

> Even the lovers of scholarship were careful to emphasize its practical advantages. At no time have Americans established schools and colleges or organized curricula within these institutions purely out of respect for learning or scholarship. Rather has the justification been consistently pragmatic and curriculum—whether in the liberal arts or in frankly vocational education—been envisaged as an instrument of utilitarian value. (pp. 19–20)

Thus, from its earliest days, American education was driven by a mix of aims and influences. Philosophy, religion, economics, and practical needs all played a part in the evolutionary process. Clearly, some of these factors constituted a governmental interest in promoting education.

Largely the poor, the oppressed, and the religiously persecuted of Europe settled this country. Education emerged as an important commodity for these pioneers as they sought both freedom and a better life in a democratic society. But the high value placed on education went well beyond self-interests. There was a common faith in the notion that education advanced civilization; and accordingly, a belief emerged that the strength of a new nation would depend on the spread of learning and enlightenment (Counts, 1952). This constituted the primary interest of governmental officials in the establishment of public schools.

Evolving Purposes

Over time, the original purposes of a common education were altered as the needs of the nation and its citizens changed and the profession of education became more enlightened. For instance, the Industrial Revolution created new needs and wants among the citizenry, leading to an emphasis on vocational education and a broadening of curriculum. Prominent philosophers such as John Dewey posed insightful questions about the nature of learners, the role of teachers, and the intentions of a public education. Wars, economic depressions, and, more recently, social ills, cultural heterogeneity, and worldwide economics helped to cast the directions of America's public schools. Partially because there is no federal system of education, and partially because there are so many avenues by which groups and individuals can affect change in the schools, the overall purposes of education have proven to be less than immutable. Change, however, does not mean a lessening governmental interest. This should be especially obvious in the midst of intense efforts to improve the nation's schools since the early 1980s.

The meandering of curricula and instructional practices between the mid-1950s and today exemplify how the aims and content of schooling can quickly be transposed. In the midst of the cold war in the late 1950s, the Soviet Union successfully launched *Sputnik I*. Americans were stunned, and perceptions that this scientific accomplishment was a threat to national security quickly became apparent. Finger pointing ensued, and the public schools often were singled out for blame. Specifically, political leaders, journalists, and even educational leaders concluded that U.S. schools had become second rate in preparing scientists and mathematicians—a judgment that was quickly tied to national security concerns. The perceived threat generated by *Sputnik I* was so great that the federal government enacted legislation that made available massive amounts of financial assistance to public education in an effort to upgrade studies in selected areas. The result was an early 1960s curriculum that stressed science, foreign languages, and mathematics. Within a few short years, however, the passage of the Civil Rights Act refocused much of the public's attention away from foreign relations and toward domestic problems. By the mid-1960s, several of the nation's major cities were

experiencing racial riots and other forms of social unrest. Again, the schools shoul-
dered a good bit of the blame for national problems—and again the federal government enacted legislation in hopes of making public education more responsive
to current needs.

Events surrounding the launching of *Sputnik I* and the passage of the Civil
Rights Act provide several insights about the ability of the federal government to
influence public elementary and secondary education:

- The federal government is likely to intervene in public elementary and secondary education when such intervention is deemed to be in the national
  interest.
- Schools are never separated from the problems of society. Whether it is
  national security, race relations, or poverty, schools are viewed as an integral
  part of the problem—and the solution.
- The purposes of U.S. education can be radically changed in a relatively short
  period of time.

Another exemplification of the power of the federal government over education is the events surrounding the promulgation of legislation for the disabled
beginning in the 1970s and continuing to this day. As special education advocate
groups applied political pressures on government officials, school administrators
observed a familiar chain reaction—one that starts with societal needs or concerns,
receives direction from federal legislation, and eventually alters elementary and
secondary school programs.

In addition to being transitory, educational goals at any given time are less
than universally embraced by the American public. Clearly, not all citizens agree
on the aims of public schooling. This discord is visible in continuing debates in
areas such as values clarification, prayer in the schools, and sex education.
Americans generally acknowledge that the public schools should address the
ever-changing needs of society and individual citizens, but there is significant dis-
cordance with respect to how this should be accomplished, the parameters of curricular responsibility, and the focus of control of public education.

Among the various conceptions of the purposes of public education, four
goals remain rather prominent (Armstrong, Henson, & Savage, 1989):

1. *Belief that the mission of public education is to promote the intellectual attainment
   of learners:* Here, emphasis is on the individual student and the acquisition
   of knowledge.
2. *Belief that the mission of public education is to create good citizens:* Here, emphasis
   is on the collective interests of society, especially those interests that relate to
   the responsibilities of being a member of a democratic country.
3. *Belief that the mission of public education is to prepare individuals for the workforce:*
   Here, emphasis is on economic issues that suggest direct connections between
   educational outcomes and the nation's economic welfare.

4. *Belief that the mission of public education is to provide individuals with learning skills:* Here, emphasis is on learning skills, mental discipline, and the development of an appreciation for learning so that students become lifelong learners.

Although each of these goals is generally accepted by society, there are persistent disagreements regarding their order of importance.

Environmental Influences

Actions of the American public, especially of those who promulgate and administer educational policy in an official capacity, are influenced by the problems of the day. As an example, the evolution of a global economy has prompted business and government leaders to stress the need for students to be prepared adequately for the workforce. A single environmental force, however, usually does not determine education priorities, because societal conditions are evaluated in the context of personal values. Table 5.1 provides examples of environmental influences that have created needs and wants for public education consumers over the past few decades.

Often in their zeal to improve education, business leaders and government officials promote ideas that are incongruous with the fundamental beliefs of many educators. In 1991, for example, the state governors attending an education conference produced six goals for American education. Their goals, to be reached by the year 2000, exemplified the range of purposes attached to public elementary and secondary schools:

1. All children in the United States will start school ready to learn.
2. The high school graduation rate in the United States will increase to at least 90 percent.
3. Students in the United States will leave grades 4, 8, and 12 having demonstrated competency in challenging subject matter, including English, mathematics, science, history, and geography; and every U.S. school will ensure that all students learn to use their minds well, so they may be prepared for responsible citizenship, further learning, and productive employment in the nation's economy.
4. Students in the United States will be first in the world in science and mathematics achievement.
5. Every adult American will be literate and will possess the knowledge and skills necessary to compete in a global economy and exercise the rights and responsibilities of citizenship.
6. Every school in the United States will be free of drugs and violence and will offer a disciplined environment conducive to learning.

Education writer Evans Clinchy (1995) observed that in writing their goals, the governors failed to explain how children incarcerated in standards-driven schools will make sense of the world. Many educators believe that students should be prepared to be leaders in their own world.

TABLE 5.1 *Examples of Factors Creating Needs and Wants in Public Education*

Factor	Implications
Cultural diversity	Both multicultural education and bilingual education have become more common in public schools.
Drug abuse	Schools have adopted prevention programs and revised discipline policies.
Changing American family	Many citizens have argued that schools have a responsibility to help students develop socially and morally.
Poverty	Schools have implemented more compensatory programs for children reared in poverty, including programs that address basic needs (e.g., breakfast programs).
Technological advancements	Both instructional methods and curriculum have been affected by the placement of computers in classrooms over the past 25 years.
Global economy	Economic forces have encouraged comparisons of educational outputs among the states and between the United States and other countries; school-to-work transition has become a focused topic.
Crime and violence	Schools are expected to provide safe environments and to educate students to obey laws and to respect each other.
Life in an information society	Schools are expected to prepare students to access and use information to solve problems.

Purposes and Control

One weighty criticism of public education is that children do not have access to equal educational opportunities. That is, from school to school and district to district, there are differences in the quality of teachers, instructional materials, facilities, and per-student spending. Some conclude that these differences reflect the philosophical and political conditions of local communities. Although this judgment is partially valid, it by no means provides a full explanation of existing inequities. Even if all citizens and communities could agree on what should be accomplished in elementary and secondary schools, many doubt that consensus would lead to standardized experiences for students. As Lawrence Cremin (1989) noted, "For all of the centralizing tendencies in American schooling—from federal mandates to regional accrediting association guidelines to standardized tests and textbooks—the experiences students have in one school will differ from the experiences they have in another" (p. 44). In part, variations in schools and districts are explained by the reality that everyday experiences in the classroom really determine what is emphasized and what is accomplished; and collectively, teachers, principals, superintendents, and school board members influence what really occurs in schools.

Control of American education is vested in legal foundations. This legal framework has three basic sources:

1. Federal and state constitutions
2. Statutes
3. Case law

Constitutions delegate authority to legislative bodies to enact laws in the interest of the public; statutes provide the actual laws; and case law establishes interpretations of constitutions and legislative acts. Historically, laws governing education have been shaped by philosophical, political, and social traditions (Alexander & Alexander, 1998). Within this framework, the development of a public school system appears to have been guided by several basic principles embraced by the public (Morphet, Johns, & Reller, 1967):

- The citizenry should be responsible for schools.
- The federal government should not have direct control over public education and should not dictate the organization and operation of schools.
- Each state should develop its own plan for providing public education.
- Direct responsibility for providing and operating public schools should be a function of local government.

These guiding principles helped shape a truly novel system of public education—one in which the balance of federal, state, and local control is ever changing.

Federal Government's Role

The role of the federal government in public education has been modified markedly since the nineteenth century. The United States Constitution does not mention education; thus, under provisions of the Tenth Amendment ("The powers not delegated to the United States by the Constitution, nor prohibited by it to the States, are reserved to the States respectively, or to the people"), education is deemed a state's right. Based largely on this interpretation, each state has the charge of establishing a system of public schools.

Many scholars have speculated about the conspicuous absence of a reference to education in the federal Constitution. Common suppositions include the following:

- Many of the framers were products of private schools, and as such, they viewed education as a family and church responsibility.

- By 1787, some states had already made provisions for public education in their state constitutions and state officials wanted to avoid federal intrusions into this activity.
- The omission of education was by default. It was simply overlooked (Grieder, Pierce, & Jordan, 1969).
- Much of the education offered in 1787 was private and limited to those who could afford it.
- Education was not a high national priority at the time (Van Scotter, Kraft, & Haas, 1979).

Omission of education in the Constitution has not prevented the federal government from becoming involved in public elementary and secondary education. However, advocates of federal interventions have generally recognized that the primary responsibility for this service belongs to the states. During latter parts of the nineteenth century and continuing through the twentieth century, federal involvement in education expanded, and as it did, concerns emerged about the possible erosion of local control. In the early 1900s, for example, political cartoons expressing the misgivings of local school officials relative to accepting federal assistance appeared in publications read by school board members and administrators. A common belief that federal assistance always came with "strings attached" exemplified concerns about a potential loss of liberty. To this day, a negative attitude about the federal government's involvement in education persists among many local educational leaders who see an imbalance between potential benefits and a loss of control.

Sources of Intervention

In the infant years of the United States, governmental powers were divided between the federal government and the states. Political and economic conditions of that era favored such an arrangement. But as the country matured, a shift from a dual federalism to national federalism occurred (Campbell et al., 1990). No longer could issues be neatly separated as either federal or state concerns. For example, the federal government became increasingly focused on protecting constitutional rights of citizens and the welfare of the nation—especially when rights or welfare appeared to be eradicated or diminished by state statutes. A gray area between state and federal jurisdiction grew rapidly and many aspects of public education fell into this zone of uncertainty.

The federal government can reach out and touch school districts through legislation, legal decisions, and policy (i.e., rules and regulations developed by agencies charged with enforcing federal statutes and court decisions). These avenues of power and authority are displayed in Figure 5.1, where they are associated with the branches of the federal government—the legislative, the judicial, and the executive (also called the administrative branch). Each branch is assigned unique functions; yet, the three intertwine to create operational and policy relationships. For instance, the courts interpret laws enacted by the legislative branch;

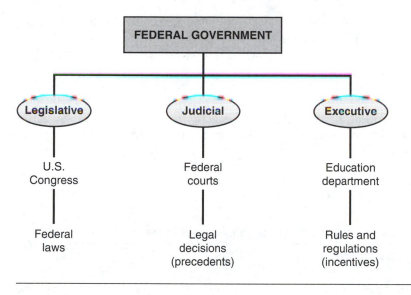

FIGURE 5.1   *Avenues of Federal Intervention*

the executive branch often influences legislation through political lobbying; and both the executive and legislative branches exercise control over judicial appointments. Each branch of the federal government is reviewed here.

Legislative.   The promulgation of laws is the most visible form of federal activity and is a function of the United States Congress. The earliest federal interventions into public education followed a pattern of providing financial assistance to create or augment programs deemed to be associated with national interests. The establishment of land grant universities in the late nineteenth century exemplifies how a national concern, in this case agriculture, resulted in the enactment of federal law in an area that was officially accepted as a state's right. Supporters of such acts did not intend to usurp the state's authority; they justified their initiatives on the view that indirect support to public education was possible without an erosion of state authority and control—a view held by many policy analysts (McCarthy, Cambron-McCabe, & Thomas, 1998).

In the past 100 years, dozens of federal laws affecting public education have been enacted. Some actually changed curriculum, others merely had a tangential effect. An examination of the action of the United States Congress in the area of education produces four overriding themes:

1. Constitutional rights of citizens
2. National security
3. Domestic problems
4. Concerns for a healthy economy

Table 5.2 provides selected examples of legislation and brief indication of how the legislation affected schools.

The role of the United States Congress is largely to translate the intent of the federal Constitution into actual practices. But intent is open to interpretation. As an example, philosophical and political disagreements frequently result in divergent opinions about the appropriateness of federal interventions. Over the past several decades, more representatives and senators have become increasingly active in elementary and secondary education policy, as this topic has become a national concern.

TABLE 5.2 *Examples of Federal Legislation Affecting Education*

Legislation	Year	Implications
Smith-Lever Act	1914	Support for teacher education in agriculture and home-making
Smith-Hughes Act	1917	Federal support for vocational education
National Youth Administration	1935	Full-time employment provided to those between ages 16 to 24 who were in school full time
National School Lunch Act	1946	Support to improve food services in schools
National Defense Education Act	1958	Financial assistance for the study of mathematics, science, foreign languages
Vocational Education Act	1963	Federal assistance to maintain, extend, and improve vocational education programs
Elementary and Secondary Educational Act	1965	Support for the disadvantaged; inducements for innovative programs; and supplemental funding for libraries and state departments of education
Education for All Handicapped Children Act	1975	Federal assistance to provide special education programs

Judicial.   The United States has a dual system of laws: federal and state. The two may conflict with each other; when they do, pertinent federal law displaces inconsistent state law (Valente, 1987). For the most part, the federal courts have jurisdiction when a federal constitutional question or a federal statute is involved, or when there is a diversity of state residence between litigants (Reutter, 1985). Since many aspects of public education involve constitutional rights, the potential for the federal courts to hear cases related to education is rather high.

The federal judicial system has three divisions: district courts, courts of appeal, and the Supreme Court. Typically, cases heard by the first two receive less public attention than those decided by the highest court. Yet, the decisions issued from all federal courts have had a profound influence on public schools and the duties assumed by administrators.

Since the mid-1950s, the federal judicial system has increasingly adjudicated education-related cases. At first glance, a number of these legal disputes appear to have been unrelated to education because they did not address commonly recognized components of schooling (e.g., curriculum, tuition, and textbooks). But they did address constitutional issues that unavoidably have implications for all public institutions (e.g., civil rights). As noted earlier, educational and social issues often are inextricably linked; as a result, schools can become the battleground for legal disputes that involve individual and group rights (Hessong & Weeks, 1991). Matters decided in federal courts have included issues such as parental rights, student rights, the rights and authority of school officials (school boards, administrators, teachers, and other employees), and the rights of racial and ethnic minorities or other protected groups (e.g., racial, gender, or age discrimination).

Legal disputes can make their way to the nation's highest court in two ways: (1) if federal or state statute is questioned under the federal Constitution and (2) if any title, right, privilege, or immunity is claimed under the federal Constitution (Alexander & Alexander, 1998). Both pathways are broad. Several landmark cases serve to explicate the power of the federal courts to influence public education. *Brown v. Board of Education*, decided by the United States Supreme Court in 1954, struck down state laws that required public schools to be racially segregated. Even though public education is a state's right, this ruling restricted the decisions of state government when those decisions were deemed discriminatory under the United States Constitution. The *Brown* decision was later extended to cover other ethnic minorities (e.g., Hispanics and Native Americans). A second cogent example pertains to teacher unions. As these organizations developed in public education, circa 1960, disputes related to membership, fees, contract interpretation, and collective bargaining were settled in federal courts. Additionally, topics such as religious freedom, the funding of education, affirmative action, and tort liabilities have made their way into the federal courts.

Constitutionally, the federal judicial system does not have the right to formulate law—rather, the courts are expected to interpret law. This issue has been central to many confirmation hearings for federal judgeships held by congressional committees. Given that the Supreme Court occasionally votes five to four, the values and beliefs of judges are deemed critical with respect to judicial interpretations.

Thus, even the best legal minds often disagree on interpretation of law and their ultimate decisions have a profound effect on society.

Executive.   The passage of laws providing federal support to education required some form of regulation by federal agencies. For many years, education responsibilities were delegated to the Department of Interior; in 1939, the Federal Security Agency assumed responsibility; in 1953, education became part of the Department of Health, Education, and Welfare; and under the Carter administration in 1979, a separate Department of Education was established. In part, the evolution to a separate department (whose head is a member of the president's cabinet) reflected the rapid growth of federal involvement in public elementary and secondary education from 1950 to 1980. Throughout the planning phases for the new department, the question of the proper federal role in public education loomed as a point of controversy.

Immediately after being formed, the Department of Education had 17,000 employees, 11,000 of whom were part of the Department of Defense overseas schools. Approximately 6,000 employees comprised the Washington, D.C., staff (Radin & Hawley, 1988). Responsibilities of the department were outlined by focused assignments given to six assistant secretaries:

1. Elementary and secondary education
2. Postsecondary education
3. Vocational and adult education
4. Educational research and improvement
5. Special education and rehabilitative services
6. Civil rights

The development of rules and regulations for enforcing federal laws remains one of the Department of Education's primary functions. The department also dispenses federal aid and grants. Often, these functions intermingle. For instance, the acceptance of federal aid places requirements on school districts to comply with standards initiated in legislation and defined by the Department of Education (e.g., awarding contracts to bidders who meet certain federal guidelines). In its brief existence, the Department of Education has generated considerable controversy. For instance, disagreements abound regarding the role this agency should play in formulating policy and laws. The department is part of the executive branch of the government and the president, subject to approval by the Congress, appoints the Secretary of Education. The mere existence of the Department of Education transmits the message that the federal government has a role in elementary and secondary public education.

Shortly after being created, the Department of Education was almost eliminated. The election of President Ronald Reagan resulted in a significant philosophical change from the previous administration with regard to the role of the federal government in education (Marcus, 1990). This shift occurred at approximately the same time that critics began to call for a massive restructuring of public schools.

Conservatives and libertarians basically oppose federal controls over public education, whereas liberals believe that such control is often essential to ensure the equality of educational opportunities within and among states.

Federal Government's Present Role

A number of authors describing the federal role in education during the early 1980s referred to the period as the "Reagan reversion" (e.g., Campbell et al., 1990). Ronald Reagan entered the presidency openly stating that the creation of the Department of Education was an error. Philosophically, he favored deregulation and a reduced role for the federal government in elementary and secondary education. His initial positions called for substantial reductions in federal expenditures and a decentralization of authority that would permit state and local units of government to have more autonomy. During the Reagan administration, the federal government for the first time in several decades retreated from the educational policy arena (Marcus, 1990).

Attempts to diminish the federal government's role in education during the early 1980s were attenuated by reform reports indicating that the nation's elementary and secondary schools were in trouble. Politicians who had advocated the elimination of the newly created Department of Education retreated in the midst of growing public concern about the quality of public schools. Legislators and governors in many states, however, did not to wait for the federal government to provide a reform agenda; rather, they aggressively enacted laws and revised existing education policies. Most of these initiatives were predicated on the belief that schools could improve by doing more of what they were already doing (Wirt & Kirst, 1997).

As reform efforts evolved during the 1980s, positions on the federal government's role in elementary and secondary education vacillated. Observing that positions were often issue sensitive, Beryl Radin and Willis Hawley (1988) noted, "The level of social agreement on the appropriate role of the federal government in education is, indeed, fragile and tends to vary from one education policy area to another" (p. 230). Overt positions taken by the two major political parties also were less than constant. Some politicians wanted the federal government to determine the reform agenda; others wanted no federal interference in state decisions. Although the federal Department of Education was not eliminated, political ideology, philosophy, and tradition, buttressed by what the Constitution does not say, have restricted federal interventions (Burke, 1990).

In troubled times, advocates for greater federal control usually become more visible. Among the arguments they put forward to defend their case are the following:

- Other nations with federal systems of education have superior results as measured by higher student test scores (e.g., Japan).
- The present system of education has resulted in schools of varying quality. The federal government has a responsibility to ensure that all children have

access to an equal education. Present conditions have been especially harmful to economically disadvantaged students.

- The record of educational achievements for state governments is inconsistent. Put simply, state governments cannot be trusted to provide good schools (e.g., it was federal intervention that put a stop to segregation).
- Federal standards would lead to a national curriculum and a national curriculum would improve student performance.
- Essential improvements are often blocked by state systems that allow taxpayers to vote on tax referenda; that is, some state systems encourage self-interests rather than the public's interest.

By contrast, many continue to argue against greater federal control. Among the more visible arguments for this group are the following:

- A widening federal role is in direct contrast to the intentions of the Constitution.
- Federal intervention will result in greater levels of bureaucracy. This will make schools less effective and less responsive to the real needs of the populace.
- The federal government will attempt to standardize educational programs; as a result, differences in community and student needs will be overlooked.
- The real improvements in education must come in the classroom. Centralizing control and authority is moving in the wrong direction. What is needed is greater authority for teachers and increased citizen participation in policy decisions.

Generally, political conservatives emphasize liberty, whereas political liberals emphasize equality. Given these diverse viewpoints and the division of power between the two main political parties, the future role of federal government in education remains uncertain.

State Government's Role

From the very earliest years, the promulgation of laws governing schools were the province of colonial legislatures—and they delegated much of this power to local agencies. The concept of local control is nested in the value of liberty, but this decentralization of authority has its critics. After more than 150 years, two essential concerns continue to linger with regard to permitting local districts to be somewhat independent: equalization of educational opportunities (i.e., providing every child within the state with equal educational opportunities) and increased standards (i.e., changing rules, regulations, and curricula in pursuit of improved programming and outcomes). Each concern generates cogent questions about the legal responsibilities of state government for public education and an appropriate mix of power and authority between state government and local school districts. Such questions and the changing economic, social, and demographic conditions of the country in the late nineteenth century contributed to decisions to expand state control over public education. Expanded state authority was particularly evident in two initiatives: the advancement of the position of state superintendent and the creation of state boards of education (Butts & Cremin, 1953).

The evolution of the state's authority over local school systems was accompanied by considerable and protracted controversy. Over time, most citizens accepted, albeit some grudgingly, that state government was a legally legitimate partner in public education (Burke, 1990). In a great many court decisions, judges have uniformly held that education is essentially and intrinsically a state function and have stipulated that public education is a matter of state and not local concern (Garber & Edwards, 1970). But these affirmations have not totally eradicated criticisms coming from school board members, educators, and other taxpayers who believe that state government ought not get overly involved in controlling public elementary and secondary schools. Disputes between state government and local school boards also reflect the perennial tensions between liberty and equality. As local autonomy increases, the likelihood of inequities also rises. This is because wealthy districts can spend more money with less tax effort than can poor districts (Kowalski & Schmielau, 2001).

Avenues for state intervention in public education are similar to those at the federal level. State government also is divided into three distinct divisions: the legislative, the judicial, and the executive. The judicial and legislative functions are quite similar at federal and state levels; however, the executive process of state government with regard to public elementary and secondary education is more complex.

Legislative

Constitutions of individual states establish the authority of the legislature to enact statutes that give direction to public education. A state legislature has almost unlimited or plenary power to determine basic policy questions within a given state (Kimbrough & Nunnery, 1976). No state may enact laws that violate provisions of either the United States Constitution or the respective state constitution. For example, a state legislature may not pass a law that would abridge the privileges and immunities granted to a citizen of the country (First Amendment rights). It may not establish a statute that would deprive a citizen of life, liberty, or property without due process (Fourteenth Amendment rights). Nor may it pass a law that would deprive a citizen of equal protection under the law (also a Fourteenth Amendment right).

Recent reform efforts have magnified the importance of state legislatures with respect to formulating education policy. Legislatures can, and often do, pass laws based on focused concerns with little or no consideration as to how their actions will affect long-term initiatives pursued by either the state department of education or local school districts. For example, state laws requiring high school graduation examinations may deter local efforts to reduce school dropout rates. Coordinating legislative and executive initiatives at the state level remains one of the great policy challenges for public education.

Judicial

The role of the state courts in providing direction and control of public education is becoming an increasingly important topic. Two areas of litigation serve to exemplify the power of state courts in matters affecting educators: collective bargaining and state funding formulas. As noted in the discussion of federal courts, the purpose of judicial review is to interpret law, not to rewrite it. Decisions rendered by state courts affect educational policy in two primary ways. First, decisions establish precedents that are likely to affect future judgments in similar cases. Second, decisions in landmark cases often lead to new legislation. In the late 1980s, for example, courts in the Commonwealth of Kentucky ruled that all previous statutes pertaining to education were invalid. This ruling was the catalyst for developing a totally new state system of public education pursued under the Kentucky Education Reform Act (KERA).

Historically, state judges have been somewhat reluctant to interfere with the authority of legislative and executive branches of state government in the area of education (Hessong & Weeks, 1991). The primary charge given to the legal branch of state government has been to determine the reasonableness of constitutional provisions and statutory law. There was little expectation that judges would question the wisdom or appropriateness of these provisions and statutes (Kimbrough & Nunnery, 1976). Despite this tradition, there are indications of increasing levels of judicial activism (i.e., more state court judges have been willing to make broad interpretations of education law) (Rebell, 1999).

Executive

In many states, the executive branch of state government exerts considerable influence over education. Several key agencies and positions are standard in all states (e.g., chief school officer, state board of education); however, the actual power and authority of the executive branch among states is less than uniform. In recent times, the key players in state-level policy for public education have been the governor, the state board of education, the chief school officer, and the state department of education.

Governor.   Because of dissimilar statutes, the power of governors to affect educational policies varies among the states. But differences in the degree to which these elected officials involve themselves in education issues go well beyond legal parameters. Partisan politics, tradition, aspirations, personality, and self-interests also are key factors. Overall, however, most recent governors have opted to be heavily involved in elementary and secondary education. In 1984, half of the nation's top state executives made education their top priority in their state-of-the-state addresses (McDonnell & Fuhrman, 1985). Little had changed 10 years later. Most were still taking positions favoring more funding for education (Hertert, 1998). However, religious groups, affluent communities, and business leaders—

groups that typically oppose increased government support—have had substantial influence on positions taken by governors (e.g., these groups usually prefer market-based solutions to education problems) (Gittell & McKenna, 1999).

Powers of a state's chief administrator over education policy may be exercised in several ways. The most obvious is vetoing legislative action. Additionally, governors frequently formulate legislative proposals and engage in political persuasion to aid the passage of bills before the legislature. In some states, governors appoint all or some members of the state board of education and the state superintendent. All governors have a responsibility for formulating and administering state budgets—a duty that clearly affects public education (Campbell et al., 1990).

State Board of Education.   By 1870, most states had some form of a state board of education (Knezevich, 1975). In some instances, this body is authorized by state constitutional provision; in other states, it is authorized by legislative action. In the earliest years of existence, state boards largely assumed the role of executing law enacted by the legislature. There is tremendous variance among the states with regard to the size and functions of these bodies. Although the primary purpose of the state board is to carry out state mandates, these bodies also formulate policy. Actual duties and responsibilities may include the following:

- Influence the development of educational policy.
- Coordinate the efforts of state government with regard to education.
- Appoint commissions and other bodies as may be necessary to administer state laws, rules, and regulations.
- Develop rules and regulations.
- Oversee the operations of the state department of education and establish policy for its operations.
- Engage in strategic planning.
- Serve as a hearing board in adjudicating grievances and due process procedures related to state educational policies, rules, and regulations.
- Recommend legislation, budgets, and other matters to the legislature or other state agencies.

State Chief School Officers.   The first state chief school officer was appointed in 1812, and since that time, all states have created a similar position. Conditions surrounding this role, however, are not uniform. In some states, for example, the chief school officer is referred to as the "state superintendent of public instruction"; in several other states, he or she is referred to as the "commissioner of education." Differences also exist in the following areas:

- Scope of duties and responsibilities (e.g., some perform largely regulatory functions, whereas others play a key role in policy development)
- Term of office (the most common term of office is four years)
- Compensation

- Requirements to hold the position (e.g., several states have or have had chief school officers who are not professional educators)
- Method of selection to the position (i.e., some are appointed to office, whereas others are elected)

The state superintendent's relationship to the state board of education also varies across the states and territories of the United States. In two states (Maine and New Hampshire) and in Puerto Rico, state superintendents have no official role on the state board of education. In the remaining states and territories, state superintendents assume one of the following roles on state boards:

- Secretary (e.g., Connecticut and New Jersey)
- Executive secretary (e.g., Delaware and Georgia)
- Chief executive officer (e.g., Illinois and Missouri)
- Ex officio member (e.g., Arkansas and Wyoming)
- Ex officio member and chair (e.g., Indiana and Oklahoma)

Typically, a state's top education executive assumes an important political role as spokesperson for public education—a role that entails building public support for schools. Through appointments, fiscal decisions, and the administration of rules and regulations, the chief school officer can exercise considerable authority.

State Departments of Education.   In reviewing the evolution of state departments of education, three distinct levels are noteworthy. Up to the twentieth century, these departments largely engaged in maintaining records. From 1900 to 1930, they assumed an inspectoral role—one in which officials determined if local school districts were complying with state laws. After 1930, many departments incorporated leadership activities—that is, proactive functions designed to improve local schools (Knezevich, 1975). Today, these agencies perform a number of important functions as exhibited by the following examples:

- Ensuring compliance with state and federal laws for schooling
- Providing technical assistance to local school districts
- Serving as an agent for the distribution of federal assistance
- Maintaining adequate statistical data
- Filing necessary reports with other governmental agencies
- Providing staff development opportunities
- Developing and publishing curriculum guides
- Administering standards for school facility development
- Administering licensing standards for practitioners
- Establishing recommendations for the state board of education and/or legislature
- Conducting needs assessments
- Completing program evaluations

- Establishing and administering accreditation standards for state licensed schools
- Providing interpretations of laws, rules, and regulations
- Administering the state funding formula

School improvement efforts are resulting in broader missions for most state departments. Today, there are growing expectations that these agencies become catalysts for change as well as regulatory agencies.

State Government's Present Role

Since the 1950s, state governments have been exerting more control and authority over public education. Two factors have been largely responsible. First, litigation involving equal educational opportunities has resulted in greater state funding for public education in many states (e.g., between 1971 and 1981, 28 states reformed their funding systems for public education). But in most instances, increased state funding has meant increased state control. Second, demands for improvement in elementary and secondary schools have been directed largely toward state government. During the 1980s, the political climate was very conducive for bold initiatives at the state level. For governors, legislators, and other state officials, the risks of acting decisively on educational reform were low—and the political costs for not doing so were high (McDonnell & Fuhrman, 1985).

The ability of state government to provide meaningful leadership in educational improvement is still in question. In reality, the promulgation of state laws, rules, and regulations are almost always mired in politics and self-interests. Additionally, evaluations of attempted innovations reveal that many contextual variables at the local level facilitate or impede state-initiated change efforts (McGuire, 1985); put another way, even the best-intentioned and best-designed state reforms encounter problems stemming from community and student differences. Starting in the 1990s, school reformers began recognizing this fact, and their efforts shifted toward change strategies that gave local district and school administrators more discretion in developing improvement initiatives. State deregulation and district decentralization are prime examples. But at the same time that state governments are allowing local district officials greater discretion in pursuing reforms, they are imposing additional accountability criteria, such as state testing programs (Kowalski, 1999).

Local School Districts

During the second half of the nineteenth century, there was a rapid expansion of the common public school. Compulsory attendance laws resulted in more students attending school, and, as this occurred, arguments for more centralized control at the state, county, and district levels were strengthened (Button & Provenzo, 1989). Today, in 49 states, legislatures generally delegate authority to local government to establish units of school organization. In essence, local districts are quasi-corporations that serve as instruments to oversee and manage public education—they are extensions of state government (Campbell et al., 1990).

Local districts may be defined by several criteria. The more common include the following:

- *Scope of services:* Districts serving all grades, K through 12, are the norm in this country; however, different configurations exist in several states. In addition to districts serving all grade levels, Illinois also has elementary districts (serving students through grade 8) and high school districts (serving students in grades 9 to 12). In a few states, local districts may have jurisdiction over two-year technical or community colleges.
- *Fiscal independence:* Local districts may or may not be required to have their budgets and tax rates established by another government agency. Those required to do so are called fiscally dependent districts; those not required to do so are called fiscally independent districts. Most states have only fiscally independent districts, a few have only fiscally dependent districts, and a few states have both.
- *Scope of territory:* The amount of territory served by local districts is not constant across the states. In some states, there is a separate school district in almost every township; in other states, there is only one school district in each county. Hawaii is the only state with a single public school system. School reorganization in the 1950s and 1960s markedly reduced the number of local districts in this country; today, there are just over 14,000 local districts.

Geographic settings may also be used (formally or informally) to describe districts. Labels such as *rural, urban, suburban,* and *city or town* are most common.

Local District Boards

Lay boards almost always govern local school districts; in several states, there are still a few districts operating under the jurisdiction of township trustees. Selecting school board members through nonpartisan elections remains the norm in this country. State statutes determine criteria for school board service; such criteria may include qualifications, term of office, and other pertinent parameters regarding legal operations and scope of authority.

The common names given to local district boards vary depending on the state, but the most common titles used include: *board of education, school board,* and *board of school trustees.* The general duties of a local school board include:

- Employing a superintendent of schools
- Approving recommendations for the employment of all other personnel
- Establishing policy for the operation of the school district

- Becoming involved in adjudicating disputes (e.g., due process hearings, grievances)
- Collectively negotiating with employee unions
- Approving budgets and expenditures
- Evaluating the superintendent of schools
- Communicating with the public at large
- Approving capital projects (e.g., new facilities)
- Levying taxes and borrowing money
- Establishing attendance boundaries
- Determining curricula

The general public does not readily understand two facts about board members: they are agents of state government and they do not possess power individually to administer schools. In part, these facts are not discerned because many board members act as local political figures and immerse themselves in the day-to-day operations of schools. Legally, however, a local board must act as a whole to exercise its powers.

Conditions surrounding the formation of the first school boards helped shape the functions of these governing bodies and their relationships with school administrations. First, the concept of meritocracy (the idea that one's social and occupational position is determined by merit, not politics or wealth) influenced decisions regarding schooling. Thus, those who had acquired special knowledge and skills were deemed qualified to lead the schools. Second, there was a strong desire to keep public education out of politics. One way to do this was to grant powers to professional leaders (administrators). Third, the growth of school administration as a field of study fostered the notion of an appropriate separation of powers in local school districts. School boards were to set policy—administrators had the charge to enforce policy without interference from the school board (Spring, 1990).

Since the early 1990s, greater attention has been given to the influence of local boards on school reform. Some policy specialists (e.g., Danzberger, 1994; Danzberger & Usdan, 1994) advocate reshaping local boards into policy boards—an action that would narrow the scope of authority given to boards. Others (e.g., Streshly & Frase, 1993) have gone so far as to question whether local boards should even exist. Regardless of the perceived problems with the present system of local district governance, the demise of the local school is most unlikely. This concept, unique to the United States, is firmly rooted in liberty ideals and supported by the vast majority of taxpayers.

District Superintendent

The nature of district-level administrative positions was discussed earlier in the book. District superintendents basically perform executive functions, but they also serve in an advisory capacity relative to policy development. The actual power and authority of these administrators are not constant. In part, differences are explained by the following factors:

- School board philosophy
- School board expectations
- Community and school district cultures
- Community and school district needs and problems
- Superintendent personality, ability, and philosophy
- Superintendent and school board relationship
- Adherence to ideal standards (e.g., codes of ethics, accreditation standards, state statutes, rules, and regulations)

These and other variables help explain why the actual roles of local district superintendents usually differ.

Present Status of Local Districts

During the 1980s, many administrators complained that local control in public education had been seriously eroded. Their conclusion was generally based on three pieces of evidence:

1. Their authority and the authority of school boards to make meaningful decisions had been incrementally restricted by political and economic developments.
2. State legislators and state departments of education officials were making most curricular decisions, and often individuals outside the education profession influenced them.
3. Judges in state and federal courts had become the real arbiters of education disputes.

These conditions, however, did not totally eradicate the power and authority of local district officials. Superintendents and boards were still able to have a pronounced effect on education outcomes in areas such as

- Support for staff development
- A willingness to raise local taxes for facilities and operations
- Visioning and planning that led to meaningful goals and objectives
- Concerted efforts to employ highly qualified administrators and teachers

In addition, local officials often provide a critical link between federal and state policymakers and local taxpayers—a connection that can be critical in ensuring that local goals and standards are congruous with broader objectives (Cross, 1999).

Unfortunately, some policymakers have become indifferent about protecting public education generally and local control specifically. Demographic, economic, and political changes, coupled with limited evidence of student learning improvements, have fueled their skepticism. American society has become increasingly pluralistic and multicultural; the structure and functions of families have changed substantially; families have become more mobile; many economic, political, and social issues have been transfigured into global concerns; and the association of federal, state, and local policy development has reached new levels of complexity. These conditions spawn doubts as to whether a system of local control that worked well in the past can effectively serve future generations. Interestingly, persons who are either opposed to or indifferent about local control are quite divided about a preferred future. Those guided primarily by the value of equality favor increased centralization in the form of greater federal and state control; those guided primarily by the value of liberty favor market-based approaches (e.g., vouchers, charter schools), which reduce the influence of government on education at all levels.

Despite intense criticism, the present system of local control is still supported widely in the United States. Many people continue to believe that smaller schools and districts that are free from excessive state controls and enjoying a symbiotic relationship with their local communities are more effective than other types of public schools. This conclusion is supported by some of the research on student achievement. Studying results from eighth-graders on the National Assessment of Educational Progress mathematics assessment, for example, researchers found that higher-achieving states had smaller schools and districts and smaller state shares of school expenditures (Walberg & Walberg, 1994). In fact, some reformers believe that education policy should move closer to, rather than retreat from, local control; they believe that school boards are more likely to produce initiatives that will result in lasting improvement (Saks, 1990).

Overall, it is unlikely that the present system of local governance for public elementary and secondary education will be eliminated. What remains in doubt is the extent to which the authority of local district officials will be increased, decreased, or modified, either through legislative actions or judicial decisions.

Intermediate School Districts

Intermediate school districts exist in a number of states and are known by various names (e.g., regional educational service agencies, regional service centers, board of cooperative educational services, etc.). In essence, these organizations are downward extensions of state authority over public education, an intermediate administrative/service agency between local school districts and the state departments of education. The creation of the position of county superintendent was the earliest form of intermediate districts. The primary function of this office was to provide services and management to weak and ineffective school districts (Knezevich, 1975). This was especially true in an era when many school districts were organized on a township basis and were controlled by the township trustee rather than a school board. In many counties, this condition resulted in numerous school districts with relatively small pupil enrollments.

Although various forms of intermediate school districts have existed for some time, they remain an enigma to many. The concept underlying this organization is rather simple: The intermediate district provides services to school districts too small or too poor to offer complete programs (Campbell et al., 1990). Through cooperative purchasing, media libraries, equipment repair, shared staff development programs, and similar functions, the intermediate district can provide cost savings and programmatic improvements.

Intermediate districts are often confused with two other forms of joint ventures. These are education service cooperatives and study councils. Cooperatives exist in some states to provide joint services (i.e., several school districts offering programs cooperatively). Typically, these ventures have a single function, special education and vocational education being the most common. Study councils, by contrast, generally conduct collaborative research, staff development, and other functions designed to provide information and services for educators rather than direct programming for students. Intermediate units differ from these two entities in that they are less restrictive in operations and exist as official extensions of state government. Some school districts simultaneously hold membership in a special education cooperative, a vocational education cooperative, a study council, and an intermediate school district. Not all states having intermediate districts require local school districts to participate in them. In Indiana, for example, membership in regional service centers is voluntary; yet, the state government encourages and financially supports these centers as extensions of the state department of education. Some states permit private schools to participate in all or some services provided by intermediate units.

The funding of intermediate districts also varies among the states; however, revenues for most are obtained through a combination of state funding and local participation fees (usually established on a per-pupil basis). Intermediate units also may receive federal funding (in the form of support for special projects and grants), private gifts, and revenues generated through designated fees (e.g., charges for equipment repair).

Governance of intermediate units is usually prescribed by state statute. The typical arrangement is for the unit to have a director or superintendent (appointed in most states, but elected in some), a staff, and a governing board. The mode is for superintendents from participating districts (or their representatives) to serve on the board; some states elect board members in a fashion similar to local school board elections. These units may be fiscally independent or they may be linked to a school district that functions as its local educational agency (LEA).

One example of the growing value of intermediate units for many school districts is the proliferation of technology in schools. Intermediate school districts can provide smaller school systems with cooperative purchasing of computers, software libraries, staff development, and even equipment repair. These are functions that smaller districts usually cannot afford to provide within their own organizations.

The degree of control an intermediate district has over local school systems varies among the states. In Illinois, for instance, regional superintendents perform certain functions commonly provided by state government (e.g., registering licenses and certificates). In the past 30 to 40 years, some states have consolidated regional units in an effort to achieve a more reasonable scale of economies (e.g., Wisconsin and Illinois). This has resulted in fewer but larger intermediate districts.

Implications for Practice

Who controls public education in the United States? The answer is more complex than most imagine. In the past 50 years, the federal government has become more than a silent partner in providing this service. Likewise, state government has increased its control. What has evolved is a novel approach to establishing policy that sets the United States apart from virtually all other countries. Control flows from a mixture of federal/state/local government where roles and shares of power are fluid.

Concerns sparked by the distribution of authority among federal, state, and local governmental agencies have taken on new prominence in an era of school reform. Many who investigate ways of improving education quickly conclude that the issue of control is paramount to meaningful reform. Three different but not necessarily mutually exclusive proposals for school improvement remain before the public:

1. *Increasing federal and state control:* Advocates argue that the current system perpetuates serious inequities in educational opportunities; more centralized governmental intervention is proposed as a solution.
2. *Making public school compete in the market economy:* Advocates believe that public schools will not improve appreciably as long as their future is guaranteed. Ideas such as charter schools, vouchers, tax credits, and choice are viewed as ways of placing schools in a competitive environment.
3. *Decreasing federal and state control:* Advocates argue that decisions about education improvement are most likely to be effective if they are made on a school-by-school or district-by-district basis. Ideas such as site-based management and teacher professionalization are viewed as ways of allowing visioning and planning to occur at the local level with only minimal intrusions from federal and state governments.

Clearly, the U.S. public and even professional educators are less than uniform in their convictions regarding the future governance of public schools. As you prepare to enter practice in school administration, you should develop a solid understanding of the following topics:

- The evolution of control in U.S. public education
- The present mixes of federal, state, and local control
- The factors affecting education policy, including the role of values
- The potential for radical changes in the coming decades

In later courses, especially in the study of school law and policy analysis, you will examine these issues in greater depth.

Regardless of claims to the contrary, public education has always been immersed in political problems defined by four primary questions:

- What is legitimate?
- Who controls decision making?
- What is the nature of competition?
- What is valued? (Wiles, Wiles, & Bondi, 1981, p. 4)

As an administrator, you will repeatedly analyze these questions as you confront different values, beliefs, needs, and wants.

For Further Discussion

1. If the United States Constitution does not mention education, why has it been held to be a state's right?

2. In the past 10 years, has the federal government become more or less involved in public education? Explain.

3. Does your state have a state board of education? If so, how are members selected and what are their terms of office?

4. What are the arguments favoring greater state control of public elementary and secondary education?

5. What are the arguments favoring greater local control of public elementary and secondary education?

6. How is the chief school officer selected or appointed in your state?

7. What is the difference between an independent and dependent school district?

8. What are the laws in your state regarding the selection of school board members for local school districts?

9. What are the primary duties of the state board of education in your state? How does the state board interface with the state department of education?

10. Why do some school board members choose to involve themselves in the day-to-day operations of schools?

11. What authority do school board members have to act independently in making decisions that affect the operations of a local district?

Other Suggested Activities

1. Have a debate in your class relative to whether local control of education should be expanded or reduced.

2. Discuss the relationships between increased professional control (e.g., teacher empowerment) and increased democratic decision making (e.g., greater citizen involvement).

3. Discuss the issue of the role of federal courts in education. Can these courts make law?

4. Trace the development of the state department of education in your state.

5. Discuss the merits and potential pitfalls of greater federal intervention into public elementary and secondary education.

References

Alexander, K., & Alexander, M. D. (1998). *American public school law* (4th ed.). Belmont, CA: Wadsworth.

Armstrong, D. G., Henson, K. T., & Savage, T. V. (1989). *Education: An introduction* (3rd ed.). New York: Macmillan.

Brubacher, J. S. (1947). *The history of the problems of education*. New York: McGraw-Hill.

Burke, F. G. (1990). *Public education: Who's in charge?* New York: Praeger.

Button, H. W., & Provenzo, E. F. (1989). *History of education and culture in America* (2nd ed.). Englewood Cliffs, NJ: Prentice-Hall.

Butts, R. F., & Cremin, L. A. (1953). *A history of education in American culture*. New York: Henry Holt.

Campbell, R. F., Cunningham, L. L., Nystrand, R. O., & Usdan, M. D. (1990). *The organization and control of American schools* (6th ed.). Columbus, OH: Merrill.

Clinchy, E. (1995). Learning in and about the real world: Recontextualizing public schooling. *Phi Delta Kappan, 76*(5), 400–404.

Counts, G. S. (1952). *Education and American civilization*. New York: Teachers College Press.

Cremin, L. A. (1989). *Popular education and its discontents*. New York: Harper and Row.

Cross, C. T. (1999). Standards and local control. *American School Board Journal, 186*(4), 54–55.

Danzberger, J. P. (1994). Governing the nation's schools: The case for restructuring local school boards. *Phi Delta Kappan, 75*(5), 67–73.

Danzberger, J. P., & Usdan, M. D. (1994). Local education governance: Perspectives on problems and strategies for change. *Phi Delta Kappan, 75*(5), 366.

Garber, L. O., & Edwards, N. (1970). *The public school in our governmental structure*. Danville, IL: Interstate Printers & Publishers.

Gittell, M., & McKenna, L. (1999). Redefining education regimes and reform: The political role of governors. *Urban Education, 34*(3), 268–291.

Grieder, C., Pierce, T. M., & Jordan, K. F. (1969). *Public school administration* (3rd ed.). New York: Ronald Press.

Hertert, L. G. (1998). What the governors propose for 1998. *School Business Affairs, 64*(7), 28–32.

Hessong, R. F., & Weeks, T. H. (1991). *Introduction to the foundations of education* (2nd ed.). New York: Macmillan.

Hill, P. T. (1990). The federal role in education: A strategy for the 1990s. *Phi Delta Kappan, 71*(5), 398–402.

Kimbrough, R. B., & Nunnery, M. Y. (1976). *Educational administration: An introduction*. New York: Macmillan.

Knezevich, S. J. (1975). *Administration of public education* (3rd ed.). New York: Harper and Row.

Kowalski, T. J. (1999). *The school superintendent: Theory, practice, and cases*. Upper Saddle River, NJ: Merrill, Prentice-Hall.

Kowalski, T. J., & Schmielau, R. E. (2001). Potential for states to provide equality in funding construction. *Equity and Excellence in Education, 34*(2), 54–61.

Marcus, L. R. (1990). Far from the banks of the Potomac: Educational politics and policy in the Reagan years. In L. R. Marcus & B. D. Stickney (Eds.), *Politics and policy in the age of education* (pp. 32–55). Springfield, IL: Charles Thomas.

McCarthy, M. M., Cambron-McCabe, N., & Thomas, S. B. (1998). *Public school law: Teachers and students' rights* (4th ed.). Boston: Allyn and Bacon.

McDonnell, L. M., & Fuhrman, S. (1985). The political context of school reform. In V. D. Mueller & M. P. McKeown (Eds.), *The fiscal, legal and political aspects of state reform of elementary and secondary education* (pp. 43–64). Cambridge, MA: Ballinger.

McGuire, K. (1985). Implications for future reform: A state perspective. In V. D. Mueller & M. P. McKeown (Eds.), *The fiscal, legal and political aspects of state reform of elementary and secondary education* (pp. 309–324). Cambridge, MA: Ballinger.

Morphet, E. L., Johns, R. L., & Reller, T. L. (1967). *Educational administration: Concepts, practices, and issues* (2nd ed.). Englewood Cliffs, NJ: Prentice-Hall.

Radin, B. A., & Hawley, W. D. (1988). *The politics of federal reorganization*. New York: Pergamon Press.

Rebell, M. A. (1999). Fiscal equity litigation and the democratic imperative. *Equity and Excellence in Education, 32*(3), 5–18.

Reutter, E. E. (1985). *The law of public education* (3rd ed.). Mineola, NY: Foundation Press.

Saks, J. B. (1990). Michael Kirst. *American School Board Journal, 177*(11), 31–33.

Sergiovanni, T. J., Burlingame, M., Coombs, F. S., & Thurston, P. W. (1987). *Educational governance and administration* (2nd ed.). Englewood Cliffs, NJ: Prentice-Hall.

Spring, J. (1990). *The American school, 1642–1990* (2nd ed.). New York: Longman.

Streshly, W. A., & Frase, L. E.. (1993). School boards: The missing piece of the reform pie. *International Journal of Educational Reform, 2*(2), 140–143.

Thayer, V. T. (1965). *Formative ideas in American education: From the colonial period to the present* (2nd ed.). New York: Dodd, Mead.

Valente, W. D. (1987). *Law in the schools* (2nd ed.). Columbus, OH: Merrill.

Van Scotter, R. D., Kraft, R. J., & Haas, J. D. (1979). *Foundations of education: Social perspective*. Englewood Cliffs, NJ: Prentice-Hall.

Walberg, H. J., & Walberg, H. J., III. (1994). Losing local control. *Educational Researcher, 23*(5), 19–26.

Wiles, D. K., Wiles, J., & Bondi, J. (1981). *Practical politics for school administrators*. Boston: Allyn and Bacon.

Wirt, F. M., & Kirst, M. W. (1997). *The political dynamics of American education*. Berkeley, CA: McCutchan.

6

Social, Political, and Historical Context of Private Education

Chapter Content _____

Historical Overview
Types of Private Schools
Status of Private Education in the United States
Resurgence of Interest in Private Education
Governance and Control of Private Schools
Political and Legal Issues
Implications for Practice

Private elementary and secondary schools in the United States have been and continue to be an important component of the nation's education system. Although approximately 88 percent of precollegiate students attend public schools, the remaining students in this country either attend private schools or are educated at home (National Center for Education Statistics, 2000a). And since 1980, reform-driven initiatives, such as vouchers and charter schools, have served to increase interest in public education alternatives. The growth in private school enrollments has two important implications for administration: a considerable number of new administrators will spend part or all of their careers working in private schools and public school administrators will be increasingly expected to collaborate with private schools.

Historically, school administration professors at public universities paid little attention to private schools. In large measure, this was because few of their students intended to work outside of public education. This condition has now changed in most states, partly because more private schools, including religiously affiliated schools, are seeking state accreditation. Accreditation standards usually require schools to employ licensed principals. Two other factors make private schools a more cogent topic for administration courses: the continued growth of private schools and the increasing levels of networking and cooperation between public and private schools. This chapter provides a general overview of private schools, including both historical and contemporary perspectives.

Historical Overview

Historically, private schools have been a refuge for those who dissented from the value system explicitly or implicitly promoted by public schools. More specifically, the establishment of private schools was often prompted by perceptions about the public school's treatment of religious values. This treatment passed through three separate but overlapping periods (Lines, 1986):

1. *The evangelical Protestant period:* This period commenced with the beginning of public schools and lasted well into the nineteenth century.
2. *The period of nondenominational religious emphasis:* This period was relatively brief and continues to be evident in some sectors even today.
3. *The secular education period:* This period became dominant in the 1970s and 1980s.

Conditions stemming from each of these phases served to increase interest in private schools.

The formation of the Catholic school system during the nineteenth century was a response to the evangelical Protestant emphasis in public schools. Values associated with this emphasis often were deemed by Catholics to be incongruous with their own religious convictions. Many of the nation's Catholics at that time were recent immigrants who did not have the financial means to enroll their children in nondenominational private schools. Consequently, they used parish resources to establish their own low-tuition schools that would promote their values. Since most Catholic immigrants resided in industrial cities, these parish schools were heavily concentrated in metropolitan areas. Even today, many major eastern seaboard cities still have large numbers of Catholic schools.

By the middle of the nineteenth century, Catholic schools were growing as rapidly as public schools. From this period until the mid-1960s, the vast majority of private schools in the United States were Catholic; over 90 percent of private school students during this period were enrolled in Catholic schools (Lines, 1986). The rapid growth of Catholic schooling made parochial education a controversial topic. Opponents of these institutions held one or more of the following beliefs:

• The expansion of parochial schools was a threat to the future of public education.
• These schools were usually inferior, overcrowded, and undesirable places for learning.

• These schools verged on being unpatriotic because cultural pluralism rather than cultural unity was stressed.

But some opponents of religious schools were simply prejudiced against certain immigrant groups and their religions.

Animosity toward religious schools in the early 1900s was exemplified by the Oregon legislature's attempt to force all children in that state to attend public schools. Although a subsequent lawsuit, *Pierce v. Society of Sisters*, resulted in the law being found unconstitutional, the action demonstrated the intensity of negative feelings that some political leaders had toward Catholic schools. The *Pierce* decision, long considered a landmark case, proved to be invaluable to the future of parochial education; over time, it has become known as the "private school bill of rights" (Lines, 1986).

Public schools responded to the rapid increase in Catholic schools by trying to replace traditional Protestant values with nondenominationalism. The underlying principle of this movement was that there was a set of core religious principles that were supported by the vast majority of the population. Consequently, these values could be identified and taught in public schools without extreme controversy. Nondenominational prayer at the start of the school day, the posting of the Ten Commandments, and Bible reading were actions characteristic of this period.

Prior to and during the nondenominational period, there were those who argued that religion, including nondenominational principles, had no place in public schools. They believed that to protect the religious freedoms of all, government-supported institutions should promote the religious principles of none. For these secularists, even supposedly nondenominational religious principles were suspect, since they might violate the beliefs of those embracing Eastern religions, or of atheists.

The influence of secularists became increasingly evident in the evolution of public education. For example, the Cardinal Principles of Secondary Education (a philosophical statement that had pronounced effect on the development of public schools) referred to "ethical character," but made no mention of religious training. The capstone events of the secularist movement occurred in the early 1960s. The *Engel v. Vitale* decision rendered by the nation's highest court held that school prayer was unconstitutional. The following year, the United States Supreme Court outlawed Bible reading in schools for all but literary, social, or historical purposes.

As schools became more secular, persons embracing traditional Protestant values responded by attempting to change the public school curriculum from its secular nature to its former evangelical roots. These individuals perceived the removal of prayer and Bible reading from schools as the "collapse of consensus concerning the basic nature and function of our institutions and the values, traditions, and purposes under girding them" (Carper, 1983, p. 135). However, the Supreme Court continued to rule in favor of secularization of schools in cases involving school prayer and other efforts to inject religious influences into the curriculum.

Failing in their efforts to reconstruct public school curriculum, some evangelical Protestants formed their own schools (Cooper, 1984). These institutions, which have variously been called evangelical, Christian, or fundamentalist Christian schools, became the fastest-growing sector of private education during the last quarter of the twentieth century. A response to a growing dissatisfaction with public schools was home schooling. By the mid-1990s, it was estimated that over one million students were engaged in this form of education (Duffey, 1998).

Some proponents of private schools (e.g., Cooper, 1984) have argued that these institutions have essentially become the nation's new public schools. Their contention is premised on the belief that private schools are better able than contemporary public schools to establish compacts with families. In most private schools, the proponents contend, families provide support, trust, and children in exchange for the schools' promotion of shared mores and values. Many parents who opt not to send their children to public schools feel public schools have broken this compact. Such feelings are reinforced by studies that indicate that religious schools produce stronger, more uniform attitudes toward religion and morality (e.g., Tritter, 1992) and that students educated in these schools tend to make different moral choices from those students educated in public schools (e.g., Norman, Richards, & Bear, 1998). Nevertheless, critics continue to point out that separating students by values and beliefs is not beneficial in a democratic society.

Types of Private Schools

Distinctions between public and private schools are not always clear. For example, many individuals erroneously believe that *magnet schools* and *charter schools* are forms of nonpublic education. The former describes a concept usually used to reduce racial isolation or to provide an academic or social focus on a specific theme (e.g., school of performing arts); most magnet schools exist in urban public school districts. The latter describes public schools operating outside the jurisdiction of a local district; because they are chartered and financially supported by the state, these institutions are public schools.

Attempts to define private schools by categorizing them have not always reduced ambiguity. Donald Erickson (1983), for example, divided private schools into four categories: high-tuition schools, religiously affiliated schools, fundamentalist schools, and other private schools. Fundamentalist schools, however, are religiously affiliated. In this chapter, private schools are divided into three general categories: parochial schools, other private schools, and home schooling. The first two contain subcategories.

Parochial Schools

A parochial school is a private institution that is owned or sponsored by a religious group. The most common sponsors have been the following religions:

- Roman Catholic
- Protestant (e.g., Baptist, Episcopal, Lutheran, Seventh Day Adventist)

- Judaism
- Muslim

A large portion of parochial schools sponsored by Protestant churches since 1980 are commonly referred to as *fundamentalist schools*. The formation and patronization of their schools are largely attributable to the following conditions (Erickson, 1983):

- Litigation perceived to have eliminated religion from public education (e.g., court decisions prohibiting prayer and Bible reading in public schools)
- Local school board policies that prohibit the teaching of creationism
- The legally protected, contemporary lifestyles of some public school teachers and administrators
- A desire to shelter children from student subcultures that promote drugs, sex, and rock and roll.

Many fundamentalist schools initially operated with very limited budgets and were located in areas such as church basements.

Often overlooked are Amish schools. In compliance with religious principles, students (called scholars) attend school only through the eighth grade (approximately age 14). The education of Amish children has long been both a political and legal issue in many states due to conflict with mandatory attendance laws.

Some parochial schools embrace both a religious and ethnic mission. One is the Hebrew day school. These schools experienced a period of significant growth in the mid-1960s and early 1970s in response to a "fever of ethnicity" that was prevalent in the United States at the time (Erickson, 1983, p. 12). Muslim schools are another type of non-Christian parochial school, and they are becoming more common as the number of Muslims living in this country is increasing.

Other Private Schools

All organized nonpublic schools not affiliated with or sponsored by a religion are placed in the category of other private schools. Many of these schools are referred to as *high-tuition* institutions. They generally serve students from affluent families; and although they are found throughout the United States, they are most prevalent along the East Coast. High-tuition schools include both day schools (students attend during the day and return to their homes in the evening) and boarding schools. The most common reasons parents elect to send their children to these schools include perceptions of academic rigor, faculty quality, and institutional reputation. Wealthy families also may be influenced by the importance of social connections their children will make at these schools (Erickson, 1983).

Other private schools outside of the parochial category include the following:

- *Japanese high schools:* The first such school in the United States opened in 1989 in a geographical area with a high density of Japanese executives. The mission was to provide students an education equal to what they would have received in their native country.

- *Inner-city private schools:* Some private schools have been created to address concerns with urban public schools. The Malcolm X Academy, an all-male school in Detroit that was created in the late 1980s, exemplifies a school in this subcategory.

- *Proprietary schools:* Some private schools are operated for the express purpose of making a profit. Arguments in favor of such schools are basically anchored in the belief that public schools have become mired in politics, making them incapable of reforming themselves (see Lieberman, 1986).

Home Schooling

Home schooling is treated as a separate category simply because it is a unique form of education taking place outside of public schools. Contrary to popular thought, home schooling is not a new concept; it actually is the oldest form of education in human history. The modern form involves students receiving home-based and family-based education. Parents who teach their children at home usually have serious objections to some aspect of public education (Marchant & MacDonald, 1992). Often, they view public schools as embracing a secular humanist philosophy. Some parents, however, are swayed by special situations or their geographic location. For example, parents may start home schooling because they believe their child is failing in a traditional school. Or, families living in remote or rural areas may opt to provide home schooling to counter excessively long trips to and from school.

Much of the controversy surrounding home schooling relates to perennial tensions between liberty and equality. Proponents argue that the option allows parents to choose freely a unique and effective education for their children; opponents counter by saying that the process causes balkanization, divisiveness, social anarchy, and segregation (Ray, 2001). Studies have suggested that home-schooled children achieve at or above the level of children educated in public schools; for example, Ray (2001) reported that home-schooled students on average scored at or above the 80th percentile in all academic subjects in 1997. However, by taking their children out of schools, home-schooling parents may be depriving them of certain resources and opportunities, such as the opportunity for peer social interaction. Proponents have reacted to these concerns by arguing that selected studies (e.g., Medlin, 2000; Ray, 2001) show that home-schooled students participate in many of the same kinds of social activity as do their peers enrolled in regular school programs. Despite the controversy that continues to surround home schooling, the process is legal in some form in all 50 states.

Status of Private Education in the United States

Although the percentage and total number of kindergarten through twelfth-grade students attending private schools decreased between 1965 and 1990, a closer look at demographic data points to significant recent growth of the private school sector. And this growth, both in the number of schools and the number of students, is projected to continue into the foreseeable future.

Figures about private school enrollments can be misleading, depending on whether the data refer to the percentage of schools or the percentage of pupils enrolled. Consider the following statistics:

- In 1998, there were approximately 27,500 private elementary and secondary schools in the United States—or approximately 25 percent of all precollegiate schools (CAPE, 2001). Growth in the percentage of private schools has been attributable to two factors: the development of new private schools and the closing of existing public schools (primarily due to consolidation). Because private schools usually have small enrollments compared to public schools, the 25 percent figure is often misinterpreted; private schools do not enroll 25 percent of all students in this country.
- In 2000, 5.9 million students of the nation's kindergarten through twelfth-grade students attended private schools (National Association of Independent Schools, 2000). This accounted for 11.2 percent of the students in this age group.
- Although private school enrollments have increased just over 230,000 pupils since 1960, the rate of growth has not kept pace with public school enrollment increases. From 1994 to 1999, enrollments in public schools increased by 5 percent at the elementary level and by 10 percent at the secondary level (National Center for Education Statistics, 2000b). Thus, despite actual increases in both the number of schools and actual enrollments, the percentage of students attending private schools is about 2.3 percent lower now than it was in 1960 (National Center for Education Statistics, 1980, 1991).

Trends in private school enrollment need to be considered in light of the fact that enrollment in private schools declined steadily for nearly three decades. In 1966, about 6.3 million students were attending private schools; in 1991, that figure dropped to about 5.2 million. Ever since 1992, private school enrollments have been increasing modestly; in 1998, they reached 5.9 million (National Center for Education Statistics, 2000b).

A breakdown of private school enrollments also is enlightening. In 1965, Catholic schools were clearly the primary provider of private education in this country—they educated 88 percent of private school students. From 1965 to 1983, however, the number of Catholic schools decreased by 30 percent and the number of students attending them decreased by 46 percent (Cooper, 1984). The decline in Catholic school enrollments can be attributed to several interrelated reasons:

- Following the Second Vatican Council of the Catholic Church, there was a significant shift in the official thinking of the Catholic Church about a variety of topics. Questions were raised about the importance of Catholic schools to the mission of the Church. The result was that many bishops and pastors no longer advocated Catholic schooling as enthusiastically as they had prior to the Second Vatican Council (especially since the schools were a drain on parish and diocesan funding).

- The Second Vatican Council also gave members of religious orders greater liberty to choose service areas. Whereas nuns had previously served almost exclusively as teachers and principals, many elected to serve in parishes, hospitals, charities, or other nonschool settings.
- The number of priests, brothers, and nuns declined. In order to staff schools, lay teachers had to be hired at salaries much higher than the schools had been providing.
- Many parishes were saddled with large convents and church buildings that needed to be replaced or renovated.
- Migration to the suburbs affected school choices made by parents. Catholic schools were not as prevalent in the suburbs as they were in urban areas, and the suburban public schools were often seen as more desirable than urban public schools (Erickson, 1983).
- Many parishes that previously relied on church collections to fund their schools could no longer do so. Tuition increases prompted some families to transfer their children to public schools.

Collectively, these and other circumstances contributed to the closing of many Catholic schools, and some of these problems remain relevant. In 1999, for example, 73 Catholic schools closed in the United States (National Catholic Education Association, 2001).

However, at the same time that some Catholic schools, especially in inner-city areas, were closing, new ones, especially in suburban areas, were opening. Declines in Catholic school enrollment began leveling in the early 1980s (Cooper, 1984); subsequently, the overall enrollment has increased. Consider the following statistics:

- From 1989–90 to 1999–2000, Catholic school enrollment in this country has increased from 2,588,893 to 2,653,038 (National Catholic Education Association, 2001).
- During 1998–99, 36 new Catholic schools started to function (McDonald, 1999).
- During 1998–99, 41 percent of all Catholic schools reported having waiting lists for admission (McDonald, 1999).

The profile of Catholic schools also has changed over time. From 1970 to 1992, the percentage of minority students attending these schools more than doubled (Brigham, 1993), and by the late 1990s, 95 percent of all Catholic schools reported being coeducational (McDonald, 1999).

While Catholic schools were experiencing enrollment declines between 1965 and 1980, the non-Catholic portion of the parochial school population more than doubled (Lines, 1986). Both Lutheran schools and conservative Jewish schools increased by over 250 percent from 1965 to 1983; however, evangelical schools, most supported by fundamentalist Protestant churches, increased by over 600 percent. Nevertheless, Catholic schools remain the primary provider of private education in the United States. A comparison of percentages of private school enrollments in for the 1989–90 school year and the 1997–98 school year is shown in Table 6.1. Compared to 1965, when nearly 90 percent of all private school enrollments were in Catholic schools, current private school enrollments are widely dispersed. Consider just two examples of growing private school enrollments not readily recognized.

- Jewish day schools, once attended almost exclusively by children from Ortho-dox families, now attract students from both the Conservative and Reformed branches of the religion. In 1998, an estimated 200,000 students attended these schools (Archer, 1998).
- Swelling immigrant populations from Asia, Africa, the Middle East, and the Indian subcontinent already have created a demand for Muslim schools (Sachs, 1998).

Overall, the growth of private schools suggests that political support for national and state legislation favoring these schools is getting broader and deeper.

Additionally, home schooling, although an alternative serving a relatively small portion of the total population of school-age children not attending public schools, is growing exponentially. In 1975, this concept was virtually nonexistent and involved only about 10,000 students (Lines, 1987); in 1995, the number of students receiving this form of education was estimated at 500,000 (Pearson, 1996). Current estimates indicate that between 1.2 and 1.9 million children are receiving home-based schooling (Ray, 2001). Despite its remarkable growth in recent decades, home schooling has received considerable criticism. Concerns have ranged from poor academic standards to concerns for social development. Often, parents send-ing their children to private schools and parents providing home schooling are allies in seeking legislation that favor their needs and wants.

TABLE 6.1   *Enrollments in Private Schools: 1989–90 and 1997–98*

	Percentage of All Private School Enrollments	
Affiliation	*1989–90*	*1997–98*
Catholic	54.5%	49.5%
Nonsectarian	13.2%	15.7%
Lutheran	4.4%	4.3%
Jewish	3.2%	3.3%
All other*	24.7%	27.2%

*Predominately schools that identify themselves as Conservative Christian or Baptist.
Source: CAPE, 2001.

As the demand for private schools increased, comparisons with public schools became more common. Both input and output data are mixed, and arguments continue as to whether private schools are superior. One area where nonpublic schools have made a significant improvement is in the area of class size. The average student/teacher ratio in private schools in 1957 was 31.5 to 1; in 1998, it was only 15.2 to 1—a ratio superior to the 1998 public school ratio of 16.5 to 1 (National Center of Education Statistics, 2000a). However, public schools have fewer teachers without college degrees (less than 1 percent, compared to 7 percent in private schools) (National Center for Education Statistics, 2000a) and more diverse student populations (in 1993, 28 percent of public school students and 17 percent of private school students were classified as minorities) (Choy, 1997).

Resurgence of Interest in Private Education

Traditionally, a substantial number of families have turned to private schools because of religious convictions (Lines, 1986). By the 1990s, however, some writers (e.g., Convey, 1991) were reporting that academic reasons had displaced religious convictions as the primary motivator. Others who have studied this issue (e.g., Newman, 1995) have concluded that Americans choose private schools for many reasons that cannot be neatly dissected—and this is even true for parochial schools. As an example, nearly 15 percent of Catholic school students are not members of the Catholic faith (National Catholic Education Association, 2001).

Since the early 1970s, a significant amount of attention has been given to studies that have produced favorable findings regarding the effectiveness of private education. For example, these studies suggest that private schools had higher academic achievement, more instructional time, fewer student absences, more effective discipline, more committed teachers, and students who do more homework and watch less television than their public school counterparts (Coleman, Hoffer, & Kilgore, 1982; Lee, 1985, 1987; Lee & Stewart, 1989; Marks & Lee, 1989; Morton, Bassis, Brittingham, Ewing, Horwitz, Hunter, Long, Maguire, & Pezzullo, 1977).

Numerous studies have also indicated that minority students attending Catholic schools have higher educational aspirations, are less likely to drop out of school, and exhibit achievement levels closer to those of white students than do minority students attending public schools (Coleman et al., 1982; Coleman & Hoffer, 1987; Greeley, 1982; Lee, 1985, 1987; Lee & Stewart, 1989; Marks & Lee, 1989). More recent data indicate that although 11.2 percent of public school tenth- through twelfth-grade students dropped out of school in 1999, only 3.2 percent of Catholic school students in these grade levels did so (National Center for Education Statistics, 2000b). Additionally, 83 percent of Catholic school graduates attend a two- or four-year institution subsequent to high school, compared to 52 percent of public school graduates (National Catholic Education Association, 2001).

Examining differences between public and private schools, Susan Choy (1997) concluded that there were many differences between the two types of institutions. She based this judgment on several findings, including the following:

- Public school students present teachers with greater challenges than do their private school counterparts, in large measure because they are a more heterogeneous population.
- The average public school teacher has more formal education and earns a higher salary than does the average private school teacher; however, teachers in both types of institutions use similar teaching strategies.
- Overall, private schools appear to offer a greater sense of community and more teacher empowerment (i.e., greater freedom in the classroom and more influence over curriculum and important school policies).
- Overall, private schools tend to provide climates more favorable to learning and personal safety—the size of the school is often a critical variable in this regard.
- Private school students typically take more advanced courses at the high school level than do public school students.

Despite these findings, Choy (1997) made two other important observations:

- Differences between public and private schools appear to be narrowing.
- Student success is not determined by whether a student attends a public or a private school; rather, success is a product of a myriad of variables, including the ability and attitudes the student brings to school.

Private schools clearly have several natural advantages with respect to institutional climate. They are formed to promote a central (frequently spiritually oriented) mission or set of values. This gives organizational members a sense of social cohesion (Erickson, 1983), of being involved in something that goes beyond self-interest. In some fundamentalist Christian schools, for example, parents are required to sign philosophical statements agreeing to have their children adhere to the values and beliefs of the sponsoring church. Because parents freely elect to place their children in private schools, these institutions are far less likely than public schools to experience fragmentation that leads to diffused purpose and cultural ambiguity.

Public school officials frequently have responded to claims of private school superiority by pointing out that general conditions surrounding private schools give them an unfair advantage. The following are among their primary arguments:

- Private schools are able to avoid serving students who have emotional, social, economic, and learning problems.
- Private schools can more easily expel students who do not comply with policies and rules.
- Private schools are not faced with the incessant conflict spawned by vast differences in parental philosophy, needs, expectations, and commitment.

Some research methodologists also have questioned the validity of studies examining private school outcomes (e.g., Cain & Goldberger, 1983). Such challenges, however, rarely affect public opinion. People either believe that standards in private schools are superior or they do not. Generally, parents believe that public schools are better with respect to supporting diversity and providing special education, but they rate private schools higher for (1) promoting religious and social values; (2) maintaining discipline, safety, and higher academic standards; and (3) having smaller class sizes (Sconyers, 1996).

Governance and Control of Private Schools

Private schools exhibit a variety of governance patterns. For example, Catholic and Lutheran systems have a governance hierarchy, whereas independent schools are generally loosely tied to the National Association of Independent Schools (NAIS). Other types of private schools are unattached to any higher authority beyond local organizing and governance groups.

Generally, private schools have fewer levels in the governing hierarchy and thus are not subject to the fragmentation that conflicting demands from trying to serve too many masters has placed on public schools. Control, authority, and decision making are generally located at the school level (Scott & Meyer, 1985).

Private school administrative staffs tend to be very small. Public schools have much larger central office administrative staffs, fostered by a web of funding sources, program requirements, and mandates (generally dictated from state or federal governments or other regulatory agencies). Some observers (e.g., Scott & Meyer, 1985) have argued that the layers of bureaucracy found in most public districts have detracted from academic program coherence.

Little detailed research has been conducted on private school governance, with the exception of Catholic schools. Most Catholic elementary schools are operated on a parish-by-parish basis. This arrangement makes these schools highly vulnerable to the adverse effects of parish resources and family migration (i.e., families moving in and out of parishes). Catholic high schools, by comparison, span parish boundaries and are operated by dioceses and religious orders. Thus, they tend to have more stable financial resources and attendance areas (Erickson, 1983).

Catholic school governance has undergone a transition during the past 25 years. Prior to the Second Vatican Council of the Catholic Church, governance of Catholic schools was carried out primarily through traditional hierarchical authority structures of bishop, pastor or religious order, and principal, in descending order of authority. Since the council, governance has evolved into more collaborative arrangements that have included parents as members of advisory committees and school boards. Under the new structure, parish school boards, usually consisting of parents whose children attend the parish school, have been developed in approximately 70 percent of the Catholic schools in the United States (Hocevar, 1991). These boards consist of two types: a board with limited jurisdiction and a consultative board. Jurisdictional boards have power over policy in certain areas of educational concern, with bishops retaining control in matters of religion and catholicity. These boards have final but not total jurisdiction. Consultative boards, on the other hand, are involved in the development of policy, but have no actual authority (Hocevar, 1991).

The parish pastor is entrusted with pastoral care for the diocese, but his relationship with the principal has not been formally delineated. Generally, the principal fulfills responsibilities such as employment, supervision, and evaluation of teachers and other school employees; the formulation of policies for consideration by the school board; oversight of the instructional program, and the preparation of a school budget. The pastor retains ultimate financial control, supervises and evaluates the principal, and oversees the religious instruction program of the school (O'Brien, 1987).

Catholic schools also have a diocesan education office, generally with a very small administrative staff (Scott & Meyer, 1985). Diocesan offices, however, have no formal authority, although superintendents may have authority if they have been appointed Episcopal vicar by the bishop. In either case, a fundamental principle of Catholic Canon Law holds that decisions regarding a parish are most appropriately resolved at the parish rather than the diocesan level (O'Brien, 1987). Informally, however, the relationship of the diocesan office with the bishop and parish pastors, and its ability to grant or withhold resources or services in some instances, give it a degree of power over individual schools regardless of whether the superintendent has been appointed Episcopal vicar. Similar to the perceptions of power loss felt by many public school administrators in response to calls for greater teacher involvement in school decision making, many bishops and religious orders have viewed the change in Catholic school governance relationships as a "diminution of their lawful authority" (Hocevar, 1991, p. 10).

Governance of other parochial schools does not follow any prescribed pattern. Some fundamentalist schools, for example, have boards of trustees; a church pastor heavily controls others. Boards of trustees almost always govern nonparochial schools. These boards have the power and authority to retain administrators and staff to operate the schools. In general, boards of trustees for all types of private schools are appointed, whereas approximately 95 percent of all public school board members in the United States are elected to office (Kowalski, 1999).

Political and Legal Issues

In many ways, the resurgence of private schools over the last quarter of the twentieth century paralleled school reform efforts. Many would-be change agents were convinced that moving public education closer to a market economy by creating real competition was central to improving all schools. Their support for concepts such as parental choice, vouchers, and tuition tax credits served to rekindle long-standing differences, both political and legal, regarding the status of private education in this country. These disputes generally fall into two broad categories: the regulation of private schools and governmental aid to private schools.

Regulation of Private Schools

During the 1970s and 1980s, the number of lawsuits involving the regulation of private schools increased substantially. In the early 1900s, for example, only 3 or 4 cases of this nature were decided in a decade; from 1980 to 1983, 51 such cases entered the courts (Lines, 1986). States generally have exercised caution in trying to control private schools. The challenge to state legislators has been to protect the state's interest in an informed citizenry while (1) respecting the fundamental right of parents to direct the education of their children, (2) protecting the religious beliefs of parents, and (3) avoiding comprehensive regulation that would deprive parents of any choice in education (Williams, 1996). For the government to intervene with parents' decisions regarding their children's education, the government must show that intervention is necessary to protect the child or the state (McCarthy, and Cambron-McCabe, & Thomas, 1998).

Concerns about racial segregation were one reason why the courts and state officials were called on to pay greater attention to regulating private schools. Critics often charged that private schools either directly or indirectly allowed white families to sidestep racial integration in public schools. In the early 1980s, James Coleman and two associates (Coleman, Hoffer, & Kilgore, 1982) wrote a book comparing public and private schools; in it, they concluded that the segregative effects of private schools had been exaggerated. Critics (e.g., Taeuber & James, 1983), however, attacked this conclusion, saying that in reality parochial and all other private schools enrolled proportionately few African American students. Another factor that drew the courts and state legislators into private school issues was the refusal of many fundamentalist school administrators to comply with state standards.

In recent years, an increasing number of private schools has attempted to gain state accreditation. In so doing, they voluntarily agree to abide by many, if not all, of the policies affecting public schools. Generalizations about state regulation of private schools are very difficult because none of the states regulates private education in the same way (Williams, 1996).

Governmental Aid to Private Schools

States provide a variety of different types of aid to private schools. Private schools receive about 26 percent of their total income directly or indirectly from government funding (Scott & Meyer, 1985). In 1985, 38 states provided public aid to education, including transportation services (23 states), the loan of textbooks (18 states), state-required testing programs (14 states), special education services (13 states), and guidance counseling (10 states) (McCarthy & Cambron-McCabe, 1987).

Public aid to private schools has been the subject of extensive litigation. Although an exhaustive treatment of relevant cases is beyond the scope of this book, several significant principles that prospective school administrators should keep in mind are highlighted here.

The primary argument against public aid to private education is that it violates separation of church and state as established by the U.S. Constitution, since most private schools are church related. The courts have approved several types of aid that primarily benefits students rather than institutions (e.g., transportation services). Court approval, however, simply means that services are constitutionally permissible; it does not mean that services must be provided (McCarthy, Cambron-McCabe, & Thomas, 1998).

One court ruling that continues to create logistical headaches for public and private schools is *Aguilar v. Felton.* In this case, the U.S. Supreme Court ruled that Title I services, which public schools are required to provide for all qualifying students regardless of school type, could not be provided by public school teachers in parochial school buildings since this constituted excessive entanglement between church and state. The Court did not strike down the provision that these services be provided for parochial school students, but rather required them to be provided in public schools or at neutral sites. It has been widely assumed that this ruling also applies to other federal programs that provide services for parochial school students (e.g., special education services) (McCarthy & Cambron-McCabe, 1987).

Recently, the concept of choice has received much attention as a reform initiative to improve education (see discussion in Chapter 12). One of the various forms of choice involves providing parents with a voucher that they can use at any school, public or private, to pay for the education of their child. The end result of the voucher system is that religiously affiliated schools receive government funding for students who choose to attend their schools, although the aid is indirect in the sense that it is first funneled through the student. At issue is whether the primary beneficiary of government funding are parents and students or religiously affiliated institutions.

The U.S. Supreme Court has ruled on several cases that hold implications for the constitutionality of choice. In *Mueller v. Allen*, the Court upheld the constitutionality of a Minnesota tuition tax credit plan that allowed parents to claim a tax deduction for educational expenses incurred for their children. The court ruled that since the benefit was provided for all students, regardless of whether they attended private or public schools, the plan "evidences a purpose that is both secular and understandable" (McCarthy & Cambron-McCabe, 1987, p. 53). In *Witters v. Washington Department of Services for the Blind* (1986), the Supreme Court ruled that aid that went directly to a student with a disability who then transmitted the funds to a religiously affiliated institution for educational services, was constitutional, since the aid was provided to the student who exercised personal choice about which institution should receive the funds. Thus, although courts have not directly ruled on the constitutionality of choice plans, it appears that in order to uphold constitutionality, plans should provide all students a choice and should provide assistance facilitating such choice directly to students or their parents rather than to the educational institution.

Implications for Practice

Scholars have noted that the lines between public and private schools are becoming increasingly blurred (Ornstein, 1989). Many private schools now promote what once were mainstream public school values, there is greater public support for private schools than for public schools, and government has become increasingly involved in the regulation of private schools. Many have argued that the private school now more closely resembles the ideal of the common school than does the public school—a school that promotes the values and beliefs of the dominant culture, where "moral instruction and civic learning occur with the greatest intensity" (James, 1985, p. 2).

Regardless of whether empirical research proves the efficacy of private schools, two issues are clear:

1. Internal and external conditions differ for public and private schools.
2. Private school patrons are more satisfied with their schools than are public school patrons.

Many of the conditions that affect public schools are beyond their control. Nonetheless, rather than practicing defensive posturing, public school administrators would do well to study the reasons for increased private school satisfaction levels and to emulate practices as appropriate and possible. Donald Erickson (1983) has noted, "One of the most compelling reasons for studying private schools may be that by isolating the factors responsible for their particular strengths . . . strategies [may be generated] for the improvement of all schools, public and private" (p. 40; bracketed wording added for clarity). One analyst has suggested that what public schools lack is "something analogous to religious commitment, an 'excitement, spiritual fulfillment and enrichment' " in the way people approach their work (James, 1985, p. 2).

The decline in the number of preschool-age children, the increased elderly population, and the growing disenchantment with public education may result in a crisis of social support for all schools (Cooper, 1984). Yet, educational authorities at different levels of governance (e.g., teaching versus administration) and in different sectors of education (e.g., public and private) often work at cross-purposes, thus fragmenting educational authority in the competition for resources and the establishment of appropriate policy (Scott & Meyer, 1985). When public and private schools war over issues such as tax relief for private school patrons, attention is diverted from increasing sums of money spent on defense and programs for the elderly (Cooper, 1984). In the interest of all children, public and private school personnel as well as constituents need to cooperate in order to present a unified front in competing with other societal groups for scarce resources.

For Further Discussion

1. One of the oft-cited reasons why families choose to patronize private schools is because of the values they promote. Discuss the issue of values instruction in public schools.

2. Should values be taught in public schools? If so, what values should be taught? Is it possible for teaching to be value free? Explain.

3. Enrollment in private schools is growing. What are the advantages and disadvantages of private school growth for education? For children? For society?

4. How do you feel public schools should respond to the growth of private education?

5. What can public schools learn from private schools? What can private schools learn from public schools?

6. What are the implications of *Aguilar v. Felton* for public school administrators?

7. Discuss the benefits and pitfalls of home schooling. What should be the responsibility of public schools to home-schooled children?

8. Discuss the concept of choice. Should vouchers be implemented to give parents a choice of schools to which to send their children?

9. Research and discuss the concepts of U.S. Japanese schools and African American male academies. What are the advantages and disadvantages of each type of school?

Other Suggested Activities

1. Some have argued that research citing the effectiveness of private schools is flawed methodologically. Review several such studies and discuss the procedures and outcomes.

2. Develop a set of interview questions for public and private school administrators based on discussion in this chapter. Interview several administrators from each category of schools and analyze and compare their responses.

3. Develop a list of advantages and disadvantages of public schools. Do the same for private schools. Compare the outcomes and discuss the implications for school administration.

4. This chapter has provided an overview of the current private school context with the concluding section suggesting several implications for practitioners. Develop a list of additional implications.

5. Spend a few hours visiting and observing in both private and public schools. Take field notes during your visit. Analyze your field notes and compare both settings. Develop working hypotheses of similarities and differences in the two types of schools and discuss what can be learned from them.

6. Review research on school choice programs. In what ways have they been successful? In what ways have they been unsuccessful?

References

Archer, J. (1998, March 18). Breaking for tradition. *Education Week*, pp. 36–41.

Brigham, F. H. (1993). *United States Catholic elementary and secondary schools, 1992–1993: Annual statistical report on schools, enrollment and staffing*. (ERIC Document Reproduction Service No. ED 360 391)

Cain, G. G., & Goldberger, A. S. (1983). Public and private schools revisited. *Sociology of Education, 56*, 208–218.

CAPE. (2001). *Private school facts*. Retrieved June 18, 2001, from the World Wide Web: http://www.capenet.org/cape.html.

Carper, J. C. (1983). The Christian day school movement. *Education Forum* (Winter), 35–149.

Choy, S. P. (1997). *Findings from The Condition of Education 1997: Public and private schools: How do they differ?* Washington, DC: U.S. Department of Education, National Center for Education Statistics.

Coleman, J. S., & Hoffer, T. (1987). *Public and private high schools: The impact of communities*. New York: Basic Books.

Coleman, J. S., Hoffer, T., & Kilgore, S. (1982). *High school achievement: Public, Catholic, and private schools compared*. New York: Basic Books.

Convey, J. J. (1991). Catholic schools in a changing society: Past accomplishments and future challenges. In *The Catholic school and society*. Washington, DC: National Catholic Education Association.

Cooper, B. (1984). The changing demography of private schools. *Education and Urban Society, 16*(4), 429–442.

Duffey, J. (1998). Home schooling: A controversial alternative. *Principal, 77*(5), 23–26.

Erickson, D. A. (1983). *Private schools in contemporary perspective*. (ERIC Document Reproduction Service No. ED 231 015)

Greeley, A. M. (1982). *Catholic high schools and minority students*. New Brunswick, NJ: Transaction Books.

Hocevar, R. A. (1991). Catholic school governance. In *Catholic school governance and finance*. Washington, DC: National Catholic Educational Association.

James, T. (1985). *Public & private schools*. (ERIC Document Reproduction Service No. ED 017 682)

Kowalski, T. J. (1999). *The school superintendent: Theory, practice, and cases*. Upper Saddle River, NJ: Merrill, Prentice-Hall.

Lee, V. E. (1985). *1983–84 National Assessment of Educational Progress reading proficiency: Catholic school results and national averages*. Washington, DC: National Catholic Educational Association.

Lee, V. E. (1987). *1983–84 National Assessment of Educational Progress writing proficiency: Catholic school results and national averages*. Washington, DC: National Catholic Educational Association.

Lee, V. E., & Stewart, C. (1989). *1983–84 National Assessment of Educational Progress proficiency in mathematics and science 1985–86: Catholic and public schools compared*. Washington, DC: National Catholic Educational Association.

Lieberman, M. (1986). *Beyond public education*. New York: Praeger.

Lines, P. M. (1986). The new private schools and their historic purpose. *Phi Delta Kappan, 67*, 373–379.

Lines, P. M. (1987). An overview of home instruction. *Phi Delta Kappan, 68*, 503–517.

Marchant, G. J., & MacDonald, S. C. (1992, April). *How home schoolers school*. Paper presented at the annual meeting of the American Educational Research Association, San Francisco.

Marks, H. M., & Lee, V. E. (1989). *National Assessment of Educational Progress proficiency in reading 1985–86: Catholic and public schools compared*. Washington, DC: National Catholic Educational Association.

McCarthy, M. M., & Cambron-McCabe. (1987). *Public school law: Teachers and students' rights* (2nd ed.). Boston: Allyn and Bacon.

McCarthy, M. M., Cambron-McCabe, N., & Thomas, S. B. (1998). *Public school law: Teachers and students' rights* (4th ed.). Boston: Allyn and Bacon.

McDonald, D. (1999). *United States Catholic elementary and secondary schools, 1998–1999: The annual statistical report on schools, enrollment and staffing.* (ERIC Document Reproduction Service No. ED 430 305)

Medlin, R. G. (2000). Homeschooling and the question of socialization. *Peabody Journal of Education, 75*(1&2), 107–123.

Morton, D. S., Bassis, M., Brittingham, B. E., Ewing, P., Horwitz, S., Hunter, W. J., Long, J. V., Maguire, J., & Pezzullo, T. R. (1977, April). *A comprehensive analysis of differences in public and parochial school student performance on standardized tests of achievement.* Paper presented at the annual meeting of the American Educational Research Association, New York.

National Association of Independent Schools. (2000, March). *NAIS fact sheet.* Washington, DC: Author. Retrieved April 19, 2001, from the World Wide Web: http://www.nais.org/nais/nafact.html.

National Catholic Education Association. (2001). *United States Catholic elementary and secondary school statistics 1999–2000.* Washington, DC: Author. Retrieved March 29, 2001, from the World Wide Web: http://www.ncea.org/PubPol/databank.shtml.

National Center for Education Statistics. (1980). *Digest of education statistics.* Washington, DC: U.S. Department of Education.

National Center for Education Statistics. (1991). *Digest of education statistics.* Washington, DC.: U.S. Department of Education.

National Center for Education Statistics. (2000a). *Early estimates of public elementary and secondary statistics: School year 1999–2000* (NCES 2000-364). Washington, DC: U.S. Department of Education.

National Center for Education Statistics. (2000b). *Digest of education statistics.* Washington, DC: U.S. Department of Education.

Newman, J. W. (1995). Comparing private schools and public schools in the 20th century: History, demography, and the debate over choice. *Educational Foundations, 9*(3), 5–18.

Norman, A. D., Richards, H. C., & Bear, G. G. (1998). Moral reasoning and religious belief: Does content influence structure? *Journal of Moral Education, 7*(1), 89–98.

O'Brien, J. S. (1987). *A primer on educational governance in the Catholic Church.* (ERIC Document Reproduction Service No. ED 289 250)

Ornstein, A. C. (1989). Private and public school comparisons. *Education and Urban Society, 21*(2), 192–205.

Pearson, R. C. (1996). *Homeschooling: What educators should know.* (ERIC Document Reproduction Service No. ED 402 135).

Ray, B. D. (2001). The modern homeschooling movement. *Catholic Education: A Journal of Inquiry and Practice, 4*(3), 405–421.

Sachs, S. (1998, November 10). Muslim schools in U.S.: A voice for identity. *New York Times,* p. 1.

Sconyers, N. (1996). *What parents want: A report on parents' opinions about public schools.* (ERIC Document Reproduction Service No. ED 400 079)

Scott, W. R., & Meyer, J. W. (1985). *Autonomy, authority, & administration: Differences in school organizations.* In *Public & private schools* (Stanford University: Institute for Research on Educational Finance and Governance; ERIC Document Reproduction Service No. ED 017 682)

Taeuber, K. E., & James, D. R. (1983). Racial segregation among public and private schools: A response. *Sociology of Education, 56*(4), 204–207.

Tritter, J. (1992). An educated change in moral values: Some effects of religious and state schools on their students. *Oxford Review of Education, 18*(1), 29–43.

Williams, L. P. (1996). *The regulation of private schools in America: A state-by-state analysis.* (ERIC Document Reproduction Service No. ED 400 609).

Witters v. Washington Department of Services for the Blind, 474 U.S. 481 (1986).

7

Organizational Dimensions of Schools

Chapter Content

Defining Organizations and Organizational Behavior
Important Concepts
Schools as Organizations
Contemporary Context for Schools
Implications for Practice

This chapter examines schools and districts as organizations. The study of organizations is both multidisciplinary and interdisciplinary (Katz, Kahn, & Adams, 1980). This means that knowledge flows from many fields of study—such as psychology, sociology, and anthropology—and that researchers and practitioners integrate this knowledge as they seek to learn more about organizations. Administrators, including those working in education, commonly study organizations and organizational behavior. The purpose is to acquire knowledge and skills necessary for analyzing individual and group behavior so that administrators can respond adequately to pervasive problems and uncertainty.

Defining Organizations and Organizational Behavior

Structure, product, and the quest for profit are attributes we readily acknowledge and associate with organizations. For example, when asked to identify organizations, people commonly respond by naming giant corporations, such as General Motors or IBM. These companies are vast, having hierarchies of authority, divisions of labor, and thousands of stockholders. But are much smaller institutions, such as churches or schools, also organizations?

Organizations have been described in many different ways. Basic definitions usually focus on two facets: the social nature of the entity and goal orientations. This is exemplified in the following two definitions:

1. "Organizations are social inventions accomplishing goals through group effort" (Johns, 1988, pp. 9–10).
2. "An organization can be defined as a social unit that has been deliberately designed to achieve some specific goals" (Reitz, 1987, p. 13).

In its most rudimentary form, organizations are viewed as integrated systems of independent structures known as groups; and in all organizations, these groups are composed of individual members (Berrien, 1976).

Some definitions have emphasized pervasiveness: "Organizations surround us. We are born in them and usually die in them. Our life space in between is filled with them. They are just about impossible to escape. They are as inevitable as death and taxes" (Hall, 1991, p. 1). Despite being immersed in organizations, many individuals do not understand how they affect personal values and beliefs, and ultimately behavior. Nor do they readily recognize that contact with and reliance on organizations extends well beyond work. For instance, myriad governmental agencies, churches, social groups, and political groups influence how people live their lives.

Some authors have used metaphors to try to explain the nature of organizations. Robert Owens (2001), for instance, summarized comparisons of organizations to the human organism. He noted that the groups and individuals within them function much like cells and molecules in our bodies. A malfunction in part of the system may have repercussions for all other parts. The components are interdependent. Over time, none is able to become self-governing. Gareth Morgan (1986) offered two other metaphors for organizations. He likened bureaucratic organizations to machines—entities where some parts were purposely designed to interface with other parts, and to do so with a minimum loss of energy. He also postulated that organizations could be viewed as systems of political activity. In this context, organizations can be studied by looking at how groups engage in conflict and vie for power. Although these metaphors provide different mental snapshots of organizations, they share several recurring themes:

• Organizations are unique entities composed of individuals and groups.
• Organizational components are interdependent.
• Human interactions in organizations make stress and conflict inevitable.

Organizational behavior is the term used to identify individual and group attitudes and behaviors (Johns, 1988). Individuals, an organization, and interaction between individuals and the organization are necessary for organizational behavior to occur. Individuals bring personal attitudes, beliefs, needs, wants, and experiences to the workplace. Through interactions with other organizational members, some of them get transformed into group goals. However, individual and group goals are not always compatible with organizational goals (see Figure 7.1).

When managers recognized that employees were likely to ignore or reject company goals if they were incongruous with personal goals, they subjected the employees to training, indoctrination, or other persuasion techniques intended to subordinate personal interests. One of the most common approaches was shaping work assignments to include only routine tasks—a strategy that was thought to reduce workers' proclivities to pursue their own interests (Hall, 1991). More recently, managers have attempted to use more productive techniques to resolve tensions between organization and employee goals. For example, some companies now offer education and training opportunities that initially benefit the employee, but ultimately benefit the organization (e.g., wellness programs).

Groups make the study of organizational behavior more complicated, because these entities constitute another dimension of human interaction. Groups are either formal (those created and sanctioned by the organization) or informal (those created by employees and not sanctioned by the organization). Individual interests and convictions are often modified through group membership, because adaptations may be necessary to retain group membership. Figure 7.2 illustrates the interactions that occur among individuals, groups, and the organization for a high school English teacher. The school affects the teacher's behavior through policy and rules, and her membership in formal and informal groups results in additional expectations (i.e., group norms). Formal groups in districts and schools can range from a teachers' union to a three-member fine arts department in a high school. Informal groups evolve as individuals sharing needs, expectations, values, beliefs, or wants find each other. For instance, a small group of teachers may be brought together because of their mutual disdain of the principal; over time, they collectively develop strategies for removing the principal from office.

Scholars studying organizational life discovered that two common problems plague administrative work: *uncertainty* and *inadequate coping strategies* (Thompson, 1967). Organizational uncertainty is created by ambiguity in philosophy, mission, and structure; that is, even the individuals and groups comprising the organization are confused about goals and preferred strategies for goal attainment. Uncertainty makes administration more difficult and risky because individuals are constantly

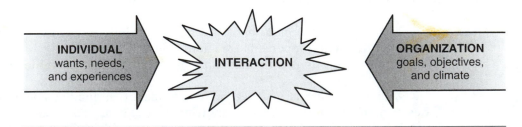

FIGURE 7.1 *Components of Organizational Behavior*

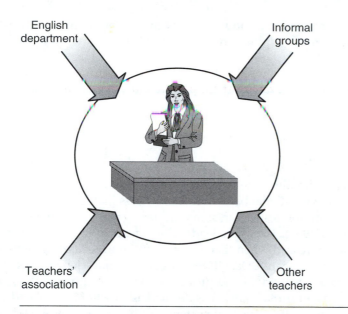

FIGURE 7.2 *Interactions for a High School English Teacher*

questioning the value of their own work and the organization's motives (March & Simon, 1958). Uncertainty has been a major problem for public schools, as evidenced by philosophical differences, opposing political agendas, and shifting social priorities. Without a solid understanding of organizational behavior, administrators are even less likely to develop coping strategies that allow them to manage uncertainty.

Important Concepts

All organizations, including schools, have some type of structure that facilitates the division of tasks or operations related to achieving goals and objectives (Knezevich, 1984), but this does not mean that all organizations are alike. Actually, they vary in size, environmental conditions, incentive systems, leadership and authority, and goals. Like human beings, organizations share certain common characteristics while still being unique. And although we can diminish the number of distinguishing characteristics by grouping organizations (e.g., manufacturing companies or schools), we can never eliminate uniqueness. For example, members of a family have fewer distinguishing characteristics than society as a whole, but the family members are certainly not all identical. In this same vein, schools can be distinguished from other families of organizations (e.g., manufacturing companies), but they continue to possess characteristics that make them unique within the family of schools. For example, small rural high schools and large urban high schools have students, teachers, and daily schedules (common characteristics) but substantially different discipline policies and extracurricular activities (unique characteristics).

The study of organizational behavior is woven through the curriculum of school administration programs. At the introductory level, students are usually exposed to five topics: organizational theory, professional organizations, organizational climate, authority, and adaptability.

Organizational Theory

Organizational theory involves the systematic ordering of knowledge accumulated in the context of organizational behavior. The process includes the study of interactions among institutional structures, individuals, groups, and the general environment (Kowalski, 1999). Too often, leaders become wed to a single view of how organizations function; and when this occurs, a full understanding of behavior is virtually impossible (Bolman & Deal, 1989). Organizational science seeks to predict, describe, and explain individual and group behavior. Its ultimate aim is the production of theory. *Administration theory* is defined as "a set of interrelated concepts, assumptions, and generalizations that systematically describes and explains regularities in behaviors in educational organizations" (Hoy & Miskell, 1982, p. 20). Theories, however, are also used to guide behavior.

Theories are either normative or descriptive. *Normative theories* are intended to prescribe (or guide) the structural, operational, and managerial characteristics of an organization; they focus on "what ought to be." Classical theory (bureaucracy), for instance, is a normative theory rooted in beliefs about human nature, rational-legal authority, and technical efficiency. *Descriptive theories* are different in that they describe "what actually occurs" in organizations. They evolved as researchers discovered that organizational life was really more complex and less predictable than first thought. In the latter half of the twentieth century, study in the behavioral sciences became central to organizational theory. In their seminal book, *Toward a General Theory of Action*, Talcott Parsons and Edward Shils (1951) exhibited how various social scientists could work together to formulate frameworks to explain behavior. Disciplines such as anthropology, psychology, political science, and sociology are indispensable in this regard. The importance of behavioral studies also is illuminated by systemic views of organizational life. As mentioned previously, an organization is much like a human organism. All parts are interrelated.

Professional Organizations

Professional organizations are institutions employing primarily individuals classified as professionals. Because educators are commonly thought to be in this group (although they may not be treated as such), schools are considered professional organizations. In true professional organizations, however, individuals are given considerable autonomy to apply knowledge and skill acquired through specialized study and practice. For example, the work of physicians in a hospital and of professors in a university usually is not supervised closely; instead, they basically are independent and loosely controlled through collegial relations (e.g., granting hospital privileges or rank and tenure).

Teachers in most schools do not enjoy the autonomy granted to most other professionals. Rather, they are subordinated to an administrative framework (e.g., principals generally control their work). This does not mean, however, that teachers are not professionals and that schools are not professional organizations. Limited autonomy simply exposes a characteristic that makes schools unique within the family of professional organizations. There are other characteristics that identify schools as legitimate members of this family. For instance, teachers, even in the most rigid schools, have considerable autonomy once they close their classroom doors—a condition that clearly separates them from assembly-line workers.

Over the past two decades, school reform efforts have focused on ideas that would increase professional autonomy. These efforts are driven by convictions that schools would become more effective if teachers and administrators were not shackled by countless laws, policies, and rules targeted toward the imaginary "average" student. If school improvement efforts in the first quarter of the twenty-first century continue on this path, research and theory on professional organizations will become an even more important element of school administration.

Organizational Climate

Organizations have leaders, policies, methods for making decisions, and other facets that collectively help establish a workplace climate. *Organizational climate* may be expressed as understandings and expectations held in common by a majority of individuals and groups. This common acceptance results in uniformity in leadership and subordinate behaviors (Frederiksen, Jensen, & Beeton, 1972). Organizational climate involves the study of individual perceptions of various aspects of an organization's environment (Owens, 2001). In its simplest form, this concept refers to the feelings a person experiences after walking into school (e.g., either feeling the climate is welcoming or hostile); at a much more complex level, the concept involves feelings about the organization's priorities.

Climate basically consists of four components (see Figure 7.3). *Ecology* includes the organization's physical attributes, such as buildings, equipment, and supplies. School buildings may be bright and exciting or dull and depressing environments. Some schools have considerable technology, whereas others have virtually none. Such characteristics are important because they affect how people feel and limit what can be done in the environment. For example, a school building that cannot be readily reconfigured to accommodate evolving curricula and teaching strategies detracts from a change-friendly climate. Because things and not people are involved, ecology is typically easier to change than either milieu or culture.

Milieu is the people dimension of an organization's climate; it includes individuals and the groups they form. Each individual brings a unique set of needs and wants to a school. In addition, people and groups differ with respect to how they

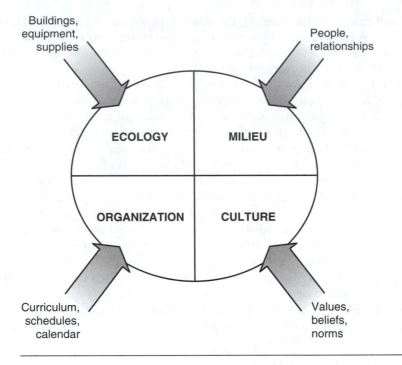

Buildings,
equipment,
supplies

People,
relationships

ECOLOGY   MILIEU

ORGANIZATION   CULTURE

Curriculum,
schedules,
calendar

Values,
beliefs,
norms

FIGURE 7.3   *Components of School Climate*

interact with each other and with persons outside of the organization. In some schools, for example, teachers spend little time interacting with each other and they generally avoid extensive contact with parents. Changing milieu in schools can be difficult for both political (e.g., unwillingness of the school board to allow administrators latitude in making personnel decisions) and legal (e.g., tenure) reasons. Often, administrators try to deal with people problems by transferring personnel or by rearranging their work areas or work groups (e.g., moving a teacher to a new grade level in an elementary school). Such actions rarely change the basic needs and wants held by individuals.

Organization refers to the organization's structural elements. The hierarchy of administration, the arrangement of schools and grade levels, the curriculum, school calendars, and even daily schedules are aspects of this facet of climate. For example, the introduction of block scheduling would be an organizational change that would probably affect perceptions of a school (either positively or negatively). Attempts to improve school climate by tinkering with organization have been rather common, largely because changes in this area of climate are generally easier to pursue (politically and economically). This is because they tend to focus on things rather than people.

The most critical element of climate is *culture.* Culture constitutes the organization's symbolic dimension. All organizations have a culture, although in some situations, it may be fragmented and difficult to determine (Deal & Kennedy, 1982). Culture consists of shared values and beliefs; it provides an invisible framework of norms that help individuals interpret everyday occurrences and sort out the confusion, uncertainty, and ambiguity of work life (Goens & Clover, 1991). Norms are standards for behavior, and beneath them are assumptions about what people in the organization hold to be true, sensible, and possible (Owens, 2001). Cultures are neither static nor easily changed (Burack, 1991). Over the past two decades, a growing number of scholars (e.g., Fullan, 1996; Sarason, 1997) have concluded that meaningful reform in education cannot occur without a substantial change in the shared values and beliefs of educators. One of the reasons culture is so difficult to change is that underlying beliefs often exist at the subconscious level (i.e., the values and beliefs have been translated into routine behaviors). Individuals may be unwilling or unable to bring these issues to the surface and discuss them objectively (Kowalski, 1997). Culture also is protected and preserved through the process of socialization—the use of routine and social pressure intended to make new organizational members comply with existing norms (Hart, 1991). When new teachers or administrators enter a school, they either conform to the new culture or are penalized (e.g., they are ostracized or leave). Among the four elements of climate, culture is clearly the most difficult to identify and change.

Organizational climate is often described along a continuum ranging from open to closed. This designation refers to the organization's disposition toward interacting with external environments. A closed climate seeks to prevent or at least limit the extent to which forces outside the organization can influence internal goals and behavior. During the Industrial Revolution, managers purposefully tried to establish closed climates. For example, steel company executives did not want their decisions restricted by government regulations (e.g., environmental pollution or safety standards). Emulating the business practices of the day, many administrators tried to create closed climates for schools (Callahan, 1962). Today, more enlightened administrators construct open climates that seek a symbiotic relationship between school and community. Especially in the case of public education, the school should be a center of community life, and efforts to isolate this institution are indefensible.

Authority

In organizations, *authority* is commonly defined as the power to make decisions that affect the behavior of subordinates (Simon, 1957). Organizations, including schools, grant authority to certain employees. For example, district superintendents have broad authority and may delegate some of it to other administrators; principals have authority to operate individual schools; even teachers have authority in areas such as controlling their classrooms, evaluating pupil progress, and assigning homework. Authority that is vested in a position is known as *legitimate power*.

Organizational authority is generally described along a continuum ranging from centralized to decentralized control (see Figure 7.4). A school district having

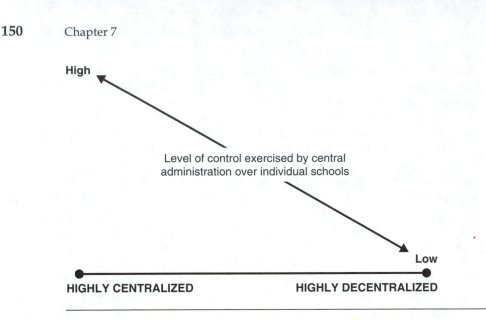

FIGURE 7.4 *Distribution of Authority in a Local School District*

high levels of centralized control is one in which a few administrators in the central office make most decisions and virtually all of the important decisions. The purpose of *centralization* is to control the organization tightly to ensure that policies and rules are applied objectively, routinely, and consistently—actions thought to provide protection against disasters, confusion, and conflict. Centralization, however, can be demoralizing for lower-level administrators and other employees who often have the knowledge necessary to make proper decisions but must defer to higher-ranking officials out of touch with the specific situations (Mintzberg, 1983).

Decentralization, by contrast, diffuses authority, dispersing it among the organization's units (e.g., giving individual principals greater autonomy in making decisions about curriculum and budgets). Daniel Brown (1990) identified three potential goals for this organizational approach:

1. Flexibility (e.g., providing schools greater latitude to address real needs and problems)
2. Accountability (e.g., permitting assessment and evaluation to occur within the subunits of the organization rather than the organization as a whole)
3. Productivity (e.g., allowing administrators to determine how human and material resources can best be deployed at the school level)

Organizations, however, are rarely centralized or decentralized entirely. Instead, they fall somewhere between these two polar positions. Michael Fullan (1999), a respected authority on education change, argues that neither centralization nor decentralization is the answer to meaningful reform, because the former often results in too much control and the latter often produces chaos. Thus, the challenge facing administrators, Fullan believes, is one of creating balance; that is, superintendents and principals need to decide what functions should be centralized and what functions should be decentralized.

Adaptability

With the deployment of technology and the demands for reform, a school either moves forward by making necessary adaptations or it falls behind. In these conditions, change is not a luxury but rather a constant in organizational life. Nevertheless, many people, including school administrators, still exert considerable energy in effort to avoid it. Why? Change is threatening or uncomfortable to many people (Hall & Hord, 2001). Teachers and administrators who believe that they are doing an excellent job see little reason to alter their practices—even when the world around them changes sufficiently so that new educational needs evolve. In the early 1980s, for example, many school administrators were slow to react to the obvious needs associated with the availability of microcomputers (e.g., putting computer labs in schools and providing staff development).

A tangled network of internal and external controls shapes public schools. State legislatures, the courts, local school boards, and community pressure groups exemplify forces that help determine the scope and quality of services provided. *Organizational adaptation* is the process of modifications carried out by administrators and other school employees in an attempt to remain relevant. Historically, public schools have not had an admirable record in making rapid adjustments to changing environmental conditions—largely because they were created as institutions of stability (Spring, 2001). In his studies of public schools, noted psychologist Seymour Sarason (1996) concluded that educators had failed to be reformers because they knew little about organizational life and even less about the work culture that controlled their behavior. Such criticisms have heightened the importance of having administrators who can lead and facilitate the process of organizational adaptation.

Schools as Organizations

As previously noted, schools possess many of the same attributes found in all organizations, yet, they are also unique entities. To better understand why schools are simultaneously similar to and different from other organizations, these institutions are examined in four frames: social, professional, political, and public.

Social Frame

The concept of a social system is based on the idea that individuals, whose relationships are more than random, create interactions that affect behavior (Hoy & Miskel, 2000). Therefore, the social nature of a district or school is determined by quantity and quality of relationships that occur in both the formal and informal organization. The formal organization consists of groups created or approved by the organization's legitimate authorities (e.g., academic departments in a high school or the certified teachers' union). The informal organization is composed of social units that form and function without approval from the organization's legitimate authorities (e.g., a group of teachers who pursue selected changes in policies and rules). Two variables are central to understanding the social nature of formal and informal groups: the *structure* and the *culture* of relationships. Structure relates to patterns of interaction (e.g., how and where members meet) and culture is comprised of the shared values, beliefs, and possibly needs of the members (Blau & Scott, 1962).

Groups in a social system are commonly called *subsystems*. The degree to which subsystems interact with and are dependent on each other varies. But because there is always some interaction, behavior rarely has a single cause. In this vein, E. Mark Hanson (1996) wrote, "The action patterns of any of these subsystems cannot be fully understood independent of its immediately linking subsystems. For instance, the actions of the history department cannot be understood independent of the constraints and demands placed upon it by the policy of the high school or by the expectations and needs of various groups of teachers" (p. 51). Put another way, an administrator cannot fully comprehend the behavior of teacher or a group of teachers unless he or she is able to view the school as a social system.

After groups are formed and membership is established, three characteristics are usually observed. First, the group's culture becomes a force affecting the behavior of its members. When members conform to the group's norms, they establish interdependence among themselves. Second, group participation satisfies some of the individual needs of members. For example, membership may provide a sense of security or prestige. Third, members share common aims. Although they may not agree on everything, they embrace goals specifically endorsed by the group (Owens, 2001). Research on small groups emphasizes the critical role the group occupies between the individual and the organization. "Small groups influence how well individuals perform, how well their needs are met, and how they view their work and the organization" (Bolman & Deal, 1989, p. 204). The group becomes the reference point for defining many work related issues.

As noted, administrators unable to analyze districts and schools as social systems have great difficulty understanding individual and group behavior. This is because they do not recognize how formal and informal groups influence job expectations (roles) and behavioral standards (norms). When educators enter practice, they experience *socialization*—the process of communicating and learning values, norms, rules, and operating procedures (Miklos, 1988). Administrators experience two types of socialization: *professional* (norms established collectively by individuals and groups comprising the school administration profession) and *organizational* (norms established by individuals and groups comprising a district or school). Professional and organizational norms may be incompatible—for example, an assistant principal may be torn between behaving ethically (a professional norm) and behaving politically (an organizational or subsystem norm). Organization members who are comfortable with the existing culture usually attempt to protect it. They do this in many ways, some of which include:

- *Selecting new administrators* (Preference is given to individuals who already embrace values and beliefs embedded in the school culture.)
- *Controlling standards for induction* (Prescribed roles and standards for acceptable behavior are communicated to new administrators.)
- *Controlling employment status* (Retention in an administrative position may depend largely on compliance with role and norms during induction.)
- *Issuing rewards and punishments* (Individuals who comply with established norms are rewarded by receiving promotions, salary increases, and greater job security; individuals who do not comply are punished by being dismissed, reassigned, or denied a salary increase.)

Socialization can be positive or negative, depending on the extent to which the organizational culture conflicts with accepted professional norms. Consequently, organizational culture plays a critical role in determining the effects of socialization.

Professional Frame

Elementary and secondary schools are frequently described as bureaucracies. In U.S. society, bureaucracy often connotes inefficiency and waste; this characterization paints a negative picture of the nation's education system. But to what extent are schools really bureaucratic? And how did they get that way?

Much of U.S. industry, especially during the Industrial Revolution, was influenced by norms intended to produce rationality and organizational efficiency. Collectively, these norms constituted the classical theory of organizational behavior. Two beliefs were foundational to the theory: Managerial authority was essential to maintaining control, and control was necessary if organizational goals were to be met. These beliefs led to the development of standard characteristics for the bureaucratic organization:

- *Hierarchy of authority:* A pyramid configuration places virtually all authority in the hands managers, especially those few at the very top of the organization.
- *Division of labor:* This process divides work into small units so that workers can be trained to repeat routine tasks.
- *Reliance on formal rules:* Work is controlled through the application of rules that specify what workers may or may not do.
- *Efficiency over interpersonal relationships:* Organizational efficiency takes precedent over personal relationships by prohibiting or discouraging managers from fraternizing with subordinates (Weber, 1947).

As U.S. industry embraced these principles during the Industrial Revolution, big-city superintendents—and eventually most other superintendents—were urged to do the same (Callahan, 1962).

Although schools and districts are often organized as bureaucracies, they are really hybrid organizations combining bureaucratic, professional, and political variables (Corwin & Borman, 1988). This fact is illustrated by the following conditions:

- In many schools, the ratio of administrators to teachers is greater than 1 to 20; principals simply cannot monitor the work of teachers continuously. Thus, teachers work in relative isolation even though the expectations for their performance are highly structured (e.g., state-prescribed goals, assigned textbooks, and evaluation policies) (Kowalski, 1995).
- In true bureaucracies, organizational subsystems are tightly coupled* to prevent subunits, groups, or individuals from acting independently. Schools are loosely coupled, meaning that principals and teachers often make decisions independently (Pellegrin, 1976).
- A certain amount of educator autonomy is justified on the grounds that administrators and teachers are professionals; as such, they should have some authority in determining student needs and in shaping instruction to meet those needs.
- Management control and rule enforcement are often less intense in schools than in factories, in part because school administrator behavior is subject to political restraints (i.e., board members or pressure groups often are able to prevent or rescind administrative decisions even when the legitimate authority to make such decisions is clearly present) (Kowalski, 1999).

In summary, schools are not true bureaucracies even though they manifest selected attributes of classical theory (Owens, 2001).

Schools are human-intensive organizations, meaning that people and not machines are prevalent in them. In addition, most of the employees are professionals. Thus, as human-intensive and professionally dominated organizations, schools are similar to hospitals or mental health clinics. Because these organizations also manifest elements of classical theory, they often are referred to as *professional bureaucracies* (Mintzberg, 1979). In some of them, administrators and employees have parallel authority; the distribution of authority between a hospital administrator and physicians is one example. In schools, however, teachers typically have much less power than do administrators and school board members over policy decisions affecting their practice and work environment (Brown, 1990).

Two characteristics are commonly used to determine whether an organization should be classified as "professional": (1) the presence of goals that relate to

---

*Coupling is a concept pertaining to the level of interdependence among units and subunits of an organization. *Tight* coupling connotes high interdependence and *loose* coupling connotes high independence.

the production, application, or communication of knowledge and (2) 50 percent or more of the staff being classified as professionals (Etzioni, 1964). Using only these criteria, schools appear to qualify. In reality, however, teachers (along with social workers and nurses) have been treated as semi-professionals, as evidenced by the fact that they enjoy less freedom from supervision and societal controls than do practitioners in more established and honored professions (Etzioni, 1964). "Practitioners of the semi-professions are not typically self-employed; rather, they are 'bureaucratized' existing within the confines of service bureaucracies and paid by means of salaries instead of client fees" (Bennett & LeCompte, 1990, p. 124).

If schools are to become true professional organizations, teachers must be given added authority to apply their knowledge and skills more independently. Two current reform initiatives are especially noteworthy in this regard. The first is *teacher empowerment*—a movement that seeks to have society treat teachers as true professionals. The second is *collegial working relationships*—a movement that seeks to establish parallel authority between administrators and teachers.

Political Frame

Another key variable that separates schools, and especially public schools, from other organizations is politics. "Politics deals with decision-making power, its distribution and limitations, among persons who are part of the organization, community, state, region, and nation" (Knezevich, 1984, p. 491). The notion that schools and school administration are apolitical is a myth. "American schools are 'political,' partly as a result of their connection to political systems of state and national governments. But schools also act as miniature political systems themselves" (Wirt & Kirst, 1997, p. 27).

In U.S. society, politics is often associated with corruption, strong-arm tactics, and other unethical behaviors; thus, administrators often have difficulty discussing the political dimensions of their work (Bauman, 1996). From an academic perspective, however, politics involves competition for scarce resources (Swanson & King, 1997). In a democratic society, such competition is pervasive. For example, administrators must constantly compete with other governmental agencies to secure resources, and administrative decisions can be vetoed at several different points (by school boards or by the courts) (Fowler, 2000). Thus, administrators must be able to function effectively in political environments.

The nature of schools as political organizations is anchored in three realities (Bolman & Deal, 1989):

1. An organization's members and clients rarely possess identical values, beliefs, needs, preferences, perceptions, and wants.
2. Organizations rarely possess sufficient resources to satisfy all their members and clients.
3. Organizational goals and decisions emerge from an ongoing process of negotiations in which the various individuals and coalitions exercise power.

All districts have experienced these conditions to some extent, but the effects have not been uniform. More precisely, the quantity and nature of political activity generated by competition for scarce resources have varied considerably (Burlingame, 1988). Another form of political tension has been omnipresent in public education: the tension between the public's desire to have professional leaders who can be trusted and their desire to have its own will carried out (Wirt & Kirst, 1997). Together, competition for scarce resources and conflicting expectations regarding the use of authority by public officials produce a political atmosphere in schools.

Public Frame

Public officials are often characterized as working in a fishbowl. This is because the media and taxpayers scrutinize their actions. As an example, parents and financial supporters usually monitor the behavior of school administrators, including those who are employed in private institutions. When they violate the law, professional standards, or community norms, their actions usually are discussed and judged publicly.

Several factors influence the public nature of education. Three of the more important ones are ownership, the relationship between schools and community life, and multiple lines of authority (Bennett & LeCompte, 1990). Taxpayers understand that in effect they are the stockholders of public schools, and even many private school patrons harbor the same thought. In addition, all schools evolve in community contexts—a condition that results in each school being a somewhat unique amalgam of values and beliefs. Thus, schools and their employees are expected to operate within the parameters of community standards and expectations. Also, schools function with multiple lines of authority, meaning that there are various ways decisions can be made and rescinded. As an example, education policy can be developed at the federal and state levels and even local pressure groups may be able to exert sufficient influence to affect major decisions. The issue of authority is the point at which the public and political frames of schools become inextricably intertwined.

The public nature of schooling is an especially cogent issue for school administrators because the condition is central to understanding this profession. The application of professional knowledge by principals and district administrators is filtered through an intricate web of community standards that may not be embraced by the entire community. And even when decisions are strongly supported by the professional knowledge base, administrators rarely have the power necessary to deter political interventions. Historically, other professions have been more protected from politics. Physicians, for instance, rarely have had to worry about public acceptance of their medical decisions. More recently, however, all professions have faced greater governmental control and political pressures. Battles in some communities over restricting abortions in local hospitals provide one example. In such instances, the medical profession usually has argued that political action should not restrict the ability of physicians to make independent decisions in relation to their patients. Although the collision of professional autonomy and community standards presents a new challenge for some professions, this same tension has always been at the center of school administration.

Contemporary Context for Schools

Public education has now been subjected to more than 25 years of intense reform efforts. Initially, policymakers tried to improve schools by forcing educators and students to do more of what they were already doing. These intensification mandates reflected a lack of understanding about the complex nature of schools, and they predictably failed (Conley, 1991). Subsequently, most reformers turned their attention to a new strategy—school restructuring. Reshaping schools involves altering one or more of the components of organizational climate; consequently, the value of understanding and applying knowledge about organizational behavior is now greater for school administrators than ever before. More precisely, contemporary practitioners need to be able to prepare schools for change and to build professional cultures.

Preparing Schools for Change

Many of the current principals and superintendents have experienced multiple attempts to change schools; and since virtually all of them have failed, these administrators tend to be cynical about the possibility of true reform. Such thinking, although understandable, has become problematic in a rapidly changing world. Unless administrators believe that meaningful improvements are necessary and possible, and unless they create institutional climates encouraging adaptations, schools are apt to become increasingly ineffective.

All too often, administrators have reacted to demands for reform rather than assuming the role of reformer. As a result, they had no vision of what they really wanted to accomplish, and their methods and goals were often unconnected (Haberman, 1994). Noted psychologist Seymour Sarason (1996) concluded that educators could not lead the process of school restructuring because they understood neither how organizations functioned nor how changes occurred within them. Lacking this critical knowledge, many district and school administrators have succumbed to convenience when pressured to produce change; that is, they tried to replicate reforms developed elsewhere. This action routinely fails for three reasons (Fullan, 1999):

1. Many important subtleties are overlooked when administrators try to replicate a change process. What really matters in making change successful may not be readily observable to the people who are observing the change.
2. Conditions under which successful change occurs are ignored or the conditions cannot be completely replicated.
3. Organizational capacity for accommodating a change initiative is often overlooked or underestimated.

The success of change depends on more than just the program or concept being pursued; the process for pursuing change and organizational climate also are critical variables. In contemporary practice, preparing a district or school for engaging in change is a major administrative responsibility.

Building Professional Cultures

As previously noted, schools are hybrid organizations possessing some bureaucratic and some professional organization characteristics—and often, the norms of the two types of organizations are in direct conflict. Organizational coupling, mentioned earlier, is a prime example. Bureaucracies are tightly coupled, whereas professional organizations are not. In professional organizations, individuals are nearly free from rules and excessive controls (Bywaters, 1991). While recognizing such realities, education scholars have been attempting to produce their own definitions of professional cultures, allowing schools to be improved within the framework of political, social, and economic conditions. Their efforts have produced some recurring characteristics of a professional school culture, such as the following:

- *Collaboration:* Encouraging educators to work collectively rather than in relative isolation (e.g., Quicke, 2000)
- *Shared decision making:* Administrators and teachers working collectively to make curriculum and instruction decisions (e.g., Howey & Collinson, 1995)
- *Knowledge about change:* Administrators and teachers understanding what change is and how it occurs (e.g., Gilley, 2000)
- *Knowledge about climate and culture:* Administrators and teachers understanding organizational climate and culture and how these characteristics enhance or inhibit change (e.g., Kowalski, 1997)
- *Individual growth opportunities:* Providing opportunities for educators to conduct research, to learn new techniques and ideas from experimentation, and to engage in advanced academic studies (e.g., Martin & Kragler, 1999)
- *Relevant and sustained staff development:* Investing in organized learning opportunities that address both organizational and individual needs (e.g., Hord & Boyd, 1995)
- *Administrative role changes:* Reconsidering the balance between management and leadership and relationships administrators have with teachers (e.g., Bredeson, 1995)

Although the need to create a new professional climate that permits schools to be more open, adaptable, and professional is widely accepted, there are still many obstacles to achieving this goal. Consider the following examples:

- Shared decision making and collaboration are often restricted by collective bargaining agreements between school boards and teachers' unions (Lieberman, 1986). Moreover, many administrators believe that professionalism and unionism are incompatible (DeMitchell & Streshly, 1996).

- The ramifications of professionalism are complex and many educators are not enthusiastic about assuming added responsibilities (Evans, 2000). Clearly, some individuals entered education because it was a highly controlled occupation; they are not inclined to make decisions or to take risks. These teachers and administrators usually resist efforts to change their role expectations and scope of authority.

- Constitutional and legislative provisions place limits on what schools can do. States have required curricula and standards for delivering curricula; and decisions about improving instruction must be made within those parameters. Although deregulation has become a popular reform strategy, many scholars (e.g., Weiler, 1990) remain skeptical about the likelihood that public schools can become truly autonomous.

- Often, school autonomy and professional autonomy are viewed as synonymous. In truth, some reformers who support the former are least interested in the latter (Good & Brophy, 1986).

- In many schools, administrators still protect information rather than share it, and existing communication channels do not allow open, two-way information exchanges (Kowalski, 1998).

- The interface of democracy and professionalism produces tension (Strike, 1993; Zeichner, 1991). As an example, many citizens are dubious about giving educators near-total authority to operate schools because they fear that doing so will negatively affect their ability to exercise power, either through their elected representatives (e.g., school board members) or through collective action (e.g., petitions and referenda).

- Existing laws, policies, and practices often prevent administrators from accepting new role expectations. Most administrators have been socialized to protect traditional responsibilities and relationships with teachers (Björk & Richardson, 1997).

- One condition associated with the public granting greater autonomy to educators is respect for professional knowledge. Historically, the public has tended to see administrators and teachers as dedicated public servants, but not necessarily as individuals possessing a unique and critical body of knowledge and skills. Hence, persons outside of the profession routinely impose controls on schools (e.g., state laws and local district policies), and they usually do so with specificity, in abundance, and without consulting with professional educators (Kowalski, 1995).

Potential obstacles to reshaping schools are not all unique to education. Increasingly, scholars in business administration also are seeking improved organizational structures for companies employing large numbers of salaried professionals (e.g., engineering firms and accounting firms). The primary question driving their inquiry is cogent to school reform: How can employees be provided the right of autonomy while ensuring adequate control of the organization (Raelin, 1989)? In all probability, the answer involves an intricate set of compromises that allow educators to have greater but not complete autonomy. Experiences in other organizations suggest that school administrators will need to focus on reward systems, communication channels, and self-regulation if they are to restructure schools in ways that permit teachers to be true professionals (Segal-Horn, 1987).

Implications for Practice

The organizational dimension of local districts and schools was summarized in this chapter. These institutions are clearly organizations, and they share certain attributes found in all organizations. Yet, districts and schools are unique among the entire population of organizations. That is, they possess distinguishing characteristics. For instance, they are subject to high levels of political intervention, they provide a service rather than a material good, and they are composed primarily of employees who are considered professionals.

When schools are placed under a microscope, within-group differences also become apparent. As an example, schools differ from one another with respect to culture, resources, attitudes, and operational procedures. Consequently, sweeping generalizations about schools are precarious. When you study any school as an organization—even the school in which you work—you should answer two cogent questions: What characteristics in this school are found in all organizations? What characteristics separate this school from other schools?

Since the early 1980s, efforts to improve education have shifted from trying to force students and teachers to do more of what they are doing to restructuring schools. This transition has increased the importance of administrators understanding organizations. Your success as an administrator will be enhanced if you understand the following aspects of organizational life:

- How individual employees interface with the organization
- How and why individuals become members of formal and informal groups
- How and why groups interact and exercise power
- How administrators can lead individuals and groups to achieve institutional goals

As administrators and teachers strive to restructure schools, they face the realization that organizational climate can either facilitate or hinder their efforts. Thus, they must understand the components of climate and have insights into ways that these components can be altered so that reform obstacles can be eradicated or bypassed. This is one reason why the study of organizational theory and behavior has become increasingly relevant for school administrators.

For Further Study

1. During the Industrial Revolution, captains of industry were able to exert considerable influence over the organizational structure of urban school systems. What conditions contributed to their ability to do this?

2. Local districts and schools are social systems. What does this mean?

3. Both formal and informal groups exist in organizations. What is the difference between a formal and informal group?

4. What is a bureaucracy? What is the purpose of bureaucratic structure?

5. What is the difference between normative and descriptive theory? What purpose does each serve in the practice of school administration?

6. Many administrators believe that professionalism and unionism are incompatible. Do you agree? Why or why not?

7. What is organizational climate? What element of climate could be identified rather easily? What is the most difficult element to identify?

8. What is the difference between the formal organization and the informal organization?

9. Historically, administrators have treated teachers as subordinates. What are some possible reasons for this behavior?

10. What are the possible advantages and disadvantages of decentralization?

11. What is teacher empowerment? Why do some reformers conclude that empowerment is essential to true school reform?

12. Administrators experience two forms of socialization: to the profession and to the workplace. How and when does each occur?

13. Some scholars have noted that democracy and professionalism generate inevitable tensions. Why is this conclusion relevant to efforts to restructure schools?

14. Should school administrators encourage or discourage large-scale inputs from individuals and groups who are officially part of the school district?

15. What are the advantages and disadvantages of a centralized system of authority in a school district?

Other Suggested Activities

1. Identify the subsystems in the district or school in which you work or reside. Determine whether they are part of the formal or informal organization.

2. Prepare a list of characteristics you would examine if you wanted to identify the culture and climate of an unfamiliar school district.

3. School systems clearly have hierarchies of authority. Discuss why this one feature alone is insufficient to determine whether the system is a bureaucracy.

4. Discuss the similarities and differences between a school and a hospital with respect to the work roles of professional employees.

5. Teaching, social work, and nursing have often been called "quasi-professions." Discuss the meaning of this label. Also provide a rationale as to why you either agree or disagree with this label.

References

Bauman, P. C. (1996). *Governing education: Public sector reform or privatization*. Boston: Allyn and Bacon.

Bennett, K. P., & LeCompte, M. D. (1990). *How schools work: A sociological analysis of education*. New York: Longman.

Berrien, F. K. (1976). A general systems approach to organizations. In M. Dunnette (Ed.), *Handbook of industrial and organizational psychology* (pp. 41–62). Chicago: Rand McNally.

Björk, L. G., & Richardson, M. D. (1997). Institutional barriers to educational leadership training: A case study. *Educational Forum, 62*(1), 74–81.

Blau, P. M., & Scott, W. R. (1962). *Formal organizations: A comparative approach*. San Francisco: Chandler.

Bolman, L., & Deal, T. (1989). *Modern approaches to understanding and managing organizations*. San Francisco: Jossey-Bass.

Bredeson, P. V. (1995). Role change for principals in restructured schools: Implications for teacher preparation and teacher work. In M. J. O'Hare & S. J. Odell (Eds.), *Educating teachers for leadership and change: Teacher education yearbook III* (pp. 25–45). Thousand Oaks, CA: Corwin.

Brown, D. J. (1990). *Decentralization and school-based management*. London: Falmer Press.

Burack, E. H. (1991). Changing the company culture: The role of human resources development. *Long Range Planning, 24*(1), 88–95.

Burlingame, M. (1988). The politics of education and educational policy: The local level. In N. Boyan (Ed.), *Handbook of research on educational administration* (pp. 439–451). New York: Longman.

Bywaters, D. R. (1991). Managing professionals. *Executive Excellence, 8*(2), 7–8.

Callahan, R. E. (1962). *Education and the cult of efficiency*. Chicago: University of Chicago Press.

Campbell, R. E., Cunningham, L. L., Nystrand, R. O., & Usdan, M. D. (1990). *The organization and control of American schools* (6th ed.). Columbus, OH: Merrill.

Clark, T. D., & Schrode, W. A. (1979). Public sector decision structures: An empirically-based description. *Public Administration Review, 39*, 343–354.

Conley, D. T. (1991). What is restructuring? Educators adapt to a changing world. *Equity and Choice, 7*(2–3), 46–51.

Corwin, R. G., & Borman, K. M. (1988). School as workplace: Structural constraints on administration. In N. Boyan (Ed.), *Handbook of research on educational administration* (pp. 209–237). New York: Longman.

Deal, T. E., & Kennedy, A. A. (1982). *Corporate cultures*. Reading, MA: Addison-Wesley.

DeMitchell, T. A., & Streshly, W. A. (1996). Must collective bargaining be reformed in an era of reform? *International Journal of Educational Reform, 5*(1), 78–85.

Drake, T. L., & Roe, W. H. (1986). *The principalship* (3rd ed.). New York: Macmillan.

Etzioni, A. (1964). *Modern organizations*. Englewood Cliffs, NJ: Prentice-Hall.

Evans, R. (2000). *The human side of school change: Reform, resistance, and the real-life problems of school change*. San Francisco: Jossey-Bass.

Fowler, F. C. (2000). *Policy studies for educational leaders: An introduction*. Upper Saddle River, NJ: Merrill, Prentice-Hall.

Frederiksen, N., Jensen, O., & Beeton, A. A. (1972). *Predictions of organizational behavior*. New York: Pergamon Press.

Fullan, M. G. (1996). Turning systemic thinking on its head. *Phi Delta Kappan, 77*(6), 420–423.

Fullan, M. G. (1999). *Change forces: The sequel*. Philadelphia: Falmer Press.

Gilley, J. W. (2000). Understanding and building capacity for change: A key to school transformation. *International Journal of Educational Reform, 9*(2), 109–119.

Goens, G. A., & Clover, S. I. (1991). *Mastering school reform.* Boston: Allyn and Bacon.

Good, T. L., & Brophy, J. E. (1986). School effects. In M. Wittrock (Ed.), *Handbook of research on teaching* (3rd ed.) (pp. 570–604). New York: Macmillan.

Haberman, M. (1994). The top 10 fantasies of school reformers. *Phi Delta Kappan, 75*(9), 689–692.

Hall, G. E., & Hord, S. M. (2001). *Implementing change: Patterns, principles, and potholes.* Boston: Allyn and Bacon.

Hall, R. H. (1991). *Organizations: Structures, processes, and outcomes* (5th ed.). Englewood Cliffs, NJ: Prentice-Hall.

Hanson, E. M. (1996). *Educational administration and organizational behavior* (4th ed.). Boston: Allyn and Bacon.

Hart, A. N. (1991). Leader succession and socialization: A synthesis. *Review of Educational Research, 61*(4), 451–474.

Hord, S. M., & Boyd, V. (1995). Professional development fuels a culture of continuous improvement. *Journal of Staff Development, 16*(1), 10–15.

Howey, K. R., & Collinson, V. (1995). Cornerstones of a collaborative culture: Professional development and preservice teacher preparation. *Journal of Personnel Evaluation in Education, 9*(1), 21–31.

Hoy, W. K., & Miskel, C. G. (1982). *Educational administration: Theory, research, and practice* (2nd ed.). New York: Random House.

Hoy, W. K., & Miskel, C. G. (2000). *Educational administration: Theory, research, and practice* (6th ed.). New York: McGraw-Hill.

Johns, G. (1988). *Organizational behavior: Understanding life at work* (2nd ed.). Glenview, IL: Scott, Foresman.

Katz, D., Kahn, R. L., & Adams, J. S. (1980). Introduction. In D. Katz, R. L. Kahn, & J. S. Adams (Eds.), *The study of organizations* (pp. 1–9). San Francisco: Jossey-Bass.

Knezevich, S. J. (1984). *Administration of public education* (4th ed.). New York: Harper and Row.

Kowalski, T. J. (1984). The debilities of MBO in educational organizations. *NASSP Bulletin, 68*(472), 119–123.

Kowalski, T. J. (1995). Preparing teachers to be leaders: Barriers in the workplace. In M. J. O'Hare & S. J. Odell (Eds.), *Educating teachers for leadership and change: Teacher education yearbook III* (pp. 243–256). Thousand Oaks, CA: Corwin.

Kowalski, T. J. (1997). School reform, community education, and the problem of institutional culture. *Community Education Journal, 25*(3-4), 5–8.

Kowalski, T. J. (1998). The role of communication in providing leadership for school restructuring. *Mid-Western Educational Researcher, 11*(1), 32–40.

Kowalski, T. J. (1999). *The school superintendent: Theory, practice, and cases.* Upper Saddle River, NJ: Merrill, Prentice-Hall.

Lieberman, M. (1986). *Beyond public education.* New York: Praeger.

March, J. G., & Simon, H. A. (1958). *Organizations.* New York: Wiley.

Martin, L., & Kragler, S. (1999). Creating a culture for teachers' professional growth. *Journal of School Leadership, 9*(4) 311–320.

Miklos, E. (1988). Administrator selection, career patterns, succession, and socialization. In N. Boyan (Ed.), *Handbook of research on educational administration* (pp. 53–76). New York: Longman.

Mintzberg, H. (1979). *The structuring of organizations.* Englewood Cliffs, NJ: Prentice-Hall.

Mintzberg, H. (1983). *Structure in fives: Designing effective organizations.* Englewood Cliffs, NJ: Prentice-Hall.

Morgan, G. (1986). *Images of organization.* Newbury Park, CA: Sage.

Owens, R. G. (2001). *Organizational behavior in education: Instructional leadership and school reform* (7th ed.). Boston: Allyn and Bacon.

Parsons, T., & Shils, H. A. (1951). *Toward a general theory of action.* New York: Harper and Row.

Pellegrin, R. J. (1976). Schools as work settings. In R. Dubin (Ed.), *Handbook of work, organization and society* (pp. 343–374). Skokie, IL: Rand McNally.

Quicke, J. (2000). A new professionalism for a collaborative culture of organizational learning in a contemporary society. *Educational Management & Administration, 28*(3), 299–315.

Raelin, J. A. (1989). An anatomy of autonomy: Managing professionals. *Academy of Management Executives, 3*(3), 216–228.

Reitz, H. J. (1987). *Behavior in organizations* (3rd ed.). Homewood, IL: Irwin.

Sarason, S. B. (1996). *Revisiting the culture of the school and the problem of change.* New York: Teachers College Press.

Sarason, S. B. (1997). NASP distinguished lecture series: What should we do about school reform? *School Psychology Review, 26*(1), 104–110.

Segal-Horn, S. (1987). Managing professionals in organizations. *International Journal of Manpower, 8*(2), 11–19.

Simon, H. A. (1957). *Administrative behavior* (2nd ed.). New York: Macmillan.

Spring, J. (2001). *American education* (10th ed.). New York: McGraw-Hill.

Strike, K. A. (1993). Professionalism, democracy, and discursive communities: Normative reflections on restructuring. *American Educational Research Journal, 30*(2), 255–275.

Swanson, A. D., & King, R. A. (1997). *School finance: Its economics and politics* (2nd ed.). New York: Longman.

Thompson, J. D. (1967). *Organization in action.* New York: McGraw-Hill.

Weber, M. (1947). *The theory of social and economic organizations* (translated by A. Parsons & T. Parsons). New York: The Free Press.

Weiler, H. N. (1990). Comparative perspectives on educational decentralization: An exercise in contradiction? *Educational Evaluation and Policy Analysis, 12*(4), 433–448.

Wirt, F. M., & Kirst, M. W. (1997). *The political dynamics of American education.* Berkeley, CA: McCutchan.

Zeichner, K. M. (1991). Contradictions and tensions in the professionalization of teaching and the democratization of schools. *Teachers College Record, 92*(3), 363–379.

8

The Roles of School in Society

The relationship between schools and society is characterized by three roles that reflect philosophical viewpoints of reproduction, readjustment, and reconstruction (Johnson, Collins, Dupuis, & Johansen, 1988). The *reproductive* role of schools encompasses transmission and preservation of the existing culture, values, traditions, and norms. *Readjustment* involves responding to changes in society and adjusting curriculum and instruction as appropriate. *Reconstruction* requires a more proactive stance, since it views the school as an agent of societal development. The reproductive role was dominant in the formative years of public education; therefore, schools were shaped as agencies of stability rather than as agencies of change (Spring, 2001). Nevertheless, these three philosophical viewpoints persist and are carried out through school purposes and goals that have been classified as political, social, economic, vocational, intellectual, and personal (Goodlad, 1984; Spring, 2001).

Similar to the interrelationship between schools and society is the interrelationship between administrators and schools. Administrators can play a critical role in shaping education philosophy by directly and symbolically emphasizing selected values and beliefs. On the other hand, existing school culture can have a profound effect on them. For example, when a principal begins working in a school, he or she faces pressures to conform to the social system's culture.

This chapter addresses the role of schools in society. Although schools undoubtedly shape and are shaped by society, there is still considerable controversy concerning the extent to which each of these should occur. That is, should schools reproduce societal culture or should they transform society? The first part of this chapter examines the reproduction role; the second part examines the reconstruction role.

Schools as a Mirror of Society

The Formative Years

In their discussion of public school leadership in the United States, David Tyack and Elisabeth Hansot (1982) provided an insightful portrait of how schools have reflected societal norms and values. They noted that as one travels across this nation, evidence of the legacy left by various periods of U.S. schooling can be observed in school building architecture. For example, the earliest facilities were influenced both by dominant philosophy and political thought. Both idealism and the Protestant ethic served to define the mission of schools as preparing individuals for leading a godly life, and to teach reading for purposes of studying the Bible and laws. Since individuals who objected to excessive government control founded this country, early American institutions, including schools, were purposely kept small and simple.

During this era, schools were elitist institutions with access to education provided only to the wealthy. In post-Revolutionary America, the elitist conception of education broadened. Schooling began to be perceived as a vehicle that could serve both religious and human needs. Many of the persons in positions of power and authority concluded that education could be used to promote political and cultural values. In essence, they saw universal schooling as a means of creating a perfect society. A tension that continues to this day in U.S. education developed almost immediately. On the one hand, some considered education to be a liberating force—a social experience that would allow individuals to determine the types of values and the type of government they wanted to embrace. This thinking was adversative to the mission of preparing virtuous, patriotic, and well-behaved citizens who would embrace the country's dominant values. Gradually, education policy was reshaped by the passionate quest for liberty. If education was to be an instrument for building a free society, then the service could no longer be treated as a luxury for the wealthy. The broadened mission made education a necessity for the masses.

The goal of universal schooling was enhanced by two other societal conditions. As large groups of immigrants came to America, they brought with them their cultural values. For those who believed that all citizens must adhere to the existing dominant values, this was a threatening situation. The common school movement—that is, ensuring that every child received a common education in public schools—was deployed as a means for dealing with this concern (Spring,

2001). Thus, universal schooling served the dual purposes of building a more perfect society and ensuring that new societal members conformed to the dominant values.

The second factor that reinforced the concept of universal schooling was suffrage. The right to vote was being extended to an ever-increasing segment of U.S. society. Suffrage required a literate society, and schools therefore became the primary vehicle for ensuring literacy (Pounds & Bryner, 1973).

While the country was struggling with new societal challenges during and immediately following the Industrial Revolution, schools became an important instrument of government and politics (Callahan, 1962). According to Ralph Pounds and James Bryner (1973), the emerging government-supported education system took on four characteristics that reflected the democratic spirit of the country:

1. There was no tuition.
2. Every citizen had access.
3. The schools were nonsectarian.
4. Provision of the service was universal.

Public schools became nonsectarian to protect the religious freedom; that is, schools as agencies of government were protected from unnecessary entanglements with organized religion. The separation of church and state continues to this day and has been the subject of great controversy, legal battles, and frequent headaches for school administrators for more than 100 years.

Although schools were nonsectarian in the sense that they were not formally associated with any religious sect, they were nonetheless grounded in religious ideology. Tyack and Hansot (1982) described the creation of a system of public schooling as a social movement that was concerned with instilling a Protestant-republican ideology in the hearts and minds of individual citizens. They noted that among school leaders there was a "common religious and political conception of the role of public education in shaping a Christian nation" (p. 5). This sense of common purpose and, in a manner, spiritual mission galvanized and mobilized the creation of a nonsectarian, universal, and free system of public schooling that remains with us to this day.

Era of Big Business

During the earliest decades of the twentieth century, the United States became an industrial society. Giant manufacturing corporations were created, drawing both immigrants and citizens residing in rural areas to major cities were the plants were located. Conditions surrounding the Industrial Revolution had a profound effect on schools:

- Growth in cities spawned the development of school districts. This new organizational structure made the management of human and material resources more demanding (Cuban, 1976).

- As schools and districts became larger, demands for administrative efficiency increased. In response, many administrators adopted the theories and principles that had guided industrial development (Callahan, 1962).
- The centrality of manufacturing to U.S. society influenced the mission and curriculum of most schools. Especially in urban areas, both federal and state government encouraged the development of vocational education.
- Large urban districts became the lighthouses of public education, and their superintendents exerted considerable influence over both the nature of schooling and the practice of school administration (Tyack & Hansot, 1982).
- The design of school buildings was guided almost entirely by efficiency; hence, many new urban schools looked like factories with uniform classrooms placed on each side of a hallway. Little consideration was given to designing facilities that would enhance the intended curriculum and instructional practices (Kowalski, 2002).

Collectively, these conditions moved public schools toward a more secular vision and economic purposes; as a result, emphasis on education as a means for achieving liberty was diminished. Both leading school administrators and the captains of industry who exerted power over them concluded that schools should be a tool for enhancing and protecting the nation's status as the world's most dominant economic force (Callahan, 1962). The challenge for education policymakers was to design a system that would achieve this goal.

The emergence of a wealthy urban elite also intensified class divisions in the United States. Vocational education, for example, was targeted largely for children from low-income families. In essence, school redesign during this era focused on differentiation rather than common denominators. That is, whereas formerly everyone had received the same education under the common school movement, students now began receiving a differentiated education based on their perceived merit. The differentiation of students according to merit changed the meaning of equality of educational opportunity in U.S. schools. Formerly, the educational system had attempted to provide an equal education for everyone and then allowed the social race for power and economic goods to begin. Under the revised system, school officials had the power to determine the type of education program each student would receive.

The practice of separating students either in overall programs or in specific courses has been especially detrimental to children from low-income families. As an example, the practice of tracking students (i.e., placing and keeping them in groups based on intellectual capacity) continues to this day in many schools, even though its adverse effects on students have been well known. For example, Jeannie Oakes (1986) noted:

> There is little evidence to support any of the assumptions about tracking. The effects of tracking on student outcomes have been widely investigated, and the bulk of this work does not support commonly-held beliefs that tracking increases student learning. . . . Students who are not in top tracks suffer clear and consistent disadvan-

tages from tracking. . . . The net effect of tracking is to exaggerate the initial differences among students rather than to provide the means to better accommodate them. (p. 14)

The separation of students was made more possible by the development of scientific means of measuring intelligence (IQ tests) and by persistent demands for operational efficiency. The continued and perhaps increasingly prevalent use of the progeny of these early measures is evident in today's schools in the variety of intelligence, achievement, competency, and other forms of standardized testing to which students are subjected.

Although the overriding societal purpose for schooling had been modified during the era of big business, schools continued to be regarded as "museums of virtue" (Tyack & Hansot, 1982). The previous era of schooling had been characterized by a spiritual focus that had provided the moral capital for the current era. This had resulted in a sharply defined sense of purpose which was now combined with a scientific management perspective and resulted in schools that were characterized by a "blend of science and missionary zeal. . . . The rhetoric of moral charisma . . . complemented . . . the language of science and evolutionary social efficiency" (Tyack & Hansot, 1982, p. 7).

Era of Diversification and Fragmentation

From the mid-twentieth century on, the hard-edged factory appearance of schools that had characterized the previous business and scientific management era changed to a sprawling, one-story structure, divided into segments, and united only by a parking lot. The typical schoolhouse designed during this era frequently resembled a shopping mall, both in appearance and in its attempt to provide something for everyone. Pluralism was cast as a supreme institutional virtue, and public schools were expected to model peaceful coexistence among diverse groups (Powell, Farrar, & Cohen, 1985). The eclectic nature of the school was intended to satisfy individual tastes and needs, but the pursuit of this goal blurred the sense of purpose that characterized earlier U.S. schools (Tyack & Hansot, 1982).

The fragmented nature of contemporary schools remains evident not only in course offerings but also in leadership and policymaking. Utilitarian social theories posit that all human behavior is determined by self-interests; therefore, education policymaking can be viewed as a process in which competing values vie for dominance (Fowler, 2000). Clearly, the self-interests of single-issue reformers multiplied exponentially over the past four or five decades. These would-be change agents have affected education policy primarily by recruiting similarly minded individuals to join their cause. These pressure groups have used primarily political and legal strategies to achieve their objectives. As an example, they have elected school board members who support their position or challenge existing policies in the courts. Although political action is pervasive in a democratic society, and has produced laudable social gains for minority groups, the resultant fragmentation and politicization has contributed to diminished clarity of education purpose.

Also contributing to fragmentation has been an increasing number of state and federal programs, frequently initiated in response to pressure from special-interest groups or in response to historical or social events. For example, the Russian launching of *Sputnik* in the late 1950s produced claims that the nation was at risk of being dominated by a foreign power. Much of the blame for this condition was directed at public education; critics claimed that the nation's elementary and secondary school system had failed to produce world-class scientists and mathematicians. The passage of the National Defense Education Act provided millions of dollars of federal support to improve programs and instruction in subjects deemed vital to national defense. Just a few years later, however, the nation faced new problems centering largely on race relations and poverty. Riots in several major cities made the public aware that the Civil Rights Act had not resolved the nation's racial and economic problems. Again, much of the blame for these social ills was directed at public schools—and again, the federal government enacted a law (the Elementary and Secondary Education Act of 1965) that provided financial support for new programs.

More recently, public schools were blamed for placing the nation at risk once again—this time the risk involved the United States falling from its lofty position as the world's number-one economic power. Actions were taken to direct public schools toward academic excellence and to hold local school boards and administrators accountable for the outcomes. At first, state legislatures relied on intensification mandates to pursue their goals; that is, students and teachers were forced to do more of what they were already doing. Critics of this strategy (e.g., Boyd, 1987; Timar & Kirp, 1989) pointed out that the initiators ignored the complexity of schools and did virtually nothing to improve the capacity of schools to change. By the early 1990s, many states had shifted to new strategies that focused on state deregulation and district decentralization in an effort to restructure the operations of schools. Some proponents of moving reform to the individual school level (e.g., Finn & Kanstoroom, 2000) argued that this strategy was one way of making administrators and teachers more accountable for education outcomes. Although well intentioned, these persistent shifts in education goals and improvement strategies serve to widen disagreements over the primary purposes of public education.

In many cases, responsibilities of schools have been expanded beyond educational functions to encompass functions such as health care, nutrition, counseling, day care, and other functions that were formerly the responsibility of the family or the church. On the social front, increased rates for teenage pregnancy, venereal disease, and the spread of AIDS resulted in mandated sex education programs. And during the 1990s, tragic incidents in which students and teachers were killed in schools led to expectations that schools would be able to prevent violent behavior.

Frederick Wirt and Michael Kirst (1989) noted that six societal core constituencies have emerged during recent years, each effecting schools and administrators:

1. *Students:* Primarily interested in issues of governance, expression, dress, behavior, and other student rights

2. *Teachers:* Primarily interested in issues of collective bargaining and personal rights
3. *Parents:* Primarily interested in issues dealing with parental involvement in school governance
4. *Taxpayers:* Primarily interested in reforming school finance, especially as it may affect them economically
5. *Minorities:* Primarily interested in issues of desegregation and equality
6. *Federal and state authorities:* Primarily interested in a variety of areas that are addressed in laws or mandates

Although this categorization is rather general, it serves to exhibit that administrators are bombarded with different wants and needs that are expressed and pursued by political groups. In addition, these groups often compete with each other in an effort to achieve their self-interests.

Overload and fragmentation also have made reform and accountability more elusive goals (Fullan, 1996). As an example, competing purposes have often divided school staffs and eroded goals—conditions that contribute to negative attitudes about the potential of achieving meaningful improvement (Peterson & Deal, 1998). Even at the individual school level, administrators often face the reality that they must pursue school improvement by working with individuals groups that have different and often competing agendas; and although the level of power possessed by these individuals and groups varies, none is void of power (Fowler, 2000).

Conflicting Values and Purposes

Public Education's Guiding Values

Historically, education policy in the United States has been guided by six primary values (see Figure 8.1). *Liberty* is deeply rooted in U.S. society and it refers to "the right to act as one chooses" (Swanson, 1989, p. 274). The centrality of this value is evidenced by the concept of local school boards, an organizational pattern for public education that is unique to the United States. Liberty, however, does not grant unrestricted powers to local districts. Typically, district-level decisions are subject to state review, especially when the state government partially or totally funds the operations in question.

Equality may be defined politically as the equal right to participate in a political system and economically to mean equal wealth (Fowler, 2000). In public education, the concept has been defined most often as meaning equal opportunity. If equality were defined as a fair and just method of distributing resources among public school students, it could be measured by variations in revenue and spending across local districts (Crampton & Whitney, 1996). In essence, an equitable state system would produce low or moderate variation in spending among local districts and minimal variations in the quality of school buildings.

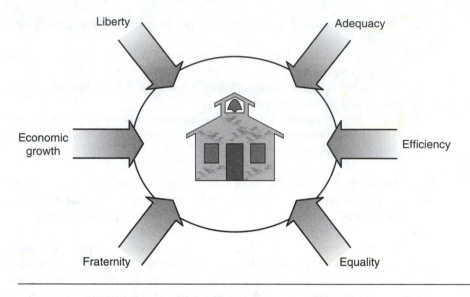

Liberty   Adequacy

Economic
growth   Efficiency

Fraternity   Equality

FIGURE 8.1   *Primary Values Shaping American Education*

Adequacy is a complex value for at least two reasons. First, the term is relative; what may be adequate in one community may be inadequate in another. Second, definitions of adequacy are constantly changing. As an example, social, economic, and political changes in society create new needs and wants. Thus, the parameters of an adequate education are dynamic (Kowalski, 2002).

Efficiency pertains to the relationship between inputs and outputs. Typically, it is achieved in one of two ways: increasing outputs while holding inputs constant and holding outputs constant while decreasing inputs. In education, efficiency often is addressed through the concept of accountability (Swanson & King, 1997). In many communities, for example, taxpayers evaluate schools on the basis of their productivity in relation to financial support.

Fraternity addresses the goal of developing a sense of community in a diverse society. "To value community is to seek a common bond that produces a sense of unity and nationhood" (Bauman, 1996, p. 85). Programs such as multicultural education are expressions of this value. The pursuit of fraternity often generates considerable tension between those forces that believe that schools should promote and celebrate diversity and those forces that believe that schools have the responsibility to teach and reinforce the nation's dominant culture.

The final guiding value is *economic growth.* This objective focuses on ways that education serves to increase the production of goods and services. Programs such as school-to-work and Tech Prep are expressions of this value. The underlying belief is that schools should prepare students to be economically productive so that they can enjoy life and contribute to the collective welfare of society.

Although each of these values continues to guide educational policy, there are conceptual inconsistencies among them. At times, they are "contradictory or even counterproductive" (Bauman, 1996, p. 85). As a result, administrators face the persistent dilemma of trying to balance conflicting beliefs (Cuban, 1988). For example, liberty promotes local decision making; however, excessive liberty almost always leads to serious inequities in tax effort and spending among local districts. This is because affluent communities are usually more willing and able to generate and spend more money for education (Kowalski & Schmielau, 2001). Although individuals and groups do not embrace the six values with the same fervor, the values continue to provide a framework for education policymaking.

Competing Purposes

Scholars have provided various classifications for what public schools are expected to accomplish. In general, the public supports two broad goals: individual development and the general welfare of society. The two represent the private and social purposes of education (Levin, 1990). Support becomes less certain, however, when these broad objectives are divided into specific purposes.

Studying the purposes of public schools since their beginning, Joel Spring (1991) identified three broad categories: political, social, and economic. Potential political goals include educating citizens, providing education to help citizens select political leaders, helping achieve political consensus by instilling a common political creed in individuals, maintaining dominant power relationships, and socializing children for the political system (Spring, 1991, pp. 6–10). From a political perspective, Spring observed that schools both exert political control and teach citizens how to exercise their political rights. Consequently, they may be both instruments of domination and a source for protecting personal freedom. Political purposes for schools may emanate from school, district, community, state, or national sources. For example, they may come from forces ranging from national political parties to state-level special-interest groups to local community pressure groups.

The social purposes of schooling, such as social control and social mobility, suggest that schools should move in very different directions (Spring, 2001). Social control involves passing on existing cultural values and norms to new generations of students. The intent is social stability—that is, to perpetuate current societal values and beliefs. Advocates argue that the perpetuation of fundamental values preserves the integrity of a society's culture that has been developed over time. Social mobility can be defined in different ways, but the concept basically refers to the ability to become upwardly mobile in society. Critical theorists and others advocating that schools should serve to reconstruct society rather than perpetuate it argue that society is clearly characterized by inequitable relationships with regard to race, class, and gender. In their eyes, educators pursuing social control use textbooks, curriculum, and instructional practices such as tracking to perpetuate existing inequitable economic relationships (McLaren, 1989; Wilbur, 1998). The strong differences of opinion regarding the social purposes of schooling stem from the fact that political and personal philosophies are involved. Thus, the advocates of social control and the advocates of social reconstruction believe that they have the high moral ground in this disagreement.

Underlying the economic purposes of education are the dual objectives of increasing national wealth and advancing technological development (Spring, 2001). Many of the national reform reports since 1980 have expressed this view. For example, *A Nation at Risk*, the report that served as a springboard for the most extensive period of school reform in our nation's history (Murphy, 1991), focused largely on the perceived failure of public education to meet these purposes. Most reform reports defined academic success almost exclusively in terms of capital accumulation and the logic of the marketplace (McLaren, 1989). This proclivity was especially offensive to those who support the idea that schools should focus primarily on compensating for the effects of economic inequalities in U.S. society.

Noted education scholar John Goodlad (1984) developed yet another classification system for education purposes. In his study, *A Place Called School*, he categorized education purposes as vocational, social, intellectual, and personal:

- *Vocational purposes* are those that prepare students for work.
- *Intellectual purposes* differ from vocational purposes in that they focus on academic skills and knowledge.
- *Social purposes* focus on preparing students for life in a complex and diverse society.
- *Personal purposes* focus on the development of individual responsibility.

Some scholars have classified school purposes according to philosophical schools of thought. For instance, Pounds and Bryner (1973) provided the following summary:

- *Humanism:* The purpose of school is to pass on unchanging truths of universe and to cultivate the intellect.
- *Essentialism:* The purpose of schools is to pass on the essential elements of established culture.
- *Social realism:* The purpose of school is to ensure that currently prevailing ideas and values are passed on to students and to help them adjust to present society.
- *Experimentalism:* The purpose of school is to develop critically minded individuals who are able to solve problems.
- *Reconstructionism:* The purpose of schools is to determine what future society should be like and to prepare students who are able to transform society into this future state.

All of these categorizations serve to exhibit that there have been and continue to be multiple purposes for public education. More important, these purposes are often discordant, resulting in philosophical and political factions.

Goals versus Purposes

Distinctions need to be made between goals and purposes. Organizational goals can be thought of as specific objectives that members of an organization are attempting to accomplish. Contrastingly, organizational purpose is a more general statement that indicates what the organization stands for and provides a rationale for the organization's existence. For example, integrating computers into the curriculum is a goal; providing students with the academic skills to function productively in society is a purpose.

Traditionally, organizational theorists have held the following to be true with regard to education goals:

- They are prospective.
- They guide action.
- Progress toward them can be measured and monitored.
- The results of measuring and monitoring can be communicated to broad audiences.
- Individuals and organizations are willing and able to make adjustments that help achieve greater congruency between goals and organizational behavior.

Recently, however, organizational theorists have questioned the accuracy of these assumptions; they argue that goals often are retrospective, constructed after-the-fact, and determined largely by happenstance (e.g., March & Olsen, 1979; Perrow, 1982; Weick, 1979). Assume, for example, that a middle school employs a new teacher to provide remedial reading instruction. Her ability and enthusiasm are largely responsible for significant student gains in this area. Yet, the principal claims that the improvement is attributable to an overall goal to improve student outputs.

Theorists also argue that progress toward goal achievement cannot be measured due to the ambiguity of what constitutes effectiveness. For example, school effectiveness is usually measured on the basis of standardized test scores. However, this criterion provides only a very limited picture of the school's true level of productivity, for it ignores the school's total mission and fails to account for variables outside of school that may affect student test performance. Even if accurate measurement can occur, accurate feedback may not be able to be designed; schools are complex social systems and any outcome is likely to have multiple causes (Hanson, 1996). Finally, even if all these conditions were met, individuals or organizations may not be willing or able to implement feedback due to lack of skill, competing agendas (e.g., insufficient time due to family commitments or other personal interests), or the loosely structured nature of schools (e.g., although schools may have elaborate, articulated curricula, what is taught in one classroom at a particular grade level may have little relationship with what is being taught in another classroom at the same grade level).

Thomas Sergiovanni (2001) has suggested that multiple goals can mean no goals, because competing interests produce fragmentation and diffuse institutional mission. Yet, the history of schooling in the United States reveals that new goals seldom replace existing goals. Moreover, two other forces serve to direct public education. One of them involves periodic shifts in political philosophy. For example, during conservative periods, private values are emphasized; during liberal periods, public values are promoted (Schlesinger, 1986). Differences in dispositions toward public education under President Carter and President Reagan exemplify this point. The other force involves critical events that produce public dissatisfaction with schooling. The launching of *Sputnik* in the late 1950s, civil unrest in the 1960s, and growing global competition in economic markets in the 1980s serve as examples.

Research findings often question the efficacy of goals but highlight the importance of purpose. David Clark and Terry Astuto (1988), for example, have referred to the goal/purpose issue as the choice leaders have between intention (i.e., achieving productivity through goal setting) and distinction (i.e., defining the core values and beliefs for which the organization stands). They noted that the literature highlights the efficacy of distinction. Indeed, it is distinction that motivates and galvanizes people (Sergiovanni, 2001). Consider the observation made by Tom Peters and Robert Waterman (1982) in their study of outstanding business organizations: "Every excellent company we studied is clear on what it stands for, and takes the process of value shaping seriously. In fact, we wonder whether it is possible to be an excellent company without clarity of values" (p. 280).

There is a nexus between organizational culture and organizational purpose. School cultures are described along two continuums ranging from weak to strong and negative to positive. Strong cultures reflect the fact that individuals comprising the organization embrace the same basic values and beliefs about education. Positive cultures reflect the fact the dominant values and beliefs are congruous with the professional knowledge base. Strong, positive organizational cultures have been linked to effectiveness in several ways:

- Culture provides an unwritten set of informal norms that inform what actions are appropriate in most situations (Deal & Kennedy, 1982). Specifically, the beliefs, values, and assumptions that constitute an organization's culture guide employee action and behavior. Actions incongruent with these cultural norms are labeled inappropriate and are discouraged; those congruent with them are labeled appropriate and are encouraged.
- In the sense that culture provides informal norms that guide action and behavior, it increases the intelligence level of the organization. New rules do not have to be developed to handle each contingency. Edward Hall (1981) referred to this as "contexting" and noted that it is similar to "programming the memory of the system" in order to help it avoid information overload in an increasingly complex environment (pp. 85–86).
- Culture provides a positive identity for employees by linking them with excellence (Deal & Kennedy, 1982; Smircich, 1983). Just as athletic teams (especially those with winning records) engender fan support, so also do organizations with strong cultures gain employee support. Employees feel pride in being

associated with an organization they, or others, perceive in a positive light. Similar to the way in which fans cheer more rabidly for a winner, employees put forth greater effort for positively perceived organizations.

- Culture provides meaning for individuals and engenders a sense of commitment that goes beyond self-interest (Smircich, 1983). When individuals accept the values, beliefs, and assumptions of the organization's culture as their own, they become "true believers" (Hoffer, 1951) in the organization's mission. Their degree of commitment to fulfilling organizational tasks resembles that of a spiritual or political activist more nearly than that of a typical organizational employee. Individual needs become subordinate to organizational needs.

Although goals may not guide organizational action to the extent that a strong organizational culture grounded in a common sense of purpose does, they do serve as symbols that portray schools as rational and legitimate to outsiders. In this vein, Thomas Sergiovanni (2001) wrote, "Under loosely structured conditions, schools don't achieve goals as much as they respond to certain values and tend to certain imperatives that ensure their survival over time" (p. 180). In the words of Tom Sawyer in an organizational parody of *The Adventures of Huckleberry Finn,* "Goals is there only so's you can tell them to people when they ask you what your goals are. You don't have to follow them or nothing like that. It don't look right if you don't have no goals" (Reitzug, 1989, p. 147).

Implications for Practice

This chapter has provided a historical perspective of the relationship between society and schools. Events during the twentieth century clearly illustrate two important facts about this relationship. First, significant changes in societal needs and wants almost always result in new directions for public schools; threats to national defense, social order, and economic dominance over the past 50 years are prime examples. Second, growing demographic diversity has helped expand the purposes of schooling. Today, the mission of many schools is fragmented and ambiguous.

Although most Americans accept two general purposes for public education (individual development and the general welfare of society), disagreements over the breadth and depth of them have produced conflict and political activity. As such, the lack of consensus over the precise purposes of education have been a barrier to school reform and a major challenge to school administrators. This is because the purposes spawn a growing number of goals, some of which are incongruent with each other and many of which are extremely difficult to measure. Overall, this condition has made the practice of school administration more complex and difficult; that is, fragmentation and political conflict have created expectations that superintendents and principals should do more than just manage people and material resources. Many of the new job requirements involve organizational leadership activities, such as shared visioning, inclusive planning, conflict resolution, consensus building, and evaluation.

For Further Discussion

1. During the formative years of public education, there was less disagreement regarding the purposes of education. Why?

2. Are public schools still mirrors of society? Why or why not?

3. What is the basic difference between purposes and goals? In what ways are these two factors connected?

4. As the United States became a more diverse society in terms of race, religion, and economic status, how were the purposes of education affected?

5. What are the causes of social fragmentation? How does social fragmentation affect the mission of public education?

6. Should schools pursue a single purpose or a multiplicity of purposes? Is it possible to have a focused direction and still provide something for everyone? Is it desirable to provide something for everyone?

7. What is the difference between the goals of individual development and the general welfare of society? Which of these goals should be the most important?

8. Should school administrators determine the purposes of their district or school? Why or why not?

9. How do critical theorists view the purposes of public education?

10. During and immediately following the Industrial Revolution, many school administrators embraced the tenets of scientific management. How did these principles affect the way schools were structured and operated?

11. What is social reconstruction? How does this purpose differ from social stability?

12. The development of education in the United States has been guided by six primary values. Why are two of them, equality and liberty, basically incompatible?

13. What is school culture? Why is this characteristic important to understanding institutional missions?

Other Suggested Activities

1. Obtain the mission statements for several districts and schools. Evaluate them in the context of this chapter's content. Determine the extent to which to they encourage social stability.

2. Discuss possible differences between private and public schools with regard to purposes and goals. How are the two categories of schools different with regard to these two variables?

3. Discuss the advantages and disadvantages of schools encouraging students to develop their own intellectual tools, to think for themselves, and to select their own moral and political values. What objections might be raised if a school embraced these goals?

4. Invite several local administrators to meet with your class to discuss their opinions about the purposes and goals of education in relation to school reform and their personal practice.

5. Identify pressure groups that have attempted to influence the purposes and goals of public education over the past decade. What purposes and goals did they pursue? What tactics did they use? To what extent were they successful?

References

Bauman, P. C. (1996). *Governing education: Public sector reform or privatization.* Boston: Allyn and Bacon.

Boyd, W. L. (1987). Public education's last hurrah? Schizophrenia, amnesia, and ignorance in school politics. *Educational Evaluation and Policy Analysis, 9*(2), 85–100.

Callahan, R. E. (1962). *Education and the cult of efficiency: A study of the social forces that have shaped the administration of public schools.* Chicago: University of Chicago Press.

Clark, D. L., & Astuto, T. (1988). Paradoxical choice options in organizations. In D. E. Griffiths, R. T. Stout, & P. B. Forsyth (Eds.), *Leaders for America's schools* (pp. 112–130). Berkeley, CA: McCutchan.

Crampton, F., & Whitney, T. (1996). *The search for equity in school funding.* NCSL Education Partners Project. Denver, CO: National Conference of State Legislatures.

Cuban, L. (1976). *The urban school superintendent: A century and a half of change.* Bloomington, IN: Phi Delta Kappa Educational Foundation.

Cuban, L. (1988). Why do some reforms persist? *Educational Administration Quarterly, 24*(3), 329–335.

Deal, T. E., & Kennedy, A. A. (1982). *Corporate culture: The rites and rituals of corporate life.* Reading, MA: Addison-Wesley.

Finn, C. E., Jr., & Kanstoroom, M. (2000). Improving, empowering, dismantling. *Public Interest, 140,* 64–73.

Fowler, F. C. (2000). *Policy studies for educational leaders: An introduction.* Upper Saddle River, NJ: Merrill, Prentice-Hall.

Fullan, M. G. (1996). Turning systemic thinking on its head. *Phi Delta Kappan, 77*(6), 420–423.

Goodlad, J. I. (1984). *A place called school.* New York: McGraw-Hill.

Hall, E. T. (1981). *Beyond culture.* New York: Doubleday.

Hanson, E. M. (1996). *Educational administration and organizational behavior* (4th ed.). Boston: Allyn and Bacon.

Hoffer, E. (1951). *The true believer: Thoughts on the nature of mass movements.* New York: Harper.

Johnson, J. A., Collins, H. W., Dupuis, V. L., & Johansen, J. H. (1988). *Introduction to the foundations of American education* (7th ed.). Boston: Allyn and Bacon.

Kowalski, T. J. (2002). *Planning and managing school facilities* (2nd ed.). Westport, CT: Bergin & Garvey.

Kowalski, T. J., & Schmielau, R. E. (2001). Liberty provisions in state policies for financing school construction. *School Business Affairs, 67*(4), 32–37.

Levin, H. M. (1990). The theory of choice applied to education. In W. H. Clune & J. F. Witte (Eds.), *Choice and control in American education* (pp. 247–284). New York: Falmer Press.

March, J. G., & Olsen, J. (1979). *Ambiguity and choice in organizations.* Bergen, Norway: Universitetsforlaget.

McLaren, P. (1989). *Life in schools: An introduction to critical pedagogy in the foundations of education.* New York: Longman.

Murphy, J. (1991). The effects of the educational reform movement on departments of educational leadership. *Educational Evaluation and Policy Analysis, 13*(1), 49–65.

Oakes, J. (1986). Keeping track: The policy and practices of curriculum inequality. *Phi Delta Kappan, 68*(1), 12–17.

Perrow, C. (1982). Disintegrating social sciences. *Phi Delta Kappan, 63*(10), 684–688.

Peters, T. J., & Waterman, R. H. (1982). *In search of excellence: Lessons from America's best-run companies.* New York: Warner Books.

Peterson, K. D., & Deal, T. E. (1998). How leaders influence the culture of schools. *Educational Leadership, 56*(1), 28–30.

Pounds, R. L., & Bryner, J. R. (1973). *The school in American society* (3rd ed.). New York: Macmillan.

Powell, A. G., Farrar, E., & Cohen, D. K. (1985). *The shopping mall high school: Winners and losers in the educational marketplace.* Boston: Houghton Mifflin.

Reitzug, U. C. (1989). Huck Finn revisited: A 19th century look at 20th century organizational theory. *Organization Studies, 10*(2), 145–148.

Schlesinger, A. M., Jr. (1986). *Cycles of American history.* Boston: Houghton Mifflin.

Sergiovanni, T. J. (2001). *The principalship: A reflective practice perspective* (4th ed.). Boston: Allyn and Bacon.

Smircich, L. (1983). Concepts of culture and organizational analysis. *Administrative Science Quarterly, 28,* 339–358.

Spring, J. (1991). *American education* (5th ed.). New York: Longman.

Spring, J. (2001). *American education* (10th ed.). New York: McGraw-Hill.

Swanson, A. D. (1989). Restructuring educational governance: A challenge of the 1990s. *Educational Administration Quarterly, 25*(3), 268–293.

Swanson, A. D., & King, R. A. (1997). *School finance: Its economics and politics* (2nd ed.). New York: Longman.

Timar, T. B., & Kirp, D. L. (1989). Education reform in the 1980s: Lessons from the states. *Phi Delta Kappan, 70*(7), 504–511.

Tyack, D., & Hansot, E. (1982). *Managers of virtue: Public school leadership in America, 1820–1980.* New York: Basic Books.

Weick, K. E. (1979). *The social psychology of organizing.* Reading, MA: Addison-Wesley.

Wilbur, G. (1998). School as equity cultures. *Journal of Curriculum and Supervision, 13*(2), 123–147.

Wirt, F. M., & Kirst, M. W. (1989). *Schools in conflict* (2nd ed.). Berkeley, CA: McCutchan.

9

Administrative Strategies and Styles

Chapter Content

This chapter examines the strategies and styles that administrators use in performing their responsibilities. Practitioner behavior is a complex topic that spans both normative and descriptive theories and models; you will study many of them as you progress toward completing your degrees and licensure programs in school administration. The intent here is to provide you with a general understanding of these topics.

Strategies and styles have commonly been associated with leadership; that is, they have been referred to as "leadership strategies" or "leadership styles." More precisely, however, strategies and styles are relevant to both components of administration—leadership and management. The failure to define leadership, especially in relation to management and administration, has been a long-standing problem in the profession (Leithwood & Duke, 1999). In large measure, a precise, enduring, and universally accepted definition for leadership has been difficult for two reasons: The needs of organizations and the role expectations for administrators are fluid (Razik & Swanson, 1995) and *leadership* is conceived by many to be a politically correct synonym for *administration*. In this book, however, leadership has been previously described as a social influence process in which a person steers members of a group or organization toward a specific goal. Conceptually, this may seem like a straightforward and relatively simple task, but it really is difficult and complex. Leadership has been called one of the most observed and least understood phenomena (Burns, 1978).

The discussion of strategies and styles begins with an overview of the complexity of leadership. The intent is to exhibit that this element of administration is more complex and challenging than management. Several common dimensions of administrative strategies and styles are introduced and explained.

Complexity of Leadership

Clearly, the various tasks performed by administrators differ with respect to difficulty and importance. As an example, consider two possible role expectations given to a middle school principal: Manage the lunch program budget and bring members of the school and community together to build a shared vision. The first task is structured and relatively simple; the latter is essentially unstructured and highly complex. In general, making decisions about how to do things is less threatening and complicated than making decisions about what should be done.

The complexity of the leadership component of administration is illustrated by the following example:

> Mr. Jones is the principal of a large elementary school in an affluent suburban area of a large city. Several weeks into the school year, Mr. Jones received a complaint from the father of a third-grade student in Mrs. Smith's class. The father told the principal that his child never had any homework. The principal said that he was aware of this, and then explained that Mrs. Smith and the other third-grade teachers did not feel that homework was appropriate for their students. The teachers believed that after spending more than six hours at school, the students would benefit more from playtime and other developmentally appropriate activities. Mr. Jones told the father that he supported allowing teachers to develop their own rules regarding homework. After the conversation, the principal notified Mrs. Smith that he had received the complaint and summarized what he had told the father.
>
> A number of weeks passed before Mr. Jones received more complaints about Mrs. Smith. This time, the parents of three other children in Mrs. Smith's classroom came to his office. They reiterated the concern about homework and also charged that the teacher had "low academic standards." They told the principal that their children spent too little time studying reading, writing, and arithmetic; consequently, the parents feared that their children would not perform well on the upcoming standardized achievement tests. Mr. Jones responded that Mrs. Smith was a competent teacher who addressed the social and emotional needs as well as the academic needs of her students.

The parents were not satisfied with the principal's response. They told the principal that the school should be concerned with academics and that parents should worry about the social and emotional needs of their children. Before they left, they warned the principal that unless changes were forthcoming in Mrs. Smith's classroom, they would express their concerns directly to the superintendent and school board.

After the meeting, Mr. Jones contemplated possible courses of action. He did not agree that Mrs. Smith had low academic standards, but he understood why the parents were concerned. In the "real" world, students were certainly rated by how well they scored on standardized tests. In addition, state funding for schools is partially affected by student performance on these state-mandated tests. He concluded that the easiest solution would be simply to tell Mrs. Smith to toughen up—to assign homework and to spend more time preparing the students for the achievement tests. But . . . was this the right thing to do?*

The decision Mr. Jones faces illustrates the problematic nature of leadership. Although Mr. Jones may fully intend to influence Mrs. Smith or the parents in a specific direction, in whose direction does he influence them? Does he support his teacher (right or wrong) or does he side with the parents? Should his decision be guided by personal conviction, political expediency, current practices in the school or district, or by professional ethics?

Donald Schön (1989, 1990) has noted three characteristics that make the work of professionals in fields such as education especially challenging. First, "minor" professions (a term used to designate professions that do not enjoy the relative freedom and prestige given to more established professions such as medicine and law) are frequently characterized by an absence of widely accepted, unambiguous purpose. The example of Mr. Jones clearly illustrates the ambiguity of purpose faced by principals. Should the goal of schooling be high test scores? Or should the goal be the development of the total person? Educational historians have observed that unlike early nineteenth-century school leaders who shared a common religious and political conception of public education's purpose, today's leaders resembles heirs "receiving a handsome legacy from a distant relative whose purposes now seem unclear or even quaint" (Tyack & Hansot, 1982, p. 4).

Second, Schön noted that social sciences (such as education) lack a basis in systematic, scientific knowledge, but even if such knowledge were available, the nature of social reality has created problems of complexity and uncertainty ill suited to traditional cause-and-effect solutions. Others have described the modern era as one characterized by "rapid and spastic change" (Bennis & Nanus, 1985, p. 10) in which traditional ways of addressing problems are ineffective. The discrepant views regarding appropriate instructional content and methodology held by Mrs. Smith, Mr. Jones, and the parents in the previously cited example exemplify the uncertainty of professional knowledge in education.

*Adapted from Kowalski (2001).

Finally, Schön argued that there are two types of problems, and leaders make choices about dealing with them. The first category includes problems that are simple, are manageable, have clear solutions, and thus lend themselves to research-based or technical solutions. Scheduling, budgeting, accounting, facilities management, miscellaneous paperwork, and other routine managerial tasks are examples. The second category includes problems that are complex, messy, and time consuming, and that rarely produce a clear-cut solution. Motivation problems, conflict, organizational direction, ethical behavior, and other human behavior issues are examples. These messy problems primarily involve leadership.

Unfortunately, the easily solved problems encountered by administrators are relatively unimportant when compared to complex problems that often have only ambiguous solutions. Nevertheless, administrators almost always have some choice in determining the types of problems they personally address, thereby allowing them discretion in how they spend their time. They can choose the "high hard ground," where work is consumed by the less complex and less important problems, or they can elect to wade through "the swamp," where the more complex and more important issues are found (Schön, 1983). Many administrators have chosen the former alternative not only because it is less risky and less taxing but also because the problems on the high ground are usually solvable. Although choosing to deal with them may provide a sense of safety, comfort, and the satisfaction of accomplishment, and although dealing with them is essential (e.g., budgets and school facilities are certainly important), the administrator must be careful not to ignore leadership. Staying out of the swamp may be personally beneficial for superintendents and principals, but this is the terrain where the truly important issues cogent to school effectiveness are found. In determining how they practice, school administrators adopt strategies and styles—and often they do so without understanding the potential consequences of their choices.

Administrative Strategies

Whereas *style* usually refers to individual behavior, *strategy* has organizational connotations. Strategy describes broader, longer-term, and more comprehensive patterns of administrator behavior (Bassett, 1970). In local school districts, for instance, an administrative strategy may focus on sharing authority or it may focus on balancing competing philosophical positions (e.g., liberty and equality).

Although strategies are usually described along a continuum with opposing positions, this does not mean that administrators must choose one over the other. Instead, administrative strategies are more accurately described as being skewed toward one of the alternatives. Two dimensions of strategy are provided here to illustrate the concept.

Locus of Control Dimension

Historically, administration in public education has been highly centralized; that is, power and authority have been concentrated in the upper echelons of local districts. In highly centralized districts, superintendents maintain tight control over principals and principals maintain tight control over teachers. Several values and beliefs are fundamental to this organizational configuration:

- Administrators in high-level positions know more than administrators in low-level positions, and administrators at any level know more than nonadministrators.
- The distribution of power and authority creates tension within the district, and the resulting conflict detracts from the district's efficiency and effectiveness.
- A hierarchy of authority is necessary to establish district goals and to coordinate efforts toward their achievement.

Organizational theorists who have studied schools (e.g., Hanson, 1996) point out that these values and beliefs are only occasionally true.

Some critics of traditional school administration have argued that centralization strategies merely reflect superintendents' self-interests; that is, superintendents maintain most of the authority and power to protect themselves from political enemies. Although this may have been true in some instances, the centralization of local districts has a more intricate root system (Kowalski, 1999). As an example, many districts became increasingly centralized in the 1960s and 1970s as a means of protection from litigation. For example, a myriad of federal and state laws affecting schools (e.g., laws dealing with civil rights, special education, and sex discrimination) created a "compliance mentality" (Tyack, 1990). Thus, centralization in most instances was used to ensure uniform compliance with laws, policies, and rules and not as a means to protect the personal power of superintendents.

Centralization also has been advanced by concerns for equality of education opportunity. As schools are given greater freedom to develop their own visions, goals, and objectives, the potential for inequities increases. This is because some communities are willing and able to spend more money on education than are others. So, as pressures increase to allow schools to chart their own courses, concerns about equity and wealth redistribution surface (Weiler, 1990).

Over the past 15 years, both deregulation (i.e., freeing schools and educators from excessive policies and rules) and decentralization have become popular reform strategies. Under decentralization, power and authority are dispersed. For example, principals and teachers have greater freedom to make decisions about their goals and their methods for achieving them. This strategy has three primary goals (Certo, 1989):

1. *Increasing flexibility:* Allowing decisions to be made at the school level permits principals and teachers to respond to emerging needs more quickly and directly.
2. *Using human resources more effectively:* Many educators have knowledge and skills that are critical to school improvement; decentralization allows them to be part of the decision-making process.

3. *Ensuring that decisions are made closest to the problems:* Principals and teachers often have better insights into what needs to be done.

The most popular decentralization strategy has been site-based management. This approach typically creates school councils that include parents as well as educators; the councils are given varying degrees of power to make decisions. Governance configurations, such as site-based management, are often adopted for different reasons. For instance, a superintendent may impose the strategy simply because it is currently the thing to do; others may be philosophically committed to the concept. Noted change theorist Michael Fullan (1999) has argued that neither total centralization nor total decentralization is appropriate. He believes that the most effective governance strategy involves a mixture of the two. In other words, superintendents and other administrators should determine which elements of the district should be centralized (to avoid chaos and legal problems) and which elements should be decentralized (to ensure that changes address the real needs and wants existing in individual schools).

Participation Dimension

Another administrative strategy employed in local districts relates to the degree to which administrators are expected to work alone or as part of a team. The pursuit of high levels of autonomy is usually grounded in two beliefs: (1) administrator autonomy promotes competition that ultimately raises district productivity and (2) administrator autonomy allows superintendents to assess and evaluate individual performance accurately. The latter argument against administrative teaming is identical to one commonly expressed against teacher teaming.

Excessive autonomy, however, can create problems. One of them is the unwillingness of administrators to share information. For example, a principal might not warn other district principals about a forthcoming problem that he or she has already experienced because the principal views the others as competitors rather than colleagues. Instead of helping his or her peers, the principal thinks, "Let them find out the hard way, just as I had to do."

Another possible dilemma that may be created by excessive autonomy is the development of political factions. In high-competition environments, individuals who perceive that they are not winning usually seek compacts with others in an attempt to strengthen their position. Over time, the district's administrative staff may be divided into several factions—a condition that is likely to intensify competition and conflict.

The alternative to administrator autonomy is teaming. "Team administration simply refers to genuine involvement—before the fact—of all levels of administration in goal-setting, decision-making, and problem-solving processes" (Duncan, 1974, p. 10). One purpose of teaming is to prevent a "we-they" attitude between district-level and school-level administrators. The potential for such divisions increases with the size and complexity of local districts.

Another perceived benefit of teaming is shared decision making. Decisions made by the entire administrative staff may produce both practical and political benefits. Pragmatically, group decision making produces both broader perspectives of the problem and a higher quantity and quality of information related to the problem. Politically, shared decision making increases the likelihood that the decision will be supported uniformly, because all administrators express a sense of ownership. Some authors (e.g., Wynn & Guditus, 1984) also contend that shared decision making creates a collective moral responsibility for the participants.

Critics of administrative teaming have identified several possible problems, including the following:

- Often, there is a disjunction between power and accountability. For example, some team members may exert considerable influence over a decision but subsequently refuse to accept responsibility when the outcomes are less effective than anticipated.
- Teaming ignores the realities of organizational life. That is, some team members may be unwilling to state their true feelings because they do not want to offend others who are in higher-level positions. In addition, these individuals may pressure other administrators to do the same in order to preserve in-group cohesion (Bernthal & Insko, 1993). Under these conditions, teaming is an illusion rather than a democratic process.
- The very nature of group decision making and shared authority increases the potential for serious conflict. Problems are especially evident in districts where administrators have not been properly prepared to employ this strategy (Meadows, 1990).
- Teamwork often requires administrators to neglect the most important aspects of their work. For example, some administrators have weekly team meetings that may last five or six hours. Because principals are forced to be out of their schools, they either spend less time on instructional leadership or they relegate this essential responsibility to others.

Recognizing the promises and pitfalls of teaming, effective superintendents often use *restricted teaming*. In other words, they purposely establish parameters for the team's jurisdiction in an effort to balance collective action with autonomy. The intent is to benefit from teaming without unduly restricting the professional practice of individual administrators.

Administrative Style

Administrative style refers more directly to individual behavior, and it has almost always been referred to as *leadership style*, even though the dimensions of this concept clearly also relate to management functions. *Style* has been defined as an action disposition, or set or pattern of behaviors, displayed by an administrator

(Immegart, 1988); it describes the way an administrator handles work responsibilities, such as human relations, supervision, and sharing power (Bassett, 1970). The most popular conception of style has centered on task versus people orientation (Stodgill & Coons, 1957). Other popular conceptions have addressed the administrator predisposition toward democratic or autocratic governance, and toward directive versus nondirective behavior.

Style is discussed here in the context of five continuums, shown in Figure 9.1. As noted with strategies, you should recognize that the polar positions on the continuums represent extremes—and actual styles are almost between rather than at these extremes. In addition to discussing the five dimensions of style, possible linkages between gender and style are also noted.

Work Orientation Dimension

A significant amount of research has been conducted on the people orientations and task orientations of organizational leaders. Administrative behavior in most situations is likely to embody both dispositions with the degree to which each is necessary, varying from situation to situation. A high-task orientation indicates that an administrator is focused on job responsibilities (e.g., enforcement of policy); a high-people orientation indicates that an administrator is focused on meeting individual needs.

One of the best-known studies conducted on leadership dispositions toward tasks and people was completed approximately a half century ago at Ohio State

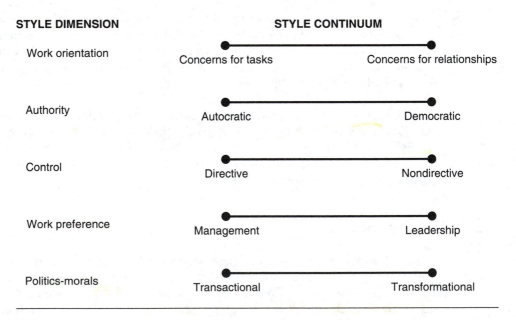

STYLE DIMENSION	STYLE CONTINUUM	
Work orientation	Concerns for tasks	Concerns for relationships
Authority	Autocratic	Democratic
Control	Directive	Nondirective
Work preference	Management	Leadership
Politics-morals	Transactional	Transformational

FIGURE 9.1   *Dimensions of Administrative Style*

University (Halpin, 1966). One of the key findings was that leaders whose behavior was high in both task orientation and people orientation were generally viewed as effective.* Research on the effectiveness of task-oriented versus people-oriented administration has not conclusively supported the superiority of either orientation. Consider several findings that reveal that each orientation may have its advantages and disadvantages:

- Leaders high in consideration (i.e., people orientation) tend to have more satisfied subordinates (Fleishman & Harris, 1962).
- The effects of consideration on group productivity vary greatly. Sometimes a high people orientation has a positive effect on productivity; other times it does not (House & Baetz, 1979).
- Leaders who are very task oriented achieve greater group productivity (Schriesheim, House, & Kerr, 1976) but experience greater employee turnover and higher employee grievance rates (Fleishman & Harris, 1962).

Many administrators have entered practice without understanding or thinking about work orientation. They almost always have been guided by preexisting personal dispositions; that is, they entered administration inclined to favor either tasks or people and their behavior was a product of that disposition. These administrators failed to reflect on the potential consequences of their leadership style. Consequently, they ignored critical questions about the appropriateness of their routine behavior. For example, should the interests of schools be balanced with the interests of people who work in them? Is it justifiable for an administrator to achieve greater organizational productivity at the expense of the satisfaction of those who do the work of the organization? Or, conversely, is it justifiable for a leader to jeopardize organizational productivity in order to keep organizational members satisfied? Increasingly, effective administrators recognize two facts: (1) both tasks and people are extremely important and (2) paying ample attention to both is most likely to produce high productivity.

Authority Dimension

A second common conceptualization of style is the extent to which administrators are either authoritarian or democratic. The tendency is to associate people-oriented administrators with a democratic administrative style and task-oriented administrators with an authoritarian style. Although this correlation may often exist, people-oriented administrators may be authoritarian, just as task-oriented administrators may be democratic.

There are distinct differences between the task-people and the authoritarian-democratic dimensions of administration. *Authoritarianism* and *democracy* refer to the extent to which followers are permitted to participate in making decisions.

---

*Halpin (1996) used the concepts *consideration* and *initiating structure* in his studies. These concepts correspond closely to and are frequently referred to as *people orientation* and *task orientation*, respectively.

Authoritarian administrators are those who allow little or no employee participation in organizational decision making and may even severely restrict teacher decision making in core technical areas (e.g., not allowing teachers to make decisions about assigning homework). Democratic administrators, on the other hand, encourage individual and group input into organizational decision making. They also encourage employees to make suggestions about how task requirements of their position might better be accomplished. Some researchers (e.g., Lewin, Lippitt, & White, 1939) identified a third category of style in this dimension: the *laissez-faire administrator*. This individual essentially is a nonadministrator; that is, people in the organization are allowed to direct their own behavior and to make decisions independently.

Studies initially conducted on the effectiveness of authoritarian versus democratic styles found that followers generally preferred democratic administrators. Authoritarian administration elicited either aggressive or apathetic behavior but, like task orientation, resulted in greater productivity (Lewin et al., 1939). However, subsequent studies have found that the initial increase in productivity experienced under authoritarian administrators diminishes sharply over time and ultimately results in lower productivity levels than in democratically led groups (Bowers, 1977). Although reviews of research on productivity levels of democratically versus autocratically led groups have been inconclusive (Bass, 1981; Jago, 1982), such reviews have consistently indicated that satisfaction and morale are likely to be higher in democratically led groups.

Opting for a purely democratic style creates a potential quandary for school administrators. Democratic administration implies a commitment to the group's goals for the organization rather than to a administrator's individual goals for the organization. This can be problematic if the administrator and the group's goals are incongruous or if the group's goals and the organization's official goals are incongruous. Consider a district that has an established goal of raising student performance on standardized tests by 5 percent over two years. In one elementary school, however, the teachers have voted not to change any instructional practices. The principal in this school faces a rather serious problem. Can he or she take measures to improve student test scores without altering the current instructional practices?

Control Dimension

Administrators also differ with respect to how they behave in implementing a decision. Directive principals, for example, tell teachers what they are supposed to do and how to do it; they then provide close supervision over implementation, especially when new programs are involved. By comparison, nondirective principals typically communicate expectations and then step back and allow teachers to implement the programs without administrative interventions.

Highly directive behavior is encouraged by classical theory, because followers are viewed as requiring close and continuous supervision (Hanson, 1996). Both standardization and routine are integral to classical theory (Sergiovanni, 2001) and thus they are also central to directive administrative behavior. Nondirective behaviors are more congruous with principles espoused by professions. That is, most education writers argue that teachers are professionals, and, as such, they should be allowed to apply their knowledge and skills within the parameters of established institutional goals. In addition to philosophical and professional dispositions, trust between the administrator and others plays an important part in determining directive behavior.

Work Preference Dimension

The responsibility dimension refers to the two basic components of administration: management and leadership. Scholars making conceptual distinctions between these two functions (e.g., Bennis & Nanus, 1985; Zaleznik, 1989) typically view *management* as focusing on *how* to do things. Chapter 2 includes a list of common school management tasks, including operating school lunch programs, budgeting, purchasing, operating the school plant, scheduling, discipline, and administering policies. *Leadership* focuses primarily on deciding *what* to do; common functions include visioning, policy development, and institutional change. Although all administrators are expected to balance management and leadership, most exhibit an action disposition, or style, that gives precedence to one of them.

Differences between management and leadership styles have been defined in many different ways. Joseph Rost (1991), for example, viewed management as largely an authority relationship involving control, supervision, and leadership as an influence relationship involving participation (e.g., shared visioning), an action orientation (e.g., the intention to pursue real change), and mutual purposes (e.g., shared goals). In the context of schools, this view of management is centered on avoiding failure (i.e., not implementing policy and not achieving prescribed goals) rather than on taking risks (i.e., planning and pursuing change).

Abraham Zaleznik (1989) discussed managers and leaders in the context of personality differences. He noted that the behavior of managers is influenced by the basic tenets of classical theory (e.g., rationality, control through rules, objectivity, and impersonal relationships with subordinates). Thus, administrators who function primarily as managers are prone to substitute process for substance; that is, they are far more concerned about how to do things than they are about making organizational improvements. By comparison, Zaleznik views leaders as visionary change agents—administrators who concentrate on what the organization can and should be.

There is a considerable disjunction between the extent to which administrators are expected to be leaders (especially as expressed in the professional literature) and the extent to which they actually manifest this style. In part, conceptual ambiguity is responsible for the gap between ideal and real behavior. For example, many practitioners believe that leadership and administration are synonymous and they conceive of administration as being primarily management. Therefore, even though they focus almost entirely on management responsibilities, they refer to themselves as leaders. Factors such as time availability, personal dispositions, past practices, and informal role expectations also explain why administrators may be inclined toward management or leadership.

Political-Moral Dimension

In his seminal work on leadership, James Burns (1978) distinguished between two types of leadership interaction: transactional and transformational. *Transactional leadership* involves an exchange between leader and follower for purposes of achieving individual objectives. Thomas Sergiovanni (2001) noted that transactional leadership requires a bargaining process: "The wants and needs of followers and the wants and needs of the of the leader are traded and a bargain is struck" (p. 136). "Each person in the exchange understands that she or he brings related motives to the bargaining process and that these motives can be advanced by maintaining that process" (Leithwood & Duke, 1999, p. 49). For example, a principal may agree to let a teacher attend a national reading conference in exchange for the teacher's work on a textbook adoption committee. In this case, the individual objective of the principal to fill committee slots is achieved, as is the teacher's individual objective of being able to attend the conference. Much of the work in organizations is accomplished through transactional leadership where tasks are completed for rewards such as money, security, or other jobs (Bennis & Nanus, 1985).

Instead of appealing to baser emotions such as fear, greed, and jealousy, the *transformational leader* seeks to influence behavior by appealing to "higher ideals and moral values such as liberty, justice, equality, peace, and humanitarianism" (Yukl, 1989, p. 210). The style is characterized by three conditions (Burns, 1978):

1. *Common goals:* Both the leader and the followers are pursuing the same goals.
2. *Ethical and moral guidance:* Both the leader and the followers are guided by ethical values and moral principles.
3. *Higher-order needs:* Both the leader and the followers are motivated by higher-order needs.

Warren Bennis (1984) noted that transformational leadership was enhanced by four competencies:

1. *Attention:* Developing a shared vision
2. *Meaning:* Communicating the vision to others
3. *Trust:* Believing in people and remaining focused
4. *Self:* Knowing personal skills and deploying them

Collectively, these competencies nurture empowerment, symbolically emphasize the importance of learning and competence, and promote a sense of community. Transformational leadership occurs at two levels: the personal level (interactions between a leader and a follower) and the organizational level (interactions between a leader and all followers). Whereas the former promotes personal growth and professionalism, the latter is often connected to reconstructing organizational culture (Yukl, 1989). Central to the moral appropriateness of culture-building behaviors are questions of process and substance. Specifically, what process is used to determine what the organization's core beliefs and values are to be? And what is the substance of the core beliefs and values?

The question of process contains several potentially problematic elements. Should the vision be determined by the leader and articulated and "sold" to followers? Or should the vision be created with input from all organizational members? If the former is the case, what happens when there are severe discrepancies between the leader's vision and the followers' visions? If the latter is the case, how does one reach consensus without a resulting product that is so watered down that it does not mean anything, or so inclusive that it provides no focus?

Simply satisfying process issues and holding a common goal is insufficient to ensuring moral appropriateness or transformation. The point has been made that democratic processes do not justify undemocratic ends, such as inequitable or dominance relationships (Quantz, Cambron-McCabe, & Dantley, 1990). For example, deciding to exclude parents from involvement in a school is not justified simply because the decision was made collectively by the faculty.

For leadership to be transformational, the substance of organizational beliefs and values must show a concern for higher-order, intrinsic, and moral motives. Transformation implies change. To engender commitment, the change must be an improvement over current affairs that appeal to the heart as well as the head. Thomas Sergiovanni (2001) noted that to be morally elevating, leadership must be concerned with psychological needs for esteem, autonomy, and self-actualization, and with moral principles such as goodness, righteousness, duty, and obligation. Thus, another dimension of style includes the degree to which administrators are transactional (essentially a political activity) and transformational (primarily a moral activity).

Gender and Administrative Style

Over the past 25 years, women have entered the study of school administration in greater numbers. In many universities, they already constitute a majority of the graduate students in this specialization. Partly for this reason, researchers have given greater attention to studying possible differences in leadership styles of male and female administrators.

In general, the literature supports the contention that the experiences and dispositions of females contribute to some gender-related style preferences. For example, authors writing in this area (e.g., Grogan, 1996; Regan & Brooks, 1995) note that women are viewed as being more democratic, more focused on leadership, more interested in instruction, and more reform minded. Often, these conditions are thought to be related to professional socialization and experiences; for example, women often have not been encouraged to become administrators and they usually have spent more time teaching before entering administration. In reviewing more recent research on women administrators, Charol Shakeshaft (1999) noted that much of research on this subject over the past decade has been qualitative in nature and centered on trying to determine if there is a nexus between gender and style. She concluded, "If it is true that women approach the job of administration in ways that differ from men, the reason why is less clear" (p. 115). Three essential questions related to this topic merit additional research:

1. To what extent do male and female administrators differ in style, given the extended pressures to improve schools by using state deregulation and district decentralization as primary strategies?
2. Are style preferences of female administrators related to innate characteristics or to the gender-related experiences?
3. To what extent are the style preferences of female administrators advantageous to meaningful school reform?

Normative Models for Administrative Style

Recognizing the importance of style, researchers have examined this topic both to provide a deeper understanding of it and to provide a guide for effective practice. With respect to the latter objective, normative models have been developed in an effort to inform administrators when style preferences are likely to be most effective. These models focus on and infuse contextual variables—the conditions surrounding the work of an administrator—into the decision process. Although the models are far from being perfect, and even though some even appear to conflict with each other, they are a valuable resource for making decisions about your behavior as an administrator.

Leading Normative Models

The potential value of normative models is anchored in the belief that effective administration requires practitioners to make conscious choices about style alternatives based on an evaluation of contextual variables. Consequently, the ability to evaluate these variables and personal flexibility and adaptability are critical characteristics; simply put, highly competent administrators almost always demonstrate style variability (Immegart, 1988).

Much of the research that has been conducted using the two-dimensional leadership theory has focused on determining in which situations administrators should be people or task oriented. One of the most widely used techniques for examining this dichotomy is the *Managerial Grid* developed by Blake and Mouton (1978). The process involves determining administrator predispositions or subordinate preferences and plotting them on a grid. The intent is to produce profiles of a leader's preferred style and the subordinates' preferences regarding their expectations of administrative style. Applied to education, for example, the process could be used to determine whether a prospective principal was inclined toward task or toward relationships. Once this is done, judgments could be made regarding congruity between organizational conditions and leadership style.

To illustrate how prevailing conditions in a high school may influence preferred administrative style for a principal, the four extreme styles identified by Blake and Mouton are related to selected contextual variables in Table 9.1.

Fred Fiedler (1967) also developed a normative model that identified preferred leadership style on the basis of three variables inherent in the situation being considered:

1. *Position power:* The strength of an administrator's influence, by virtue of his or her position, is described as being either strong or weak.
2. *Task structure:* The nature of the task is described as being either structured or unstructured.
3. *Leader and member relationships:* The administrator's personal relationship with others is described as being either good or poor.

Once ratings for these variables are established, the administrator chooses either a task or a people orientation as the most appropriate style to adopt for that situation. Details of the model are shown in Table 9.2.

TABLE 9.1   *Contextual Factors in a School Favoring Principal Dispositions Using Blake and Mouton's Extreme Styles*

Principal Style Disposition	*Selected conditions favoring disposition*
Low task and low concern for teachers	Pressure for the school to be productive is low; teachers (individually and collectively) have little power; emphasis on employee morale is low; collaboration between administration and teachers is considered relatively unimportant.
Low task and high concern for teachers	Pressure for the school to be productive is high low; teachers (individually and collectively) have considerable power; emphasis on employee morale is high; collaboration between administration and teachers is considered relatively important.
High task and low concern for teachers	Pressure for the school to be productive is high; teachers (individually and collectively) have little power; emphasis on employee morale is low; collaboration between administration and teachers is considered relatively unimportant.
High task and high concern for teachers	Pressure for the school to be productive is high; teachers (individually and collectively) have considerable power; emphasis on employee morale is high; collaboration between administration and teachers is considered relatively important.

TABLE 9.2   *Conditions Favoring Task or Relations Using Fiedler's Model*

Position Power	Task Structure	Leader-Member Relations	Style Orientation
Strong	Structured	Good	Task
Weak	Structured	Good	Task
Strong	Unstructured	Good	Task
Weak	Unstructured	Good	Relations
Strong	Structured	Poor	Relations
Weak	Structured	Poor	Relations
Strong	Unstructured	Poor	Relations
Weak	Unstructured	Poor	Task

Source: Adapted from Fiedler (1967).

Paul Hersey and Kenneth Blanchard's (1977) situational leadership theory promotes the idea that the degree of task orientation or people orientation depends on the maturity levels of the followers with regard to the specific task to be accomplished. They identified two types of maturity:

1. *Job maturity:* An employee's level of ability to perform is influenced by education and experience.
2. *Psychological maturity:* An employee's level of motivation is expressed by the need to achieve and the willingness to accept responsibility.

Psychological maturity is especially prone to vary depending on work assignment; for example, a teacher's level of motivation usually varies depending on the task being addressed. Hersey and Blanchard's model also employs four leadership styles:

1. *Directing:* Telling people what they should do and training them to do it; the style is effective when employees are not motivated and when they are relatively unskilled.
2. *Coaching:* Showing people how to do things; the style is effective when employees are motivated but relatively unskilled.
3. *Supporting:* Encouraging individual efforts; the style is effective when employees are skilled but not very motivated.
4. *Delegating:* Allowing others to work independently; the style is effective when employees are highly motivated and highly skilled.

After interfacing maturity levels with leadership styles, the model's authors concluded that low levels of maturity require a greater emphasis on tasks (i.e., either directing or coaching styles), and high levels of maturity require a greater emphasis on relationship behaviors (i.e., supporting or delegating).

Other models focus on helping administrators determine when they should be democratic or autocratic. Victor Vroom and Philip Yetton's normative contingency theory (1973), for example, uses five leadership styles, ranging from the administrator making the decision alone (highly autocratic style) to the administrator functioning as a group facilitator (highly democratic style). The appropriate style for a given problem is determined by using a flowchart that plots the answers to questions based on seven situational factors:

1. *Quality requirement:* Is it important that the decision be made quickly? Is it important to keep employees stimulated? Is it important to keep employees informed through participation?
2. *Sufficiency of information:* Does the administrator have sufficient information to make a good decision?
3. *Degree of structure:* To what extent is the problem structured?
4. *Necessity of acceptance:* To what extent is it necessary for employees to accept the decision?
5. *Likelihood of acceptance in the absence of participation:* How likely is it that employees and others affected will accept the decision if they are not involved in making it?
6. *Congruence between organizational and individual goals:* To what extent do others share the organizational goals that are central to the problem being addressed?
7. *Potential for conflict:* To what extent are preferred solutions likely to generate conflict among individuals in the organization?

The questions are answered sequentially. By following the prescribed flowchart, the administrator is guided to select the preferred style for the situation.

Jan Muczyk and Bernard Reimann (1989) distinguished between the act of making a decision and the process of executing the decision. In their conceptualization, the authoritarian-democratic dimension refers to the extent to which the leader involves employees in making decisions, whereas the leader's style in executing a decision falls on a continuum from directive to nondirective. Thus, their conceptualization has four distinct leadership styles:

1. *Authoritarian and nondirective leaders* provide employees little input into decision making, but great discretion in how to execute decisions.
2. *Authoritarian and directive leaders* allow neither input into decision making nor employee discretion in how to execute decisions.
3. *Democratic and nondirective leaders* permit and solicit employee input into decision making and allow great discretion in how to execute decisions.
4. *Democratic and directive leaders* permit and solicit employee input into decision making, but allow little discretion in terms of executing a decision.

Muczyk and Reimann believe that situational factors determine when each of the four styles is most appropriate. Table 9.3 provides an overview of preferred-style situations.

TABLE 9.3 *Summary of Conditions Related to Authority and Direction*

Situation Factors	Preferred Style			
	Authoritarian Directive	Authoritarian Nondirective	Democratic Directive	Democratic Nondirective
Time dimension				
Quick action required	X	X		
Time for consensus			X	X
Task complexity				
Simple		X		X
Complex	X		X	
Task structure				
Unstructured	X		X	
Highly structured		X		X
Employee experience				
Low	X		X	
High		X		X
Employee reliability				
Low	X		X	
High		X		X
Participation benefits*				
Low	X	X		
High			X	X
Substitutes for formal leadership				
Low	X		X	
High		X		X
Level of trust in employees				
Low	X			
High			X	X

*Benefits may be educational, motivational, or political (e.g., increasing ownership in the decision).

A much less complex model, known as the *Maier model* (Maier & Verser, 1982), uses two discrete elements to determine the extent to which administrators should be democratic when solving problems. The elements are *decision quality* (the need to achieve organization goals and maintain control) and *decision acceptance* (the level of subordinate commitment needed to implement solutions). The administrator is guided by the following recommendations:

- *When quality is high and acceptance is low:* The administrator is encouraged to make the decision alone or with the assistance of an expert (e.g., external consultant).
- *When quality is low and acceptance is high:* The administrator is encouraged to form representative groups and allow the groups to make a decision.

- *When both quality and acceptance are high:* The administrator is encouraged to form problem-solving groups consisting of individuals who have special knowledge and skills and he or she works with the group to reach a decision.
- *When both quality and acceptance are low:* The administrator has a wide range of choices, and usually personal preferences determine how the decision is made.

Assume, for example, that a principal is trying to improve student standardized test scores in a middle school. Decision quality is high because there is a clear need to improve the school's overall performance (as expressed by the community, school board, and superintendent). But the decision acceptance dimension also is high because any change in curriculum or instruction requires teacher support (as specified by the contract with the teachers' union and by the political nature of the community). Therefore, the Maier model encourages the principal to appoint highly knowledgeable and highly influential individuals (including himself or herself) to a committee that will make recommendations for raising student test scores.

Overall, research indicates that if tasks are clear and highly structured, there does not seem to be much benefit in soliciting employee input into how the tasks should be accomplished, since a clear conception of this already exists. However, when tasks are ambiguous, complex, or ill defined, or when subordinates are ego involved with the task, employee input is of greater benefit (House, 1971). Subordinate participation also is of greater value when employees exhibit a willingness to participate, see benefits accruing from their participation, and receive satisfaction from participation (Duke, Showers, & Imber, 1980; House & Baetz, 1979).

Promises and Pitfalls of Normative Models

One of the primary advantages of normative models is that they can sensitize administrators to the fact that they should adjust their styles based on situational variables. For those who have the opportunity to use normative models properly, they provide a structured format for selecting style alternatives. Therefore, using these models is certainly better than "flying by the seat of your pants."

Normative models, however, do not guarantee success. In fact, research across a wide range of organizations has repeatedly found that administrators rarely use them to make decisions about their behavior (Owens, 2001). In addition, administrators who attempt to use normative models heuristically are likely to confront several problems:

- Administrators often are unsure of the criteria they should use to rate a particular variable in relation to a specific situation. Consider the principal who is having difficulty determining whether his position power is strong or weak in relation to implementing block scheduling. The principal realizes that he can make conditions more difficult or unpleasant for teachers who do not accept the decision, but he also knows that these employees may have the power to retaliate if he does so. In addition, his position power may vary from one group of teachers to another. Thus, how does this principal rate his position power given that he has only two choices—strong or weak? Or how does the principal rate staff maturity in relation to block scheduling when some have high maturity toward a task, some have moderate maturity, and some have low maturity?

- Often, there are contextual factors that have a direct bearing on leadership style in schools that are not addressed in a specific model. For example, community factors, personal beliefs and experiences, and characteristics of the institutional context often have a direct influence on principals' behaviors (Dwyer, Barnett, & Lee, 1987). And even if the most essential situational factors could be identified, how does the leader determine in which situations these factors constitute the critical mass necessary to dictate one leadership style over another?

- The work of school administrators is frequently frenetic, fragmented, and unpredictable. Therefore, superintendents and principals often do not have the luxury of retrieving the models and studying them prior to deciding how they will behave.

- There are lingering questions regarding the inflexibility of some administrators. That is, some individuals may not be able or willing to alter their styles even when using normative models. Rather than changing their orientations (i.e., from task to people or from autocratic to democratic) when confronted with a unique problem, most administrators make adjustments within their established styles. For example, a task-oriented principal may become less so rather than becoming people oriented.

Even though professors of school administration recognize that practitioners may not use normative models extensively, they address them in their courses so that students gain a deeper understanding of the complex nature of administrative behavior. The models provide a framework that allows leadership style to be examined in the context of situational variables, and this knowledge clearly can have a positive influence on one's ability to be an effective practitioner. In addition to normative models for administrator behavior, practitioners may be influenced by a variety of decision-making models.

Implications for Practice

In performing their responsibilities as leaders and managers, administrators use strategies and styles. Often, they do so without purposeful planning; and when this is true, they are in a weak position to evaluate the effectiveness of their actions and to make appropriate behavior adjustments. The content of this chapter defines the concepts of strategy and style and provides examples of each. Understanding the dimensions of each concept helps you to observe and evaluate the behavior of administrators and to consider how you prefer to behave once you are in an administrative position.

Your exposure to normative models for leadership style at this point is not designed to be comprehensive. Rather, the intent was to provide sufficient examples so that you have a basic understanding of normative models with respect to (1) their nature in relation to contextual variables, (2) how they should be used, and (3) their potential pitfalls. Most of all, you should consider why it is important for contemporary practitioners to be flexible and adaptable.

For Further Discussion _____

1. Why is the management component of administration considered to be less complex than the leadership component?

2. Why is it important to define leadership?

3. Some studies have indicated that a people-oriented administrative style results in greater employee satisfaction, but that a task-orientation style results in greater productivity. Do you think that these findings justify a principal focusing exclusively on school goals? Why or why not?

4. What is the difference between a strategy and a style? Is it possible for a district's style to be incompatible with an individual administrator's style?

5. What purposes do normative models for administrative style serve?

6. What is a contextual variable? Why are such variables important to determining a preferred administrative style?

7. What is the difference between being democratic and being nondirective?

8. What are some possible reasons why administrators pay little attention to normative-style models?

9. Why is transactional leadership considered political and transformational leadership considered moral?

10. Is it possible for a principal to be both transactional and transformational? Why or why not?

Other Suggested Activities _____

1. Analyze your personal leadership style. Do you perceive yourself to be more people oriented or task oriented? More democratic or authoritarian? More directive or nondirective? Check with several of your colleagues to determine whether their perceptions of you match your own.

2. Discuss the concept of transformational leadership. Is this concept realistic in most districts and schools? Why or why not?

3. Discuss your opinions regarding gender and leadership style. Try to identify the sources of these opinions.

4. Imagine that your class is a committee of administrators appointed by the superintendent to develop guidelines for decisions that will be addressed by the district's administrative team. What types of decisions would you recommend be included and excluded?

References

Bass, B. M. (1981). *Stodgill's handbook of leadership.* New York: Macmillan.

Bassett, G. A. (1970). Leadership style and strategy. In L. Netzer, G. Eye, A. Graef, R. Drey, & J. Overman (Eds.), *Interdisciplinary foundations of supervision* (pp. 221–231). Boston: Allyn and Bacon.

Bates, R. J. (1987). Corporate culture, schooling, and educational administration. *Educational Administration Quarterly, 23*(4), 79–115.

Bennis, W. B. (1984). The four competencies of leadership. *Training and Development Journal, 38*(8), 14–19.

Bennis, W. B., & Nanus, B. (1985). *Leaders: The strategies for taking charge.* New York: Harper and Row.

Bernthal, P. R., & Insko, C. A. (1993). Cohesiveness without groupthink. *Group and Organization Management, 18*(1), 66–87.

Blake, R. R., & Mouton, J. S. (1978). *The new managerial grid.* Houston: Gulf Publishing.

Bowers, D. G. (1977). *Systems of organization: Management of human resources.* Ann Arbor: University of Michigan Press.

Burns, J. M. (1978). *Leadership.* New York: Harper and Row.

Certo, S. C. (1989). *Principles of modern management: Functions and systems* (4th ed.). Boston: Allyn and Bacon.

Cornett, J. W. (1990). Utilizing action research in graduate curriculum courses. *Theory into Practice, 29*(3), 185–195.

Duke, D. L., Showers, B. K., & Imber, M. (1980). Teachers and shared decision-making: The costs and benefits of involvement. *Educational Administration Quarterly, 16*(1), 93–106.

Duncan, R. (1974). Public Law 217 and the administrative team. *Indiana School Boards Journal, 20*(2), 9–12.

Dwyer, D. C., Barnett, B. G., & Lee, G. V. (1987). The school principal: Scapegoat or the last great hope? In L. T. Sheive & M. B. Schoenheit (Eds.), *Leadership: Examining the elusive* (pp. 30–46). Reston, VA: Association for Supervision and Curriculum Development.

Fiedler, F. E. (1967). *A theory of leadership effectiveness.* New York: McGraw-Hill.

Fleishman, E. A., & Harris, E. F. (1962). Patterns of leadership behavior related to employee grievances and turnover. *Personnel Psychology, 15*, 43–56.

Fullan, M. G. (1999). *Change forces: The sequel.* Philadelphia: Falmer Press.

Grogan, M. (1996). *Voices of women aspiring to the superintendency.* Albany: SUNY Press.

Halpin, A. W. (1966). *Theory and research in administration.* New York: Macmillan.

Hanson, E. M. (1996). *Educational administration and organizational behavior* (4th ed.). Boston: Allyn and Bacon.

Hersey, P., & Blanchard, K. H. (1977). *Management of organizational behavior: Utilizing human resources* (3rd ed.). Englewood Cliffs, NJ: Prentice-Hall.

House, R. J. (1971). A path-goal theory of leader effectiveness. *Administrative Science Quarterly, 16*, 321–338.

House, R. J., & Baetz, M. L. (1979). Leadership: Some empirical generalizations and new research directions. *Research in organizational behavior* (vol. 1). Greenwich, CT: JAI.

Immegart, G. L. (1988). Leadership and leader behavior. In N. J. Boyan (Ed.), *Handbook of research on educational administration* (pp. 259–277). New York: Longman.

Jago, A. G. (1982). Leadership: Perspectives in theory and research. *Management Science, 28*(3), 315–336.

Kowalski, T. J. (1999). *The school superintendent: Theory, practice, and cases*. Upper Saddle River, NJ: Merrill, Prentice-Hall.

Kowalski, T. J. (2001). *Case studies on educational administration* (3rd ed.). New York: Longman.

Leithwood, K., & Duke, L. D. (1999). A century's quest to understand school leadership. In J. Murphy & K. Seashore Louis (Eds.), *Handbook of research on educational administration* (2nd ed.) (pp. 45–72). San Francisco: Jossey-Bass.

Lewin, K., Lippitt, R., & White, R. K. (1939). Patterns of aggressive behavior in experimentally created "social climates." *Journal of Social Psychology, 10,* 271–299.

Maier, R. F., & Verser, G. C. (1982). *Psychology in industrial organizations* (5th ed.). Boston: Houghton Mifflin.

McLaren, P. (1989). *Life in schools: An introduction to critical pedagogy in the foundations of education*. New York: Longman.

Meadows, B. J. (1990). The rewards and risks of shared leadership. *Phi Delta Kappan, 71*(7), 545–548.

Muczyk, J. P., & Reimann, B. C. (1989). The case for directive leadership. In R. L. Taylor & W. E. Rosenbach (Eds.), *Leadership: Challenges for today's manager* (pp. 89–108). New York: Nichols Publishing.

Owens, R. G. (2001). *Organizational behavior in education* (6th ed.). Boston: Allyn and Bacon.

Quantz, R. A., Cambron-McCabe, N., & Dantley, M. (1990). Preparing school administrators for democratic authority: A critical approach to graduate education. *The Urban Review 24*(3), 243–262.

Razik, T. A., & Swanson, A. D. (1995). *Fundamental concepts of educational leadership and management*. Englewood Cliffs, NJ: Merrill, Prentice-Hall.

Regan, H. B., & Brooks, G. H. (1995). *Out of women's experience: Creating relational leadership*. Thousand Oaks, CA: Corwin Press.

Rost, J. C. (1991). *Leadership for the 21st century*. New York: Praeger.

Schön, D. A. (1983). *The reflective practitioner*. New York: Basic Books.

Schön, D. A. (1989). Professional knowledge and reflective practice. In T. J. Sergiovanni & J. H. Moore (Eds.), *Schooling for tomorrow: Directing reforms to issues that count* (pp. 188–206). Boston: Allyn and Bacon.

Schön, D. A. (1990). *Educating the reflective practitioner: Toward a new design for teaching and learning in the profession*. San Francisco: Jossey-Bass.

Schriesheim, C. S., House, R. J., & Kerr, S. (1976). Leader initiating structure: A reconciliation of discrepant research results and some empirical tests. *Organizational Behavior and Human Performance, 15,* 197–321.

Sergiovanni, T. J. (2001). *The principalship: A reflective practice perspective* (4th ed.). Boston: Allyn and Bacon.

Shakeshaft, C. (1999). The struggle to create a more gender-inclusive profession. In J. Murphy & K. Seashore Louis (Eds.), *Handbook of research on educational administration* (2nd ed.) (pp. 99–118). San Francisco: Jossey-Bass.

Stodgill, R. M., & Coons, A. E. (1957). *Leader behavior: Its description and measurement*. Columbus, OH: Bureau of Business Research, The Ohio State University.

Tyack, D. (1990). Restructuring in historical perspective: Tinkering toward utopia. *Teachers College Record, 92*(2), 170–191.

Tyack, D., & Hansot, E. (1982). *Managers of virtue: Public school leadership in America, 1820–1980*. New York: Basic Books.

Vroom, V. H., & Yetton, P. W. (1973). *Leadership and decision-making*. Pittsburgh: University of Pittsburgh Press.

Weiler, H. N. (1990). Compartive perspectives on educational decentralization: An exercise in contradiction? *Educational Evaluation and Policy Analysis, 12*(4), 433–448.

Wynn, T., & Guditus, C. W. (1984). *Team management: Leadership by consensus*. Englewood Cliffs, NJ: Prentice-Hall.

Yukl, G. A. (1989). *Leadership in organizations* (2nd ed.). Englewood Cliffs, NJ: Prentice-Hall.

Zaleznik, A. (1989). *The managerial mystique: Restoring leadership in business*. New York: Harper and Row.

10

Behavior, Decision Making, and Reflective Practice

Chapter Content

The previous chapter provided information that demonstrated how administrative behavior could be influenced by organizational strategies and individual styles. Students preparing to be practitioners often ask: How will I know if my style will be effective? This cogent question does not lend itself to a simple and direct answer. As demonstrated in the previous chapter, the effectiveness of strategies and styles depends partially on contextual variables (i.e., the conditions under which they are used). This fact explains why a principal who has been highly successful in one school can be an utter failure in another school even though he or she uses identical strategies and styles. Inflexible administrators eventually encounter situations when their tried and true behaviors do not produce positive results—and they often are bewildered when this happens. The failure to make appropriate behavioral adaptations is often caused by narrow perspectives of administration (e.g., believing that there is only one right way to do things) and an inability to relate problems to context in order to select appropriate behaviors (Kowalski, 2001).

Administrative behavior would be a less complex topic if strategy and style decisions were simply a matter of personal preference. This is not the case, however. There are a number of forces that push and shove practitioners to mold their behavior, and often, these forces are not recognized or are misunderstood. For example, the formal organization (e.g., school board), the informal organization (e.g., teacher coalitions), and the community (e.g., political pressure groups) almost always are able to exert influence over administrative behavior because of the political nature of schools.

This chapter examines three additional topics that should help you understand administrative behavior. The first is descriptive behavior paradigms—that is, models that provide explanations of why administrators behave in certain ways. The second is decision making. Since decisions are the nucleus of administrative activity, the manner in which they are made is an essential component of administrative behavior. Last, this chapter addresses the potential effects of experience. More precisely, the process of reflective practice is explained and advocated as a mechanism for personal and professional growth.

Descriptive Models of Administrative Behavior

What causes administrators to be autocratic or democratic or directive or nondirective? In some instances, behavior is the product of conscious choices based on both theoretical knowledge and accumulated wisdom. But as noted in the previous chapter, research has repeatedly revealed that administrators rarely determine style on the basis of normative models. Given this reality, scholars have been intensely interested in explaining administrative behavior. Their inquiries have produced several valuable theories.

Personal Needs and Dispositions

Initial efforts to understand administrative behavior focused on personal variables. For example, researchers in the first half of the twentieth century often examined possible relationships between administrative styles and personality traits. In general, these efforts failed to establish a nexus between personal traits and successful practice, but they did serve to reveal that an administrator with certain traits could be effective in one situation and ineffective in another (Yukl, 1989).

Since the 1960s, one of the most widely used models in administration across all disciplines has been Douglass McGregor's *Theory X* and *Theory Y*. Influenced by content theories of motivation, McGregor (1990a, 1990b) concluded that managerial strategies and styles were largely the product of the views managers had of their subordinates. He divided managers into two categories based on their fundamental dispositions toward workers. The first group's disposition was called Theory X and it was predicated on the following assumptions about the average worker:

- Most workers have a negative disposition toward work and will try to avoid it when possible.
- Most workers are not especially intelligent, and therefore a manager can easily lead them.

- Most workers must be forced to work and then they must be closely supervised.
- Most workers want to be directed by someone in authority because this alleviates responsibility for making decisions (McGregor, 1990a).

The second group's disposition was called Theory Y and it was predicated on opposite assumptions about the average worker.

- Most workers view work as a natural activity; any negative views about work are attributable to past experiences and not to innate characteristics.
- Most workers can be highly committed to organizational objectives if they are motivated and rewarded properly.
- Most workers seek and accept responsibility if conditions in the organization are favorable (McGregor, 1990b).

According to Theory X, administrators are task oriented, autocratic, and highly directive. According to Theory Y, administrators are more flexible; they attempt to balance tasks with relationships, balance organizational and personal goals, and empower employees by giving them greater autonomy (e.g., either through decentralizing governance or through delegation of tasks and responsibility).

Personal and Situational Variables

Most theorists reject the conclusion that individual beliefs or characteristics are the sole determinants of administrative strategies and styles. Instead, they believe that these factors are influenced by a combination of role expectations and individual personality. Over the last half century, the model developed by Jacob Getzels and Egon Guba (1957) has been used consistently in relation to this perspective. It identifies two dimensions of work in a social system: the nomothetic and the idiographic. The *nomothetic* dimension represents the school's normative expectations shaped by the school's history and culture, formal roles, and resultant role expectations. The *idiographic* dimension represents personal dispositions that include the individual, the individual's personality, and the individual's need dispositions (i.e., what the individual needs to achieve from work). According to the model, administrative preferences for strategy and style are an intricate mix of the two dimensions. Thus, administrative behavior is viewed as being a function of institutional role (defined by the expectations it produces) and the personality of a role incumbent (defined by the person's need dispositions). Getzels (1958) expressed this relationship by using the following formula:

$$B = f(R \times P)$$

where B = observed behavior
       R = institutional role
       P = personality of the role incumbent

The mix of personality and institutional role varies both among and within types of organizations. For example, some organizations provide little leeway for the personal dimension to affect behavior; being an officer in the military is an example. By comparison, other organizations impose relatively few role expectations, allowing the individual considerable leeway to self-determine behavior; being a design architect in an architectural firm is an example. Role expectations for school administrators are not uniform largely because local districts are not all alike. Whereas some districts impose many role expectations on principals, others impose relatively few.

Getzels's views of administrative behavior were subsequently expanded to include two additional dimensions: organizational culture (Getzels & Thelen, 1960) and communities (Getzels, 1978). The *organizational culture* dimension addresses the ethos of the organization as expressed by the shared values of the individuals in it. Administrators, like all other employees, are subjected to socialization; that is, they are pressured to accept shared values and beliefs—even when those values and beliefs are in conflict with the prescribed organizational role or individual need dispositions. The *communities* dimension addresses the potential influence of stakeholder groups that hold common cognitive and affective norms and values. These norms and values are expressed via the various ways in which the communities interact with the district or school.

Given the range of potential influences, leadership style is indeed a complex issue. Administrators must reconcile potential conflicts among needs and expectations that may emanate from the following sources:

- Personal needs and dispositions
- Organizational role expectations
- Organizational culture norms
- Norms, values, and expectations embedded in various stakeholder communities

Reconciling differences and making appropriate adaptations to them depend largely on two conditions: the administrator's ability to recognize when adaptations are necessary and the administrator's willingness to be flexible.

Value of Descriptive Models

Assume that a principal does not devote sufficient time to instructional leadership activities and his or her superintendent wants to take positive action to correct the situation. Descriptive theories provide the superintendent with a framework for identifying potential variables that may be affecting this principal's behavior—variables such as personal needs and dispositions, formal role expectations, school culture norms, parental expectations, and the influence of outside pressure groups. However, descriptive theories do not provide the superintendent with information about the extent to which each of these variables is responsible for the behavior in question. The superintendent would have to probe deeper to acquire this information by studying the principal and contextual variables.

Students often misinterpret the use of theoretical models. Instead of viewing them as tools, some expect theory to provide precise and foolproof answers. In the case of administrative behavior, descriptive models may not be infallible for the following reasons:

- Administrators do not share a common set of need dispositions; therefore, making generalizations about individual characteristics is precarious.
- Contextual variables are not constant across communities, districts, schools, and problems.
- Since contextual variables are not static, conditions surrounding the behavior of an administrator may be different from day to day.

Descriptive models of behavior also help us understand the primary forms of conflict that occur in an administrator's life. For example, James Lipham (1988) noted that the Getzels-Guba model helped clarify the following:

- *Role-personality conflict:* Conflict caused by differences between the administrator's needs-dispositions and the organization's role expectations
- *Role conflict:* Conflict caused by differences in the role expectations expressed by various individuals and groups in and out of the organization (e.g., differences between the expectations expressed in the formal job description and those expressed by teachers through the school's culture)
- *Personality conflict:* Conflict caused by the administrator having opposing needs and dispositions (e.g., the administrator has a need to be both controlling and well liked)

Models also may help us see how misinterpretations of role expectations, needs, and dispositions can be another source of conflict. For example, conflict can be generated when the superintendent and a principal interpret the same job description in different ways.

Administration and Decision Making

Another aspect of the complexity of administrative behavior is the nature of decision making. Every phase of administrative responsibility involves making choices. Some of them are relatively simple and unimportant, such as deciding whether to write a letter today or tomorrow. Others are difficult and may have lifelong consequences, such as deciding whether to recommend a teacher for dismissal. Given the pervasive nature of decision making in administrative work, both normative and descriptive models have been developed to guide practice.

Rational Models

Traditionally, decision-making research has been predicated on the dual assumptions that it is an orderly, rational process of choosing from alternative means of accomplishing objectives and that the process is logical and sequential (Owens, 2001). Rational models are normative in that they prescribe a "scientific" approach to making decisions and they are reflective of the tenets of classical theory. Such models are built on the following assumptions:

- Administrators can and will be rational when making decisions.
- Administrators can and will be unbiased when making decisions.
- Administrators can identify and evaluate all alternative solutions, making it possible for them to select the ideal decision.

Although there are multiple rational models, Daniel Griffiths (1959) suggested that generically they should include the following activities:

- Recognizing, defining, and limiting the problem
- Analyzing and evaluating the problem
- Establishing criteria or standards for judging whether a solution is acceptable
- Collecting data
- Formulating and selecting a preferred solution and testing it
- Putting a preferred solution into effect

Peter Drucker's model (1974), one of the most widely recognized, contains the following steps:

- Defining the problem
- Analyzing the problem
- Developing alternative solutions
- Deciding on the best solution
- Converting the decision into actions

The primary advantage of rational models is that they provide a linear recipe that is easy to follow; this fact alone often makes them attractive to administrators. Nevertheless, rational models are far from perfect, primarily because their foundational assumptions are not valid. For example, Herbert Simon (1957) argued that in order to make objectively rational decisions, an individual must

- View all decision alternatives in panoramic fashion prior to making a decision
- Consider all consequences that would follow each choice
- Assign values to each alternative and select one alternative from the set

Simon (1957) added that actual behavior falls short in at least three ways:

1. Rationality requires a choice from among all alternatives when in actuality only a few of the alternatives come to mind.

2. Rationality requires a complete knowledge of all the consequences that will follow each choice when in actuality knowledge of consequences is only fragmentary.
3. Values attached to consequences can only be imperfectly anticipated.

In districts and schools, assumptions underlying rational models are attenuated by conditions such as these:

- The political nature of contextual variables reduces rationality and objectivity (Slater & Boyd, 1999). This interference is often referred to as *contextual rationality* (March & Simon, 1993)—recognition that administrative decisions are affected by a myriad of influences in and outside of the school.
- Administrators rarely have complete information, an exhaustive list of alternative solutions, or totally unbiased dispositions (Browne, 1993). Thus, decisions in school districts are usually made in the context of mixed motives, ambiguities, and limited information—characteristics that lessen the potential effectiveness of rational paradigms.

Studies of administrative behavior revealed that decision makers made less than ideal decisions, even when they followed linear models. Their failure to make the ideal decision was largely attributable to the fact that they did not have sufficient time and resources to apply the model as intended. In addition, decision makers often did not frame the problem correctly nor did they have access to complete information (Zey, 1992). These problems led to the development of *bounded rational models*.

Although bounded models retain linearity, they are constructed on the assumptions that decision makers are not totally unbiased, that they do not have access to complete information, and that they rarely make ideal decisions. These core assumptions promote the idea of *satisficing*. James March and Herbert Simon (1958) described this concept as "the difference between searching a haystack to find the sharpest needle in it and searching the haystack to find a needle sharp enough to sew with" (pp. 140–141). In essence, satisficing involves the tendency of decision makers to select something less than ideal (Hellreigel & Slocum, 1996). Therefore, bounded models reflect recognition of the following conditions:

- Complete information is not typically available to the decision maker.
- Decisions are usually made in the context of conflicting values and interests.
- Bias rarely can be eliminated.
- Administrators often make decisions by selecting the first available satisfactory course of action rather than endlessly pursuing the ideal course of action.

In summary, bounded models prescribe an orderly approach yet recognize that uncertainty, values, competing interests, and biases affect the outcomes.

Ethical Models

Like rational models, ethical models are normative. But rather than being guided by assumptions of rationality and objectivity, ethical models are guided by moral and professional standards. They are premised on the belief that administrative decisions are more than factual propositions in that they include preferences for achieving desired conditions (Simon, 1997). For example, eliminating prejudice from public schools prompts administrators to meld moral judgments (e.g., treating every one as equals) and factual information.

Ethical administration is rooted in values. These values may be personal or part of a shared moral code (e.g., a code of ethics for an administrative group). They provide an administrator with a structured rationale for making decisions (Hitt, 1990). In an ethical framework, administrators are encouraged to balance the interests of society, students, employees, and the organization (district or school) rather than making politically expedient decisions favorable to the organization, powerful individuals or groups, or decision maker. Kenneth Blanchard and Norman Vincent Peale (1988) proposed a simple mechanism for determining whether a decision is ethical:

- Is the decision legal?
- Is the decision balanced?
- How will the decision make me feel about myself? (p. 27)

In school administration, ethical decisions extend beyond legal considerations to include areas such as abuses of power, discrimination, nepotism, violating confidentiality, and playing politics for purposes of self-interest (Howlett, 1991). Ethical decision-making models encourage administrators to examine their thoughts and feelings about the nature of schools and their work in them (Mitchell & Tucker, 1992). That is, they direct attention to what schools are all about and the way schools should ideally function in a democratic society.

Participatory Models

A third normative model focuses on shared decision making. Like ethical decision making, values and beliefs drive participatory models. This is especially true with regard to determining the role teachers and community representatives should play in school governance. The following four beliefs are foundational to participatory models (Estler, 1988):

- Participation leads to increased productivity.
- Administrators need to consider both ethics and individuals when making decisions.
- The decision-making process of a school should reflect the values of a democratic society.
- Participation increases employee consciousness with respect to their rights.

In addition, group decision making can broaden information, knowledge, and skills that affect the problem in question.

Two of the more common methods for making participatory decisions are consensus and voting. The former requires participants to agree on a common decision—a process that usually requires some degree of negotiation. The latter is more direct, easier to use, and quicker, but it results in winners and losers—an outcome that often creates political problems for implementing the decision.

Both advantages and disadvantages have been suggested for participatory decision making. The presumed advantages include

- A broader spectrum of viewpoints results in better decisions.
- An educational experience is provided for the participants (those involved are exposed to both information and process).
- Support for the decision is enhanced (the participants typically develop a sense of ownership).
- The range of knowledge and skills is increased (the capabilities of the group almost always outweigh the individual administrator's capabilities).
- Involvement in decision making is motivating for the participant because he or she is able to express creativity and initiative (Owens, 2001).

The presumed disadvantages include

- The process is often inefficient (it usually requires more time than autocratic decisions).
- There is a tendency to make mediocre decisions in favor of group cohesion (the group members care more about getting along with each other or appeasing the administrator than they do about the quality of their work) (Reitz, 1987).
- Just one or two influential group members are often responsible for the making the decision (some group members are intimidated and do not participate in the intended fashion) (Janis, 1982).
- Groups are often prone to expressing biases and committing errors, as are individual decision makers (Carroll & Johnson, 1990).
- There is little evidence to support claims that group decision making yields political benefits (e.g., heightened support) (Conway, 1984).

Participatory decision making has increased in popularity over the past several decades. One reason is political philosophy; many citizens favor liberty-driven provisions for school reform, such as site-based management. Another reason is professional convictions; administrators believe that broader participation can lead to improved decisions and the process is congruous with teacher professionalization. Still another reason is practical politics; broad participation increases the likelihood of support for the decision.

Political Models

Political models are basically descriptive in that they reveal how decisions are often made in schools, but they also can be normative in that they encourage administrators to act politically. Rather than being rational, objective, and focusing on organizational goal achievement, many administrative decisions are shaped by self-interests or special-group interests (Estler, 1988). That is, individuals and groups compete for scarce resources that can be used to satisfy their needs and wants. Often, they have sufficient power to influence administrative decisions.

Every decision faced by a school administrator has four dimensions: students, employees, the organization (school or district), and the community. Normative approaches suggest that administrators should give equal consideration to each dimension by objectively examining evidence and making a rationale decision. But in the real world of school administration, this often does not occur because the political power of each dimension is unequal. Consider a highly transactional principal who receives a request from a teacher to take a personal leave day the Friday before spring break starts. District policy prohibits teachers from using this benefit either on the day before or the day after a scheduled vacation. The teacher in question, however, is the union president. The principal knows that finding a way to grant the request—even if it must be done dishonestly—is likely to produce a personal political benefit. Without considering the potential effects on the organization (e.g., setting precedent) or on students (e.g., not ending a key unit properly before the break), she advises the teacher to sidestep the policy by reporting that he is ill instead of using a personal leave day. Her decision to resolve the issue in this manner is purely political (and unethical).

Although local school districts may have bureaucratic designs, they actually function as social and political entities in which power and authority are shared and distributed among various formal and informal groups (Hanson, 1996). Political influences on decision making are evidenced by the following (Giesecke, 1993):

- Districts and schools are usually loosely coupled organizations; that is, many individuals and groups act independently.
- Administrators assess the real distribution of power so that they know when and with whom they can bargain.
- Bargaining, coalition building, and incremental strategies are common strategies when difficult decisions must be made.

Balancing ethical values and political realities is one of the most difficult assignments faced by administrators.

Garbage Can Model

Observing how decisions are really made in schools, researchers have noted that in many instances solutions actually precede problems. How is this possible? At any given time, organizations, including schools, are like a container (garbage can) holding three critical elements: preferred solutions, problems, and fluid participation (Cohen, March, & Olsen, 1972). When events create opportunities for change (called *choice opportunities* within this model), a preferred solution and a particular problem find a sponsor. "That is, a participant, or a coalition of participants, decides to use extensive time and energy to promote a particular solution to a specific problem. That participant or coalition may prevail because other participant sponsoring other problems and solutions reduce their participation and drop out from involvement all together" (Hanson, 1996, p. 144). The shifting involvement of people constitutes the fluid participation.

Several prevalent conditions in districts and schools lead administrators to make decisions in the manner described by the garbage can model. Foremost among them are the presence of ambiguous and often competing goals. As noted earlier in the book, the public embraces many purposes for education and this condition contributes to substantial confusion regarding the parameters of effective education. Hence, each district and school must establish clearly defined goals and criteria for measuring their attainment—and many districts and schools have not done so. In the absence of a widely accepted vision and long-range objectives, administrators and other decision makers often apply their favored solutions to problems when conditions provide them with this opportunity.

Consider a principal who wants to implement block scheduling in a high school. Knowing that there is likely to be considerable resistance or indifference to her idea, she waits until a choice opportunity occurs. When the scores on the state-mandated achievement tests fall below expected levels, she seizes the opportunity to promote block scheduling as a preferred solution; and other individuals and coalitions supporting other problems and solutions retreat.

The garbage can model is another depiction of what really occurs in schools. As a descriptive model, it shows that administrative decisions are not always objective, linear, and rational. Rather, decisions are often predicated on a solution in search for a problem that can be implemented when conditions are favorable.

Reflective Practice

Earlier, administrative behavior was described as a product of individual personality and role expectations; although organizational culture and external communities affect administrative behavior, their influence falls within the parameters of these two broad categories. In professions, practitioners also are expected to shape their behavior using the knowledge base they have acquired through formal study and experience. Thus, professional knowledge is an ideal intervening variable (see Figure 10.1).

However, components of the professional knowledge base, theory and artistry, are viewed, acquired, and used in different ways by administrators.

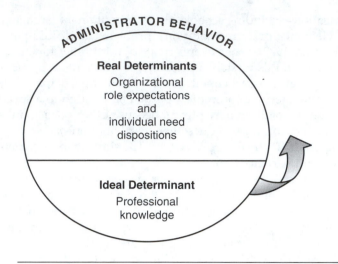

FIGURE 10.1   *Ideal and Real Determinants of Administrator Behavior*

Thomas Sergiovanni (2001) has noted that principals tend to fall into three broad categories in this regard:

- Those who treat administration as a nonscience (These principals reject the value of theory and research and rely on tacit knowledge, intuition, and more transcendental factors.)
- Those who treat administration as an applied science (These principals believe that theory and research are linearly linked to practice.)
- Those who view administration as a craftlike science (These principals believe that practice is characterized by interacting reflection and action episodes.)

Whereas the first group errs in rejecting all scientific knowledge, the second group errs in the opposite direction, because they assume that known scientific or technical solutions will resolve their problems. Increasingly, scholars conclude that the most effective practitioners are those who treat administration as a craftlike science, because both their knowledge and artistry are essential to good practice, especially when problems defy textbook solutions.

Donald Schön (1983) has promoted the concept of professional reflection as a means for dealing with the reality that more than technical knowledge is necessary to resolve complex and ambiguous problems found in all professions. He identified three intermediate zones of practice:

1. *Uncertainty:* Problems faced by administrators do not always occur as well-informed structures.
2. *Uniqueness:* Problems faced by administrators often are not discussed in textbooks.

3. *Value conflict:* Solutions often are supported by individuals and groups holding conflicting values.

In addition, the context of problems is critically important for school administrators, because effective solutions often depend on context analysis (i.e., accurately evaluating the conditions under which a problem occurs and is addressed) (Erlandson, 1992).

As professionals engage in the daily routine actions of their practice, they frequently cannot describe how they know what to do next or why they take the actions they do. They are guided by an embedded, tacit knowledge of their practice. Occasionally, however, they must improvise or modify their routine actions in response to external stimuli. For example, teachers make on-the-spot adjustments in their lesson plans or their line of questioning, based on immediately prior student responses. When this occurs, the professional is engaging in *reflection in action*. Schön (1987) differentiated between "knowing in action" and "reflecting in action." The former is embedded in theoretical knowledge; the latter represents artistry that becomes critically important when problems and challenges are unique and less than rational. Artistry is developed through experience, especially when administrators take the time to mentally evaluate the extent to which their actions were effective. Over time, professionals encounter certain types or elements of situations on a recurring basis. They build an implicit repertoire of techniques and strategies for responding to them. Simultaneously, they develop mental images of expected outcomes. When things go as planned and expected results materialize, no further thought is given to the event. However, occasionally surprises occur. Expected results do not materialize as they had previously in seemingly similar situations. These unexpected results trigger both reflection in action and reflection on action, causing the individual to think about what is causing the unanticipated consequences, both as they are occurring and later after the heat of the moment has dissipated. The individual begins to evaluate contextual variables, attempting to determine the unique dimensions of the most recent experience.

Reflective practice, however, entails more than casual thoughts about work experiences. It is the application of experiential learning—a process that involves four stages: (1) having an experience, (2) making observations of and reflecting on the experience, (3) abstractly reconceptualizing based on the experience, and (4) engaging in experimentation (Kolb, 1984). Done properly, reflection not only guides problem solving but it also helps administrators develop problem-finding skills.

Consider the reflective practice heuristic shown in Figure 10.2. It addresses the examination of an event, and the thoughts that occurred prior to, during, and after the event. Imagine that a middle school principal is considering how to deal with a first-year teacher who often arrives several minutes late for her first-period class. The teacher's performance in other areas is very promising. The principal's thoughts and actions related to this matter are separated into three frames. The first contains (1) the principal's plan for how he intends to deal with this problem and (2) the principal's personal thoughts during planning. In many cases, this

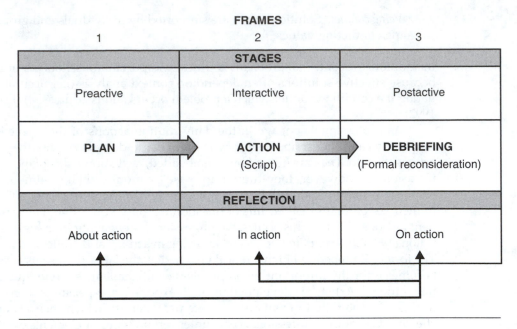

FIGURE 10.2   *A Heuristic Model for Reflective Practice*
Source: Adapted from Cornett (1990) and Reitzug and Cornett (1991).

planning period consists of only a few seconds or minutes; for example, the principal is immersed in other problems or he simply is not prone to planning his actions. In other cases, principals may spend considerable time in this frame before they act; for example, the principal may want to consider alternatives for at least several days before acting.

The second frame contains a "script" of the actual encounter between the principal and the teacher. It contains not only audio and visual images of what occurred but also the principal's mental images. For example, how did the principal perceive the teacher was reacting to their meeting? Did the teacher appear to be concerned and committed to eliminating the problem?

The third frame contains the principal's thoughts about the action after it has occurred; that is, it involves debriefing. The frame includes spontaneous reactions (e.g., the principal's immediate reaction about the effectiveness of his action) and deeper reflections about the matter. These deeper reflections involve purposefully integrating thoughts and insights about his actions in the first two frames with the outcome after more than just his impressions are available as evidence (e.g., the principal is able to observe whether the teacher has started arriving on time or he receives feedback from the teacher's department chair).

A variety of other more specific factors can be examined during the debriefing that occurs in frame 3. For example, the principal could examine whether role contextual factors and personal beliefs had affected his behavior in this matter. This activity is usually productive because factors such as community locale, socioeconomic status, ethnic composition of the community, transience, level of parental support, institutional resources, and personal beliefs and experiences often influence administrative behavior (Dwyer, Barnett, & Lee, 1987). While considering this broader range of variables, the principal might ask himself the following role, personality, and knowledge base questions:

- *Institutional role:* Did I consider community and institutional factors before acting? If so, which ones? Which factors actually influenced my behavior and to what extent? Were there other unique circumstances that affected by decision? To what extent has this experience changed the weight that I will give to variables in the future?
- *Personal need dispositions:* What personal beliefs and needs affected my actions? Were these beliefs congruent with my espoused beliefs? Were my personal needs congruent with my role expectations? To what extent did my personal beliefs or needs take precedent over my espoused beliefs or organizational role expectations? To what extent has this experience altered my personal beliefs or needs?
- *Knowledge base:* What elements of the professional knowledge base were cogent to this issue? To what extent were my beliefs and needs congruent with the knowledge base? To what extent were my role expectations congruent with the knowledge base? To what extent were my actions congruent with the professional knowledge base? Did my knowledge base change as a result of this experience, and if so, how?

During the debriefing, the principal also could restate the problem and develop alternative solutions that he did not consider initially. The following are questions he might ask at this point:

- *The problem statement:* Did I begin by defining the problem? If so, did I define accurately? If not, what problems were created by this omission? Could the problem have been defined differently? Did I realize that the manner in which I framed the problem was going to affect my behavior? Looking back, how would I frame the problem now?
- *Alternative decisions or actions:* Was my action appropriate in relation to the problem? Did my action produce the intended outcome? Did I develop and evaluate alternative solutions? If not, why not? Given the nature of the problem, were there alternative solutions that I did not consider? What were these alternatives? Why didn't I consider them?

This more formal postevent reflection is essential if the principal is to maximize the potential for professional growth. Even occasional formal reflection is likely to be beneficial.

Unfortunately, many administrators do not engage in formal reflection. As noted earlier, some express the disposition that professional knowledge has no value. Others view reflection as too time consuming; for them, the cost-benefit ratio does not justify the process. In both instances, these individuals fail to view administration as a profession and to view themselves as professionals. True professionals engage in continuous learning and grow intellectually as a result. As Schön (1987) observed, the most effective practitioners in every profession are those who grow through experience; as a consequence, their knowledge base is dynamic and their artistry empowers them to deal with unique and highly complex problems.

Implications for Practice

This chapter examined descriptive models of administrative behavior, decision making, and reflective practice. Each of these topics is relevant to understanding how administrators behave, especially in relation to the choices they make.

First, you should understand how the study of administrative behavior evolved. Initially, it was thought to be a matter of personal needs and dispositions. When the importance of situational variables became obvious, efforts were made to integrate organizational expectations with personal needs and dispositions. Organizational culture and external communities that can influence education were subsequently added to the list of primary variables.

Second, you should be aware of the importance of decision making to school administration. Decision-making models provide a mechanism for describing, explaining, understanding, and directing practitioner behavior. Unfortunately, some administrators either have not studied them or they have chosen not to use them. An understanding of decision-making models will broaden your understanding of administrative behavior and better prepare you to act in difficult situations.

Third, you should understand how professional reflection cultivates artistry. Some administrators capitalize on experience and use it to enhance their professional growth; these practitioners are prone to see every challenge and every decision as somewhat unique. Other administrators ignore the value of experience; these practitioners usually exhibit routine and highly predicable behavior. Clearly, the former are better prepared to deal with complex and unstructured problems.

For Further Discussion

1. How do individual needs and dispositions affect administrative behavior?

2. What is likely to occur when an individual's personal needs and beliefs are incongruous with the role expectations of his or her employing organization?

3. Do you think it is possible for individuals to modify their leadership style based on situational factors, or do you feel that leadership style is ingrained, similar to one's personality? Explain your answer.

4. Is it possible for an administrator to have two needs that are in conflict with each other? Why or why not?

5. What do you feel are the key contextual factors that inform which leadership style is most appropriate for a situation?

6. How does school culture differ from organizational role expectations? How might culture affect administrator behavior?

7. What are the differences between rational decision-making models and bounded models?

8. What are the assumptions underlying rational decision making? Do you agree or disagree with these assumptions?

9. To what extent are ethical decision making and political decision making compatible?

10. Some administrators reject the value of theoretical knowledge and research. What is likely to guide the behavior of these administrators?

11. Some administrators are guided entirely by technical knowledge (models and theory). Is this a problem? Why or why not?

12. What is reflective practice? How does it promote artistry? How does it promote professional growth?

Other Suggested Activities

1. Discuss administrators with whom you have worked. To what extent were they guided by technical knowledge or intuition?

2. When a principal accepts an assignment in a new school, he or she is likely to be unfamiliar with that school's culture. Discuss ways that the new principal might discover the basic values and beliefs of that culture.

3. Discuss the decision-making models that were presented in this chapter. Identify the models that are most congruous with your own values and beliefs.

4. A distinction was made in the chapter between *reflection on action* and *reflection in action*. Outline the differences between the two.

5. If an administrator does not engage in reflection, what is likely to be the effect of experience on professional practice? Discuss the range of answers generated by this question.

6. Use the reflective practice heuristic shown in Figure 10.2 to study your teaching or administrative decision making in relation to a recent problem or challenge.

References

Blanchard, K. H., & Peale, N. V. (1988). *The power of ethical management*. New York: John Wiley & Sons.

Browne, M. (1993). *Organizational decision making and information*. Norwood, NJ: Ablex.

Carroll, J. S., & Johnson, E. J. (1990). *Decision research: A field guide*. Newbury Park, CA: Sage.

Cohen, M. D., March, J. G., & Olsen, J. P. (1972). A garbage can model of organizational choice. *Administrative Science Quarterly, 17*(1), 1–25.

Conway, J. A. (1984). The myth, mystery, and mastery of participative decision making in education. *Educational Administration Quarterly, 20*(3), 11–40.

Cornett, J. W. (1990). Utilizing action research in graduate curriculum courses. *Theory into Practice, 29*(3), 185–195.

Drucker, P. F. (1974). *Management: Tasks, responsibilities, practices.* New York: HarperBusiness.

Dwyer, D. C., Barnett, B. G., & Lee, G. V. (1987). The school principal: Scapegoat or the last great hope? In L. T. Sheive & M. B. Schoenheit (Eds.), *Leadership: Examining the elusive* (pp. 30–46). Reston, VA: Association for Supervision and Curriculum Development.

Erlandson, D. A. (1992). The power of context. *Journal of School Leadership, 2*(1), 66–74.

Estler, S. (1988). Decision-making. In N.J. Boyan (Ed.), *Handbook of research in educational administration* (pp. 305–319). White Plains, NY: Longman.

Getzels, J. W. (1958). Administration as a social process. In A. W. Halpin (Ed.), *Administrative theory in education* (pp. 150–165). New York: Macmillan.

Getzels, J. W. (1978). The communities of education. *Teachers College Record, 79,* 659–682.

Getzels, J. W., & Guba, E. G. (1957). Social behavior and the administrative process. *School Review, 65,* 423–441.

Getzels, J. W., & Thelen, H. A. (1960). The classroom as a social system. In N. B. Henry (Ed.), *The dynamics of instructional groups* (pp. 53–83). Chicago: University of Chicago Press.

Giesecke, J. (1993). Recognizing multiple decision-making models: A guide for managers. *College & Research Libraries, 54*(2), 103–114.

Griffiths, D. E. (1959). *Administrative theory.* New York: Appleton-Century-Crofts.

Hanson, E. M. (1996). *Educational administration and organizational behavior* (4th ed.). Boston: Allyn and Bacon.

Hellreigel, D., & Slocum, J. W. (1996). *Management* (7th ed.). Cincinnati: Southwestern College Publishing.

Hitt, W. D. (1990). *Ethics and leadership: Putting theory into practice.* Columbus, OH: Battelle Press.

Howlett, P. (1991). How you can stay on the straight and narrow. *Executive Educator, 13*(2), 9–21, 35.

Janis, I. L. (1982). *Groupthink: Psychological studies of policy decisions and fiascoes* (2nd ed.). Boston: Houghton Mifflin.

Kolb, D. A. (1984). *Experiential learning: Experience as the source of learning and development.* Englewood Cliffs, NJ: Prentice-Hall.

Kowalski, T. J. (2001). *Case studies on educational administration* (3rd ed.). New York: Longman.

Lipham, J. M. (1988). Getzels's models in educational administration. In N. J. Boyan (Ed.), *Handbook of research on educational administration* (pp. 171–184). New York: Longman.

March, J. G., & Simon, H. (1958). *Organizations.* New York: John Wiley.

March, J. G., & Simon, H. (1993). *Organizations* (2nd ed.). Cambridge, MA: Blackwell Publications.

McGregor, D. (1990a). Theory X: The integration of individual and organizational goals. In J. Hall (Ed.), *Models of management: The structure of competence* (2nd ed.) (pp. 11–18). Woodlands, TX: Woodstead Press.

McGregor, D. (1990b). Theory Y: The integration of individual and organizational goals. In J. Hall (Ed.), *Models of management: The structure of competence* (2nd ed.) (pp. 19–27). Woodlands, TX: Woodstead Press.

Mitchell, D. E., & Tucker, S. (1992). Leadership as a way of thinking. *Educational Leadership, 49*(5), 30–35.

Owens, R. G. (2001). *Organizational behavior in education* (6th ed.). Boston: Allyn and Bacon.

Reitz, H. J. (1987). *Behavior in organizations* (3rd ed.). Homewood, IL: Irwin.

Reitzug, U. C., & Cornett, J. W. (1991). Teacher and administrator thought: Implications for administrator training. *Planning and Changing, 21*(3), 181–192.

Schön, D. A. (1983). *The reflective practitioner*. New York: Basic Books.

Schön, D. A. (1987). *Educating the reflective practitioner: Toward a new design for teaching and learning in the profession*. San Francisco: Jossey-Bass.

Sergiovanni, T. J. (2001). *The principalship: A reflective practice perspective* (4th ed.). Boston: Allyn and Bacon.

Simon, H. A. (1957). *The new science of management decisions*. New York: Harper.

Simon, H. A. (1997). *Administrative behavior: A study of decision-making processes in administrative organizations* (4th ed.). New York: Simon & Schuster.

Slater, R. O., & Boyd, W. L. (1999). Schools as polities. In J. Murphy & K. Seashore Louis (Eds.), *Handbook of research on educational administration* (2nd ed.) (pp. 323–336). San Francisco: Jossey-Bass.

Yukl, G. A. (1989). *Leadership in organization* (2nd ed.). Englewood Cliffs, NJ: Prentice-Hall.

Zey, M. (1992). *Decision making: Alternatives to rational choice models*. Thousand Oaks, CA: Sage.

11

Important Aspects of Practice

Certain facets of leadership and management are found in all organizational settings. This chapter examines four that are especially important in education institutions. The first, *motivation,* has become increasingly essential in the current environment of school reform, because organizational change in general and decentralization strategies in particular require administrators to understand human behavior. For example, knowledge of concepts such as drives, needs, and expectations help administrators in building shared visions and in restructuring schools accordingly.

The second topic, *communication*, took on new importance when the United States first moved from being a manufacturing society to an information-based society. Today, modern technologies allow superintendents and principals to access and use large quantities of information; this allows them to identify and solve problems more quickly and accurately than in the past. Consequently, the potentialities of technology have served to redefine definitions of effective practice; however, communication has unfortunately remained one of the most neglected areas of study in school administration (Kowalski, 1998a).

The third process discussed in this chapter is one of the most perplexing for practitioners—the seemingly contradictory norms of political leadership and ethical leadership. For many administrators, practice includes an endless chain of situations in which they must choose between *doing the right thing* and *doing the expedient or personally beneficial thing*. The need to make such choices is rather common in public education, where local school boards are political sounding boards and administrators are the source of professional guidance.

Last, this chapter examines the need for administrators to *manage their time*. Often, administrators complain that their jobs are overwhelming—indeed, some spend 70 or more hours per week either at work or doing work-related tasks. Not managing time effectively frequently results in difficulties such as conflict between work and family obligations, neglect of complex but exceedingly important responsibilities, excessive levels of stress, and even decisions to leave administration. Yet, there are thousands of practitioners who are able to structure their time so as to minimize the negative effects of these problems.

Motivation

Organizations are formed when tasks needing to be accomplished are too complex for one individual to achieve (Argyris, 1964). Thus, all organizations exist to serve some purpose, and they are composed of more than one person. You should now recognize that individuals comprising the organization have their own needs, and these personal needs may or may not be in harmony with the organization's goals. When they are not, the administrator's task of directing people toward achieving the organization's purposes is especially challenging.

In striving for efficiency and accomplishment, organizations develop rules, regulations, standard operating procedures, and other mechanisms prescribing how individuals in the organization are expected to comport themselves. In districts and schools, these control mechanisms are found in policy manuals and teacher handbooks, and administrators are assigned the responsibility of enforcing them. Although this specific duty is well understood and straightforward, it is nevertheless a source of constant tension and conflict. This is because the organization's need for standardization and the employee's desire for autonomy are basically incompatible.

Chris Argyris (1957) has likened the relationship between employees and organizations to a developmental continuum from infancy to adulthood. He noted that the more formally structured the organization, the more its tendency is to force employees to be like infants (i.e., dependent and submissive). Adults, on the other hand, seek autonomy, independence, and control over their immediate worlds. Discussions in recent years about school site-based management and teacher empowerment have been based in part on efforts to establish greater congruence between the adult developmental needs of teachers and the way schools are governed.

Principals, superintendents, and other administrators face the challenge of motivating teachers and other employees when these individuals are not naturally inclined to fulfill the organization's needs. For example, a high school teacher's need to be autonomous may lead her to resist department-imposed policies that restrict the ways in which she can teach her classes. In classical theory, the resolution of this conflict is quite simple; only the organization's goals matter, so employees who disobey policies and rules should be replaced. In the case of the teacher, she would be told to follow the department rules or face disciplinary action or even dismissal. In the real world of education, however, many administrators do not treat teachers as if they were assembly line workers in a factory; and even those who do face legal and political realities that preclude the use of such coercion.

Understanding Motivation

Administrators study motivation so that they gain a deeper understanding of organizational behavior—knowledge essential to being able to influence people in a positive manner. There are a myriad of motivational theories that reflect two basic conceptualizations of motivation. The first view is represented by a cycle that describes motivation as the linear relationship among needs, drives, and incentives (see Figure 11.1). The second view is represented by motivational patterns—elements of observable behavior that describe motivation. These patterns include the following (Owens, 2001):

- *Direction:* The pattern of choices an individual makes when confronted with an array of possible alternatives

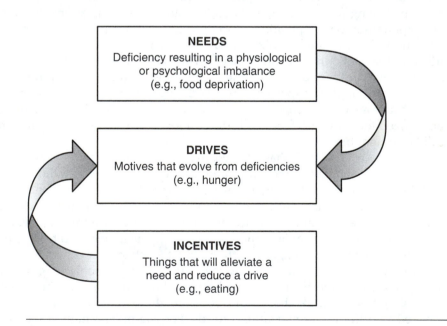

FIGURE 11.1 *The Motivation Cycle*

- *Persistence:* The perseverance exhibited in a particular behavior
- *Intensity:* The amount of effort or energy given to a particular behavior

Consider a teacher faced with the prospect that several students will fail his mathematics class unless their performance improves significantly. He has choices in responding to this concern. One of them is to do nothing more than remind the students that they are failing. Offering to tutor the students after school, giving them remedial homework assignments, and meeting with the parents are examples of other possible choices. The action the teacher selects indicates the direction of his behavior. Assume that he chooses to help the students after school but does so for only two weeks. The length of the activity indicates the persistence of his behavior. Perhaps he tutors the students for only two weeks, but he works intensely with them during this period—usually spending about two hours every day helping them. His behavior during these remedial sessions indicates the intensity of his behavior. Collectively, his decision to help the students and his subsequent behavior while helping them reveals the extent of his motivation.

In essence, motivation reveals why people are energized, activated, and directed to achieve certain goals. Mark Hanson (1996) noted that four essential questions are involved in analyzing motivation:

- What energizes human behavior?
- What directs or channels that behavior?
- How is that behavior sustained?
- How is that behavior terminated? (p. 195)

Because people in schools do not share the same motivations, either in degree or kind, administrative tactics do not have the same effect on people. Consequently, effective administrators use a variety of motivational techniques, recognizing that each individual is unique with respect to the extent that he or she must reconcile differences between school objectives and personal needs and dispositions. The choice of techniques should be guided by motivation theories. These tools are broadly divided into two categories—content theories and process theories—as shown in Figure 11.2.

Content Theories

"Content theories are based on the notion that things within us generate motivation" (Hanson, 1996, p. 195). According to content theories, all human beings possess the same categories of needs and drives, and these categories exist in a hierarchy of lower-level and higher-level needs.

One of the most widely recognized content theories is Maslow's *hierarchy of needs.* Abraham Maslow (1970) theorized that the behavior of individuals is motivated by a number of needs that range from basic physiological needs (food, clothing, and shelter) at the lowest level to self-actualization at the highest level. Intermediate-level needs are security and safety (physical and financial), social

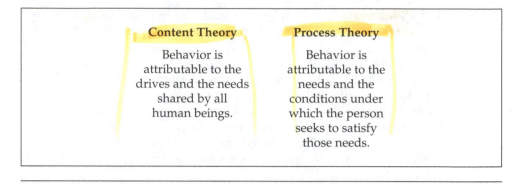

FIGURE 11.2   *Types of Motivation Theories*

affiliation (love, belonging, acceptance), and esteem. According to Maslow, once a need has been satisfied, it no longer serves as a motivator, with the next higher-level need becoming the primary motivator. For example, consider a teacher who seeks to become an administrator. She has fulfilled basic physiological needs and has achieved personal and professional acceptance by others that satisfies her need for social affiliation. Thus, her primary motivator is determined to be at the next level in the hierarchy—that is, she views administration as a means for achieving esteem or as a way of receiving peer recognition. In other cases, individuals seeking to be administrators may already have achieved adequate esteem as teachers; they may view becoming a principal as a way to achieve greater autonomy so that they have broadened opportunities for self-actualization.

Frederick Herzberg, Bernard Mausner, and Barbara Snyderman (1959) have provided a different conceptualization of job motivation, commonly referred to as Herzberg's *two-factor theory.* It stipulates that two separate sets of variables are responsible for motivation and employee satisfaction. These sets have been termed *motivators* and *hygiene factors.* Motivators include achievement, advancement, the work itself, growth, responsibility, and recognition. Hygiene factors include the work environment (e.g., the ecology of the workplace), the type of supervision, salary, job security, status, and attitudes and policies of superiors. Simply stated, improving hygiene factors causes employees to be less dissatisfied but does not motivate them to better job performance; only motivators can lead employees to perform better and feel more job satisfaction (see Figure 11.3). Thus, hygiene factors are thought to affect behavior between dissatisfaction and no dissatisfaction; motivators are thought to affect behavior between no dissatisfaction and satisfaction.

Content theories have achieved great popularity and are widely accepted. However, research supporting the most popular of them, Maslow's hierarchy, has been quite limited (Miskel & Ogawa, 1988). And Herzberg's theory, although probably the most widely used in administration, has been subjected to consistent criticisms (e.g., Solimon, 1970).

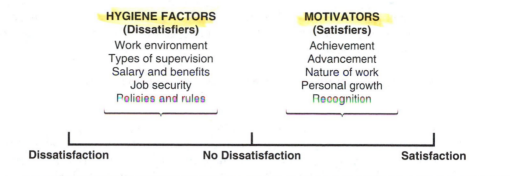

FIGURE 11.3   *Range of Dissatisfaction and Satisfaction in Herzberg's Two-Factor Theory*

Process Theories

Process theories view motivation as a combination of the person's needs and the conditions under which the person seeks to satisfy those needs. These theories reject two basic beliefs of content theories: that human behavior is solely a response to innate instincts and drives and that people possess a common hierarchy of needs (Hanson, 1996). Process theories are more complex than content theories because personal conditions are combined with environmental conditions.

One of the most widely recognized process theories is Vroom's *expectancy theory*. Victor Vroom (1964) based his theory on several assumptions:

- People enter organizations with expectations that affect their behavior in the organization. These expectations reflect a combination of individual and environmental forces.
- People have choices in the way they behave.
- People comprising the organization do not share the same expectations.
- Choices are reflective of personal expectations and the desire to maximize personal benefits.

Vroom believed that people viewed two levels of outcomes from their behavior. The first level determined whether behavior resulted in task performance; the second level determined if task performance resulted in a reward. For example, a principal is told by the superintendent to implement block scheduling in a high school. The first-level outcome of this initiative is actually being able to put block scheduling into place. The second-level outcome is any direct or indirect reward the principal receives for having complied with the superintendent's directive.

In expectancy theory, a person's level of motivation is determined by assigning points to three variables:

- *Valence:* A person's preference for a particular outcome (i.e., the attractiveness of a goal)

- *Expectancy:* The perceived relationship between effort and performance (i.e., the extent to which an individual believes that effort will produce a desired performance level)
- *Instrumentality:* The perceived relationship between performance and reward (i.e., the relationship between first- and second-level outcomes)

Each variable is scored from 0 to 100 percent. In the case of the high school principal directed to implement block scheduling, valence represents the degree to which she views implementing block scheduling as an attractive initiative. If it is highly attractive, the valence score will be at or near 100 percent. The expectancy score reflects the principal's beliefs that she can accomplish the task; the higher the score, the greater the belief that she can implement block scheduling. Finally, instrumentality represents the extent to which the principal believes she will be rewarded for successfully completing this assignment. The collective score for the three variables reveals the principal's level of motivation.

Process theories, such as Vroom's expectancy theory, help administrators understand behavioral choices. In the context of modern practice, it has not been uncommon to ask or even demand that teachers do something they are unprepared to do. For example, the infusion of computers into schools in the early 1980s was highly threatening to many school employees because they were not computer literate. Their motivation to use computers was likely reduced by doubts about their ability to use this technology properly.

Motivation and the Exercise of Power

Motivation is also broadly categorized as being intrinsic and extrinsic. *Intrinsic motivators* relate to inner thoughts and feelings being a primary cause of behavior and are associated with cognitive and humanist psychology. *Extrinsic motivators* relate primarily to rewards and punishments and are associated with behavioral psychology (Owens, 2001). Behaviorist views, in particular, involve the exercise of power—that is, the ability of one individual to get other individuals to do something. Therefore, distinctions between line motivation and power are often imprecise.

Power in organizations has many sources, and, contrary to popular belief, administrators are not the only persons who have it. Gary Yukl (1989) separated power sources into three categories:

- *Position power* (e.g., formal authority, control of information, control of rewards and punishments)
- *Personal power* (e.g., personal relationships, knowledge, charisma)
- *Political power* (e.g., coalition support, control over decisions)

John French and Bertram Raven (1968) provided one of the most widely used typologies for the bases of power in social systems. Its five categories—*legitimate, punishment centered, reward centered, expert,* and *referent*—and examples of application using a situation in which a principal exercises power over a teacher with regard to a lunchroom supervision assignment are shown in Table 11.1.

Although the examples in Table 11.1 indicate that each form of power produces the desired outcome for the principal, this does not mean that all five types of power are equally potent or durable. The five forms are listed in the table in order of typical potency and durability, with the least potent and least durable listed first. In other words, relying on one's official position or threatening people may work in the short term, but administrators may quickly exhaust this source of power. The most potent and durable forms of power are personal rather than positional; they depend on abilities, relationships, and perceptions. Some scholars (e.g., Abbott & Caracheo, 1988) have argued that there are only two types of power in organizations: *legitimate power* and *prestige power*. This is because they view punishment and reward as ways of exercising power rather than as types of power, and they see both expertise and charisma as elements of prestige power.

Regardless of the typologies used, an administrator's understanding of human behavior, and especially of motivation, is highly relevant to the exercise of

TABLE 11.1   *Examples of French and Raven's Five Types of Power*

Type of Power	Description	Example
Legitimate	Position-based power	A teacher agrees to supervise the lunchroom because he respects a principal's authority to make such assignments.
Coercive	Power based on threatening punishment	A teacher agrees to supervise the lunchroom because the principal said that refusal to do so would result in a negative statement in his performance evaluation.
Reward	Power based on offering or promising rewards	A teacher agrees to supervise the lunchroom because the principal promises to assign him to a better classroom next year.
Expert	Knowledge-based power	A teacher agrees to supervise the lunchroom because he believes that the principal knows what is best for the school and for him.
Referent	Power attributable to factors such as friendship, loyalty, and charisma	A teacher agrees to supervise the lunchroom because he views the principal as a loyal friend and an ideal principal.

power. Although administrators are not the only individuals possessing power in a district or school, they are the only individuals who possess *legitimate* power and they are the only individuals who are expected to *use* power.

Motivation and power are essential concepts for leaders in all types of organizations, but they are especially cogent to education because of the many structural incompatibilities found in schools. Put another way, school administrators are expected to lead people toward fulfilling shared visions and goals under conditions where purposes and goals are often contradictory. For example, professionalism promotes teacher empowerment and discretion but demands for accountability promote administrative control (Ogawa, Crowson, & Goldring, 1999). Likewise, principals are expected to help teachers grow professionally and, at the same time, to make summative judgments about their employment status (Clark & Astuto, 1988).

Because teachers work in relative isolation and cannot be supervised continuously, they have the ability to respond to change initiatives by being overtly compliant but covertly resistant. This is one reason why coercion and threats rarely have had a lasting effect on individual teacher behavior or school reform. It is also the reason why motivation is so important to administrative work. Two factors are critical to effectively moving people to improve schools: *motivation theory*, which explains conflicts between individual and organizational needs and how and why individuals make choices in the face of this conflict, and the effective use of power.

Communication

Clearly, individuals will sacrifice a great deal to organizations that provide meaning to their lives. Given the noble, service nature of education, developing meaningful districts and schools would seem a relatively easy task for administrators to achieve. After all, most parents, teachers, and administrators have the best intentions of students in mind. What, then, prevents many administrators from developing shared visions, positive school cultures, and school restructuring?

In part, the answer is communication. On the surface, the process of communication seems to be a relatively straightforward responsibility; in reality, it is not. Jerome Lysaught (1984) noted "problems of language, and meaning, and their transmission are among their [administrators] most important, persistent, and ubiquitous organizational difficulties. More frequently than not, failures in communication lie at the heart of problems in organization, goal-setting, productivity, and evaluation" (p. 102). As administrators increasingly use cultural change strategies in an effort to restructure schools, the importance of communication is becoming more and more apparent (Kowalski, 1998b).

Elements of Communication

Administrators must keep in mind a number of considerations related to communication. Harold Lasswell (1948) has succinctly stated these as, "Who says What, to

Whom, in Which channel, with What effect?" (p. 37). An additional consideration administrators may want to add is, "When should it be said?" Lasswell's formulation, however, captures only one side of the communication equation. The other side might be stated as, Who heard What, from Whom, When, through Which channel, with What effect? This dual formulation of communication illustrates a number of aspects of the communication process. Communication includes a sender, a receiver, a sent message, a time when it was sent, a medium, and an outcome.

Administrators often take communication for granted and give the process little thought in daily practice. This attitude almost always produces serious problems. Effective communication requires conscious thought to the following dimensions:

- *Status:* Communication is either *formal* (a letter from the principal to a parent) or *informal* (a discussion between the principal and student in the hallway). Administrators obviously use both; however, situational conditions need to be weighed to determine which is more appropriate.
- *Form:* Communication is either *verbal* or *nonverbal*. The former entails speaking and listening, whereas the latter pertains to gestures, facial expressions, and other actions that convey messages without using words.
- *Action:* Communication either involves *sending information* or *receiving information*. The former requires encoding skills (e.g., preparing a memorandum so the intended message is clear), whereas the latter requires decoding skills (e.g., interpreting a message accurately).
- *Clarity:* Communication can be *clear* or *ambiguous* depending on the quality of encoding and decoding. Clarity usually depends on the nature of the message, the encoding ability of the sender, and the decoding ability of the receiver(s). For example, some principals send written announcements to parents that contain terms the parents are unlikely to understand. This lack of attention to clarity reduces the effectiveness of the communication.
- *Direction:* Communication can be *top down, horizontal,* or *bottom up*. Top-down communication involves supervisors sending information to subordinates; horizontal communication involves information exchanges among peers; and bottom-up communication involves subordinates sending information to supervisors.
- *Flow:* Communication can either be *one way* or *two way*. In the former, information is only distributed, whereas in the latter, information is both distributed and received.

Historically, communication in districts and schools has been largely top down and one way. This is because administrators believed that (1) they should disseminate information on a need-to-know basis and (2) there was little value in receiving information from anyone other than supervisors or other higher-level officials (e.g., officials with the state department of education). Over the past 50 years, the debilities of one-way communication have become quite apparent. Even executives in large businesses have discovered that they must continuously interact with their environments if their goods or services are to satisfy real needs and wants. In the case of public education, the rationale for two-way communication is even more compelling; the schools belong to the people and therefore people have a right to be heard and to express their beliefs.

One other element of organizational communication that needs to be noted is the method that is used for distributing information. Distribution processes are called *channels*, and they may be formal or informal. A district or school establishes formal communication channels; a format for distributing information about school closings is an example of a formal channel. Informal channels are developed without administrative direction. They exist in all organizations and reflect employee demands for information that they believe they cannot receive through formal channels—at least not as fast as they would like. Informal channels may be nothing more than a school's "rumor mill."

Using Communication Effectively

Administrators do not become effective communicators by chance. Rather, knowledge of communication and conscious thought to using that knowledge are required. Consider a principal who has been directed by the superintendent to involuntarily transfer a teacher to another school. The principal has to make several critical decisions about completing this assignment, and the choices she makes will determine the effectiveness of the communication. The following three questions are especially cogent:

- *How should the message be sent?* The principal can convey the message to the teacher in several different ways—for example, through a formal letter, a routine memorandum, an email message, a telephone conversation, a third-party contact (e.g., having an assistant principal or department chair tell the teacher), or a face-to-face conference. A wide array of personal, professional, political, and legal factors should be weighed before deciding which medium is most appropriate. In some cases, more than one medium may be needed, such as having a face-to-face conference and giving the teacher a formal letter during the conference.
- *When should the communication occur?* A number of factors could be weighed in deciding when to present the message to the teacher. Some are legal (e.g., complying with state law, district policy, and the master contract with the teachers' union), some are professional (e.g., determining when to send the message, given the teacher's responsibilities to students), and some are political (e.g., determining when to send the message based on an attempt to avoid or reduce conflict).
- *What quantity of information is necessary?* The principal needs to decide how much to say in the message. For instance, this could range from simply saying, "I hereby notify you that you are being transferred to another assignment effective . . ." to providing both a legal explanation and a personal note (e.g., an expression of sorrow that the transfer must take place). More than a

few principals have discovered that the content of the message can result in either legal or political problems.

There are a number of other common problems that administrators should avoid. Here are the more important ones and strategies for overcoming them:

- *Communication oversights:* Administrators often fail to send information to all parties who should receive it. This problem is especially common in school-to-home communication. Creating a written schedule of regular (and frequent) written communication with various audiences is one effective technique. Another is to maintain a log of communication problems.
- *Inadequate attention to effect:* Administrators often fail to determine if a communication has produced its intended effect. This is especially true of communication that does not occur face to face. Frequently, messages are not decoded in the intended manner; for example, using emotion-producing terms such as *redistricting* and *reductions-in-force* produce contextual noise (the effect of situational conditions that influence decoding) and result in a discrepancy between the sent message and the received message (Lysaught, 1984). When it is critically important to determine if the message was decoded properly, face-to-face communication is essential. This is because the administrator can ask questions about the message and observe nonverbal behavior. In situations where face-to-face exchanges are not possible, the administrator should ask the receiver to respond to the message by sharing his or her interpretation of it.
- *Information overload:* Often, administrators are confronted with more information than they can manage. Problems resulting from this condition include omitting (e.g., failing to process information), queuing (e.g., not processing information until time is found to do so), filtering (e.g., incorrectly determining that some information may be nonessential), generalizing (e.g., reducing the specificity of information by skimming through it), employing multiple channels (e.g., having a secretary read communication to determine its relevance even though the secretary may not be properly qualified to do so), and escaping (not dealing with information, such as tossing letters in the wastebasket without reading them) (Miller, 1960).
- *Excessive use of informal channels:* Although administrators cannot totally eradicate informal communication channels, they may be able to control the extent to which they are used. They usually want to do this because messages transmitted through informal channels may be terribly misleading or even inaccurate. Such problems often require administrators to expend considerable time and energy correcting misperceptions. The most effective strategy for controlling the use of informal channels is the maintenance of multidirectional and two-way channels that provide consistently accurate and ample information.
- *Lack of trust:* Honesty is extremely important to communication. No matter how well structured and delivered, a message can fail to produce its intended

effect if the sender is not trusted. Any gain from lying is likely to be temporary but the potential loss of credibility is high—the sentence for lying can be
a loss of public respect and trust (Howard & Mathews, 1994). Thus, honesty
is always the best policy.

- *Poor listening skills:* Some administrators either do not think that it is important to listen to others or they are not very skilled at doing so. Poor listening skills include problems such as not capturing details, daydreaming
while someone else is talking, not paying attention when a subject is of little
interest, and being distracted easily. Becoming a good listener involves commitment, the skill to capture deeper meanings in messages, improved comprehension and memory, and the skill to ask clarifying questions (Spaulding
& O'Hair, 2000).

- *Failing to work properly with the media:* Given the nature of school administration, contact with reporters is inevitable. Often, administrators are unprepared
to deal with negative news, blame reporters for reporting news inaccurately,
and avoid contact with reporters. They make mistakes such as trying to speak
"off the record" or answering "no comment" to critical questions. Administrators who have positive relationships with the media usually have media relations plans and understand the role of journalism and journalists (Kowalski,
2000).

Importance of Communication

The relevance of communication should be viewed in two dimensions. From a personal perspective, there is compelling evidence that communication is a key variable in determining *effective practice*. This certainly is not surprising, since the
administrative work centers on human interactions. Deficiencies in this area of practice are virtually impossible to hide, because people readily detect when a principal
has poor writing skills, poor verbal skills, or poor listening skills. In addition, the
application of knowledge almost always involves some facet of communication.
Thus, it is no surprise that studies almost always identify poor communication
skills as a primary reason for dismissal (e.g., Davis, 1998) and communication proficiency as a primary reason for success (e.g., Mahoney, 1996; O'Hair & Reitzug, 1997).

Communication also is vital to *organizational success*. Administrative communication styles and skills often influence how people treat each other, how they
solve conflict, and how they exchange information. The symbolic and direct effects
of administrative communication on behavior in schools are especially noteworthy.
The relationship between school culture and communication is reciprocal; that is,
communication is both a tool for shaping school culture and a reflection of school
culture (Kowalski, 1998b). Clearly, communication is a key variable both in establishing shared visions and in building support for them (Thurston, Clift, & Schacht,
1993).

Administrative communication also is critical in relation to information
exchanges between schools and their broader communities. During organizational

change, for example, administrators are expected to provide accurate information in order to prevent those who are less informed from making and interpreting educational news. By using communication effectively, administrators can "confront inaccurate and unfavorable reports and explain or qualify difficult-to-understand or distorted content" (Spaulding & O'Hair, 2000, p. 138).

Ethical Practice

Professions commonly establish ethical norms for practitioners, and education is no exception. Teachers and administrators, however, constantly face conflicting expectations that their work should be guided by a knowledge base and that their work should be guided by the will of the people (Wirt & Kirst, 1997). In essence, educators are expected to be both professionals and public servants who are guided by political power. This has led some to conclude that education is not a true profession and that work in schools is largely political. Others, however, continue to argue that education is a unique profession in which professional knowledge is applied in public and political contexts. This latter perspective shapes expectations that administrators should be politically effective within the parameters of ethical and moral practice.

Taxonomy of Ethical Issues

Success in school administration is a relative term. Some measure it by the amount of money a practitioner earns; others measure it by focusing on managerial efficiency; and still others measure it in terms of political survival. From a professional perspective, however, success is highly reliant on maintaining ethical standards in service to others.

The most common conception of ethics centers on illegal acts, such as embezzlement, or gross faults of character, such as dishonesty (Kimbrough & Nunnery, 1988). Practitioners with this narrow perspective often pay little attention to ethics, because they view themselves as law-abiding individuals. Illegalities, however, are only one aspect of ethical behavior, and they are the more easily understood and avoided component of ethical behavior. Some authors (e.g., Howlett, 1991) have even argued that professional ethics actually begin where laws of right and wrong end. Interestingly, some elements of ethical norms have become law over the past 50 years—possibly because professions were doing an inadequate job of controlling practitioner behavior. Prime examples include discrimination laws, right to privacy laws, and sexual harassment laws.

Increasingly, scholars have argued that ethics are rooted in the fundamentals of school administration and extend to establishing appropriate practice (e.g., Leithwood & Duke, 1999) and moral school environments (e.g., Capper, 1993; Starratt, 1991). The fundamental ethical issues of school administration have been identified as "the application of power, the shaping of people and organizations, the search for better values . . . and the unending . . . questioning of the justification of the administrator's power and choices" (Greenfield, 1991, p. 3). Harold Hodgkinson (1991) noted that "values, morals, and ethics are the very stuff of leadership and administrative life" (p. 11). For purposes of discussion, ethics are discussed in the context of three categories:

1. *Nonroutine issues of morality and personal practice:* This category includes ethical choices administrators confront on an irregular basis where one choice may result in personal pleasure or personal (as opposed to professional) gain. Examples include misuse of funds, sexual indiscretion, and certain conflicts of interest.
2. *Nonroutine issues of professional practice:* This category includes ethical choices administrators confront on an irregular basis that deal with professional matters. Examples include nepotism, yielding to influential constituents in order to avoid trouble, and improperly terminating teachers (e.g., recommending dismissal for a teacher who has never received proper guidance and professional assistance to improve performance).
3. *Daily issues of administrative practice:* This category includes the routine misuse of power. Examples include coercion, treating people unfairly simply because they are disliked, showing favoritism, and disrespecting the rights and needs of others.

As previously noted, the first category is the least ambiguous with respect to making ethical decisions, since legal guidelines and social expectations exist that address these issues. Problems in the second category can have serious consequences and be extremely problematic, intense, and focused during the time they are occurring. However, decisions in this category extend over a limited time period. That is, they may emerge, intensify over a period of time to the point where a choice must be made, and then lose intensity as the choice is implemented and gradually accepted. Problems in the third category may not have the intensity nor the immediate grave repercussions of problems in the second category; however, they are constant and are likely to have a more pervasive, long-term effect on the organization than problems from either of the other two categories. Essentially, these problems get at the essence of administration.

Ethical Issues of Daily Practice

Leadership was described in the first chapter of this book as a social influence process in which a person steers members of a group or organization toward a specific goal or direction. Axiomatic in this definition is the concept of *directionality*— that is, the responsibility of leaders to move organizations in some direction. Embedded in directionality are ethical issues dealing with the determination of organizational direction and the influencing of organizational members to pursue this direction.

How should direction and purpose be developed in schools? There are basically three ways in which organizational direction is determined. The first is *highly autocratic;* the administrator determines the direction, dictates it to organizational members, and establishes accountability systems to ensure implementation. The second is *somewhat democratic;* the administrator seeks limited input from others, ultimately makes decisions about organizational directions, and then tries to persuade others to accept them. The third is *quite democratic;* the administrator involves everyone or representatives of all groups in determining organizational direction and then provides others substantial autonomy to pursue implementation.

All three variations are rife with potential ethical dilemmas primarily because of the contradictory expectations of democratic leadership and management control. Autocratic principals usually exert too much control, thus raising ethical concerns regarding the treatment of people. Highly democratic administrators usually exert too little control, thus raising ethical concerns about adequately protecting students and the rights of the community. In the third approach, principals appear to be striking a balance between being autocratic and democratic, but this may not be true. Some scholars (e.g., Bates, 1987; Foster, 1986) have suggested that these principals may simply be manipulative, and as such, their behavior may be more intrusive of followers' rights than simple autocracy. Richard Bates (1987) wrote that those who embrace a manipulative strategy "are arguing for a shift from traditional forms of bureaucratic control, toward techniques of ideological control. . . . Such a shift toward ideological control implies intervention of managers in the very consciousness of workers" (p. 83). The argument is that selling followers on a purpose or direction is an underhanded way of accomplishing one's personal agenda.

Professionalism and the need for control are most likely to be balanced in an ethical manner through the use of directed autonomy in the absence of manipulation. This means that teachers and the broader school community participate in creating a shared vision and they freely support the vision's goals. It also means that teachers are given considerable discretion to determine the most appropriate procedures for achieving the goals. Last, it means that administrators and teachers are accountable for outcomes—a condition that promotes controls other than traditional management (e.g., cultural norms, peer evaluation, collective responsibility).

One of the most essential ethical questions is: To what extent do administrators have a responsibility to change individual beliefs and values in the effort to achieve organizational goals? Most scholars agree that manipulating teachers and others for the sake of achieving personal or imposed organizational goals is unethical. Thomas Sergiovanni (1991) argued that the true test of moral leadership is whether the competence, well-being, and independence of school employees are enhanced by an administrator's behavior. Thus, the moral reason for involving others in organizational direction setting and decision making is not to make them feel good about being part of a democratic organization, but to provide the opportunity for them to become more critically reflective about the purposes of education, schooling, and the role of their personal practice. Essentially, ethical practice demands that educators continually ask themselves: What serves as the warrant for our decision making and action?

Robert Starratt (1991) has proposed a model of ethical practice that consists of three components: the ethic of critique, the ethic of caring, and the ethic of justice. The concept of *critique* involves the study of practice, with particular attention given to power relationships involved in policy and practice. For example, whose interests are served by a decision? At least four separate sets of interests are at stake in any administrative decision: the interests of the school (or district), the interests of the administrator, the interests of the faculty (and other employees), and the interests of the students (and the broader community). Making less than balanced decisions is unethical. Say, for example, that a principal is faced with the decision to impose new discipline rules that are terribly prescriptive and rigid. The teachers favor implementation because the new policy reduces the need for them to recommend disciplinary actions; parents and counselors, however, oppose implementation because the rules would restrict consideration of a student's total record and personal needs in imposing discipline. Even though the principal believes that the parents and counselors are correct, he adopts the new rules because he fears political repercussions from the teachers' union if he does not.

The ethic of *caring* acknowledges the right of individuals "to be who they are" and requires those who care for them to encounter them "in their authentic individuality" (Starratt, 1991, p. 195). It focuses on human relationships, such as cooperation, shared commitment, and friendship. A principal who dislikes a teacher and treats her unfairly simply because of her political views would be violating the ethic of caring.

The ethic of *justice* demands that attention be given to both the rights of individuals and the common good (Starratt, 1991). The primary foci are democratic participation and equal access to programs and resources. Consider a high school principal who arbitrarily allocates resources to departments without faculty input. Being a former physical education teacher and coach, his staunchest supporters are in the health and physical education department. By consistently giving that department more resources than the others, he is behaving unethically.

In summary, ethics are one of the most ambiguous elements of school administration and yet one of the most important. The degree to which administrators abide by ethical and moral standards not only affects the future of education as a profession but it also influences what schools will be in the future and the processes that will be used in reconfiguring them. William Greenfield (1995) aptly observed that one of the conditions that separates school administration from other types of leadership and management is work context—that is, schools are uniquely moral institutions.

Time Management

One of the biggest challenges faced by administrators is managing time in a manner that allows them to accomplish those tasks that are most important. This is especially noteworthy in light of the fact that studies often reveal a discrepancy between the responsibilities principals consider to be important and the responsibilities that actually consume most of their time (e.g., Whitaker & Turner, 2000). In the past, studies of managerial work in general (e.g., Mintzberg, 1973) and the principalship in particular (e.g., Wolcott, 1973) have found that administrative work is characterized by many brief encounters—generally several minutes or less in length. Administrative work also is fragmented (Rosenblatt & Somech, 1998; Wright, 1991); that is, the administrator deals with many different issues during the course of the day but sees few of these to immediate completion. For many superintendents and principals, the average day is characterized by one crisis after another.

Despite the frenetic nature of administrative work, it is clear that some choice is exercised in determining what will receive attention. The fact that some principals are able to spend 50 percent or more of their time on instructional leadership is one piece of evidence supporting this conclusion. Clearly, however, degrees of freedom are determined largely by contextual factors; for example, a principal in an elementary school with only nine teachers is apt to have more opportunities to make choices about time management than is an elementary principal (without an assistant principal) in a school with 20 teachers. Most often, school culture is the most potent determinant of how principals choose to spend their time; values and beliefs embedded in a school's culture provide norms for the principal's behavior (Peterson, 1999).

Time-Management Strategies

The first step to effective time management is planning. In the absence of a plan, administrators are vulnerable to being pushed and shoved from one unanticipated situation to another. The primary purpose of a time-management plan is to reduce the proclivity to be reactive; that is, the intent is to move an administrator to be proactive instead of reactive. The following are other suggestions for time management.

- *Learn to delegate:* Administrators who tend to have the greatest difficulty with time are those who try to do everything.
- *Learn to say no when it is appropriate to do so:* Tending to the most important responsibilities requires administrators to say no to some opportunities. For example, a principal may have to decline an invitation to attend a service club picnic so that he or she has time to create more time to complete classroom observations.
- *Set goals and priorities:* Determining what is important requires thoughtful planning; attending to the most important responsibilities requires setting priorities.
- *Cluster activities:* Some responsibilities can be combined. For example, a principal may be able to meet with all department chairs collectively to discuss budgets rather than meeting with each chair individually.

- *Set deadlines:* The frenetic pace of administration often leads to procrastination. Eventually, uncompleted tasks accumulate, making it even more impossible for an administrator to address important duties.
- *Emphasize brevity:* Communication with others does not have to be lengthy to be effective. Also, administrators should learn to stop meetings and conversations at a point when they cease to be productive.
- *Use technology:* Various technologies, such as personal computers and fax machines, provide an opportunity for administrators to save time.
- *Seek necessary resources:* Attending to important responsibilities requires human and material resources. For example, many principals may require additional help if they are to function as instructional leaders.
- *Evaluate time allocation decisions:* Administrators can learn to manage time more effectively by studying their own behavior. This not only includes reviewing the choices that were made but also examining the reasons for the choices.
- *Use a daily priority list:* A simple note detailing the priorities for a given day can be a useful tool. The note should be developed the day before and reviewed at the start of the workday.
- *Filter what is unimportant:* Screening telephone calls and email and separating junk mail from important letters are ways that administrators can filter the communications they receive.
- *Stay on task:* No matter how well conceived, a time-management plan will fail if administrators are unable to stay focused. This is especially true if the most important tasks involve activities that are unpleasant, challenging, or highly complex. For example, a principal may avoid observing a teacher's classroom by immersing himself or herself in the job of counting lunchroom proceeds.
- *Avoid doing some else's work:* Administrators often fall victim to doing the work of others. For example, a teacher may ask the principal to call a parent because a student is not doing homework. Doing so might enhance the principal's relationship with the teacher, but it detracts from the principal's ability to complete his or her own work.

Importance of Time Management

Time management, like communication, serves both organizational and personal goals. At the organizational level, administrators are unlikely to achieve their role expectations unless they learn to be in control of how they spend their time and unless they make the right choices regarding how they should spend their time. Most people, including many administrators, are inclined to do what they feel comfortable doing. So, they often elect structured tasks over unstructured tasks, simple tasks over complex tasks, and nonthreatening tasks over risk-laden tasks. But in so doing, they often neglect the responsibilities that are most critical to school effectiveness.

At a personal level, administrators desire to be effective—they seek recognition, accomplishment, and personal fulfillment from their work. These objectives are thwarted by poor time-management skills, resulting in additional stress, frustration, and a fatalistic attitude toward being an effective leader. Thus, the ability to manage time is a career-enhancing skill, and especially so in school administration, where the latitude to make time-allocation choices increases as individuals move to higher-level positions.

Implications for Practice

The four topics addressed in this chapter are not new issues for school administrators. However, they have become increasingly important in modern practice. Later in your studies of school administration, you should have opportunities to examine them in greater depth. The purpose here was to introduce you these topics and to explain why they are fundamental to work in schools.

Motivation theories help you know how drives, needs, experience, and situational variables serve to shape behavior. Arguably, administrators have always needed to know something about motivation so that they could understand their own behavior and help others to improve their performance. Now, however, most superintendents and principals are facing the challenge of organizational change. In this context, using effective motivational techniques has assumed new levels of importance. Although such knowledge does not ensure that a principal will be able to get teachers to accept change, it does help explain why some individuals are ready for change and others are not—information that permits leaders to select effective change strategies.

Similarly, communication has always been cogent to administrative work, but in modern practice, the expectations for knowledge and application have increased markedly. Transition to an information age, movement toward shared decision making, and the need for schools to be open to their external environments are but a few of the reasons why this is so. Today, effective practice entails the ability to use information to identify and solve problems in collaborative contexts. This requires administrators to transmit, receive, interpret, and use information through open, multidimensional communication channels.

The fact that administrators must apply their knowledge in highly political situations is one of the distinguishing characteristics of school administration. This reality has prompted some practitioners to view themselves as politicians rather than as professionals. This is most unfortunate, given the moral nature of schools. The challenge for administrators is not to choose between ethical and political behavior, but rather to apply ethics in the context of political situations.

Last, you should realize that most administrative jobs extend beyond the standard 40-hour workweek and require practitioners to manage a myriad of unanticipated problems. Adjustment to these conditions depends largely on one's ability to manage time. Those who ignore time management usually end up meandering from one problem to the next; their day is characterized by a series of reactions. On the other hand, highly effective administrators make sure that they address what really matters in schools—and often this consists of unstructured, complex tasks, such as collaborating with teachers to construct improved programs.

For Further Discussion

1. What is the difference between content and process theories of motivation?

2. Why is it important for administrators to have an understanding of motivation?

3. What is the relationship between motivation and the exercise of power, especially in relation to using rewards and threats of punishment?

4. Both formal and informal communication channels are found in districts and schools. What is the difference between them?

5. Communication channels may be one way or two way. What is the difference between them? Which is preferable for schools? Why?

6. One of the keys to effective communication is selecting the correct medium for a message. Why is the manner in which a message transmitted so important?

7. What is nonverbal communication? Why should administrators have an understanding of nonverbal behavior?

8. Often, ethics are viewed in terms of legal behavior. Is this an accurate and sufficient depiction of ethics in school administration? Why or why not?

9. In what ways, if any, does the exercise of power relate to ethical practice?

10. What is the difference between political behavior and ethical behavior? How should administrators reconcile this difference?

11. Why is it especially important for principals and other administrators to manage how they spend their time?

12. Time management can produce positive effects for a principal's school and for the principal. How might it benefit the school? How might it benefit the principal?

Other Suggested Activities

1. Discuss the ways in which a principal could use technology to enhance communication in a middle school.

2. Using Herzberg's two-factor theory, discuss the extent to which an elementary school principal could change the attitude of a dissatisfied teacher by assigning her to a new grade level and a new classroom.

3. Discuss French and Raven's five bases of power in relation to ethical practice.

4. Invite a superintendent and a principal to visit your class to discuss the political contexts of their work and the extent to which these conditions affect ethical practice.

5. Discuss the possible reasons why some administrators do not engage in time management.

6. Develop a list of characteristics that describe an assistant superintendent for curriculum who is a highly effective communicator.

References

Abbott, M., & Caracheo, F. (1988). Power, authority and bureaucracy. In N. J. Boyan (Ed.), *Handbook of research on educational administration* (pp. 239–257). New York: Longman.

Argyris, C. (1957). *Personality and the organization: The conflict between system and individual.* New York: Harper.

Argyris, C. (1964). *Integrating the individual and the organization.* New York: John Wiley.

Bates, R. J. (1987). Corporate culture, schooling, and educational administration, *Educational Administration Quarterly, 23*(4), 79–115.

Capper, C. A. (1993). *Educational administration in a pluralistic society.* Albany: SUNY Press.

Clark, D. L., & Astuto, T. A. (1988). Paradoxical choice options in organizations. In D. Griffiths, R. Stout, & P. Forsyth (Eds.), *Leaders for America's schools* (pp. 112–130). Berkeley, CA: McCutchan.

Davis, S. H. (1998). Why do principals get fired? *Prinicpal, 28*(2), 34–39.

Foster, W. (1986). *Paradigms and promises: New approaches to educational administration.* Buffalo, NY: Prometheus Books.

French, J., & Raven, B. (1968). The bases of social power. In D. Cartwright & A. Zander (Eds.), *Group dynamics: Research and theory* (pp. 259–269). New York: Harper and Row.

Greenfield, T. B. (1991). Foreword. In C. Hodgkinson, *Educational leadership: The moral art* (pp. 3–9). Albany: SUNY Press.

Greenfield, W. D., Jr. (1995). Toward a theory of school administration: The centrality of leadership. *Educational Administration Quarterly, 31*(1), 61–85.

Hanson, E. M. (1996). *Educational administration and organizational behavior* (4th ed.). Boston: Allyn and Bacon.

Herzberg, F., Mausner, B., & Snyderman, B. (1959). *The motivation to work.* New York: John Wiley.

Hodgkinson, H. (1991). *Educational leadership: The moral art.* Albany: SUNY Press.

Howard, C. M., & Matthews, W. K. (1994). *On deadline: Managing media relations.* Prospect Heights, IL: Waveland Press.

Howlett, P. (1991). How you can stay on the straight and narrow. *Executive Educator, 13*(2), 19–21, 35.

Kimbrough, R. B., & Nunnery, M.Y. (1988). *Educational administration: An introduction.* New York: Macmillan.

Kowalski, T. J. (1998a). Communication in the principalship: Preparation, work experiences, and expectations. *Journal of Educational Relations, 19*(2), 4–12.

Kowalski, T. J. (1998b). The role of communication in providing leadership for school reform. *Mid-Western Educational Researcher, 11*(1), 32–40.

Kowalski, T. J. (2000). Working with the media. In T. J. Kowalski (Ed.), *Public relations in schools* (2nd ed.) (pp. 272–293). Upper Saddle River, NJ: Merrill, Prentice-Hall.

Lasswell, H. D. (1948). The structure and function of communication in society. In L. Bryson (Ed.), *The communication of ideas* (pp. 39–51). New York: Harper & Brothers.

Leithwood, K., & Duke, D. (1999). A century's quest to understand school leadership. In J. Murphy & K. Seashore Louis (Eds.), *Handbook of research on educational administration* (2nd ed.) (pp. 45–72). San Francisco: Jossey-Bass.

Lysaught, J. P. (1984). Toward a comprehensive theory of communication: A review of selected contributions. *Educational Administration Quarterly, 20*(3), 101–127.

Mahoney, J. (1996). The secrets of their success. *Executive Educator, 18*(7), 33–34.

Maslow, A. H. (1970). *Motivation and personality.* New York: Harper and Row.

Miller, J. G. (1960). Information, input, overload, and psychopathology. *American Journal of Psychiatry, 116*(8), 697–711.

Mintzberg, H. A. (1973). *The nature of managerial work.* New York: McGraw-Hill.

Miskel, C., & Ogawa, R. (1988). Work motivation, job satisfaction, and climate. In N. J. Boyan (Ed.), *Handbook of research on educational administration* (pp. 279–304). New York: Longman.

Ogawa, R. T., Crowson, R. L., & Goldring, E. B. (1999). Enduring dilemmas in school organizations. In J. Murphy & K. Seashore Louis (Eds.), *Handbook of research on educational administration* (2nd ed.) (pp. 277–296). San Francisco: Jossey-Bass.

O'Hair, M. J., & Reitzug, U. C. (1997). Restructuring schools for democracy: Principals' perspectives. *Journal of School Leadership, 7*(3), 226–286.

Owens, R. G. (2001). *Organizational behavior in education* (6th ed.). Boston: Allyn and Bacon.

Peterson, K. D. (1999). Time use flows from school culture. *Journal of Staff Development, 20*(2), 16–19.

Rosenblatt, Z., & Somech, A. (1998). The work behavior of Israeli elementary school principals: Expectations versus reality. *Educational Administration Quarterly, 34*(4), 505–532.

Sergiovanni, T. J. (1991). *The principalship: A reflective practice perspective* (2nd ed.). Boston: Allyn and Bacon.

Solimon, H. M. (1970). Motivator-hygiene theory of job attitudes: An empirical investigation and attempt to reconcile both the one- and the two-factor theories of job attitudes. *Journal of Applied Psychology, 54*, 452–461.

Spaulding, A., & O'Hair, M. J. (2000). Public relations in a communication context: Listening, nonverbal, and conflict-resolution skills. In T. J. Kowalski (Ed.), *Public relations in schools* (2nd ed.) (pp. 137–164). Upper Saddle River, NJ: Merrill, Prentice-Hall.

Starratt, R. J. (1991). Building an ethical school: A theory for practice in educational leadership. *Educational Administration Quarterly, 27*(2), 185–202.

Thurston, P., Clift, R., & Schacht, M. (1993). Preparing leaders for change-oriented schools. *Phi Delta Kappan, 75*, 259–265.

Vroom, V. H. (1964). *Work and motivation.* New York: John Wiley.

Whitaker, T., & Turner, E. (2000). What is your priority? *NASSP Bulletin, 84*(617), 16–21.

Wirt, F. M., & Kirst, M. W. (1997). *The political dynamics of American education.* Berkeley, CA: McCutchan.

Wolcott, H. J. (1973). *The man in the principal's office.* New York: Holt, Rinehart and Winston.

Wright, L. V. (1991). Instructional leadership: Looking through schoolhouse windows. *Theory into Practice, 30*(2), 113–118.

Yukl, G. A. (1989). *Leadership in organization* (2nd ed.). Englewood Cliffs, NJ: Prentice-Hall.

12

Demands for School Reform

Chapter Content _____

Educational reform has been advocated at numerous times since the founding of the first public schools in the United States. The many frustrations produced by previous reform movements created an atmosphere of skepticism and gave rise to questions as to whether sufficient improvement could ever be achieved. What is really wrong with our schools? Are they as bad as critics claim? Can meaningful change be accomplished? And why do the demands for school reform keep surfacing? Although there are many different perspectives regarding how these questions should be answered, most everyone agrees that improvements are necessary.

The current reform era is unusual in that it has been sustained for more than two decades. During this time, reformers have modified their definitions of problems, identified new change targets, and embraced new change strategies. But schools have proven to be highly resistant; in most cases, those working in schools have proven that they are at least as likely to change reforms as they are to be changed by them (Cuban, 1998). Administrators entering practice in the next few years can expect the issue of reform to be pervasive in their work. This chapter examines the context of current society and the tensions created by the competing goals of excellence and equity. In addition, the evolution of school reform since 1983 is reviewed.

Society and Schools in the Twenty-First Century

Changing global and societal conditions spawn demands for educational reform, and this fact is clearly visible in the current efforts to make schooling more effective and relevant. Being aware of how the world has changed enhances one's understanding of why change is necessary. Two facets of contemporary society are presented here to exemplify how conditions outside of schools set the agenda for school reform.

Demographic Trends

During the formative years of the nation's public school system, the United States was a rural society in which family, church, and community provided for many needs of youth. Today, by contrast, the nation is an urban society and many children are reared in fragmented families that live in inner-city areas or suburbs where there is little or no true community environment. The United States also has become a much more diverse society racially. In 1976, 24 percent of all elementary and secondary students were classified as minorities; by 1992, that percentage had increased to 33 percent and it is still rising (National Center for Education Statistics, 1997). Consider the following facts that illustrate the effect of this transition:

- Until 1960, most children grew up in traditional families that consisted of a father, a stay-at-home mother, and one to three siblings. In the first decade of the twenty-first century, however, half of all children are expected to be living apart from their biological fathers (Popenoe, 1996).
- In 1976, 15.5 percent of all students enrolled in elementary and secondary schools were African American; by 1992, that percentage had increased to 16.5 percent. In 1976, 6.4 percent of all students were Hispanic, but by 1992, that percentage had doubled to 12.3 percent. The figures for actual increases in the number of students in these categories are even more revealing. The number of African American students grew 4 percent from 1976 to 1992, but the number of Hispanic students grew an astonishing 86 percent in that same period (National Center for Education Statistics, 1997).
- Minority students are far more likely than white students to live in families where one or both parents are missing. In the late 1990s, 60 percent of African American students, 29 percent of Hispanic students, and only 11 percent of white students lived in one-parent families (National Center for Educational Statistics, 1997).
- In the late 1990s, 12.5 percent of white children enrolled in schools lived in poverty; however, the percentage of African American students living in poverty was 43.8 percent (National Center for Education Statistics, 2000).

These statistics reveal two important conditions: The number of minority students is increasing and minority children are much more likely than white children to live in one-parent and low-income families.

Most of the nation's largest school districts already have so-called minority-majorities. In some, the number of students living in poverty is over 80 percent (Kowalski, 1995). Poor children living in fragmented families have become increasingly dependent on government agencies—and especially schools—to meet their basic needs. However, most of these children are enrolled in school districts where the tax base is being eroded as businesses and factories relocate to safer and more tax-friendly environments. Current demographic trends suggest that the United States is becoming a bipolar society with children living in low-income families concentrated in inner-city school districts.

School-Related Problems

At a time when expectations are mounting for schools to provide greater services to students, many districts are operating outdated and overcrowded schools. Political and economic support is also a problem for virtually all districts; less than 30 percent of a typical district's taxpayers have children enrolled in public elementary and secondary schools (Stratton, 1995). Consider these additional facts that illustrate the problems faced by contemporary schools:

- Enrollment in elementary and secondary schools grew considerably after World War II and peaked in 1971. From 1971 to 1984, however, total elementary and secondary school enrollment decreased every year. But in 1985, it started increasing again and by the mid-1990s, total enrollment in public schools reached record levels (National Center for Education Statistics, 2000). This enrollment pattern has resulted in a growing number of overcrowded school buildings (Kowalski, 2002).
- Projections indicate that school enrollment figures will continue to rise. For example, kindergarten through grade 8 enrollments rose from 29.9 million in fall 1990 to an estimated 33.5 million in fall 2000 (National Center for Education Statistics, 2000). Overall, school enrollment is projected to rise from 46.4 million in 1997 to 48.3 million by 2007 (4 percent increase). During this same period, total private school enrollment is expected to increase 3 percent, rising from 5.9 million to 6.1 million (National Center for Education Statistics, 1997).
- Nearly 50 percent of all elementary and secondary school buildings need to be remodeled or replaced—and many of these buildings are in large, urban districts where financial resources for rebuilding infrastructures are often minimal (Kowalski, 2002). The National Center for Education Statistics (1997) reported the following facts in this regard: (1) the average age of a school building in the United States in 1995 was about 42 years; (2) nearly one-third of the schools were constructed prior to 1950, almost half were built between 1950 and 1969, and only 10 percent have been built since 1985; and (3) nearly three-fourths of the schools have had at least one major renovation.
- Approximately 5 percent of all high school students in the late 1990s dropped out of school each year. This figure compounds, since many of these students never return to school. Approximately 13 percent of all young adults in the

late 1990s had never completed high school (National Center for Education Statistics, 2000).

- About 57 percent of public schools reported a criminal incident to police in 1996–97, including a serious violent crime or a less serious crime such as a fight without weapons, theft, or vandalism. Serious violent crime was reported to police by 10 percent of the nation's schools (National Center for Education Statistics, 2000).
- Students and parents in many large urban districts speak 40 to 50 different languages (Glass, 2000).
- Technology had a dramatic impact on schools during the 1980s and 1990s. For example, the percentage of schools having access to the Internet increased from 35 to 95 percent in just five years after 1994 (National Center for Education Statistics, 2000).

The ultimate effectiveness of the education system is influenced by conditions in both society and schools. In fact, schools are a mirror of society as well as a predictor of societal problems. Students who drop out of school, for example, will earn much less money over the course of their lifetimes than those who remain in school. Thus, high dropout rates present serious economic concerns for individual states and the nation. Likewise, a nexus between not finishing high school and being incarcerated is well established; it is estimated that approximately 80 percent of the people in prisons are school dropouts (Hodgkinson, 1989).

Most citizens readily understand that movement to a global economy and an information-based society has created new expectations for schools. They are far less likely to recognize how unresolved social problems have the same effect. Educators are not responsible for poverty or family conditions, but they must address the needs of students who are affected by these problems. And educators are not responsible for the decaying infrastructure of the nation's school buildings, but they must work in these conditions. These facts are essential to understanding the conditions that surround the protracted demands for school reform, and they are essential to understanding why many reform ideas reproduced rather than transcended some of society's greatest needs (Reyes, Wagstaff, & Fusarelli, 1999).

Tensions between Excellence and Equity

Differences in public opinion regarding purposes of public education can be traced to the development of the nation's earliest schools. During the common school era, circa 1830 to 1840, varying interpretations of public expectations of education were already visible. Chronicling this period, Joel Spring (1990) wrote:

> On the one hand, there are those who see the common school period as a battle between liberals and conservatives for the establishment of a school system that would be of great benefit to all members of society. On the other hand, some historians argue that common schools were established to protect privileged economic

and religious positions in society. These broad differences in historical interpretation contain elements of the debate that continues to this day about whose interests
are served by public schools. (p. 75)

Values and beliefs that created individual perceptions of public education
became increasingly diversified as the United States grew in population, welcoming immigrants with varying ethnic, religious, and cultural experiences. To this day,
many local communities find it difficult to establish commonly accepted goals for
schooling. Is it surprising, then, that reform has proven to be elusive at the state
and national levels?

After the passage of the Civil Rights Act in 1964, the attention of the citizenry
was drawn to human rights issues. In particular, the nation became aware of how
poverty and race were associated with achievement gaps. Thus, equity became
the primary education goal—especially in urban school districts (Passow, 1995).
The federal government began waging a war on poverty and the federal courts
became increasingly involved in desegregation lawsuits. These actions occurred
in the social context of an unpopular war being fought in Viet Nam and race-related
riots destablizing some the nation's largest cities.

The pursuit of equal educational opportunities had multiple facets, as exemplified by the following actions:

- Curricula were broadened to infuse courses that stressed the multicultural
  nature of U.S. society, the effects of poverty, and human relations.
- Greater emphasis was placed on reducing dropout rates by diversifying
  educational programs; for example, some schools adopted mini-courses that
  allowed students to pursue personal interests outside of boundaries of traditional academic courses.
- Federal support was provided to bolster the education of children living in
  poverty.
- Educators were encouraged to emphasize the affective domain of education
  in an effort to influence the feelings of students toward schools and society.

By the mid-1970s, however, equity was being pushed to the back burner. The
war in Viet Nam had ended, some economists had declared that the gap between
rich and poor was narrowing, and the movement of the baby boomers through the
schools resulted in substantial enrollment declines in many local districts (Reyes
et al., 1999). In this revised social context, critics resurrected concerns about the academic quality of schools. They noted that student test scores had actually declined
despite increased federal support (Dye, 1992) and that forced busing not only failed
to desegregate schools but it also drew attention away from education quality and
deeply divided communities (Reynolds, 1986). The major critics included government officials, many business leaders, and even local school board members. Concluding that well-intentioned experiments with affective education had damaged
the academic productivity of schools, they demanded that educators get "back to
basics." Amidst the criticisms, the confidence of the U.S. public wavered sufficiently,

and schools found themselves immersed in yet another era of emphasis on educational excellence (Finn, 1991).

Following the sudden shift from equity to excellence in the early 1970s, teachers and administrators were inundated with new state laws and policies such as those requiring minimum competency testing. These changes further eroded the status of teachers as professionals.

> Being able to work with relatively little direct supervision, escaping bureaucracy by closing the door, was one of the most attractive features of the occupation. The back-to-basics movement and minimum competency testing changed the situation drastically, ushering in an era of standardized teaching, testing, and grading. Teachers now feel pressure from their bosses, school board members and administrators, to teach by the cookbook. (Newman, 1990, p. 94)

Equity has been described as "the pressure to make each school responsive to the particular needs of its community constituency" and *excellence* as "the pressure to ensure that the general needs of the country are being met" (Bacharach, 1990, p. 3). Movement away from equity-based social issues during the 1970s exemplifies how quickly and radically the focus of public education can be changed. Such transitions have been common throughout the history of public education, largely because the basic values guiding public policy are often incompatible (e.g., equity and excellence; liberty and equity).

Radical philosophical shifts have had a destabilizing effect on public education. Educators are usually required to implement new courses, use new instructional methodologies, and respond to new accountability standards. Yet, the basic structure of their work environment is not affected; that is, after multiple reform movements, schools are still organized much as they have always been. Reluctance to change the infrastructure of schools is rooted in a fundamental belief shared by most educators—reform movements have little chance of succeeding.

Tensions between equity and excellence are still very visible, and they sustain philosophical differences regarding the purposes of education. For example, some policymakers argue that schools should prepare individuals for the workforce; others believe that schools should prepare students for higher education; and still others argue that schools should be a vehicle for social reconstruction. Recognizing the debilitating effects of philosophical divisiveness, Philip Schlecty (1990) predicted that reform efforts, no matter how well conceived, would be attenuated if reformers did not reach consensus on the purposes of schooling.

Public schools were once considered highly effective. But this was at a time when only select portions of the population were served, and at a time when family, church, neighborhoods, and other social units provided those portions of a child's development and education not directly addressed in the context of formal schooling. The development of morals, ethics, and civic responsibility occurred more naturally in this environment. Our schools remain largely as they were in that era; yet, the communities in which they exist, and the needs of persons they serve, have changed radically. Problems created by this institutional inertia are central to understanding current reform efforts.

Efforts to resolve tensions between equity and excellence have been made more difficult by the unwillingness of parents, communities, churches, the business community, and other agencies to accept responsibility for their contributions to the nation's present state of affairs (Finn, 1991). As a result, schools not only receive imputations they deserve for failing to remain relevant but they also are blamed for a whole host of societal and economic maladies.

The First Wave: 1983–1987

With the publishing of *A Nation at Risk* in 1983, the National Committee on Excellence in Education is credited with commencing the current round of educational reform efforts. Actually, the shift away from equity issues had begun nearly seven to eight years earlier; this report merely legitimized quality and excellence as contemporary priorities (Finn, 1991). *A Nation at Risk* alarmed the public by advancing the hypothesis that U.S. schools had placed the national economy and security in a state of risk because too many students were failing to acquire basic skills. The report's content characterized the country's public education as mediocre and declining. Influential policymakers immediately accepted the conclusion that the effectiveness of schools was at a new low despite the glaring absence of evidence to support this judgment (Hawley, 1988). In part, timing was a critical factor with respect to the report's widespread acceptance; it had been released during Ronald Reagan's first term as president. From an education perspective, some writers (e.g., Marcus, 1990) referred to those four years as the "Reagan Reversion" because President Reagan had entered office committed to reducing the federal government's involvement in public education—a commitment that included the intent to dismantle the newly-created Department of Education.

From approximately 1983 to 1987, many other reform reports were published; virtually all echoed the principal conclusions reached by the National Commission on Excellence. The persistent criticisms in the midst of a shrinking federal interest in public education prompted many governors to pursue education reform at the state level (Krotseng, 1990); collectively, school-improvement initiatives advanced during this five-year period constituted the first wave of modern reform efforts.* Although variations existed from state to state, the actions of would-be reformers were influenced by the same assumptions that made students the targets of reform (Kirst, 1988):

- A decline in the quality of education had affected international and interstate economic competition negatively.
- Low expectations for students were the primary cause for the decline in academic excellence.

---

*The literature on school reform contains differing opinions regarding the number of waves of school reform that have occurred since 1983. Regardless of whether authors divide the reform movement into two or three waves, virtually all agree that the first wave occurred during the period from 1983 to 1987.

• A desired level of excellence could be achieved without changing the fundamental structure of schools.

In addition, first-wave reform ideas relied almost exclusively on intensification mandates as a change strategy; that is, states forced educators to do more of what they were already doing. The most common change initiatives included the following:

- Lengthening the school year
- Lengthening the school day
- Increasing high school graduation requirements (including more required courses in basic subjects such as English, science, and mathematics)
- Requiring statewide achievement tests
- Requiring summer school remediation programs

Starting in approximately 1985, the reformers shifted some of their attention to educators. Now, in addition to seeing lazy students as a primary cause of low productivity, they also pointed fingers at incompetent administrators and teachers. Proposed remedies focused on increasing standards for entry into the profession (e.g., improving professional preparation and requiring testing for licensure) and increasing controls over educators once they entered practice (e.g., requiring closer supervision and increasing accountability) (Hanson, 1991).

By the mid-1980s, however, skeptics were already challenging the notion that intensification and more rigid standards for the teaching profession would produce excellence. They noted that an intricate network of social, political, and economic problems affected the productivity of public education; and by defining the problem as simply lazy students and incompetent teachers, reformers were proposing inadequate and misguided solutions. In addition, some scholars (e.g., Boyer, 1985) warned that the increased role for state government in education could unwittingly produce a bureaucratic model that left teachers and principals more accountable and less empowered.

Although the cumulative benefits of intensification mandates are still being debated, it appears that the more direct and simple initiatives met at least some of their goals. Students were spending more time in school and they were taking more courses in mathematics and science at the high school level (Hawley, 1988). As an example, the mean number of mathematics courses completed in high school rose from 2.6 in 1982 to 3.4 in 1998, and the number of science courses rose from 2.2 to 3.1 (National Center for Education Statistics, 2000). In addition, funding for public elementary and secondary education increased substantially from 1983 to 1987; expenditures in general and starting teacher salaries increased by approximately 25 percent during this period (Kirst, 1988). Despite these gains, Al Shanker (1988), who was then president of the American Federation of Teachers, issued the following warning to first-wave reformers:

> Undoubtedly, many able youngsters who have been too casual about their education will respond positively to greater demands, but we can also easily imagine how other kids, who cannot function in the current system, will react to even tougher

standards. Tightening the current system probably will mean a better education for some students but increased frustration and failure for many others who, before reform, might have put in enough seat time to get a diploma. (p. 367)

Intensification mandates basically ignored both liberty and equity. The arena for formulating educational policy shifted from school boards to state legislatures, and this occurred at a time when there was increasing recognition that local decision making would be beneficial in terms of addressing real education needs across local communities (Passow, 1988). In most instances, equity is enhanced through central-ization because the state typically emphasizes equal educational opportunities across local districts. But during the first wave, state government officials either totally ignored equity or they treated it as an appurtenant reform objective. Observ-ing this oversight, John Gardner (1984) asked a troublesome and crucial question: Could U.S. schools be both equal and excellent? By the end of 1987, however, many policy experts were no longer asking questions—they were passing judgment. They argued that meaningful reform was impossible unless issues of equity were a pri-mary consideration. One of them wrote, "With one-fourth of our children growing up in poverty and one-third members of minority groups, we cannot afford to con-sider the education of such children a side issue" (Metz, 1990, p. 143).

The Second Wave: 1988–

During the first wave, many politicians were more interested in creating an illu-sion of change than they were in finding meaningful solutions to a highly complex problem (Rubin, 1984). But the illusions neither improved education outputs appre-ciably nor mollified a dissatisfied public. Facing these realities, many policy elites (individuals having the most influence over the reform agenda) began searching for ideas—and in doing so, they became more interested in listening to voices from within the education profession. The tensions between excellence and equity received more attention as this occurred.

At the same time, philosophical, legal, and political forces were refocusing on tensions between liberty and equality. First-wave reforms included significant increases in state spending on education, but the allocation of these scarce resources ignored uneven economic conditions among local districts. Thus, policymakers faced the persistent concern that not all community constituents would equally ben-efit from the rash of laws generated by a quest for excellence (Scheurich & Imber, 1991). In addition, reformers could no longer ignore the fact that school improve-ment initiatives were unlikely to succeed unless forces in the local community, including educators and school board members, were supportive of them.

The second wave, initiated in approximately 1988, was characterized by three new commitments:

1. *An investment in children:* Reformers began to realize that threats and higher standards would not make many students at risk improve their academic per-formance. Therefore, reformers became willing to pursue broader initiatives.

2. *An investment in teaching strategies:* Reformers began to realize that educators had to be involved in setting the reform agenda. If teachers and administrators were to be given greater autonomy, then efforts were needed to attract and retain more competent teachers (Hawley, 1988).
3. *Working more closely with local districts:* Instead of relying entirely on mandates, reformers attempted to forge a shared agenda with local districts. The state would continue to set expectations, but local districts would have more freedom with respect to pursuing them (Saban, 1997).

These commitments led to the adoption of three new strategies:

1. *State deregulation:* Local districts were given greater leeway to determine how reforms should be pursued.
2. *District decentralization:* Individual schools were given greater leeway to determine how reforms should be pursued.
3. *Professionalism:* Educators were given greater authority to determine how reforms should be pursued.

Historically, teachers have had little control over the services they render (Sarason, 1990). If the primary strategies in the second wave were to succeed, the reformers had to sustain efforts to improve the education profession and the profession's image in U.S. society. For example, teachers had to be educated and socialized to assume added responsibility in areas such as organizational planning, organizational change, decision making, and evaluation (Timar, 1989), and the public needed to view educators as true professionals (Petrie, 1990). This meant that administrative roles had to be reconsidered. Principals, for example, would need to become true instructional leaders capable of mobilizing and coordinating professional talent (Glickman, 1991). To do this, principal preparation would need to be reformed so that more attention was given to curriculum, instructional theory, conflict management, and communication (Johnson & Snyder, 1989–90).

Influential and politically powerful individuals outside the education profession largely shaped first-wave efforts. A more diverse group, including many prominent leaders within the education profession, molded second-wave reforms. Educators tended to favor decentralized reforms geared to individual communities and schools, erected on shared power, and directed toward quality and equity rather than quality and efficiency. Whereas first-wave ideas were "simple, uniform, universal, and abrupt," the ones advanced by educators "emphasized handcrafted, school-specific changes, the sort that are almost certain to be slow, gradual, and uneven" (Finn, 1991, p. 42).

Whereas students and teachers were the primary targets in the first wave, school climate was placed in the cross hairs in the second wave. The overall goal was to achieve school improvement by allowing people in the local community—and even in individual schools—to determine how the school should be structured and organized, how decisions should be made, and how compromises should be reached among competing values and beliefs. The failure of past reforms is largely explained by the highly resilient culture of public education—a culture that has shaped the minds and hearts of educators (Sarason, 1996). Most scholars who have studied change in schools (e.g., Fullan, 1999; Hall & Hord, 2001) agree that school restructuring depends on the ability and willingness of educators to comprehend organizational culture and to modify it as conditions warrant.

Implications for Practice

The topic of school reform is expected to remain at the center of school administration for at least the next decade. Accordingly, you should have a basic understanding of modern school improvement efforts. This includes knowledge of the following topics:

- Conflicting values and their influence on education goals
- Differing perceptions regarding the purposes of education
- The targets of school reform
- Change strategies and their effectiveness with schools
- The reasons why change has been so elusive
- The transitions and assumptions that are guiding current reform efforts

This general information provides a foundation for your further studies in administration and school reform.

As an administrator, you will find change to be pervasive in your work. Some changes are minor and require little thought and they produce few repercussions. Other initiatives, such as cultural change, may continue for decades. During the first wave of modern reform ideas, principals and superintendents essentially sat on the sidelines where they were forced to react rather than to help build new goals, programs, and strategies. During the second wave, new role expectations evolved. As state deregulation and district decentralization became more popular strategies, and as educators became more involved in making reform decisions, the role of administrators in the reform movement became less managerial and more developmental. More precisely, administrators are now expected to lead and facilitate school restructuring—roles that require them to be change agents.

For Further Discussion _____

1. What causes tension between excellence and equity? How have reformers reacted to this tension?

2. Why does centralization tend to enhance equity and decentralization tend to jeopardize equity?

3. During the first wave of school reform, who were the primary reformers?

4. How did first-wave reformers define the problems of public schools?

5. How did first-wave reformers view educators?

6. School officials often used staff development as a means of preparing teachers to implement change. Under what circumstances is staff development likely to be ineffective with respect to this goal?

7. How does school culture serve as a change barrier?

8. What role did prominent education scholars play in the first and second reform waves?

9. What is the difference between state deregulation and district decentralization?

10. One of the current strategies for improving schools is professionalization. What is professionalization and how is it expected to contribute to school improvement?

11. Scholars argue that reform requires the internal and external capacity to change districts and schools. What is the difference between internal and external capacities?

12. Business leaders tend to look at education from an economic perspective. What does this mean?

Other Suggested Activities

1. Determine whether your state promulgated school reform laws and policies from 1983 to 1987. Then determine whether the laws and policies were indicative of first-wave reforms described in this chapter.

2. Discuss whether it is possible to pursue excellence and equity at the same time.

3. Develop a list of purposes for public education. Determine which purposes are most important to you.

4. Assume you are a principal and you must develop a vision for your school. How would you proceed? Who would you involve?

References

Bacharach, S. B. (1990). Education reform: Making sense of it all. In S. Bacharach (Ed.), *Education reform: Making sense of it all* (pp. 1–6). Boston: Allyn and Bacon.

Boyer, E. L. (1985). In the aftermath of excellence. *Educational Leadership, 46*(6), 10–13.

Cuban, L. (1998). How schools change reforms: Redefining reform success and failure. *Teachers College Record, 99*(3), 453–477.

Dye, T. R. (1992). *Understanding public policy* (7th ed.). Englewood Cliffs, NJ: Prentice-Hall.

Finn, C. E. (1991). *We must take charge.* New York: The Free Press.

Fullan, M. (1999). *Change forces: The sequel.* Philadelphia: Falmer Press.

Gardner, J. W. (1984). *Excellence.* New York: W. W. Norton.

Glass, T. (2000). Changes in society and schools. In T. J. Kowalski (Ed.), *Public relations in schools* (2nd ed.) (pp. 30–45). Upper Saddle River, NJ: Merrill, Prentice-Hall.

Glickman, C. (1991). Pretending not to know what we know. *Educational Leadership, 48*(8), 4–10.

Hall, G. E., & Hord, S. M. (2001). *Implementing change: Patterns, principles, and potholes.* Boston: Allyn and Bacon.

Hanson, E. M. (1991). Educational restructuring in the USA: Movements of the 1980s. *Journal of Educational Administration, 29*(4), 30–38.

Hawley, W. D. (1988). Missing pieces in the educational reform agenda: Or, why the first and second waves may miss the boat. *Educational Administration Quarterly, 24*(4), 416–437.

Hodgkinson, H. (1989). *The same client: The demographics of education and service delivery systems.* Washington, DC: Institute for Educational Leadership.

Johnson, W. L., & Snyder, K. J. (1989–90). Instructional leadership training needs of administrators. *National Forum of Educational Administration and Supervision Journal, 6*(3), 80–95.

Kirst, M. W. (1988). Recent state education reform in the United States: Looking backward and forward. *Educational Administration Quarterly, 24*(3), 319–328.

Kowalski, T. J. (1995). *Keepers of the flame: Contemporary urban superintendents.* Thousand Oaks, CA: Corwin Press.

Kowalski, T. J. (1999). *The school superintendent: Theory, practice, and cases.* Upper Saddle River, NJ: Merrill, Prentice-Hall.

Kowalski, T. J. (2002). *School facility management* (2nd ed.). Greenwood, CT: Bergin & Garvey.

Krotseng, M. V. (1990). Of state capitals and catalysts: The power of external prodding. In L. Marcus & B. Stickney (Eds.), *Politics and policy in the age of education* (pp. 243–262). Springfield, IL: Charles Thomas.

Marcus, L. R. (1990). Far from the banks of the Potomac: Educational politics and policy in the Reagan years. In L. Marcus & B. Stickney (Eds.), *Politics and policy in the age of education* (pp. 32–55). Springfield, IL: Charles Thomas.

Metz, M. H. (1990). Hidden assumptions preventing real reform: Some missing elements in the educational reform movement. In S. Bacharach (Ed.), *Education reform: Making sense of it all* (pp. 141–154). Boston: Allyn and Bacon.

National Center for Education Statistics. (1997). *The condition of education, 1997.* Washington, DC: U.S. Department of Education.

National Center for Education Statistics. (2000). *Digest of education statistics, 2000.* Washington, DC: U.S. Department of Education.

Newman, J. W. (1990). *America's teachers.* New York: Longman.

Passow, A. H. (1988). Whither (or wither?) school reform? *Educational Administration Quarterly, 24*(3), 246–256.

Passow, A. H. (1995). Nurturing potential talent in a diverse population. In E. Flaxman & A. H. Passow (Eds.), *Changing populations, changing schools* (pp. 59–80). Chicago: University of Chicago Press.

Petrie, H. G. (1990). Reflections on the second wave of reform: Restructuring the teaching profession. In S. Jacobson & J. Conway (Eds.), *Educational leadership in an age of reform* (pp. 14–29). New York: Longman.

Popenoe, D. (1996). *Life without failure.* New York: The Free Press.

Reyes, P., Wagstaff, L. H., & Fusarelli, L. D. (1999). Delta forces: The changing fabric of American society and education. In J. Murphy & K. Seashore Louis (Eds.), *Handbook of research on educational administration* (2nd ed.) (pp. 183–201). San Franciso: Jossey-Bass.

Reynolds, W. B. (1986). Education alternatives to transportation failures: The desegregation response to a resegregation dilemma. *Metropolitan Education, 1,* 3–14.

Rubin, L. (1984). Formulating education policy in the aftermath of the reports. *Educational Leadership, 42*(2), 7–10.

Saban, A. (1997). Emerging themes of national educational reform. *International Journal of Educational Reform, 6*(3), 349–356.

Sarason, S. B. (1990). *The predictable failure of educational reform.* San Francisco: Jossey-Bass.

Sarason, S. B. (1996). *Revisiting the culture of the school and the problem of change.* New York: Teachers College Press.

Scheurich, J. J., & Imber, M. (1991). Educational reforms can reproduce societal inequities: A case study. *Educational Administration Quarterly, 27*(3), 297–320.

Schlecty, P. C. (1990). *Schools for the twenty-first century: Leadership imperatives for educational reform.* San Francisco: Jossey-Bass.

Shanker, A. (1988). Reforming the reform movement. *Educational Administration Quarterly, 24*(4), 366–373.

Spring, J. (1990). *The American school: 1642–1990* (2nd ed.). New York: Longman.

Stratton, J. (1995). *How students have changed: A call to action for our children's future.* Arlington, VA: American Association of School Administrators.

Timar, T. (1989). The politics of school restructuring. *Phi Delta Kappan, 71*(4), 264–276.

13

Responses to Student Needs and Public Dissatisfaction

The final report on the current reform movement may not be written for another 10 to 20 years, partly because ideas and evidence regarding effectiveness are still evolving and partly because the public's interests in specific reforms have been fleeting. Although citizens expect schools to respond to the problems of the day by making adaptations, their interest often wanes when new and more threatening problems emerge (Timar & Kirp, 1987). In addition, educators face the conflicting expectations of preserving and improving society (Reyes, Wagstaff, & Fusarelli, 1999). At the practical level, these conflicting roles often create considerable controversy in areas such as sex education and bilingual education.

First, this chapter examines the reasons why reform has been an elusive goal for public education. Second, selected reforms are discussed to demonstrate the range of different perspectives that influence school-improvement initiatives. The examples are divided into two broad categories: market-driven reforms and school restructuring. Market-driven reforms are basically predicated on the assumption that schools will improve if policy decisions move from the public-sector economy to the market economy. School restructuring entails socially driven reforms concerned with improving opportunities for students. Whereas market-driven reforms are anchored in the belief that competition produces improvement, restructuring is anchored in the belief that schools must be reconfigured to address evolving social and educational needs.

Failure and an Unfinished Agenda

The political and social climate of the modern reform era, especially during the formative years in the mid-1980s, is important to understanding why public school reform has been so problematical. The following contextual factors are especially cogent:

- *Federal government's role:* Philosophical divisions over the purposes of education are reflected in the shifting role of the federal government over the past 25 years. As control of the administrative and legislative branches of government changed, so too did the emphasis on guiding values for public education. Thus, the federal government has been less than consistent in emphasizing excellence, equity, and liberty.
- *Technology:* The rapid development of technology served to redefine effective practice in both teaching (Donlevy & Donlevy, 1997) and administration (Mehlinger, 1996).
- *The business community:* Beginning in the early 1980s, top business executives became some of the most vocal critics of public education. Their access to elected officials, their financial resources, and their economic perspectives made them a powerful voice in the school reform movement (Cuban, 1992).
- *The media:* Dissatisfaction with schools and attempted reforms were given considerable media coverage, and reporters played a key role in shaping public opinion (Feir, 1995).
- *Funding:* Often, there was little or no nexus between state reform efforts and state funding policies (Hertert, 1996). This was because many policymakers and taxpayers believed that schools could be improved without funding increases, although proponents of this view provided little or no evidence to support the claim.
- *Political coalitions:* Most reform initiates, although state centered, were developed or supported by national networks consisting largely of elected officials and business leaders. Until the very late 1980s, traditional education interest groups had relatively little influence on reform (Feir, 1995).

As change initiatives failed to meet expectations, they were rarely replaced. Instead, new ideas were layered on top of them. For example, many of the intensification mandates promulgated between 1983 and 1987 remain in effect even though the primary targets and strategies for school improvement are now different.

Reasons for Failure

Education reform has recurred periodically since the late nineteenth century, suggesting that most change initiatives were either ineffective or effective only for a brief time. In part, reform has been elusive because it involves change—and the very process of change is unpopular and disconcerting. But in the case of public education, there were substantive barriers as well. Following are some of the more important ones:

- *Conflicting values:* Larry Cuban (1988) postulated that reform efforts often failed because problems were framed incorrectly. That is, the problems were viewed as being simple and solvable when they "were instead persistent dilemmas involving hard choices between conflicting values. Such choices seldom get resolved but rather get managed; that is, compromises are struck until the dilemmas reappear" (p. 329).
- *Ineffective strategies:* Two primary approaches have been used to change schools: the use of power and coercion and the introduction of new ideas through staff development. The former approach has never really worked well in public education because reliance on laws, regulations, and mandates flies in the face of conventional wisdom (Finn, 1991). Teachers and administrators obviously have the power to derail such efforts, and they resent being treated as nonprofessionals. The latter approach proves effective only when the change initiatives are congruous with the basic values and beliefs of educators.
- *Flawed assumptions:* Not only did many reformers frame problems incorrectly but they also often relied on myths rather than empirical evidence (Pogrow, 1996). Thus, their perspectives on critical issues such as professional preparation, the existing knowledge base, and organizational change were at best narrow and at worst incorrect.
- *An imbalance between risk and reward:* Although many proposed changes required administrators and teachers to take risks, no effort was made to develop an appropriate reward system. Instead of actually holding individual educators accountable for student outcomes, the traditional system rewarded them for adhering to routine behaviors (Glickman, 1991; Shanker, 1990). That is, the reward structure in public schools had not been oriented toward rewarding performance (Boyd, 1988a).
- *Fragmentation:* Michael Fullan (2000) called fragmentation one of the primary barriers to large-scale reform. Reforms have often been contradictory in nature, poorly implemented, and eventually abandoned (Orlich, 1989). Many of the ideas were disjointed and ignored the fundamental questions surrounding the purposes of schooling (Soltis, 1988).
- *Inadequate funding:* A number of prominent leaders wanted the general public to believe that schools could be radically improved without additional funding. Although such notions have obvious political merit, they are not supported by the facts. Those who argue that money is not the problem ignore

realities concerning poverty, cultural diversity, and the range of societal problems that have seriously complicated the missions of schools. Clearly, one of the greatest problems with reform efforts has been the notion that schools can be markedly improved without any additional funding (Boyd, 1988b).

- *Short attention span:* As noted at the beginning of this chapter, enthusiasm for reforms tends to diminish when new problems evolve, even though the old problems have not been solved (Timar & Kirp, 1987). Thus, many citizens may not be as deeply committed to school reform as reformers have been led to believe; rather, their initial support for school reform may be associated with the felt need to alleviate discomforts and fears created by such things as economic downturns, illegal drugs, and violence.
- *Failure to address total student needs:* Student performance in school is affected by social and personal conditions, and this fact has often been ignored in school reform. A child who comes to school abused and hungry, for instance, is unlikely to achieve at a level commensurate with his or her potential unless social services are coordinated so that the total needs of the student are met (Smrekar & Mawhinney, 1999). Thus, some reform initiatives have failed to live up to expectations because the underlying causes of poor academic performance were never really addressed.
- *Failure to address school culture:* The traditions of public education are strong, and even intense and prolonged criticism has not produced change. Studying this issue, noted psychologist Seymour Sarason (1996) concluded that behavior in schools was controlled by a long-standing culture that was passed from one generation of educators to the next through socialization. He argued that reformers have basically ignored culture and that educators are incapable of reshaping their own culture because they know little about organizational life and change processes.

An Unfinished Agenda

Pointing to the history of public education, cynics believe that the current quest for school reform, despite being protracted, will gradually fade away, leaving schools much as they were in 1980. Because change initiatives have often been unconnected to the real work of teachers and to improvement in student learning (Seashore Louis, Toole, & Hargreaves, 1999), many educators share this viewpoint. Even so, there are reasons to believe that this era of reform is different.

Clearly, the insights and conclusions guiding reforms changed as educators were given an opportunity to participate in policy development during the second wave. As a result, policymakers outside the profession have gained a more accurate understanding of basic problems and possible solutions. Following are some of the most important transitions that occurred between the first and second waves (see Figure 13.1 concerning a broader range of differences between first wave reforms and contemporary reforms):

- *Fragmentation to coordination:* Reformers recognize that fragmented individual tasks are insufficient to produce lasting school improvement (Soltis,

	First Wave →	Current Reform Efforts
Reform targets:	Students and educators	Schools
Primary change approach:	Fix broken parts	Restructure
Primary change strategy:	Intensification mandates	Cultural change
Primary governance strategy:	Centralized control	Decentralized control
Power and authority:	Autocratic	Democratic
Locus of policy development:	State	Local district and school
Coupling of reform ideas:	Fragmented	Coordinated
View of schools as organizations:	Rational, ordered	Irrational, complex

FIGURE 13.1   *Transitions between First-Wave Reforms and Contemporary Reforms*

1988); consequently, greater effort is now being given to coordinating change initiatives. In addition, policymakers are giving more thought to integrating school improvement with social services—especially in areas where there are high concentrations of students at risk.

- *Renovation to reconstruction:* At least through the first wave of reform, most reformers believed that they could improve schools sufficiently by fixing broken parts. In addition, the programs they advocated were largely cosmetic and did little to change school climate. Current reforms are shaped by the assumption that the organization of the school, the distribution of authority, decision making, and school culture need to be altered if schools are to become more effective (Bauman, 1996).
- *Autocratic to democratic:* Democratic processes reflected in shared visions, school councils, and shared decision making have replaced autocratic processes in which power elites mandated change (Bauman, 1996).
- *People to institution:* Whereas students and educators were the primary targets of first-wave reforms, more recent efforts have focused on school climate (Kowalski, 1999); consequently, reformers now believe that schools cannot be improved sufficiently unless they are restructured.
- *Order to complexity:* Assumptions of rationality and order characterized first-wave reforms; subsequent initiatives have been more prone to view communities and schools as being complex, unpredictable, and dynamic (Seashore Louis et al., 1999). This revised perspective has encouraged reformers to move away from traditional, linear planning models.

Strategy transitions reveal the fact that reform is now being guided by a new set of assumptions, including the following:

- *Neither total centralization nor total decentralization suffices.* Complete centralization invalidates liberty and provides too much control; complete decentralization invalidates equity and provides too little control (Fullan, 1999; Timar & Kirp, 1989). Historically, conflict between primary values guiding public policy has led to compromise; thus, reform becomes more likely when centralization and decentralization are appropriately balanced.

- *The most critical elements of reform are likely to be accomplished at the local level.* If reforms are to address teaching and learning, then change initiatives need to be tailored to the real needs in local communities. Visioning and planning at the local level are more likely to produce this outcome than are national or state visions and plans (Seashore Louis et al., 1999). However, neither deregulation nor decentralization diminishes the legal responsibility of state government to set broad goals and expectations and to hold local districts accountable for meeting them.

- *External connections are essential to visioning and planning.* Schools, just as other organizations, must be able to identify and solve real problems that affect success. Doing this requires "across-boundary collaboration," allowing school officials to shape reforms with broad involvement from individuals inside and outside the organization (Fullan, 1999).

- *Schools cannot be sufficiently improved unless organizational cultures are reshaped.* What actually occurs in classrooms on a daily basis is heavily influenced by school culture. Improving schools requires underlying values and beliefs to be identified and discussed; those detrimental to school improvement need to be altered (Sarason, 1996).

- *Educators must develop the internal capacity to change.* The potential benefits of professionalism and democratic decision making are attenuated if educators are incapable of or unwilling to assume the responsibilities inherent in these concepts (Seashore Louis et al., 1999). Unfortunately, many educators, including administrators, have known far too little about the nature of organizations and the essence of organizational culture (Sarason, 1996).

- *External resources must support change efforts.* Change often fails when it is not widely supported by the public (political support) and when it is not adequately funded (economic support) (Swanson & King, 1997). It also fails when reform inside the school is disconnected from a student's life outside the school. Therefore, external resources serve two critical functions in relation to school improvement programs: sustaining them and complimenting them.

- *Balancing excellence, liberty, and equity is essential.* Policy for public education has always been guided by basic values that are widely supported in society— even when the values compete with each other (Swanson & King, 1997). Consequently, tensions between excellence and equity and between liberty and equity need to be resolved through compromise if reforms are to be widely accepted by educators and society.

Reform through Market-Oriented Concepts

Many major reform ideas "are anchored in consumer- or market-oriented ideologies" (Murphy, 1999, p. 405). In the public sector of the economy, elected officials or trustees—individuals who are expected to act in the best interests of entire communities—make decisions about the allocation of scarce resources. In the market, individual consumers, based on personal needs and interests, make such decisions. The purpose of the public-sector economy is to ensure that vital services are not subjected to the whims and economic means of individual citizens. Thus, the military, police protection, fire protection, schools, and similar services function in this economy.

Critics, however, argue that keeping schools in the public-sector economy ensures their status as a quasi-monopoly—a condition that they believe allows school officials to be inefficient and schools to be mediocre. Those favoring market-driven approaches for government services have waged several arguments in this vein:

- Considerable evidence shows that government agencies are inefficient and frequently incur unnecessary losses (Hemming & Mansoor, 1988). Stories about the military purchasing toilet seats for $10,000 serve as an example.
- Public managers, such as school administrators, lack property rights or profit motives in the successful performance of the organization (Boyd, 1988a). Thus, public administrators lack incentives to increase organizational productivity.
- Public organizations (including schools) receive tax-supplied budgets independent of satisfying consumers (Boyd, 1988a). Schools typically receive funding increases even when productivity declines.
- Increases in government spending rarely result in improved services. That is, problems are not eradicated by new government programs and increased allocations, and in some instances, they are even aggravated (Savas, 1987).
- The fundamental beliefs in which the public-sector economy is rooted are either false or exaggerated. For example, government officials (including school board members) often make political or self-serving decisions instead of objectively caring for the needs of communities or society.

After 1983, market-based concepts grew in popularity, partly because advocates usually presented their ideas in philosophical rather than economic terms. For example, school choice addresses both a basic value (liberty) and an economic concept (achieving improvement through increased competition in the market). The idea that parents should have greater freedom to select schools for their children obviously was more popular than the idea that a vital social service such as education should be subjected to supply-and-demand conditions shaped by individual consumer decisions.

Choice Programs

Choice programs are predicated on several assumptions. The first is that there is a relationship between wealth and education choices that allows wealthy families to have many choices and poor families to have none. For example, wealthy families can opt to live in areas served by outstanding districts and schools; poor families are usually trapped in areas where the schools are riddled with problems. Wealthy families can take advantage of private schools; poor families cannot afford the tuition. The second assumption is that given a choice, most parents will opt to send their children to the best available school; that is, they will make informed choices on behalf of their children. Third, choice will create competition among schools—a condition that will eventually force poor schools to improve or to be closed. In their book, *Politics, Markets, and America's Schools,* John Chubb and Terry Moe (1990) argued that public education is a massive bureaucracy requiring restructuring and competition to remain effective. They hypothesized that parental choice would force schools to change in positive ways. Faced with competition, they concluded, administrators and teachers would literally be forced to improve.

The term *choice* has been used generically and this has caused considerable confusion because there are several forms of choice. The type of program developed depends on the intentions, assumptions, and commitments of the policymakers (Raywid, 1992). One version, *intra-district choice,* allows parents to send their children to any school within the district in which they legally reside. Districts providing this option almost always place some restrictions on the program. For example, parents may not be able to send their children to another school if the transfer results in overcrowding or racial imbalances. Or parents may be required to provide transportation if they transfer their children to another school. Larger school districts have often created magnet schools (special theme schools designed to attract students who would otherwise not enroll at this location) as part of an intra-district choice program. Proponents of intra-district choice have argued that the program increases liberty and promotes competition among schools without moving the funding of education and policy decisions into the market economy.

The second form of choice is referred to as *inter-district choice.* Here, parents can elect to send their children to any public school in the state in which they legally reside without paying tuition. Parents who elect to send their children to private schools get no benefits under this program. In terms of restrictions and purposes, statewide programs are a larger-scale version of intra-district programs. Parents have more choices, competition among local districts is expected to evolve, and the funding of education and policy decisions are not moved to the market economy.

The third version of this concept is *total choice.* This adaptation empowers parents to send their children to any school, public or private, in their state of legal residence. State support is either funneled to the parents (usually in the form of a voucher or tax credit) sent to the school in which the student enrolls. Total choice intentionally pulls education funding away from the public-sector economy; therefore, policymakers who prefer to have governmental services in the market economy have favored it.

Critics of choice programs, especially total choice, have pointed to a number of potential problems:

- Parents often choose private schools solely on the basis of religious faith; choice programs therefore provide a mechanism for funding parochial schools (Witte, 1995).

- Many families use choice to escape racially integrated schools; thus, choice plans can be an enabling force for segregation (Margonis & Parker, 1995).
- Families that take advantage of choice are those that least need access to the program—that is, middle- and upper-class families (Witte, 1995).
- If not properly structured, choice programs can be discriminatory toward special education students; that is, many private schools may refuse to admit students who have special needs (McKinney & Mead, 1996).
- Regardless of intent, schools participating in choice programs can, and do, refuse to enroll certain students (Witte, 1995).
- The self-interests of wealthy and powerful individuals and not the will of the people are often responsible for choice legislation (Mazzoni, 1991).

Despite these concerns, many policymakers have remained very interested in school choice as a means of moving public school funding away from the public-sector economy. Some cities (e.g., Milwaukee) and states (e.g., Florida) already have experimented with full choice programs.

By 1990, more than 20 states either passed choice legislation or were considering doing so (Association for Supervision and Curriculum Development, 1990). Beyond the more traditional arguments that center on the need for competition, some proponents also contend that choice is needed if we are to destroy the myth that there is "one best method" for educating children (Raywid, 1987). Choice, according to them, would likely produce competing philosophies, curricula, and instructional methods. Supporters also suggest that school choice promotes bonding between schools and parents—a condition deemed to be lacking in many public schools.

Four conditions have been suggested as a framework for determining the effectiveness of choice programs (Clinchy, 1989):

1. There must be sufficient diversity among available schools for parents to have a real choice.
2. Schools must have the leeway to be sufficiently diverse—a condition that requires autonomy (i.e., some degree of state deregulation and district decentralization).
3. The degree of choice afforded to all families should be reasonably equal.
4. The program should be sufficiently funded to ensure that it will function as intended.

Funding is an especially important consideration because many choice advocates believe that the concept can be implemented without additional state spending on education.

Vouchers and Tax Credits

Vouchers are another market-driven concept. "In a voucher system, governments subsidize students' education directly by distributing vouchers that parents then use to purchase educational services" (Adams & Kirst, 1999, p. 471). A voucher may be used to pay for tuition up to the maximum amount specified. When a student enrolls in a school, the voucher is typically given to the school as a whole or partial tuition payment. School officials then redeem the vouchers to receive the state support.

Noted economist Milton Friedman is credited with developing this concept in the mid-1950s. Friedman believed that providing education and paying for it were separate functions; thus, he concluded that states could pay for even private education without violating constitutions. He argued that vouchers would produce three desirable outcomes (Alexander & Salmon, 1995):

1. Parents would have greater freedom to choose (a liberty-based argument).
2. Public education would lose its status as a monopoly.
3. Increased competition would result in improved education.

Another market-driven concept involves giving parents of private school students a tax credit to offset tuition costs. This approach has generally been less controversial than total choice or vouchers, probably because the aid to parents is indirect. Like total choice and vouchers, the purposes of tuition tax credits are to increase parental options and to force public schools to compete with private schools for students.

Objections to both vouchers and tuition tax credits are the same as those articulated for choice. The most prevalent objections have involved potential violations of the separation of church and state, economic segregation, and racial segregation.

Charter Schools

As noted earlier in this book, public education is delivered through local districts in 49 states. A charter school bypasses this governance structure; it is "an independent school of choice, freed from rules but accountable for results" (Manno, Finn, & Vanourek, 2000, p. 737). Charter schools are often described as hybrid institutions—a combination of public and private schools. Like other public schools, they are supposed to be open to all students, they receive state funding, and they are held accountable by the state. But charter schools also possess two critical characteristics of private schools: They are independent (as opposed to being part of a local district) and they are institutions of choice (i.e., parents elect to send their children to these schools) (Manno et al., 2000).

Organizations comprising the traditional establishment in public education have been generally opposed to charter schools. The objections have centered on the belief that many of these schools do not meet their obligations as publicly funded institutions—a condition that is almost always ignored by policymakers when they make comparisons between the productivity of charter schools and traditional public schools. More specifically, charter schools have been accused of the following:

- Practicing selective admissions (e.g., Watkins, 1999)
- Avoiding service to special education students (e.g., McKinney, 1996)

- Cutting corners by reducing basic services such as student transportation (e.g., Dykgraaf & Lewis, 1998)
- Being quick to expel undesirable students (e.g., Watkins, 1999)
- Undermining the need to provide high-quality education for all students (Molnar, 1996)

Critics also charge that charter school legislation, if not sufficiently restrictive, permits public revenues to be used to support churches (in cases where churches operate charter schools) and encourages economic and racial segregation.

By 1997, 21 states had enacted charter school legislation, but their laws and policies were not uniform (Banks, Huston, Murphy, & Muth, 1996). Thus, the degree to which charter schools were required to abide by the same standards as traditional public schools varied. Influenced by lobbyists favoring market concepts, several states have given charter holders considerable leeway to function as private schools. Because of differences in ways that charter schools are organized and operate (e.g., some are operated as for-profit institutions), it is not surprising that evidence regarding their effectiveness has been mixed. Studying selected charter schools, Seymour Sarason (1998) concluded that many of them will fail or fall short of their goals due to politics, resistance from vested interests (primarily teachers' unions, school board organizations, and administrator groups), and a lack of knowledge related to creating and maintaining a positive school culture.

Reform through Restructuring

The concept of restructuring has been interpreted in different ways, ranging from top-down, ruthless retrenchment to power sharing and professionalism (Hargreaves, 1994). For some, restructuring has become synonymous with specific reform initiatives, such as empowerment, decentralization, and professionalism (Tyack, 1990). Restructuring is treated here as a socially driven, broad strategy that is primarily focused on transforming organizational structure, traditional political alignments, instructional practices, and institutional culture. Unlike market-driven concepts, restructuring does not attempt to move schools away from the public-sector economy. To exemplify the way this strategy has been employed, three restructuring concepts are examined here.

Site-Based Management

During the 1960s and 1970s, centralization became even more pervasive in public education because of district consolidation, union contracts, federal legislation (e.g., civil rights laws), the increased use of litigation to adjudicate equity-related disputes, and increased federal and state regulations. David Tyack (1990) noted that circumstances during these two decades created a compliance orientation for many administrators—a condition he labeled *fragmented centralization*. The persistent flow of new laws, government regulations, and judicial decisions made school board members and superintendents apprehensive about granting excessive autonomy to employees. For example, allowing principals complete freedom to employ teachers could result in inconsistent practices that induce discrimination lawsuits against local districts.

During the 1980s, reformers became increasingly critical of centralization. They argued that the real needs of students varied not only from district to district but also from school to school. Therefore, "one-size-fits-all" laws and policies—common attributes of highly centralized systems—were viewed as barriers to true reform, and interest in decentralization was rekindled. "Policy analysts note that proposals for delegating decision making to individual schools and sharing authority among principals, teachers, parents, and community representatives tend to go through reiterative cycles that are in accord with state centralization or decentralization policies" (Björk, 2001, p. 289). The professional literature (e.g., Brown, 1990) suggests that organizations pursue decentralization paradigms in an effort to achieve one or more of the following goals:

- *Higher levels of flexibility:* Allowing schools to make decisions based on the real needs of students
- *Accountability:* Holding individual schools more accountable for the decisions that are made
- *Productivity:* Increasing student learning by virtue of school-based decision making

The most popular form of decentralization, *site-based management,* is shaped by two key concepts: autonomy and shared decision making (David, 1989). In the typical site-based school, you would find a school council consisting of teachers, parents, and even students. This council would have the authority to make decisions in areas that previously were the domain of the school board, superintendent, or principal. The range of authority relegated to school councils varies substantially depending on laws and the philosophy of the school board and superintendent. The general principles of site-based management are rooted in three assumptions about school improvement:

1. Meaningful change is most likely to occur at the school level rather than at the school district or state level.
2. For change to occur, individual schools must be given a certain degree of leeway to implement broad policies and goals.
3. Shared decision making creates a sense of community and a necessary level of commitment to bring about lasting change.

Charles Achilles (1994) called site-based management education's response to industrial downsizing, a shift from an assembly-line mentality to quality and service.

Rather than a specific program, site-based management is a broad construct. Five variables serve to identify differences in implementation from one school to another (Brown, 1990):

1. *Structure:* How authority has been realigned
2. *Flexibility:* The extent to which modifications can be made easily and rapidly
3. *Accountability:* The extent to which the school council, principal, and faculty are held responsible for the decisions that are made
4. *Productivity:* Differences in the quality of decisions and student outcomes
5. *Change:* The extent to which the concept has move the school away from traditional organization, teaching practices, political alignments, and culture

As is the case with any innovation, site-based management generates concerns relative to authority and responsibility. The following have been some of the more frequent criticisms:

- Involving large numbers of people in decisions politicizes the process and does not necessarily lead to better decisions (Conway, 1984). For example, council members are apt to form factions and compete for power and influence.
- Merely creating councils does not ensure shared decision making; there is little evidence that site-based management has lived up to its promises in this regard (Malen, 1999). For example, some school councils are merely rubber stamps for the principal, whereas others rarely make decisions.
- Allowing schools considerable autonomy fosters inequity. For example, schools with effective councils and principals often develop productive programs, whereas others do not. Over time, this unevenness in program quality results in legitimate questions about equal access to educational opportunities for all students in the district.
- Democracy and professionalism—two facets of site-based management—are basically incompatible and will produce considerable conflict (Zeichner, 1991). For example, a majority decision on a textbook adoption may be at odds with what is best in the eyes of the teachers.
- The use of councils contributes to role ambiguity. In some instances, principals find themselves being accountable to as many as 10 or 12 individuals who comprise the council (Ford, 1992).
- Without changing the fundamental beliefs and values that have made schools bureaucratic-like institutions, the development of school councils is only cosmetic (English, 1990).
- Often, decisions made by councils are disjointed and unrelated to a shared vision (Midgley & Wood, 1993). This is especially likely when councils have weak leadership and when they work without a long-term agenda.
- The decentralization of decision making may actually undermine the use of knowledge rather than promote it—especially when it occurs without

appropriate guidance from district-level personnel. Left alone, school councils may make decisions predicated on self-interests and personal biases rather than on research and best practice (Corcoran, Fuhrman, & Belcher, 2001).

The last point is especially meaningful because it reveals the tensions that exist between professionalism and democracy. Often, decisions supported by the knowledge base are politically unpopular, and administrators find that they must compromise between what they know to be the best course of action and an acceptable course of action. In essence, critical choices are often guided by emotion rather than rationality and objectivity.

Professional Development Schools

The concept of professional development schools was developed by the Holmes Group, a consortium of teacher education universities, in response to growing demands for improved teacher education. Conceptually, the professional development school was to be analogous to the teaching hospital in medical education. The primary intents were as follows:

- Build a synergistic relationship between schools and teacher preparation programs.
- Create a restructured school environment in which teachers and administrators function as true professionals (Anderson, Rolheiser, & Gordon, 1998).
- Develop learning communities (Levine, 1997).
- Foster professionalism and professional accountability (Levine, 1998).
- Develop innovative teaching practices.
- Disseminate information about research and successful practices (Stallings & Kowalski, 1990).

Thus, professional development schools always have a university partner or sponsoring institution, and the school provides a site for pre-student teaching and student teaching experiences.

In some respects, professional development schools are an extension of the laboratory school concept in that they provide environments where staff development, experimentation, and research are encouraged (Stallings & Kowalski, 1990). Like site-based management, professional development schools typically rely on a council or coordinating committee; however, less emphasis is typically placed on community involvement.

Criticisms of professional development schools have focused on the following concerns:

- University and school personnel often work in different cultures, and when they are brought together, considerable conflict is likely (Pritchett, 1999).

- Often, university personnel and school personnel have different motives, and a lack of trust deters their work (Davis, 1999).
- Teachers who are already overburdened with work are expected to devote considerable time to working with teacher education interns.
- Teacher education interns conduct a considerable amount of the instruction, and this often leads to student and parental dissatisfaction (Pritchett, 1999).

Creating a professional learning community is the nucleus of the professional development school, and to date, there is no evidence as to whether these schools have been able to erect new cultures to sustain this reform. There is evidence, however, that these schools have enhanced collegiality and research opportunities (Kochan, 1998).

Integrative Services

The concept of integrative services is premised on the belief that many children are unable to learn in school because of social, economic, emotional, physical, and psychological problems (Dryfoos, 1996). Basically, two approaches have been proposed for addressing the total needs of students. The first is the *full-service school*—an organizational configuration that integrates educational, medical, and social services (MacKenzie & Rogers, 1997). With this approach, students are able to see physicians, dentists, psychologists, social workers, and other specialists without leaving the school building. The second approach involves integration of social services without placing all service providers directly in the school. This concept, often referred to as *school-linked integrative services,* describes a configuration in which the school is an equal partner with other human service agencies (Smrekar & Mawhinney, 1999).

Full-service schools face several substantial barriers. Three are particularly noteworthy:

1. *Unanswered questions about governance:* Who will be responsible for coordinating the work of health-care providers? Will administrators in these schools assume the same role as hospital administrators in relation to health-care providers or will their relationship be different?
2. *Unanswered funding questions:* Who will provide the resources to remodel and expand schools so that necessary clinical settings are provided? How will expanded services provided in schools be funded? Who will control the funds after they are made available?
3. *Unanswered questions about liability:* How will the provision of health-care services in a school affect risk management? To what extent will administrators and teachers be held accountable for problems that may occur in the delivery of these services?

There are additional barriers that affect both approaches to integrative services. The most notable include the following:

- *Taxpayer opposition to expanded services:* Many taxpayers already believe that society has become too dependent on government services; conservatives are especially inclined to oppose ideas that expand government programs in areas such as welfare and health care.
- *Student eligibility for services:* Who determines whether students require health-care services? Will all students be eligible to receive free services? Until these and other related questions are answered, assessing the extent of public support for integrated services will be virtually impossible.
- *Organizational opposition:* Most public agencies continue to have bureaucratic-type structures—a condition that prompts administrators to be apprehensive about collaborating with other agencies.
- *Professional opposition:* Efforts to involve the government more deeply in health care evoke disputes among health-care providers.

Integrative services require collaboration between public schools and other agencies. As such, problems endemic to these relationships also are relevant.

School Partnerships

Another concept that has enjoyed renewed popularity during this reform movement has been partnerships. In 1983, only 17 percent of the schools were engaged in such ventures, and by 1989, this figure rose to 40 percent (Marenda, 1989); in 1990, it was estimated that there were over 140,000 school-business partnerships (Rigden, 1991). Obviously, the growth of partnerships paralleled public disfavor with education. In simple terms, *partnerships* are joint ventures involving a district or school and some other organization or group developed to pursue mutual interests.

Education leaders have had different motives for pursuing partnerships. Some wanted additional resources; others wanted positive publicity and the political support it might produce; and still others were truly pursuing school improvement. Philosophically, public institutions in a democratic society are expected to maintain a symbiotic relationship with their communities—and partnerships provide one vehicle for achieving this goal.

The three most common partners for public schools have been communities or community groups, businesses, and colleges and universities. Table 13.1 shows examples of projects in each category.

Partnerships exist at different commitment levels, a factor that determines the extent to which an organization maintains autonomy (i.e., the right to act independently). Basically, school partnership ventures fall into one of the following four categories:

1. *Networking:* Partners merely share information; there is no reduction in autonomy.

TABLE 13.1   *Examples of Partnership Programs*

Partner Category	Examples of Partnership Ventures
Community agencies or groups	A citizenship program in a high school with the city council; a tutoring program in an elementary school with a parents' group; a recreation program in an elementary school with the local YMCA
Business or industry	A technology development program in a middle school with a utility company; a career development program in a middle school with a local bank
College or university	Development of science teaching materials between a school district and university; a joint adult education program involving a high school and community college

2. *Coordination:* Partners have a formal agreement that stipulates they will coordinate their activities; typically there is little or no reduction in autonomy.
3. *Cooperation:* Partners have a formal agreement and collaborate on only certain aspects of designated programs or processes; some degree of autonomy is maintained.
4. *Collaboration:* Partners have a formal agreement and commit to sharing power and authority for designated programs or processes.

Collaborative arrangements involve the greatest amount of risk, but they tend to produce the most lasting relationships.

Partnerships are like a marriage. When each partner is able to grow and prosper, the marriage is healthy. But when the relationship is plagued by selfishness, inadequate resources, unresolved conflict, and impatience, conflict becomes dysfunctional. In the case of schools, additional factors have proven to be essential for successful partnerships (Kowalski, 1999):

- *Incremental development:* Start with simple projects that are likely to produce success and move gradually to more complex projects.
- *Trust:* The partners are unconcerned about hidden agendas or unethical practices.
- *A shared vision and philosophy:* The partners agree on what should be accomplished and how things should be accomplished.
- *Mutual benefits:* The relationship is not one sided; both partners receive direct benefits.
- *Recognition:* Both partners enjoy positive publicity.
- *Governing board support:* The governing boards in both organizations are enthusiastic about the venture and fully support it.

Even though partnerships between schools and businesses are often success-ful, many school administrators remain cautious. First, they fear that corporate managers might use these joint ventures as a venue for imposing business values on the schools—for example, evaluating the success of programs solely in relation to economic efficiency. Second, they fear that the public may misinterpret the extent to which public school officials can or should raise money privately. For example, some taxpayers may believe that school districts should get resources from every business and industrial operation so that they become less dependent on taxes. And third, they are leery about the extent to which partners will be sufficiently patient. Many business executives expect to see quick results for investments, and this often is impossible in education.

Implications for Practice

There are many reasons why reform has been a difficult task for public education. One of the most important involves long-standing differences regarding the pur-poses of schooling. As you consider the barriers discussed in this chapter, evaluate the extent to which they have hindered improvements in your community's schools. Also, think about the extent to which taxpayers in your community sup-port meaningful change in public schools.

The public and many educators have the tendency to talk about reform initia-tives as if they were all alike. This is a mistake, because over the past two decades, very different philosophies and ideas have surfaced. Some reform proposals stem from an economic perspective and are grounded in the belief that competition guar-antees improvement. Other proposals stem from social and professional perspec-tives and are based on the belief that schools should be reconfigured as true learning communities. Proposals in the latter category have often generated questions regarding the extent to which school reform must be supported by broader initia-tives that address social and economic problems that place many students at risk of becoming education casualties.

The second wave of school reform has included broader reform strategies such as restructuring; however, the notion that schools can be improved by tinker-ing with programs and delivery systems is still very much evident. Ideas such as block scheduling, Tech Prep, and distance learning have been implemented with only a limited affect on the governance structure and culture of a school—and to date, evidence of their influence on improving student learning is quite limited. Although there have been many reform ideas and strategies, only one reform agenda remains relevant: "improving teaching and learning for all" (Firestone et al., 1991, p. 245).

How has more than two decades of proposed reforms affected practice in school administration? One outcome has been a heightened emphasis on leader-ship in the literature and in professional preparation. Gradually, this emphasis also has become visible in the role expectations articulated by people who employ administrators. Because much of the reform in education is expected to occur at the local level, contemporary principals and superintendents are expected to have the technical, human, and analytical skills necessary to restructure school climates; and they are expected to be visionary leaders and competent managers.

For Further Discussion _____

1. During the current reform movement, political coalitions have played an important role in shaping policy. What forces cause these coalitions to form? How are these coalitions able to exert political influence?

2. What is the difference between inter-district and intra-district choice?

3. What beliefs are associated with trying to move public education from the public-sector economy to the market?

4. What is the difference between vouchers and tax credits? Which option usually evokes the greatest criticism or concern?

5. Three types of choice were discussed in this chapter. To what extent does each type create competition for public schools?

6. What is the difference between networking and collaboration? Could each qualify as a partnership? Why or why not?

7. What assumptions are associated with decentralization concepts, such as site-based management?

8. What is a charter school? Do all states have uniform laws regarding charter schools?

9. Two recurring criticisms of market-oriented reforms involve violations of church and state and economic and racial segregation. How might charter schools and vouchers contribute to each of these problems?

10. Some administrators remain cautious about establishing partnership ventures with school districts. Why?

11. Why is it important for partnership ventures to be mutually beneficial?

12. What factors contributed to increased centralization in public education during the 1960s and 1970s? What criticisms of centralization were resurrected in the 1980s?

13. What are the purposes of a professional development school? To what extent could these purposes alter the climate of schools?

14. Many experts agree that meaningful reform will not occur unless the culture of schools is altered. Why do they reach this conclusion?

15. How might site-based management create equity concerns in a school district?

16. What is the difference between a full-service school and school-linked integrative services? What conditions have prompted some reformers to propose them?

Other Suggested Activities

1. Discuss the possible tensions between schools becoming more democratic and more professional.

2. Determine whether your local schools have established partnerships. What conclusions might you draw from the following: (a) the purpose of the partnerships, (b) the duration of the partnerships, and (c) the extent to which the partnerships are publicized?

3. Compare and contrast site-based management with the professional development school concept.

4. Earlier in the book, school climate was described as having four components: ecology, milieu, organization, and culture. Identify several examples of possible reform barriers in each of these components.

References

Achilles, C. (1994). Democracy and site-based administration: The impact on education. *NASSP Bulletin, 78*(558), 12–21.

Adams, J. E., & Kirst, M. W. (1999). New demands and concepts for educational accountability: Striving for results in an era of excellence. In J. Murphy & K. Seashore Louis (Eds.), *Handbook of research on educational administration* (2nd ed.) (pp. 463–490). San Francisco: Jossey-Bass.

Alexander, K., & Salmon, R. G. (1995). *Public school finance.* Boston: Allyn and Bacon.

Anderson, S., Rolheiser, C., & Gordon, K. (1998). Preparing teachers to be leaders. *Educational Leadership, 55*(5), 59–61.

Association for Supervision and Curriculum Development. (1990). *Public schools of choice: ASCD issues analysis.* Alexandria, VA: Author.

Banks, D., Huston, P., Murphy, M., & Muth, R. (1996, April). *Charter schools: Let the games begin.* Paper presented at the annual conference of the American Educational Research Association, New York.

Bauman, P. C. (1996). *Governing education: Public sector reform or privatization.* Boston: Allyn and Bacon.

Björk, L. G. (2001). The role of the central office in decentralization. In T. J. Kowalski (Ed.), *21st century challenges for school administration: The 2001 Yearbook of the National Council of Professors of Educational Administration* (pp. 286–309). Lanham, MD: Scarecrow Press.

Boyd, W. L. (1988a). Policy analysis, educational policy, and management: Through a glass darkly. In N. Boyan (Ed.), *Handbook of research on educational administration* (pp. 501–522). New York: Longman.

Boyd, W. L. (1988b). How to reform school without half trying: Secrets of the Reagan administration. *Educational Administration Quarterly, 24*(3), 299–309.

Brown, D. J. (1990). *Decentralization and school-based management.* Philadelphia: Falmer Press.

Chubb, J. E., & Moe, T. M. (1990). *Politics, markets, and America's schools.* Washington, DC: Brookings Institution.

Clinchy, E. (1989). Public school choice: Absolutely necessary but not wholly sufficient. *Phi Delta Kappan, 71*(4), 289–294.

Conway, J. M. (1984). The myth, mystery, and mastery of participative decision making in education. *Educational Administration Quarterly, 21*(1), 11–40.

Corcoran, T., Fuhrman, S. H., & Belcher, C. L. (2001). The district role in instructional improvement. *Phi Delta Kappan, 83*(1), 78–84.

Cuban, L. (1988). Why do some reforms persist? *Educational Administration Quarterly, 24*(3), 329–335.

Cuban, L. (1992). The corporate myth of reforming public schools. *Phi Delta Kappan, 74*(2), 157–159.

Cuban, L. (1998). How schools change reforms: Redefining reform success and failure. *Teachers College Record, 99*(3), 453–477.

David, J. L. (1989). Synthesis of research on school-based management. *Educational Leadership, 46*(8), 45–47; 53.

Davis, M. D. (1999). The restructuring of an urban elementary school: Lessons learned as a professional development school liaison. *Early Childhood Research & Practice, 1*(1), 6–10.

Donlevy, J. G., & Donlevy, T. R. (1997). Teachers, technology, and training. Perspectives on education and school reform: Implications for the emerging role of the teacher. *International Journal of Instructional Media, 24*(2), 91–98.

Dryfoos, J. G. (1996). Full-service schools. *Educational Leadership, 53*(7), 18–23.

Dykgraaf, C. L., & Lewis, S. K. (1998). For-profit charter schools: What the public needs to know. *Educational Leadership, 56*(2), 51–53.

English, F. W. (1990, October). *Can rational organizational models really reform anything? A case study of reform in Chicago.* Unpublished paper presented at the annual meeting of the University Council for Educational Administration, Pittsburgh.

Feir, R. E. (1995). *Political and social roots of education reform: A look at the states in the mid-1980s.* (ERIC Document Reproduction Service No. ED 385 925)

Finn, C. E. (1991). *We must take charge.* New York: The Free Press.

Firestone, W. A., Fuhrman, S. H., & Kirst, M. W. (1991). State educational reform since 1983: Appraisal of the future. *Educational Policy, 5*(3), 233–250.

Ford, D. J. (1992). *Chicago principals under school based management: New roles and realities of the job.* (ERIC Document Reproduction Service No. ED353 632)

Fullan, M. (1999). *Change forces: The sequel.* Philadelphia: Falmer Press.

Fullan, M. (2000). The three stories of education reform. *Phi Delta Kappa, 81*(8), 581–584.

Glickman, C. (1991). Pretending not to know what we know. *Educational Leadership, 48*(8), 4–10.

Hargreaves, A. (1994). Restructuring restructuring: Postmodernity and the prospects for educational change. *Journal of Education Policy, 9*(1), 47–65.

Hemming, R., & Mansoor, A. M. (1988). *Privatization and public enterprises.* (Occasional Paper No. 56). Washington, DC: International Monetary Fund.

Hertert, L. (1996). Systemic school reform in the 1990s: A local perspective. *Educational Policy, 10*(3), 379–398.

Kochan, F. K. (1998). Benefits of professional development schools: The hidden message in the forest. *Professional Educator, 20*(3), 1–6.

Kowalski, T. J. (1999). *The school superintendent: Theory, practice, and cases.* Upper Saddle River, NJ: Merrill, Prentice-Hall.

Levine, M. (1997). Can professional development schools help us achieve what matters most? *Action in Teacher Education, 19*(2), 63–73.

Levine, M. (1998). Professional development schools: More than a good idea. *Teaching and Change, 6*(1), 8–20.

MacKenzie, D., & Rogers, V. (1997). The full service school: A management and organizational structure for 21st century schools. *Community Education Journal, 25*(3–4), 9–11.

Malen, B. (1999). The promises and perils of participation on site-based councils. *Theory into Practice, 38*(4), 209–216.

Manno, B. V., Finn, C. E., & Vanourek, G. (2000). Beyond the schoolhouse door: How charter schools are transforming U.S. public education. *Phi Delta Kappan, 81*(10), 736–750.

Marenda, D. W. (1989). Partners in education: An old tradition renamed. *Educational Leadership, 47*(2), 4–7.

Margonis, F., & Parker, L. (1995). Choice, privatization, and unspoken strategies of containment. *Educational Policy, 9*(4), 375–403.

Mazzoni, T. L. (1991). Analyzing state school policymaking: An arena model. *Educational Evaluation and Policy Analysis, 13*(2), 115–138.

McKinney, J. R. (1996). Charter schools: A new barrier for children with disabilities. *Educational Leadership, 54*(2), 22–25.

McKinney, J. R., & Mead, J. F. (1996). Law and policy in conflict: Including students with disabilities in parental-choice programs. *Educational Administration Quarterly, 32*(1), 107–141.

Mehlinger, H. D. (1996). Achieving school reform through technology. *TECHNOS, 5*(1), 26–29.

Midgley, C., & Wood, S. (1993). Beyond site-based management: Empowering teachers to reform schools. *Phi Delta Kappan, 75*(3), 245–252.

Molnar, A. (1996). Charter schools: The smiling face of disinvestment. *Educational Leadership, 54*(2), 9–15.

Murphy, J. (1999). New consumerism: Evolving market dynamics in the institutional dimension of schooling. In J. Murphy & K. Seashore Louis (Eds.), *Handbook of research on educational administration* (2nd ed.) (pp. 405–419). San Franciso: Jossey-Bass.

Orlich, D. C. (1989). Education reforms: Mistakes, misconceptions, miscues. *Phi Delta Kappan, 70*(7), 512–517.

Pogrow, S. (1996). Reforming the wannabe reformers: Why education reforms almost always end up making things worse. *Phi Delta Kappan, 77*(10), 656–663.

Pritchett, D. N. (1999). *Planning procedures and leadership role of the principal in professional development schools.* Unpublished Ed.D. dissertation. Muncie, IN: Ball State University.

Raywid, M. A. (1987). Public choice, yes: Vouchers, no! *Phi Delta Kappan, 70*(10).

Raywid, M. A. (1992). What kind of choice? Issues for system designers. *Equity and Choice, 9*(1), 6–10.

Reyes, P., Wagstaff, L. H., & Fusarelli, L. D. (1999). Delta forces: The changing fabric of American society and education. In J. Murphy & K. Seashore Louis (Eds.), *Handbook of research on educational administration* (2nd ed.) (pp. 183–201). San Franciso: Jossey-Bass.

Rigden, D. W. (1991). *Business-school partnerships: A path to effective restructuring* (2nd ed.). New York: Council for Aid to Education.

Sarason, S. B. (1996). *Revisiting the culture of the school and the problem of change.* New York: Teachers College Press.

Sarason, S. B. (1998). *Charter schools: Another flawed educational reform?* New York: Teachers College Press.

Savas, E. S. (1987). *Privatization: The key to better government.* Chatham, NJ: Chatham House.

Seashore Louis, K., Toole, J., & Hargreaves, A. (1999). Rethinking school improvement. In J. Murphy & K. Seashore Louis (Eds.), *Handbook of research on educational administration* (2nd ed.) (pp. 251–276). San Franciso: Jossey-Bass.

Shanker, A. (1990). A proposal for using incentives to restructure our public schools. *Phi Delta Kappan, 71*(5), 344–357.

Smrekar, C. E., & Mawhinney, H. B. (1999). Integrated services: Challenges to linking schools, families, and communities. In J. Murphy & K. Seashore Louis (Eds.), *Handbook of research on educational administration* (2nd ed.) (pp. 443–462). San Franciso: Jossey-Bass.

Soltis, J. F. (1988). Reform or reformation? *Educational Administration Quarterly, 24*(3), 241–245.

Stallings, J., & Kowalski, T. J. (1990). Professional development schools. In R. Houston (Ed.), *Handbook of research on teacher education* (pp. 251–266). New York: Macmillan.

Swanson, A. D., & King, R. A. (1997). *School finance: Its economics and politics* (2nd ed.). New York: Longman.

Timar, T. B., & Kirp, D. L. (1987). Educational reform and institutional competence. *Harvard Educational Review, 57*(3), 308–330.

Timar, T. B., & Kirp, D. L. (1989). Education reform in the 1980s: Lessons from the states. *Phi Delta Kappan, 70*(7), 504–511.

Tyack, D. (1990). Restructuring in historical perspective: Tinkering toward utopia. *Teachers College Record, 92*(2), 170–191.

Watkins, T. (1999). The charter challenge. *American School Board Journal, 186*(12), 34–36.

Witte, J. F. (1995). Three critical factors in the school choice debate. *Social Science Quarterly, 76*(3), 502–505.

Zeichner, K. M. (1991). Contradictions and tensions in the professionalization of teaching and the democratization of schools. *Teachers College Record, 92*(3), 363–379.

14

Transforming the School

In his enlightening book, *Teaching the Elephant to Dance: Empowering Change in Your Organization*, James Belasco (1990) likens the evolution of organizational behavior to the training of elephants: "Trainers shackle young elephants with heavy chains to deeply embedded stakes. In that way the elephant learns to stay in its place. Older elephants never try to leave even though they have the strength to pull the stake and move beyond. Their conditioning limits their movements with only a small metal bracelet around their foot—attached to nothing" (p. 2). Many organizations, too, are bound by constraints that are more imagined than real—limitations that restrict creativity and change. A majority of public schools, unfortunately, have been among them. Administrators in these schools have not been prepared to take risks or to make changes, and their behavior has been influenced by norms predicated on the beliefs that schools ought not—and cannot—change.

The previous two chapters detailed society's demand for school improvement and the evolving nature of attempts to respond to it. This chapter provides an extension of that discussion by examining the process of change. Although the goal of school reform and the process of change are intertwined (Fullan & Stiegelbauer, 1990), the latter is more pervasive than the former. In today's world, the only constant is change. Therefore, understanding organizational change is pivotal to the study of school administration.

This chapter addresses the nature of organizational change, especially in relation to educational institutions. The process of change is discussed and the common barriers to and strategies for achieving it are identified and explained. Culture is identified as a key element in transforming districts and schools, and the strategy of culture change is described.

Organizational Change

Everyone has life-changing experiences, but not all of them are permanent. Consider a high school student who unintentionally drives through a stop sign on the way to school and has an accident. The incident causes the student to be cautious and defensive when behind the wheel of an automobile; however, this instinctive response is only temporary. After just several weeks of accident-free driving, the student reverts to careless habits, because his basic beliefs and values about driving were not altered. Changing behavior in schools is no different. Administrators can usually induce temporary behavior changes (through the promise of rewards or through threats of punishment), but unless the basic values and beliefs of teachers and other employees are reshaped, they revert to the routine behaviors once the pressure to change has subsided.

Defining Change

Change is not something pursued solely for its own purposes. That is to say, it is not a product—it is a process (Belasco, 1990). Change is a medium for adaptation. It may be beneficial or harmful; it can be short lived or permanent; it can be rapid or gradual; it can be planned or unexpected. But change, like conflict, is an inevitable aspect of organizational life. Pantheist philosopher Heraclitus observed, "The only thing that is permanent is change."

Change is an essential element of organizational development—a systematically planned, sustained effort of self-study and improvement (Schmuck & Runkel, 1994). School administrators, for example, are expected to identify and meet evolving needs and wants and to implement necessary improvements. In recent years, the acceleration of change in the world and U.S. society has made this responsibility increasingly difficult.

Change in schools always involves or concerns individuals and groups, but its effect on the institution per se may be temporary or permanent, minimal or substantial. Often, changes that occur in schools are not perceptible to the general public. For example, most taxpayers are unlikely to know that the local high school has implemented a student peer-tutoring program. Many changes that occur in schools generate little attention and produce little conflict. However, attempted transformations of values and practices are a different matter, as evidenced by disputes over issues such as student health clinics, sex education, and outcome-based education.

Change in Education Institutions

Students of school administration are often confused when they read seemingly contradictory conclusions regarding the extent to which schools have been adaptive organizations. For example, some authors (e.g., Tyack & Tobin, 1994) note that schools have remained basically unchanged despite repeated reform efforts, whereas others (e.g., Ginsberg, 1995) argue that schools have experimented rather freely with new ideas, such as team teaching and open space schools. In truth, both characterizations are correct.

Gene Hall and Shirley Hord (2001) offer an explanation as to why schools appear to be both intractable and adaptive. They observed that many education innovations have been "adopted, tried out, and subsequently rejected—only to cycle around and be readopted some years later in a 'new and improved' form" (p. 20). For example, team teaching as proposed for schools in the 1960s and team teaching today (common in middle schools) are very similar concepts; both are predicated on the belief that teachers can be more effective if they do not work in isolation. In large measure, team teaching was abandoned in the late 1960s because many educators never changed their fundamental beliefs that established norms for teaching behavior. The recurring nature of reforms suggests that change fails not because of the substance of the ideas, but because of the context in which it is pursued. Thus, public schools have experienced a multitude of incremental changes, but few of them have been able to reconstruct the organization or its normative frameworks.

Discussing failed reforms, Rodney Ogawa, Robert Crowson, and Ellen Goldring (1999) concluded that schools are caught in a web of enduring internal and external dilemmas that serve to derail change initiatives. These dilemmas are shaped by what appear to be contradictory choices related to key internal and external variables. The more detrimental internal issues include the following:

- *Goals:* Tensions between the purposes of schools and the individual needs and self-interests of people who work in schools
- *Task structures:* Tensions between the formal organization (as developed by people holding legitimate authority) and the informal organization (as developed by people who possess other forms of power)
- *Hierarchy:* Tensions between centralization (top-down control) and decentralization (bottom-up control)
- *Professionalism:* Tensions between bureaucracy (emphasizing managerial control) and professionalism (emphasizing individual practitioner responsibility)

The more detrimental external issues include the following:

- *Persistence:* Tensions between protecting the status quo (preserving the purposes and structure of public schools) and making adaptations (restructuring schools so that they are more responsive to evolving needs and wants)

- *Boundaries:* Tensions between protecting the integrity of the organization (preserving traditional control mechanisms) and dealing with environmental uncertainty (experimenting with new control mechanisms that may allow schools to adapt to changing environmental conditions more quickly)
- *Compliance:* Tensions between technical compliance (developing rational structures that enhance efficiency) and institutional compliance (developing structures to gain social legitimacy)

Collectively, these dilemmas serve to exhibit the extent to which schools are affected by disagreements centering on purposes, politics, and philosophy. Educational reform has usually failed to reach its goals because reformers choose between conflicting demands rather than pursuing initiatives designed to ameliorate differences between them (Ogawa et al., 1999). Consider, for example, tensions between centralization and decentralization. Legal constraints prevent states from relinquishing control over local districts and local boards from relinquishing control over individual schools. Conversely, politics and philosophy prevent states and local districts from exercising absolute control. In this vein, total centralization provides too much control; total decentralization provides too little control (Fullan, 1999). Thus, the challenge for reformers is not one of choosing centralization or decentralization, but rather it is one of balancing the two organizational concepts. That is, reformers need to determine which functions need to be centralized and which functions need to be decentralized.

The dilemma of persistence is especially important, because in the real world of schools, administrators must choose between being change agents and being protectors of the status quo (Clark & Astuto, 1988). Throughout much of the history of public schools in the United States, administrators have adhered to the latter role (Knezevich, 1984), largely because society has viewed schools as agencies promoting social stability (Spring, 2000). Given this history, it is not surprising that most pervasive and lasting modifications in public education have come from external forces (Tyack, 1990). Legislation for people with disabilities resulting in inclusion, school desegregation court orders resulting in inter-district busing, and gender-equity legislation resulting in increased programs for female students are prime examples.

However, the expectation that schools should be primarily reactive institutions began to change in the last half of the twentieth century as social values, issues of equity, and politics suggested that schools had to prepare students for life in an evolving society. Robert Owens (2001) wrote the following: "Educational organizations are expected not only to be vehicles for social change; they are expected also to preserve and transmit traditional values to younger members of society at the same time they are expected to prepare them to deal with an ever-changing world. Thus, schools, and other educational organizations must confront not merely change but rather the integration of stability *and* change" (p. 183). In contemporary practice, administrators face considerable conflict generated by the dual expectations of preserving the dominant culture and of building a new generation of schools.

At a less complex level, educational change has been studied in relation to three key variables: *change source, change type,* and *time orientation* (see Figure 14.1). Consider the differences between the following two situations that resulted in changes in the scheduling procedures at high schools:

- *Adoption of a block schedule:* Washington High School adopted a block schedule. The advocates for this change were the principal and the faculty, and they worked together to plan the transition to this scheduling format for two years. Workshops and orientation sessions were conducted for faculty, students, and parents to prepare them for the change. The adoption of block scheduling in this high school exemplifies an internally driven, planned, and primarily evolutionary change.
- *Adoption of a split daily schedule:* Lincoln High School had to adopt a split schedule after a tornado destroyed part of the facility. The students were divided into two groups: Group A attended school from 7:00 A.M. to 12:00 P.M.; Group B attended school from 12:30 P.M. to 5:30 P.M. This scheduling change was the only feasible way for the principal to ensure that the school could continue at the present site. The adoption of split schedule in this high school exemplifies an external, unplanned, and spontaneous change.

A major difference between external and internal change relates to administrative choices. In the former, change is usually required (either through mandates or through catastrophes); in the latter, change is usually optional. Because schools were created and sustained as agencies of social stability, administrators have not been especially encouraged to initiate or support changes that could threaten this role.

Dimension	Options
Source of change:	Internal (initiated in the organization) or External (initiated out of the organization)
Type of change:	Evolutionary (gradual and incremental) or Radical (sudden and sweeping)
Time required:	Short term (usually less than two years) or Long term (usually three or more years)

FIGURE 14.1 *Critical Dimensions of Change*

Resistance to Change

Resistance to change has been described as "any attempt to maintain the status quo when there is pressure to change" (Zaltman & Duncan, 1977, p. 63). Arguably, there have been many changes in public schools over the past century; for example, the curriculum is broader, facilities are much better, and technology has modified the teaching/learning process. Yet, the basic structure of schools—the organizational patterns, the distribution of power, and the divisions of curriculum—remain much as they were decades ago.

General Resistance

Most public schools possess certain qualities that inhibit change. For example, educators historically have been preoccupied with maintaining peaceful environments (i.e., atmospheres that avoid turmoil); and as a result, schools have developed an institutional character that generally treats change as disruptive and counterproductive (Blumberg, 1980). The concept of organizational character is often used to describe aggregate strengths and weaknesses that reveal the true nature of an organization—especially in relation to its sense of identity. Organizational character is perceptible in the following areas (Wilkens, 1989):

- *Vision:* Does the organization have a common understanding of purpose and identity? Do employees have a sense of "who they are"?
- *Fairness:* Do employees have motivational faith in administrators because they trust them?
- *Ability:* Do employees have motivational faith in administrators because of their knowledge and skills?
- *Distinctive skills:* How is the organization's competence characterized in terms of tacit customs, networks of experts, and technology?

Schools, like other organizations, maintain a framework that gives meaning to human activity; as an example, policy, regulations, and curriculum help give structure and meaning to the work of teachers, students, and administrators. Change threatens this framework; in essence, it threatens the social system (school) itself (Marris, 1975). When people inside the school have little or no understanding of the purposes or potentialities of change, they almost always develop high levels of anxiety and resistance (Fullan & Stiegelbauer, 1990).

The conviction that the organization and structure of schools is sacred is deeply embedded in the culture of public education (Sarason, 1996)—a condition that has prevented schools from becoming purpose-driven organizations. In purpose-driven organizations, form follows function; in other organizations, function follows form (Pascarella & Frohman, 1989). For example, in a purpose-driven middle school, goals for mathematics (function) would determine how the curriculum would be structured (courses) and delivered (class periods and instructional methods). In the typical middle school, however, the courses and class periods (form) are predetermined, and teachers must adjust their activities accordingly. And when form is viewed as being sacred, little meaningful change is possible.

Specific Barriers

Organizational character and culture are not the only obstacles to change in schools. Other impediments can be broadly divided into three categories (Connor & Lake, 1988):

1. *Barriers to understanding:* Pertain to information deficiencies
2. *Barriers to acceptance:* Pertain to philosophical or professional incongruity
3. *Barriers to acting:* Pertain to human or material resource deficiencies

Barriers in each category were visible in the resistance of educators to first-wave reforms. First, teachers and principals often did not understand why state officials had embraced certain mandates or they were unclear as to how the mandates were supposed to be implemented. For example, educators in one state were confused regarding how and when increased requirements for high school graduation were to be implemented. Second, teachers and principals rejected many of the mandates because they had little or no faith in them. Many educators, for instance, did not readily believe that lengthening the school year or the school day would have an appreciable effect on student learning. Third, educators were often expected to carry out the mandates without being given adequate training or resources. One state, for example, required mandatory summer school programs for students who scored below the set standard on the statewide proficiency test; however, no additional state support was given to districts for this purpose.

Often, just one barrier is sufficient to attenuate the effectiveness of a reform. In 1984, for instance, a state enacted a mandate limiting the enrollment of kindergarten and first-grade classes to 18 students. Although the teachers in these two grades understood the mandate and its intentions, and they supported the initiative enthusiastically, they were unprepared to take advantage of the situation. When they found themselves with only 18 students instead of 30, most continued to teach as they had in the past.

Barriers related to understanding, accepting, and acting also have been visible in attempts to decentralize governance in local districts. For instance, site-based management threatens some principals because they do not understand the concept or its purposes. Other principals understand the concept but oppose it because they are required to change their behavior (e.g., a principal may not want to relinquish power and control to decision-making committees). And some principals understand and accept the concept but lack the necessary resources (e.g., funds and facilities) to implement it properly.

Understanding and acceptance also can be problems outside the school. For instance, many citizens support school reform globally but resist it locally. That is, they believe that schools in general need to be reconfigured, but they are reluctant to support alterations to their local schools—especially when the alterations create inconveniences. Consider the following case that involved a school serving as a pilot site for implementing site-based management:

The school board in a local district voted unanimously to employ a superintendent who had established a national reputation for his work with site-based management, because they wanted to implement the concept. A year later, one of the elementary schools was selected to serve as a pilot site to experiment with ways that the concept could be implemented in this specific community. Parents of students enrolled in the selected school voiced strong support for the initiative, and they were generally proud that "their" school was chosen.

Within the first month of implementation, the principal sent a recommendation to the superintendent, requesting that the school be allowed to dismiss students at noon on Wednesdays for the remainder of the school year so that the faculty could have time to engage in staff development and related activities. If approved, the students were to be given homework assignments to compensate for lost classroom time. The superintendent not only obtained unanimous board approval for the recommendation but she was also granted a waiver from the state, which allowed the principal's recommendation to be implemented.

When the decision to reserve Wednesday afternoons for staff development was announced publicly, support for site-based management among parents eroded rapidly. Many of them had to make arrangements for child care on Wednesday afternoons; and even if they were able to do so, they had to pay for the service. In essence, they were supportive of site-based management up to the point that the process appeared to affect them negatively.

Listing all the barriers that fall under the broad categories of understanding, acceptance, and acting is virtually impossible. The following, however, are some of the more common obstacles found in schools:

- *Lack of involvement in setting the agenda:* Regrettably, teachers and principals—the individuals most responsible for implementing change in schools—are often excluded from the critical functions of visioning and planning. Consequently, they either do not understood the purposes of change or they reject the validity of change (Vogt & Murrell, 1990).
- *Lack of information about the agenda:* People who must implement change are not sufficiently informed about the change and the reasons why it is being pursued (Vogt & Murrell, 1990).
- *Lack of conviction:* Many educators believe that change is neither necessary nor possible—a condition that prompts them to concentrate on building defenses to change (Hall & Hord, 2001).

- *Disenchantment and alienation:* Tunnel vision, a problem commonly caused by working in relative isolation, prevents many teachers from viewing the school in a context broader than their own classrooms and compartmentalized work. Because these educators know little about the total environment in which they work, the ability of schools to make appropriate adaptations is seriously reduced (Koberg, 1986).
- *Discontinuity of leadership:* Many districts and schools suffer from a lack of continuity in important leadership positions. Because successful change in schools is typically a long-term evolutionary process, destabilization attenuates the potential for successful adaptations (Kowalski, 1995).
- *Insufficient time and resources:* Most schools do not have the human and material resources necessary to implement meaningful change (Basom & Crandall, 1991).
- *Inadequate preparation to deal with the complexity of change:* Most educators are incapable of changing schools because they know too little about organizational behavior and even less about organizational change (Sarason, 1996).
- *Ineffective or insufficient use of the professional knowledge base:* Educators often ignore research and effective practices in pursuing change (Sarason, 1996).

Change Strategies

Scholars studying administrative behavior in organizations have identified several common strategies that have been used to pursue change. Robert Chin and Kenneth Benne (1985) grouped them into three categories:

1. *Empirical-rational strategies:* Administrators make two key assumptions: Employees will behave rationally and employees are motivated by self-interests. Thus, when change is shown to be in their best interest, employees will implement it.
2. *Normative-reeducative strategies:* The primary administrative assumption underlying this approach is that change requires employees to alter their normative orientations to behavior patterns. This is accomplished by exposing employees to new knowledge and skills that hopefully will affect values and beliefs.
3. *Power-coercive strategies:* This approach is premised on the assumption that most members of the organization are unwilling or incapable of producing change. Thus, economic or political force must be used.

Table 14.1 provides a comparison of the three strategies in relation to the intent to implement block scheduling and teacher teaming in a district's middle schools. Empirical-rational approaches often fail for one simple reason: People do not always act rationally. Power-coercive strategies usually fail because educators

TABLE 14.1   *Comparison of Change Strategies in Relation to Implementing Changes in Middle Schools*

Strategy	Administrative Actions	Anticipated Outcome
Empirical-rational	Principals demonstrate how teachers will benefit personally from block scheduling and team teaching.	Teachers accept what they are told, act rationally and in their own interests, and implement the proposed changes.
Normative-reeducative	Teachers attend workshops that demonstrate how they can use longer instructional periods and collaboration to improve student learning.	Influenced by the new knowledge and skills, teachers change their values and beliefs about protecting the status quo and support the proposed changes.
Power-coercive	Teachers receive a mandate from the principals telling them that they must implement block scheduling and team teaching.	Teachers implement the proposed changes, fearing disciplinary action if they do not.

resent being forced to do things differently—and the condition of their work environment (e.g., control over the classroom) gives them the power to resist. Normative-reeducative strategies have been used extensively in education; however, that does not mean that they have been highly effective. Teachers often attend workshops, return to school enthusiastic about implementing new ideas, and then abandon these ideas after their enthusiasm wanes after just weeks or months. Why? The answer relates to school culture. If the values and beliefs shaping an innovation are incongruous with the underlying values and beliefs that shape a school's behavioral norms, teachers eventually discover this fact and protect the norms by abandoning the idea. Assume that teachers attend workshops on teacher teaming and return to school intent on implementing the idea. Collaboration, however, is not supported by the school's prevailing norms; instead, the independence of teachers is valued and emphasized. In essence, teachers who returned from the workshop must choose between conforming to the existing norms and their interest in teaming. If the school's culture is sufficiently strong (i.e., most teachers in the school adhere to the same set of values and beliefs), the former will dominate.

Recognizing this fundamental weakness in the normative-reeducative change strategy, a growing number of scholars (e.g., Rossman, Corbett, & Firestone, 1988; Sarason, 1996) have proposed the use of a cultural change strategy. This approach is an extension of the normative-reeducative strategy in that it focuses on the acquisition of new knowledge and skill, but unlike normative-reeducative strategy, the ultimate purpose is to reshape fundamental values and beliefs responsible for behavioral norms.

Culture Change

During the 1980s, educators contributed to reform largely by reacting to initiatives authored by others rather than by rebuilding the cultures of their work environments. The negative consequences were described as follows:

> School people have surely not prospered, or even benefited, from "received" culture and imposed wisdom. Yet school inhabitants have lived as though they were unsophisticated natives ministered to by well-meaning missionaries who exude paternalism. Practitioners have had their shortcomings and inadequacies catalogued and classified and, sadly, have come to accept the blueprint of their deficiencies as though they had drawn it themselves. They have become passive and dependent in pursuit of their own voices. (Cooper, 1988, pp. 45–46)

The reactionary nature of educators is attributable to several circumstances, the two most obvious being past practice (shaping role expectations) and limited knowledge about organizational culture and its effects on behavior (creating apprehensions about recreating culture).

Recognizing the problems associated with schools having had an imposed culture, leading reformers within the profession concluded that all change efforts would have limited value unless they were accompanied by appropriate modifications to organizational culture. Consequently, the topics of organizational culture and organizational change have received considerably more attention in professional preparation in recent years. The purpose here is to provide basic information regarding these two pivotal issues.

Complexity of Culture Change

Organizational transformation is an emerging field of study that has its origins in organizational development. The two are distinctively different, however. Whereas organizational development concentrates on the unfolding, refining, and strengthening of behaviors, roles, attitudes, motives, beliefs, and values, organizational transformation focuses on totally recreating these characteristics (Fletcher, 1990). In part, the materialization of organizational transformation is a reflection of the instability of our world and society. Change is occurring at an ever-accelerating rate, and organizations are literally forced to keep pace. Those that fail often face extinction.

Cultural change strategies are terribly complex. One reason is that "deeply embedded basic assumptions are difficult, if not impossible, to articulate" (Firestone & Seashore Louis, 1999, p. 298). As demonstrated earlier in the book, a school's culture contains tried and true solutions that have been passed on from one generation of educators to the next. Often, teachers and administrators are not even aware of the values and beliefs guiding their own behavior because they have been transformed into routine behaviors. In addition, educators are often reluctant to express their true assumptions because they are grounded in professionally indefensible or politically incorrect beliefs. For instance, educators rarely articulate the assumption that many students are doomed to fail no matter what the school does for them; yet, actual behavior suggests that this belief is deeply seated in many school cultures.

Culture gets reinforced over time through the selection and socialization of new members. For example, shared values and beliefs guide teacher employment decisions and determine the parameters for acceptable performance among probationary teachers. The same process of socialization shapes the behavior of new administrators (Hart, 1991). When an individual becomes a principal, he or she also encounters pressures to conform to the existing norms. The power to select and evaluate new members in the organization sustains culture and ensures that underlying assumptions are passed on from one generation of administrators and teachers to the next.

Basic Values and Beliefs

As noted earlier in the book, organizational culture consists of three layers: artifacts, tacit values and beliefs, and underlying values and beliefs. The last of these layers is the deepest, least visible, and most relevant, and it contains a myriad of values and beliefs that can be reduced to four primary categories (Joyce & Murphy, 1990):

1. *Decision-making norms:* For example, values and beliefs about who should participate in making decisions and about how decisions should be made
2. *Ideas about research and scientific inquiry:* For example, values and beliefs about the importance of theory to effective practice and about the need for educators to be research consumers
3. *Views of students and learning:* For example, values and beliefs about the ability of all students to learn and succeed in school and about individualization, grouping, and testing
4. *Relationships:* For example, values and beliefs about the ideal relationships between administrators and teachers and about the way teachers should treat each other

The last of these categories also addresses issues of power and authority. Collectively, the four categories constitute a framework for normative behavior in schools.

Engaging others in open and candid discussions of values and beliefs may seem like a rather simple and straightforward task, but it is not. Many underlying assumptions exist at the subconscious level and they are only perceptible in routine behaviors. Even when this is not the case, educators often are reluctant to reveal them, fearing that they are not acceptable, either professionally or politically. Therefore, discussions of values and beliefs usually must begin with discussions of real behavior. For example, what causes teachers to not individualize instruction? What causes them to oppose inclusion? Or what causes them to use corporal punishment?

In most schools, people have become comfortable with the status quo, and therefore any suggestion of change is threatening. Change is especially disconcerting, however, when culture and the distribution of power are the targets.

Consequently, proposed changes that are incongruous with the prevailing culture and proposed changes that seek to alter the distribution of power in the organization spark considerable resistance (Dalin & Rolff, 1993). In the case of schools, such resistance does not always relate to a fear of losing power; for example, some principals and teachers have resisted site-based management because it may increase their authority and responsibility.

Time Dimension

Changing culture is a long-term process. Persistence is necessary because much of what occurs in schools is "embedded in structures and routines and internalized in individuals, including teachers" (Fullan & Stiegelbauer, 1990, p. 143). Massive and quick efforts to reshape an organization's culture are laden with potential problems. When attempted in educational settings, superintendents or principals usually feel compelled to condemn many past practices as a prerequisite to establishing new norms, values, and beliefs. Revolutionary transformations are rarely successful, and they are likely to alienate veteran employees. In observing business leaders who attempted to impose quick and radical change, Alan Wilkens (1989) observed that these initiatives often needlessly destroy an organization's character. Because change is imposed swiftly, key employees are demoralized and their opposition to change becomes only more intense. Instead of totally destroying an institution's culture and character, some experts (e.g., Smith & Slesinski, 1991) have suggested a simple and effective alternative: Get employees to commit to (1) doing old things better, (2) doing new things, and (3) building a flexible, adaptable, always-improving organization.

The time dimension of cultural change is especially important in public education, because the tenure of administrators is relatively brief. Often, administrators new to the organization must spend one to two years just to identify and analyze the existing culture. Then, engaging others in conversations about values and beliefs and relating needs, relating real needs to existing norms, and reshaping norms may take three to five additional years. This is one reason why schools that change principals every few years are unlikely to modify institutional culture.

Culture and Restructuring

Culture is the primary determinant of a school's character and quality (Owens, 2001); however, the other three elements of organizational climate (ecology, milieu, and organization) also are important. Collectively, the elements of climate tell employees "what is expected" of them; therefore, they are instrumental in determining whether administrators function as change agents. Cues come from rewards, punishments, job descriptions, environmental factors, social interactions, and many other contextual variables that serve to reinforce established norms. Climate is pervasive and touches all functions of the school, including personal interactions, student learning, and personal growth (Norton, 1984).

Can schools be restructured without changing organizational culture? The answer to this question is both yes and no. Experiences over the past 25 years have demonstrated that the ecology, milieu, and organizational structure of schools can be reshaped independently. For example, technology has been infused into the classroom (ecological change), teachers and administrators in many schools have become more collegial (social context change), and experiments with schedules and calendars have been executed successfully (organizational changes). However, educators revert to their old practices unless the modifications are sustained by legal requirements (unwilling compliance) or normative modifications (willing compliance) (Darling-Hammond, 1988).

A nexus between school culture and school effectiveness provides the strongest argument for pursuing cultural change. Consider the following characteristics of effective schools identified by Stewart Purkey and Marshall Smith (1985):

- A sense of community where teachers and administrators work toward common goals
- Collaborative planning that permits teachers to have a collegial relationship with the principal
- The acceptance of common goals by those who work in the school
- A belief that the school is capable of identifying and solving problems
- A linkage to the community
- Democratic decisions based on consensus
- A greater degree of responsibility placed on the professional staff

These characteristics reflect a set of values and beliefs that can be reinterpreted rather easily as cultural elements (Firestone & Corbett, 1988). Rather than concluding that effective schools exhibit unique characteristics, it is more accurate to conclude that they possess unique cultures as reflected by these characteristics. Despite the fact that relatively little is known about the precise effects of these values and beliefs and about how they become a part of the school's normative structure, the linkage between readiness for change (a cultural condition) and institutional effectiveness is quite clear.

Implications for Practice

As an administrator, you need to recognize that change is a process rather than a specific goal. You also should understand why recurring cycles of reform have failed to change the basic structure of schools and the behavior of educators. Schools, like other organizations, face a myriad of potential change barriers, but the most potent are those that are rooted in institutional culture.

Over time, reformers and administrators have relied on three primary strategies to pursue their goals. The potential effectiveness of each paradigm was attenuated under conditions in which the proposed changes were incongruous with the normative structure of the institution. As the school reform agenda shifted to school restructuring circa 1990, Theodore Sizer (1991) wrote, "Challenging long-held assumptions, negotiating compromises, being decisive about what's truly important—these and other exacting processes are the seeds out of which can grow fundamental, lasting improvement of our schools" (p. 32). He added, however, that these processes would be both difficult and painful for administrators because educators were not convinced that such action was necessary. More recently, Seymour Sarason (1996) concluded that educators were probably incapable of transforming schools because they knew little about organizational behavior, change processes, and institutional culture.

The quest to restructure schools—and thus, the quest to build new school cultures—is serving to reshape role expectations for district and school administrators. This fact is illustrated by the following transitions in ideal role expectations:

- From failure-avoidance management to risk-taking leadership
- From political behavior to moral and ethical behavior
- From reliance on legitimate power to reliance on expert power
- From treating teachers as subordinates to treating them as peer professionals
- From focusing on conflict reduction to focusing on relevant organizational adaptations
- From being reactive managers to being visionary leaders

In essence, administrators are being encouraged to be purpose-driven leaders—that is, individuals who passionately embrace certain values that create shared visions and who are capable of building mutual trust by demonstrating high levels of selflessness (Pascarella & Frohman, 1989).

For Further Discussion

1. Give examples of how schools have been expected to provide both change and stability. Why is it difficult for schools to do both?

2. What are some reasons why teachers might resist change in general?

3. What are some reasons why teachers might resist change initiatives that seek to treat them as true professionals?

4. What is the difference between rational-empirical and normative-reeducative change strategies?

5. Why have normative-reeducative strategies often failed?

6. During the 1980s, policymakers often used power-coercive strategies to advance their ideas. Why are such strategies unlikely to produce lasting change in public schools?

7. Why is it often difficult to engage teachers in discussions of their shared values and beliefs?

8. How does a school culture sustain itself?

9. Some experts have concluded that educators are incapable of rebuilding schools because they know little or nothing about organizational behavior, change processes, and institutional culture. Do you agree? Why or why not?

10. What is the difference between organizational culture and organizational character? Is it possible to rebuild culture while preserving character? Explain.

11. What is the difference between culture and climate? Is it possible to change climate without changing culture? Explain.

12. To what extent does school restructuring serve to redefine the ideal role of school administrators?

Other Suggested Activities

1. One popular reform concept is site-based management. Using your local school district as a point of reference, identify potential barriers to understanding, acceptance, and acting that might prevent this concept from being implemented.

2. Identify and discuss several values and beliefs about student as learners that affect the behavior of teachers.

3. Identify and discuss several values and beliefs about public schools that prevent meaningful reform.

4. This chapter addressed the time dimension of cultural change. Discuss the relevance of time in relation to current conditions surrounding the tenure of school administrators.

References

Basom, R. E., & Crandall, D. P. (1991). Implementing a redesign strategy: Lessons from educational change. *Educational Horizons, 69*(2), 73–77.

Belasco, J. A. (1990). *Teaching the elephant to dance: Empowering change in your organization.* New York: Crown.

Blumberg, A. (1980). School organizations: A case of generic resistance to change. In M. Milstein (Ed.), *Schools, conflict, and change* (pp. 15–29). New York: Teachers College Press.

Chin, R., & Benne, K. D. (1985). General strategies for effecting changes in human systems. In W. G. Bennis, K. D. Benne, & R. Chin (Eds.), *The planning of change* (4th ed.) (pp. 22–43). New York: Holt, Rinehart and Winston.

Clark, D. L., & Astuto, T. A. (1988). Paradoxical choice options in organizations. In D. E. Griffiths, R. T. Stout, & P. B. Forsyth (Eds.), *Leaders for America schools* (pp. 112–130). Berkeley, CA: McCutchan.

Connor, P. E., & Lake, L. K. (1988). *Managing organizational change.* New York: Praeger.

Cooper, M. (1988). Whose culture is it, anyway? In A. Lieberman (Ed.), *Building a professional culture in schools* (pp. 45–54). New York: Teachers College Press.

Crowson, R. L., & McPherson, R. B. (1987). Sources of constraints and opportunities for discretion in the principalship. In J. Lane & H. Waldberg (Eds.), *Effective school leadership* (pp. 129–156). Berkeley, CA: McCutchan.

Dalin, P., & Rolff, H. G. (1993). *Changing the school culture.* London: Cassell.

Darling-Hammond, L. (1988). Policy and professionalism. In A. Lieberman (Ed.), *Building a professional culture in schools* (pp. 55–77). New York: Teachers College Press.

Firestone, W. A., & Corbett, H. D. (1988). Planned organizational change. In N. Boyan (Ed.), *Handbook of research on educational administration* (pp. 321–340). New York: Longman.

Firestone, W. A., & Seashore Louis, K. (1999). Schools as cultures. In J. Murphy & K. Seashore Louis (Eds.), *Handbook of research on educational administration* (2nd ed.) (pp. 297–322). San Francisco: Jossey-Bass.

Fletcher, B. R. (1990). *Organizational transformation theorists and practitioners.* New York: Praeger.

Fullan, M. (1999). *Change forces: The sequel.* Philadelphia: Falmer Press.

Fullan, M. G., & Stiegelbauer, S. (1990). *The new meaning of educational change* (2nd ed.). New York: Teachers College Press.

Ginsberg, R. (1995). The new institutionalism, the new science, persistence and change: The power of faith in schools. In R. Crowson, W. Boyd, & H. Mawhinney (Eds.), *The politics of education and the new institutionalism* (pp. 153–166). Washington, DC: Falmer.

Goens, G. A., & Clover, S. I. (1991). *Mastering school reform.* Boston: Allyn and Bacon.

Hall, G. E., & Hord, S. M. (1987). *Change in schools: Facilitating the process.* Albany: State University of New York Press.

Hall, G. E., & Hord, S. M. (2001). *Implementing change: Patterns, principles, and potholes.* Boston: Allyn and Bacon.

Hart, A. W. (1991). Leader succession and socialization: A synthesis. *Review of Educational Research, 61*(4), 451–474.

Joyce, B., & Murphy, C. (1990). Epilogue: The curious complexities of cultural change. In B. Joyce (Ed.), *Changing school culture through staff development* (pp. 243–250). Alexandria, VA: Association for Supervision and Curriculum Development.

Knezevich, S. J. (1984). *Administration of public education* (4th ed.). New York: Harper and Row.

Koberg, C. S. (1986). Adaptive organizational behavior of school organizations: An exploratory study. *Educational Evaluation and Policy Analysis, 8*(2), 39–146.

Kowalski, T. J. (1995). *Keepers of the flame: Contemporary urban superintendents.* Thousand Oaks, CA: Corwin Press.

Lewis, J. (1987). *Re-creating our schools for the 21st century.* Westbury, NY: J. L. Wilkerson.

Marris, P. (1975). *Loss and change.* New York: Anchor Press.

Miller, L. (1988). Unlikely beginnings: The district office as a starting point for developing a professional culture for teaching. In A. Lieberman (Ed.), *Building a professional culture in schools* (pp. 167–184). New York: Teachers College Press.

Norton, M. S. (1984). What's so important about school climate? *Contemporary Education, 56*(1), 43–45.

Ogawa, R. T., Crowson, R. L., & Goldring, E. B. (1999). Enduring dilemmas of school organization. In J. Murphy & K. Seashore Louis (Eds.), *Handbook of research on educational administration* (2nd ed.) (pp. 277–296). San Francisco: Jossey-Bass.

Owens, R. G. (2001). *Organizational behavior in education* (7th ed.). Boston: Allyn and Bacon.

Pascarella, P., & Frohman, M. A. (1989). *The purpose-driven organization.* San Francisco: Jossey-Bass.

Purkey, S. C., & Smith, M. S. (1985). School reform: The district policy implications of the effective schools literature. *Elementary School Journal, 85,* 353–389.

Rossman, G. B., Corbett, H. D., & Firestone, W. A. (1988). *Change and effectiveness in schools: A cultural perspective.* Albany: State University of New York Press.

Sarason, S. B. (1996). *Revisiting the culture of the school and the problem of change.* New York: Teachers College Press.

Schmuck, R. A., & Runkel, P. J. (1994). *The handbook of organizational development in schools and colleges* (4th ed.). Prospect Heights, IL: Waveland Press.

Sergiovanni, T. J. (1991). *The principalship: A reflective practice perspective* (2nd ed.). Boston: Allyn and Bacon.

Sizer, T. R. (1991). No pain, no gain. *Educational Leadership, 48*(8), 32–34.

Smith, R. C., & Slesinski, R. A. (1991). Continuous innovation. *Executive Excellence, 8*(5), 13–14.

Spring, J. (2000). *American education* (9th ed.). New York: McGraw-Hill.

Tyack, D. (1990). Restructuring in historical perspective: Tinkering toward utopia. *Teachers College Record, 92*(2), 170–191.

Tyack, D., & Tobin, W. (1994). The "grammar" of schooling: Why has it been so hard to change? *American Educational Research Journal, 31*(3), 453–479.

Vogt, J. F., & Murrell, K. L. (1990). *Empowerment in organizations: How to spark exceptional performance.* San Diego: University Associates.

Wilkens, A. L. (1989). *Developing corporate character: How to successfully change an organization without destroying it.* San Francisco: Jossey-Bass.

Zaleznik, A. (1989). *The managerial mystique: Restoring leadership in business.* New York: Harper and Row.

Zaltman, G., & Duncan, R. (1977). *Strategies for planned change.* New York: John Wiley and Sons.

15

Women and Minorities in School Administration

Chapter Content _____

Through the first half of the twentieth century, the literature on school administration contained little information about women and members of racial or ethnic minority groups in the profession. However, greater attention was given to this topic after major court decisions and legislation in the 1950s and the 1960s created an environment in which equity became a political, legal, and social agenda. Government intervention initially was predicated on the reality that certain individuals did not have equal access to professions, and this included entry to positions such as the principalship and superintendency.

The term *underrepresentation* has been used commonly to define a condition in which members of a group represented in administrative roles are at a level below their representation in the general population or in the education profession. In this vein, the percentage of women, African Americans, and Hispanic Americans in the principalship or the superintendency is well below the level of representation in the population—and especially in the case of women, it is well below the level of representation in the teaching profession. The purposes of this chapter are to examine the history of underrepresentation and to demonstrate the relevance of this topic to practice in the profession.

Women and Minorities in Education

Virtually all school administrators come from the ranks of teachers, primarily because most states require applicants for administrative licenses to have had experience in this position. Consequently, the history of women and members of racial and ethnic minorities in teaching is relevant to understanding the extent to which these individuals are represented in administration.

Women in Teaching

In the earliest schools, teachers were predominantly men. John Rury (1989) offered the following description of those times: "Teachers as a group in colonial America were overwhelmingly white and male, largely middle-class and young, and often (though not always) well educated—at least by seventeenth- and eighteenth-century standards" (p. 11). The teaching profession remained predominately male until the latter part of the nineteenth century, when population growth spawned urbanization and the development of city school districts.

Unlike conditions in rural one-room schoolhouses, elementary and secondary school students were separated in urban districts—an action made possible by higher enrollments and encouraged by an ever-expanding curriculum. The establishment of grammar schools, institutions that typically served students through eighth grade, had a profound influence on the future of women in teaching. In general, those charged with the responsibility of employment had avoided hiring women because of a perception that they would be unable to control older students. The one-room schoolhouse format required teachers to be responsible for a relatively large group of students, including some in their teens. The creation of grammar schools lessened this concern, resulting in school officials being less apprehensive about employing women in teaching positions (Clifford, 1989). In fact, the separation of younger students into their own schools was probably the single-most critical event resulting in a larger number of women entering teaching.

Industrial growth in urban settings also influenced decisions to employ women in teaching positions. The expansion of industry and commerce created a multitude of new jobs, many of which paid far more than teaching. Male teachers, most relatively well educated for that time period, were often recruited by industry. Many left education to pursue more lucrative careers in the private sector of the economy (Rury, 1989)—a development that increased the demand for teachers.

During the last three-quarters of the twentieth century, two significant trends were discernible with regard to women in the teaching force:

1. The influx of women into teaching that commenced near the turn of the century proved to be more than a short-term phenomenon. Over the first three decades of the twentieth century, the number of women who entered teaching steadily increased. Women entered the teaching ranks so rapidly that by 1940, only one in five teachers was male—a remarkable shift from the condition that existed prior to urbanization. This trend was diverted for a period of time following World

War II and the Korean War. A number of men who were veterans of the armed services took advantage of the G.I. Bill (legislation that gave financial assistance to veterans to continue their education) and became teachers. Despite this increased entry of men into the profession during the 1950s and 1960s, teaching remained predominantly a female occupation (Ortiz & Marshall, 1988). In 1968, about 30 percent of the nation's teaching force was male—an increase of about 5 percent from 1940.

2. The percentage of female teachers who married and remained in the profession increased. In the first half of the twentieth century, women generally left teaching if they decided to marry and raise a family. In 1930, only 18 percent of the female teachers were married; by 1960, only 29 percent were unmarried (Clifford, 1989). Since 1950, women who marry tend to stay in the profession—many take only brief absences to bear children (Rury, 1989). The retention of married females in the teaching profession expanded the pool of highly experienced female teachers (those with 10 or more years of experience) and increased the average age of the teaching force.

During the 1970s and 1980s, new career opportunities opened to women. As a result, many of them entering college during these two decades chose to major in business or other disciplines that enhanced their opportunities to enter professional schools in law, dentistry, or medicine. Education as well as nursing faculty realized that for the first time they had to compete to attract the most capable female students. Despite the fact that women now had greater access to all professions, many of them still elected to become teachers. From 1985 to 1990, for example, women constituted 78 percent of the new hires in the teaching profession; in 1990, women still constituted 70 percent of the nation's teaching force (Feistritzer, 1990). This latter figure continued to rise in the early 1990s, reaching 73 percent by 1994 (National Center for Education Statistics, 1999).

Although women constitute a substantial majority in the teaching profession, there are several indications of lingering discrimination—especially in relation to job treatment and compensation. Several writers, for example, have speculated about political and economic consequences stemming from the workforce in education being dominated by women. Dee Ann Spencer (1986), for instance, arrived at the following conclusion after studying the history of women in teaching: "The historical development of the structure of schools and the predominance of women in teaching has led to the quasi-professional status of teaching" (p. 13). Spencer added that the belief that women are responsible for teaching being treated as a quasi-profession is embedded in societal prejudice that women require supervision in the workplace.

Women also have been blamed unjustly for the relative low salaries paid to teachers in general. This attribution is embedded in the belief that taxpayers are unwilling to pay women higher salaries because historically many have earned second incomes in their families. More enlightened analysts, however, argue that problems of status and compensation run deeper than gender-related prejudice.

For example, Geraldine Clifford (1989) aptly pointed out, "Teaching has been underpaid throughout history, regardless of the gender of the majority and the method of paying for teaching" (p. 317). In truth, women have been primarily victims, not the causes, of society's unwillingness to compensate educators as true professionals. And despite regulated salary schedules and other structures to ensure pay equity, women still appear to be experiencing wage discrimination within the profession. A study using 1987 data, for example, found that the cost of being female was approximately 5 percent of the annual contract (Verdugo & Schneider, 1994). Today, discrepancies in salaries are diminishing. Thirty-five years after the passage of the Equal Pay Act in 1963, national data across all occupations revealed women's wages increased from 59 percent of men's wages in 1964 to 76 percent of men's wages in 1998 (Castro, 1998).

Minorities in Teaching

Teaching has long been considered an attractive occupation for first-generation college graduates, especially those coming from lower and lower-middle economic groups. This fact is especially noteworthy because of the nexus between race and economic status—that is, members of racial minorities comprise a large percentage of low-income groups. Thus, college students of African heritage frequently selected teaching as a realistic career goal. This was true even when job opportunities for African Americans were restricted; throughout the first half of the twentieth century, aspiring African American teachers realized that their greatest employment opportunities were in predominantly rural, segregated schools serving students of African heritage exclusively or primarily (Perkins, 1989).

Ironically, civil rights legislation and subsequent litigation initially reduced both the demand and supply for African American teachers. Demand was lowered especially in southern states because racially segregated schools (the primary workplaces for these educators) were forced to close. Minorities had to compete directly with nonminority applicants in locations where a certain number of African American teachers previously had been ensured employment. Unfortunately, laws and court orders that forced the closure of segregated schools could not totally eradicate prejudice, and when making employment decisions, school boards and administrators who responded to school integration with spiteful obedience hired relatively few minority teachers.

From a supply perspective, the government's intervention into civil rights opened career doors for minority college students. Rather than becoming teachers, many students of African descent opted to major in business, preprofessional studies for law and medicine, and areas related to government and social justice—decisions that paralleled those of women. Consequently, education employers could no longer depend on the best and brightest minority candidates entering teaching (Perkins, 1989).

Through the 1970s, the enrollment of African Americans in higher education steadily increased, and although these students had more realistic career choices than in the past, many continued to pursue teaching careers. In part, their interest in the education profession was attributable to changing employment prospects. By the mid-1970s, a large number of school districts were becoming more diverse racially and economically. Enlightened school board members and administrators realized that there was a pressing need for minority teachers to be role models in these schools. Consequently, the demand for African American teachers was substantially greater than the supply, and many districts engaged in rigorous campaigns to recruit minority teachers. By 1980, individuals of African descent constituted nearly 10 percent of the nation's teaching force—the highest proportion in history (Rury, 1989). Nevertheless, serious concerns about adequate representation remained, largely because minority teachers were not distributed evenly throughout the educational system. Most were still employed in either urban or rural schools serving predominately minority students.

Over the last 25 years, the percentage of college students who are minorities has increased. From 1976 to 1997, the percentage of minority students increased from 16 percent to 27 percent, with the bulk of the increase being attributable to students of Latin (Hispanic) ancestry and Asian ancestry. The percentage of African American students fluctuated during most of the early part of the period, before rising slightly to 11 percent in 1997 (National Center for Education Statistics, 1999). During the period from 1977 to 1989, however, the number of African American undergraduate students choosing to major in education fell dramatically. In 1977, African Americans were more likely than white students to major in education, but by 1989, the reverse was true. In 1989, the highest concentration ratio of African American undergraduate majors was found in business. The concentration ratio for Hispanic American students selecting an education major also has declined steadily since 1981. In 1989, education had the lowest concentration ratio for Hispanic Americans enrolled in undergraduate school. Social and behavioral sciences, humanities, natural sciences, computer science/engineering, and business all had higher concentration ratios (National Center for Education Statistics, 1991). Hispanic Americans represented 3 percent of the teaching force in the early 1990s, even though they comprised nearly 10 percent of the population (Mack & Jackson, 1993).

Data for new teacher hires between 1985 and 1990 show that only 5 percent were African Americans (Feistritzer, 1990). Recent supply-and-demand studies indicate that the need for new teachers will be greatest in urban and poor communities (e.g., Yasin, 1999)—areas most likely to employ minority teachers.

Historically, the involvement of Native Americans and Hispanic Americans in the teaching profession has been limited. In part, blame lies with public education itself for the ways it has treated both groups. The use of boarding schools, for example, essentially kept Native American students out of mainstream schools. Many Hispanic Americans also felt abused by public education. For example, Hispanic American parents sometimes saw administrators looking the other way rather than enforcing compulsory attendance laws. Some saw their children being classified as "whites" so that school districts could meet legal requirements related to desegregation (i.e., Hispanic American students were pawns used to prevent Anglo-Saxon white children from being mixed with African American children in desegregated schools) (Valverde & Brown, 1988). These experiences did not foster perceptions that teaching would be a good career choice.

In 1975, only 1.7 percent of elementary teachers and 1.5 percent of secondary teachers in the United States were of Hispanic descent. In that same year, only three-tenths of 1 percent of elementary teachers and two-tenths of 1 percent of secondary teachers were Native Americans (Ortiz, 1982). Data for new hires in teaching between 1985 and 1990 revealed the following:

- American Indians: less than 1 percent
- Asian/Pacific Islanders: 1 percent
- African Americans: 5 percent
- Hispanics: 2 percent (Feistritzer, 1990)

These figures reflected virtually no gains for these groups from the mid-1970s.

In the latter half of the 1980s, alternative licensing and certification programs were used in some states to improve minority representation in teaching. Among the new hires with alternative certificates during this period, 10 percent were African Americans, 16 percent were Hispanic Americans, and 1 percent were Native Americans (Feistritzer, 1990). Although they were allowed to teach, people with alternative licenses or certificates had little effect on increasing minority administrator pools, because many states still required traditional certification or licensure as prerequisite for administrative practice.

Concerns in Administration

To answer the question of whether women and minorities are underrepresented in school administration, two common points of comparisons have been made. The first is a comparison of teacher data to administrator data (percent of teachers who belong to a given group as opposed to the percent of administrators who belong to the same group). The second is a comparison of student data to administrator data (percent of students who belong to a given group as opposed to the percent of administrators who belong to the same group). Most often, comparisons for women have been based on the former technique, whereas comparisons for minorities have concentrated on the latter. The National Center for Education Statistics (1999) reported that approximately 49 percent of the total school enrollment of students between ages 5 and 17 was female, and the following minority group public school enrollments existed in the fall of 1997:

- African Americans: 17 percent
- Hispanic Americans: 14.4 percent
- Asian or Pacific Islander Americans: 3.9 percent
- Native Americans or Alaskan Native Americans: 1.2 percent

Sheer numbers present only one dimension of underrepresentation—there also is a qualitative aspect to the concern that addresses the types of school administration positions occupied by women and minorities. Flora Ortiz and Catherine Marshall (1988) eluded to the qualitative dimension of underrepresentation: "Women, especially minority women, but even minority men, continue to occupy the lowest positions in the administrative hierarchy, white males the higher and the more powerful positions" (p. 127).

Charol Shakeshaft (1999) recently commented that the United States lacks a "reliable, uniform, nationwide database that lets us know just how many women are in school administration and at what levels" (p. 99). Nevertheless, available data have consistently supported contentions of underrepresentation for both women and minorities. A 1990 study (Jones & Montenegro, 1990), for example, reported that men occupied 96 percent of superintendencies, 77 percent of deputy/assistant superintendencies, 88 percent of high school principalships, and 71 percent of elementary principalships. The most recent national study sponsored by the American Association of School Administrators reported that women held 13.2 percent and racial minorities 5.1 percent of all local district superintendencies in the country (Glass, Björk, & Brunner, 2000). An analysis of several national studies found that between 1984 and 1994, female representation in the administrator workforce increased from 21.4 percent to 34.5 percent (Zheng & Carpenter-Hubin, 1999). Despite these gains, however, underrepresentation clearly remains a problem.

Craig Richards (1988) offered three reasons why educators and society should be concerned about the underrepresentation of women and minorities in school administration:

1. *Equity is a legal requirement.* Title VII of the Equal Employment Opportunity Act and affirmative action require employers to seek equitable representation of women and minorities.
2. *Employment practices are part of the hidden curriculum.* Students learn much from what is called the *hidden curriculum* (i.e., things learned by students but not part of the formal curriculum of the school). Underrepresentation sends a number of messages to students about opportunity, prejudice, and other critical issues that influence student choices in life.
3. *Schools are a mirror of society.* Schools provide symbolic messages about values and beliefs to U.S. society and to the remainder of the world. Underrepresentation simply sends the wrong messages to society about equal opportunity and the equality of all citizens.

Characteristics, Placements, and Barriers

Often, it is difficult to separate issues of women and minorities because many women in school administration also are members of minority groups. Nevertheless, the two concerns are discussed separately here. Although empirical data verify that women and minorities are underrepresented in the practice of school administration, far less is known about the specific causes of this condition (Motaref, 1987; Yeakey, Johnston, & Adkison, 1986). The following review examines the causes of underrepresentation and eludes to questions that remain to be answered.

Women

Research on women in school administration continues to evolve. The earliest studies sought to determine the extent to which women had entered administration and the nature of their positions; subsequent studies addressed the characteristics of female administrators and why they were underrepresented in schools. More recently, much of the research has been qualitative, focusing on personal experiences and the effects of gender on behavior and effectiveness in organizations (Shakeshaft, 1999). The purpose here is to provide a basic understanding of the extent to which women have entered school administration and why they remain underrepresented in the profession.

Characteristics.   Because teaching is almost always a prerequisite to entering school administration, several researchers have looked at differences between men and women with regard to this variable. Collectively, this line of research has produced findings and conclusions indicating that women have had more teaching experience before entering administration. For example, a mid-1970s study found that the average female had 15 years of experience before assuming an administrative post, whereas the average male had only 5 to 7 years of experience (Gross & Trask, 1976). Another study looking specifically at superintendents found that three-fourths of the women, compared to only two-thirds of the men, had more than 5 years of teaching experience (Schuster & Foote, 1990).

Differences in previous experience suggest that women have had to provide more solid evidence of success in previous positions. A study of seven female high school principals in the Washington DC area, for instance, reported that all of the women had experience as assistant principals and all taught at least six years before obtaining an entry-level administrative position (Featherson, 1988). The hypothesis that employers demand higher qualifications of female applicants is also supported by findings that female superintendents tend to have higher IQs, higher levels of academic achievement, and are more likely to hold the doctorate than male superintendents (Schuster & Foote, 1990).

What motivates women to become administrators? Sakre Edson (1988) concluded that three factors were rather common:

1. A need for change and challenge
2. A positive assessment of management potential
3. An overriding concern for children's welfare

A study of female administrators in New York state found two primary motives among women entering administration: increased challenges and a feeling of being able to do better than people occupying these positions (Sulowski, 1987).

Although several researchers have associated underrepresentation of women in school administration with a lack of motivation, Charol Shakeshaft (1989) has taken exception with this conclusion: "Although it is true that women have traditionally applied less often than men for administrative positions and that women, more often than men, need to be encouraged to enter administration, there is little evidence that the reasons for this can be found in lower aspiration and motivation" (p. 86). Although men and women are considered to have the same level of motivation with respect to entering administration, research demonstrates that men and women frequently have different motivations. For instance, women often enter education initially because of a desire to be close to children and because they are convinced they can make a difference; as such, many do not desire positions that remove them entirely from the instructional process (Shakeshaft, 1988). Not all research, however, supports the existence of different motivations. A study of 153 administrators in Los Angeles, for instance, found that although minor differences existed, the individuals essentially shared the same basic motivations to become administrators regardless of gender (Brandes-Tyler, 1987).

One of the most promising areas of inquiry deals with comparing male and female administrative behaviors, especially with respect to those characteristics that have been found to be associated with effective schools. The following citations suggest that there are important differences between the behaviors of male and female administrators:

- Female administrators have been found to associate more highly with teachers and students (Fauth, 1984).
- Female superintendents have been more inclined to get involved in instructional programs, they communicated in less formal ways, and they exercised less control over meeting agenda and outcomes (Pitner, 1981).
- Female principals were more likely to require teacher conformity to their standards and they were more likely to monitor parent/teacher conferences and other contacts made between the school and homes (Gross & Trask, 1976).
- Female principals generally had closer supervisory relationships with teachers (Charters & Jovick, 1981).
- Female principals were more likely to use democratic procedures when making important decisions (Smith, 1978).
- Female administrators generally were more likely to concentrate on tasks closely aligned with instructional activities (Ortiz & Marshall, 1988).

In part, these gender-related variations in administrative behavior may be attributable to differences in role expectations. That is, people may expect female and male administrators to behave differently predicated on social norms. Often, women are expected to be loving and caring and men are expected to be stern and demanding. The notion that role expectations contribute to differences in actual behavior is supported by limited research findings. For example, employees in one study rated female administrators using participative and democratic behaviors more favorably than males employing the same behaviors. Such an outcome suggests that ratings may have been influenced by gender-related role expectations (Astin & Leland, 1991).

Placements. Historically, women have tended to occupy two types of administrative positions: elementary school principal and district-level jobs focusing on curriculum and instruction. Studies indicate that they are gradually making gains in two other key positions: the superintendency and the high school principalship. As noted earlier, the most recent data reported by the American Association of School Administrators indicated that just over 13 percent of the district superintendencies were held by women (Glass et al., 2000)—a percentage substantially higher than 3.4 percent reported by Effie Jones and Xenia Montenegro in 1990. Data for the high school principalship are less clear, largely because many researchers have used the category of secondary principal—a decision that makes it impossible to separate middle schools, junior high schools, and high schools. A 1988 national survey found that only 12 percent of high school principals were women (Wyatt, 1992), whereas a more recent study in New York state reported that 23 percent of secondary school principals were females (Shakeshaft, 1999). In addition, an analysis of several national studies indicates that women are making gains in the principalship in general; among principals with fewer than 5 years of administrative experience, more than 38 percent were female (Zheng & Carpenter-Hubin, 1999). Between 1987–88 and 1993–94, the representation of female principals in public schools increased from 25 to 34 percent (National Center for Education Statistics, 1997).

In what types of communities and districts do female administrators get employed? Very little research has been conducted on this topic. Examining conditions in the late 1980s, Stephen Jacobson (1989) reported that women were most likely to be found in large, urban districts. They were twice as likely to be in these settings than in rural and small-town districts; the frequency of placements in suburban districts fell between the extremes.

Barriers. Barriers to women in school administration are typically discussed as being either internal or external. "Internal barriers include aspects of socialization, personality, aspiration level; individual beliefs and attitudes; motivation; and self-image. External barriers researched were sex-role stereotyping, sex discrimination, lack of professional preparation, and family responsibilities" (Shakeshaft, 1981, p. 14). Internal barriers relate to aspects of personality, values, and attitudes of the individual; external barriers are environmental circumstances that mediate entrance into administrative positions (Leonard & Papa-Lewis, 1987). Several of the more recognized barriers are discussed here.

Mobility commonly has been identified as an intrinsic barrier, although there have been circumstances where one could argue that it was both intrinsic and extrinsic. Summarizing her research on 142 women administrators, Sakre Edson

(1988) noted both the importance of mobility and a changing attitude toward factors that made it a cogent issue. She wrote:

> Without doubt, the married women in this study feel an added burden in trying to assess the importance of their own career goals and personal needs with those of their husbands and children. They realize there is an element of risk involved in the broadened horizons they now have for themselves. But for these women, the past decision of automatically putting their careers on hold for their husbands' jobs is just that—a thing of the past. (p. 60)

Changing values and beliefs in society appear to have made mobility less of a barrier in recent years. Especially in situations involving higher-level, higher-paying positions, mobility often is less of a barrier than it was 30 or 40 years ago.

Negative attitudes toward career opportunities have been another intrinsic barrier for many women (Marshall, 1984). The fact that school administration has been, and continues to be, a white, male-dominated profession obviously affects career planning. In a review of research, Patricia Leonard and Rosemary Papa-Lewis (1987) also cited level of training, aspiration levels, a lack of confidence and initiative, and low self-image as internal constraints.

Sponsorship and *mentoring,* considered external barriers, have been studied on numerous occasions. These factors are associated with influential others promoting candidates for administrative positions. Sponsors or mentors have usually been school administration professors or high-visibility practitioners who have many political contacts; both groups have been comprised primarily of white males who have tended to offer the greatest support to other white males (Shakeshaft, 1989). As a result, even some well-qualified women have suffered a lack of sponsorship in a white, male-dominated profession (Ortiz & Marshall, 1988). Studies of career barriers often reveal that women have had difficulty gaining access to both the formal and informal male networks (e.g., Funk, 1986).

Closely related to the sponsorship issue is another external barrier: the *separation of the work of educators by gender* (sex-role stereotyping). Within administration itself, there is a tendency to see some positions as male or female jobs. The high school principal and business manager are examples of the former, and the elementary principal and curriculum specialist are examples of the latter (Schmuck & Wyant, 1981). On a broader basis, administration is often viewed as work for men and teaching as work for women. Flora Ortiz and Catherine Marshall (1988) described the ill effects of sex-role stereotyping:

> The effective separation of education into two professions, based considerably on gender, placed status and power in the hands of relatively few male administrators, who attended more to managing the enterprise than enhancing the technical core practiced by many. The separation is perpetuated in best-selling textbooks on school administration, in research that uses frameworks derived from theory on organizational control, and in long-standing reward systems and distributions of power that favor managers over the instructors. (p. 138)

Employers often placed females at a disadvantage by skewing job requirements toward managerial skills, politics, and the control of students—tasks not viewed as work for women (Wheatley, 1981). Sex-role stereotyping also can be an intrinsic barrier when an individual's personal perceptions, beliefs, and values lead to a separation of jobs based on gender.

Discrimination continues to be an external barrier for some women. Overt discrimination—simply not hiring women because they are women—persists despite laws prohibiting such actions. Not all discrimination, however, is readily discernible. Some life-related conditions also limit equal access, albeit in more subtle and less detectable ways. Encountering a lack of family support to pursue a career in administration, socializing women not to pursue administrative careers, and experiencing gender bias in professional books and research while in graduate school are examples of covert discrimination (Shakeshaft, 1989).

Minorities

Minority candidates seeking to enter school administration find that they encounter experiences different from those of whites (Valverde & Brown, 1988). The nature of these differences are central to understanding why members of racial and ethnic minority groups are underrepresented in school administration and what must be done to eradicate the problem. Overall, there is evidence that minorities are making gradual gains, with the greatest gains occurring in the principalship and the lowest gains occurring in the superintendency (Montenegro, 1993). Again, the discussion of underrepresentation focuses on characteristics, placements, and barriers.

Characteristics.   Compared to research on women, there is relatively little information available about characteristics of minorities entering school administration. One issue that has been explored is entry into the teaching profession. Many minority educators initially have been employed to teach bilingual education, Spanish, physical education, or special programs for students at risk—assignments that often have had little prestige. In addition, such programs frequently were located in remote areas of school buildings, making it more probable that teachers assigned to them would be isolated from the mainstream of professional, social, and political activity. Consequently, these teachers received less encouragement to enter administration and had fewer opportunities to exhibit leadership capabilities (Ortiz, 1982).

The literature contains many indications that the career paths of minorities and white males are different. Two factors appear especially cogent:

1. As noted earlier, there are a growing number of schools, particularly inner-city schools, that have student enrollments classified as minority-majorities. As might be expected, this demographic condition creates a high demand for minority educators. Thus, minority candidates often have found employment benefits, such as salary and position level, most attractive in these settings. Also, employers are prone to place minority administrators in schools where their services are in greatest demand. Several studies have shown that at virtually all stages of their careers, minority administrators tend to be placed in minority schools (e.g., Ortiz, 1982; Wilkerson, 1985).

2. The need for minority administrators (expressed through both affirmative action and the need to have role models) has been consistently greater than the supply over the past 40 years. Thus, school officials often have given race special consideration in employment decisions—even in relation to traditional criteria such as academic degrees, experience, and even licensing. As a result, minorities often enter administration with less experience than do whites—a circumstance that is opposite the experience of females. For example, Edward Chance (1989) found that Native American administrators had less experience teaching than did non-Native American administrators.

Studies of African American administrators have identified determination to be a key career factor. For example, one study found that African American female administrators were able to overcome a number of serious obstacles by maintaining a high level of self-esteem and determination (Spence, 1990). Another found that African American male superintendents were highly motivated and shared a career orientation that helped them focus on professional goals (Cadman, 1989).

Since affirmative action has played a role in creating job access for minority candidates, opinions regarding the utility of equity laws have been another area of inquiry. One study, for example, determined that many minority women aspiring to administrative positions expressed confidence that they could overcome any ill effects caused by quotas. The author of this study commented, "Even though they know their minority status is useful in securing administrative employment, some believe—that once hired—their competencies will win over those who doubted their worth" (Edson, 1988, p. 175). Many minority candidates have not apologized for any legal advantage they may have enjoyed in reaching administrative positions, because they view affirmative action as a necessary counteraction to race-related barriers such as discrimination.

Placements.   As noted earlier, minority educators have been most prevalent in districts or schools with high minority student enrollments. This pattern has been evident for other minority groups as well. And since minority populations have been heavily concentrated in large cities, minority administrators have been overwhelmingly employed in urban school districts (Jacobson, 1989; Rossi & Daugherty, 1996).

Flora Ortiz (1982) noted that minorities often enter administration by being placed in positions related to sponsored projects—positions such as the director of Title I programs or the coordinator of remedial reading programs. She also noted that although minority principals have been placed primarily in minority schools, central office administrators and school board members have tended to treat them differently than their white counterparts. For instance, she found that minority principals were often excluded from informal groups, especially when such groups engaged in social activities.

In 1990, 12.5 percent of all administrators and 3.4 percent of the superintendents in the United States were members of minority groups (Jones & Montenegro, 1990). In 1994, the figure for minorities in all administrative positions in elementary and secondary education increased to 15.7 percent (National Center for Education Statistics, 1997).

Representation of Hispanic Americans and Native Americans in school administration appears to have been influenced by cultural issues. Both groups have historically resented attempts by public schools to acculturate them to white Anglo-Saxon values and beliefs. Native Americans, for instance, are not adverse to Western education; they simply view it in a perfunctory manner because it is seen as an attempt to acculturate rather than educate (DeJong, 1990). Negative perceptions, deeply ingrained in culture, affect the career choices of many Hispanic Americans and Native Americans. Minorities in general have not been highly encouraged to enter the education profession by their own families, communities, and peers (Gordon, 2000).

Barriers. Repeatedly, studies focusing on minority school administrators raise the issue of sponsorship. Minorities are far less likely to be sponsored than are whites. Problems created by a lack of sponsorship have been compounded by blockages to socialization (Ortiz, 1982; Polczynski, 1990); that is, minorities aspiring to be administrators often have not gained access to informal social situations. The primary reason has been the lack of mentors or sponsors.

Discrimination has been a major barrier for minorities (Spence, 1990; Valverde & Brown, 1988). The following passage summarizes this concern:

> The larger body of organizational literature suggests, irrespective of attitudes and training programs, that no real change will occur until it is accompanied by broader societal change. That is, the basic problem of the exclusion of minorities and women from administrative positions is the subordinate role of women and minorities in all parts of society. (Yeakey, Johnston, & Adkison, 1986, p. 137)

One lingering form of discrimination entails informal job contacts—a process by which hiring officials are influenced by personal recommendations from higher-ranking individuals in the school district (Hudson, 1994). Many minority educators also perceive that as they attempt to acquire higher-level positions in administration, discrimination is likely to play an increasingly significant role (Edson, 1988). That is to say, the more successful a minority person is with regard to obtaining higher-level positions, the more likely he or she is to encounter discrimination.

Seeking Solutions to Underrepresentation

Eradicating barriers to women and minorities has remained a critical issue in school administration at least for the past 25 years. Unfortunately, the task is difficult and requires efforts on many fronts. This includes action by government agencies, state agencies, local districts, the profession, and individuals.

Legal Interventions

The federal government has assumed an active role in resolving societal problems that involve constitutional issues, and its most significant contribution has been legislation (Gupton & Del Rosario, 1997). Civil rights laws are a prime example. Americans are generally divided over the extent to which government should provide solutions to social problems, and they are divided over specific programs that attempt to eradicate the effects of discrimination. In recent years, for example, there has been a political backlash against imposed quotas. Ideally, discrimination problems should be eradicated in a democratic society for philosophical reasons; but at a more realistic level, laws have played a pivotal role in protecting the victims of prejudice. The tone set by all three branches of government has had and will continue to have a significant influence on employment practices in school administration.

Professional Preparation

Social institutions and the education profession also have promoted equity for women and minorities. Universities, albeit to varying degrees, have taken steps to increase the presence of women and minorities in school administration programs. The more common strategies have included:

- Identifying promising undergraduate students and offering them counseling to pursue a career in school administration
- Providing scholarships to members of underrepresented groups
- Modifying recruitment efforts that fail to attract sufficient numbers of women and minorities
- Creating new recruitment efforts specifically targeted to minorities
- Vigorously enforcing affirmative action
- Employing more female and minority professors to serve as role models
- Offering seminars, lectures, and workshops highlighting opportunities for women and minorities in school administration

Charol Shakeshaft (1989), Jill Blackmore (1989), and other writers have argued that academic revisions are another necessary action. Historically, the study of school administration has been shaped by male experiences—a perspective concentrating primarily on factors such as power and control. In order to attract more females to the profession, these writers believe that a more inclusive perspective of school administration needs to be provided in professional preparation. More specifically, female perspectives and experiences should be infused. Other recommendations cogent to professional preparation include the following:

- Bringing women and minority administrators to speak to graduate classes
- Placing women interns with women administrators and minority interns with minority administrators

- Requiring a course on equity and schooling (Shakeshaft, 1990)
- Exposing the gatekeepers (those who control entry into the profession) to empirical data
- Examining selection and promotion practices
- Providing support and counseling for career planning (Leonard & Papa-Lewis, 1987)

But despite an array of ideas, less than 30 percent of the doctoral programs in the mid-1990s had specific procedures for recruiting students from underrepresented groups (Hackmann & Price, 1995).

The Workplace

Public school systems exhibiting a concern for equity have concentrated largely on recruitment programs for underrepresented teachers and administrators. These efforts have included attempts to attract candidates from other school districts as well as to identify current employees who have the potential and interest to enter administration. The efficacy of these programs often depends on the extent to which the school board and superintendent are truly committed to eradicating underrepresentation. If they simply respond to political pressures and legal requirements, or if they just seek to score political points, the initiatives are usually ineffective and disappear after a relatively short time.

A few progressive districts have established sponsorship programs. This approach entails assigning a veteran administrator to a teacher who aspires to enter administration. The administrator serves as a sponsor and possibly as a mentor. Local districts, especially smaller ones, often find it impossible to fund vigorous recruitment programs adequately. Thus, they have collaborated with other agencies, such as universities and community groups, to carry out this initiative (Klauke, 1990).

Professional Organizations

Professional organizations also have made efforts to address the underrepresentation of women and minorities in school administration. The American Association of School Administrators (AASA), for example, has established designated offices (e.g., a deputy superintendent to oversee issues pertaining to women and minorities) and committees (e.g., AASA Women Administrators Committee), and has helped sponsor special projects (e.g., Assisting Women to Advance through Resources and Encouragement [AWARE]).

Professional organizations, especially at the state level, often assist with the establishment of networks—support groups that help underrepresented practitioners to find employment and to deal with job-related problems. The networks enhance communication between practitioners and professors, thus facilitating their collaborative efforts to increase the number of female and minority practitioners.

Mentors and Sponsors

Women and minorities who have entered administrative positions have demonstrated the efficacy of mentoring (Razik & Swanson, 1995); they frequently admit that mentors and sponsors helped them to enter the profession and to advance their careers. In most instances, highly respected administrators assumed this role out of a sense of professional commitment or personal friendship, and often these individuals have not been the same gender, race, or ethnic group as those they guide.

Mentors provide encouragement, help the aspiring educator to build confidence, and demonstrate friendship, mutual respect, trust, and openness (Pence, 1989). Sponsors play a key role in overcoming social and political barriers. A more concerted effort to provide mentors through organized programs at the local district level would ensure that more women and minorities could experience this advantage (Tallerico, 2000).

Society

The most difficult challenges for eradicating underrepresentation are at the societal level. This is because values, beliefs, and cultural norms are involved. As the United States continues to become an increasingly diverse society, prejudice and racial discrimination are likely to become even greater problems.

The fact that most school administrators work in public schools is a highly relevant issue because school boards, serving as representatives of the public, exercise considerable power regarding entry into the profession. Thus, actions within the profession will have only a limited effect if they are not paralleled by more favorable societal conditions.

Implications for Practice

Professors and practitioners face a myriad of unresolved issues pertaining to women and minorities in school administration. The fact that these groups have been and continue to be underrepresented affects both the image of the profession and the practice of school administration. Thus, you should have an understanding of this topic as you move forward with your studies in school administration—and this includes knowledge of the social and professional dimensions of this problem. Anyone aspiring to be an administrator should understand the extent of this problem and its relevance from both a social and professional perspective.

The public school system in the United States remains a primary force for preparing students to function effectively in a diverse society. As such, those who lead these institutions should be committed to fairness and equal opportunity—and they should serve as role models and mirror the composition of society. Student attitudes and beliefs are affected by both the formal and hidden curricula; the decisions made regarding the distribution of power and authority in social institutions provide symbolic messages about what ideas and practices are valued.

As you consider the content of this chapter, reflect on the reasons why women and minorities have not been represented in school administration. Also consider the extent to which you are personally concerned about this issue.

For Further Discussion _____

1. What does underrepresentation mean?

2. Historically, what factors encouraged women and minorities to enter the teaching profession?

3. Informal contacts often influence employment decisions in school administration. Why do informal contacts serve to perpetuate underrepresentation?

4. How did school desegregation cases and civil rights law affect African American educators in the 1950s and 1960s?

5. Do you see the underrepresentation of women and Hispanic Americans in school administration to be equally important concerns? Why or why not?

6. Women have most often entered administration in two types of positions. What are they? Why have women had greater access to these positions than to others?

7. Some studies have suggested that minority teachers often enter teaching in assignments that isolate them from the mainstream of activity in schools. Why is this finding important to understanding underrepresentation in school administration?

8. Why has mobility been a common barrier for women in school administration? Why has mobility often affected men and women differently?

9. How can local districts play a more active role in eradicating underrepresentation?

10. How can the education profession play a more active role in eradicating underrepresentation?

11. What is the difference between sexism and racism? How has each affected underrepresentation?

12. The issue of underrepresentation has both quantitative and qualitative dimensions. What is the difference between the two?

Other Suggested Activities _____

1. Debate the issue of job quotas. Is this a reasonable approach to eradicating underrepresentation? Why or why not?

2. Determine what your state-level organizations for school administrators are doing to promote women and minorities for administrative positions.

3. Obtain data from your local district regarding the percentage of women and minorities in administrative positions now and 10 years ago. Also inquire if specific actions have been taken to deal with underrepresentation. Discuss the outcomes.

4. Some states have responded to underrepresentation by either offering alternative licensing or waiving license requirements for members of underrepresented groups. Debates the merits of these actions.

5. Invite a minority administrator and a female administrator to speak to your class. See if they agree or disagree with common assumptions about barriers to entering school administration.

References

Astin, H. S., & Leland, C. (1991). *Women of influence, women of vision.* San Francisco: Jossey-Bass.

Blackmore, J. (1989). Educational leadership: A feminist critique and reconstruction. In J. Smyth (Ed.), *Critical perspectives on educational leadership* (pp. 93–130). Philadelphia: Falmer.

Brandes-Tyler, K. (1987). *A comparison of motivational differences between women and men to become educational administrators.* Unpublished Ed.D. dissertation, University of LaVerne, California.

Cadman, R. O. (1989). *Career patterns and successes of black superintendents in the Commonwealth of Virginia.* Unpublished Ed.D. dissertation, University of Virginia.

Castro, I. L. (1998). *Equal pay: A thirty-five year perspective.* (ERIC Document Reproduction Service No. ED 419 966)

Chance, E. W. (1989). *The BIA/contract school administrator: Implications for at-risk Native American students.* (ERIC Document Reproduction Services No. ED 331 682)

Charters, W. W., & Jovick, T. D. (1981). The gender of principals and principal-teacher relations. In P. Schmuck, W. Charters, & R. Carlson (Eds.), *Educational policy and management of sex differentials* (pp. 307–331). New York: Academic Press.

Clifford, G. J. (1989). Man/woman/teacher: Gender, family, and career in American educational history. In D. Warren (Ed.), *American teachers: Histories of a profession at work* (pp. 293–343). New York: Macmillan.

DeJong, D. H. (1990). *Friend or foe? Education and the American Indian.* Unpublished M.A. thesis, University of Arizona.

Edson, S. K. (1988). *Pushing the limits: The female administrative aspirant.* Albany: State University of New York Press.

Fauth, G. C. (1984). Women in educational administration. A research profile. *Educational Forum, 49*(1), 65–79.

Featherson, O. (1988). *Case studies of female secondary school principals.* Unpublished Ed.D. dissertation, George Washington University.

Feistritzer, C. E. (1990). *Profile of teachers in the U.S.—1990.* Washington, DC: National Center for Education Information.

Funk, C. (1986). *The female executive in school administration: Profiles, pluses, and problems.* (ERIC Document Reproduction Services No. ED 285 282)

Gips, C. J. (1989). *Women's ways: A model for leadership in democratic schools.* (ERIC Document Reproduction Services No. ED 314 860)

Glass, T., Björk, L., & Brunner, C. (2000). *The study of the American school superintendent 2000: A look at the superintendent of education in the new millennium.* Arlington, VA: American Association of School Administrators.

Gordon, J. A. (2000). *The color of teaching.* New York: Routledge/Falmer.

Gross, N., & Trask, A. E. (1976). *The sex factor and the management of schools.* New York: John Wiley & Sons.

Gupton, S. L., & Del Rosario, R. M. (1997). *An analysis of federal initiatives to support women's upward mobility in educational administration.* (ERIC Document Reproduction Services No. ED 409 632)

Hackmann, D., & Price, W. (1995, February). *Preparing school leaders for the 21st century: Results of a national survey of educational leadership doctoral programs.* Paper presented at the Annual Convention of the American Association of School Administrators, San Francisco.

Hudson, M. J. (1994). Women and minorities in school administration: Re-examining the role of informal job contact systems. *Urban Education, 28*(4), 386–397.

Jacobson, S. L. (1989). School management: Still a white man's game. *Executive Educator, 11*(11), 19.

Jones, E. H., & Montenegro, X. P. (1990). *Women and minorities in school administration.* (ERIC Document Reproduction Services No. ED 273 017)

Klauke, A. (1990). *Preparing school administrators.* (ERIC Document Reproduction Services No. ED 326 939)

Leonard, P. Y., & Papa-Lewis, R. (1987). The underrepresentation of women and minorities in educational administration: Patterns, issues, and recommendations. *Journal of Educational Equity and Leadership, 7*(3), 188–207.

Mack, F. R., & Jackson, T. E. (1993). *Teacher education as a career choice of Hispanic high school seniors.* (ERIC Document Reproduction Services No. ED 358 087)

Marshall, C. (1984). The crisis in excellence and equity. *Educational Horizons, 63*(1), 24–30.

Montenegro, X. (1993). *Women and racial minority representation in school administration.* Arlington, VA: American Association of School Administrators.

Motaref, S. (1987). *Women in educational administration: An analytical synthesis and summing up of what we know and don't know.* Unpublished Ph.D. dissertation, Florida State University.

National Center for Education Statistics. (1991). *The condition of education 1991 (Volume 2), Postsecondary Education.* Washington, DC: U.S. Department of Education.

National Center for Education Statistics. (1997). *Public and private school principals in the United States: A statistical profile, 1987–88 to 1993–94.* Washington, DC: U.S. Department of Education.

National Center for Education Statistics. (1999). *Digest of Education Statistics, 1999.* Washington, DC: U.S. Department of Education.

Ortiz, F. I. (1982). *Career patterns in education: Women, men and minorities in public school administration.* New York: Praeger.

Ortiz, F. I., & Marshall, C. (1988). Women in educational administration. In N. Boyan (Ed.), *Handbook of research on educational administration* (pp. 1123–1142). New York: Longman.

Pence, L. J. (1989). *Formal and informal mentorships for aspiring and practicing administrators.* Unpublished Ph.D. dissertation, University of Oregon.

Perkins, L. M. (1989). The history of blacks in teaching: Growth and decline within the profession. In D. Warren (Ed.), *American teachers: Histories of a profession at work* (pp. 344–369). New York: Macmillan.

Pitner, N. J. (1981). Hormones and harems: Are the activities of superintending different for a woman? In P. Schmuck, W. Charters, & R. Carlson (Eds.), *Educational policy and management of sex differentials* (pp. 273–295). New York: Academic Press.

Polczynski, M. A. (1990). *From barriers to challenges: The black and white female experience in educational administration.* Unpublished Ph.D. dissertation, Marquette University.

Razik, T. A., & Swanson, A. D. (1995). *Fundamental concepts of educational leadership and management.* Englewood Cliffs, NJ: Merrill, Prentice-Hall.

Richards, C. (1988). The search for equity in educational administration. In N. Boyan (Ed.), *Handbook of research on educational administration* (pp. 159–168). New York: Longman.

Rossi, R., & Daugherty, S. (1996). *Where do minority principals work?* (ERIC Document Reproduction Services No. ED 396 433)

Rury, J. L. (1989). Who became teachers? In D. Warren (Ed.), *American teachers: Histories of a profession at work* (pp. 9–48). New York: Macmillan.

Schmuck, P. A., & Wyant, S. H. (1981). Clues to sex bias in the selection of school administrators. In P. Schmuck, W. Charters, & R. Carlson (Eds.), *Educational policy and management of sex differentials* (pp. 73–97). New York: Academic Press.

Schuster, D. J., & Foote, T. H. (1990). Differences abound between male and female superintendents. *The School Administrator, 2*(47), 14–16, 18.

Shakeshaft, C. (1981). Women in educational administration: A descriptive analysis of dissertation research and paradigm for future research. In P. Schmuck, W. Charters, & R. Carlson (Eds.), *Educational policy and management: Sex differentials* (pp. 9–31). New York: Academic Press.

Shakeshaft, C. (1988). Women in educational administration: Implications for training. In D. Griffiths, R. Stout, & P. Forsyth (Eds.), *Leaders for America's schools* (pp. 403–416). Berkeley, CA: McCutchan.

Shakeshaft, C. (1989). *Women in educational administration* (updated edition). Newbury Park, CA: Sage.

Shakeshaft, C. (1990). Administrative preparation for equity. In H. Baptiste, H. Waxman, J. Walker de Felix, & J. Anderson (Eds.), *Leadership, equity, and school effectiveness* (pp. 213–223). Newbury Park, CA: Sage.

Shakeshaft, C. (1999). The struggle to create a more gender-inclusive profession. In J. Murphy & K. Seashore Louis (Eds.), *Handbook of research on educational administration* (2nd ed.) (pp. 99–118). San Francisco: Jossey-Bass.

Smith, J. (1978). Encouraging women to enter administration. *NASSP Bulletin, 62,* 114–119.

Spence, B. A. (1990). *Self-perceptions of African-American female administrators in New England public schools.* Unpublished Ed.D. dissertation, University of Massachusetts.

Spencer, D. A. (1986). *Contemporary women teachers.* New York: Longman.

Sulowski, S. (1987). *A descriptive profile of female line administrators in New York state.* Unpublished Ed.D. dissertation, Teachers College, Columbia University.

Tallerico, M. (2000). Why don't they apply? Encouraging women and minorities to seek administrative positions. *American School Board Journal, 187*(11), 56–58.

Valverde, L. A., & Brown, F. (1988). Influences on leadership development among racial and ethnic minorities. In N. Boyan (Ed.), *Handbook of research on educational administration* (pp. 143–158). New York: Longman.

Verdugo, R. R., & Schneider, J. M. (1994). Gender inequality in female-dominated occupation: The earnings of male and female teachers. *Economics of Education Review, 13*(3), 251–264.

Wheatley, M. (1981). The impact of organizational structure on issues of sex equity. In P. Schmuck, W. Charters, & R. Carlson (Eds.), *Educational policy and management of sex differentials* (pp. 255–271). New York: Academic Press.

Wilkerson, G. J. (1985). *Black school administrators in the Los Angeles Unified School District: Personal perspectives and current considerations.* Unpublished Ed.D. dissertation, University of San Francisco.

Wyatt, L. (1992). *Secondary principalships: Where are the women?* (ERIC Document Reproduction Service No. ED 352 731)

Yasin, S. (1999). *The supply and demand of elementary and secondary school teachers in the United States.* (ERIC Document Reproduction Service No. ED 436 529)

Yeakey, C. C., Johnston, G. S., & Adkison, J. A. (1986). In pursuit of equity: A review of research on minorities and women in educational administration. *Educational Administration Quarterly, 22*(3), 110–149.

Zheng, H. Y., & Carpenter-Hubin, J. (1999). *Exploring gender differences in America's school administrator workforce: Statistical evidence from national surveys.* (ERIC Document Reproduction Service No. ED 432 817)

16

Planning Your Career

Chapter Content

Personal Career Planning
Changing Attitudes and Assumptions
Building an Individual Plan
Implications for Practice

Educators who consider school administration as a career face two critical questions: Why do I want to be an administrator? What do I want to do as an administrator? These two queries have become increasingly important because the nature of schools as a workplace and society are changing. All too often, aspiring administrators ignore these questions because they are willing to gamble that life's good fortune will protect them and lead them to fulfilling jobs. They begin applying for administrative positions without considering how their new responsibilities interface with personal ability, personality, and interests. And often, their view of administrative work is inaccurate, reflecting perceptions they developed as students and teachers rather than present and anticipated conditions.

Personal career planning can be a powerful tool for ensuring that you pursue the types of positions that allow you to be successful and satisfied. Thus, the appropriate time to start the process is now—the point at which you begin the formal study of school administration. This chapter examines career planning and the changing values and beliefs regarding career decisions. In addition, suggestions for effective career planning and for obtaining your first position in school administration are provided.

Personal Career Planning

Definition

The concept of career has been defined in different ways. Some descriptions focus on work alone. These definitions view career as "the evolving sequence of a person's work experiences over time" (Arthur, Hall, & Lawrence, 1989, p. 8). Other descriptions are more encompassing in that they include the nature of the work assignment and its effects outside of the workplace. For example, *career* also has been defined as "the activities and positions involved in vocations, occupations, and jobs as well as related activities associated with an individual's lifetime of work" (Zunker, 1990, p. 3). In professions, the broader definition is more cogent because the nature of work not only affects your earnings but it also contributes to personal prestige and respect.

Personal career planning in school administration is an individual activity that helps you address six critical tasks:

1. Engaging in self-assessment
2. Gaining an accurate perception of various positions in administration
3. Developing career goals
4. Developing strategies for attaining goals
5. Examining the potential relationships between work and personal life
6. Continuously evaluating the relevance of your career goals

The process does not end when you obtain your first administrative assignment; rather, it is continuous, providing purpose and direction for choices you make throughout your career (Steele & Morgan, 1991).

The product of individual career planning is a *personal career action plan*—a document that contains accurate self-assessment data, occupational data, goal statements, and evaluation criteria. Its purpose extends beyond helping you get a job. An action plan should also help you grow within a job. This is possible because you have a deeper understanding of your personal definition of success—that is, what you must do to satisfy your employer and yourself. Effective planning extends all the way to retirement.

Personal career planning requires a commitment and the acceptance of personal responsibility. This is because the process is totally voluntary and personal. Others can provide advice and direction, but highly successful individuals take responsibility for their own action plans (Graen, 1989). Even your closest friends and colleagues may not have a clear understanding of the values, beliefs, wants, needs, and motivations that create satisfaction for you. Therefore, their ability to guide your career choice is usually limited.

Value of a Personal Plan

Why develop a personal career action plan? Countless graduate students who have studied school administration have asked this question. Unfortunately, many of them determine that the potential benefits do not justify the time required. Some are individuals who view career success as largely a matter of "being in the right place at the right time." Others offer a variety of excuses that range from not having sufficient time to not being unable to obtain all the necessary information. These rationalizations sidestep the reality that career paths in school administration are neither linear nor predictable.

Over time, virtually every school administrator experiences peaks and valleys that spark opportunities or self-doubt. For example, a highly successful principal may be offered a better-paying job in another school district, or perhaps conflict with teachers may prompt a principal to think about changing jobs. Career decisions are often stressful, and this is especially true when a person has no plan that allows a specific decision to be made in the context of lifelong goals. Recognizing the difficulties associated with relying on intuition alone to make critical career decisions, Richard Buskirk (1976) cited three cogent reasons why a personal career action plan is beneficial:

1. It helps you encounter uncertainty.
2. It provides you with emotional peace of mind.
3. It is a yardstick to measure how you are doing.

More specific purposes of a personal career plan include:

- *Providing a personal understanding of needs and wants related to work:* The plan causes you to engage in introspection and to seek linkages between your personal life and your work life.
- *Providing a better understanding of career opportunities:* Planning requires information. By engaging in this process, you learn more about school administration, opportunities, rewards, and common employment practices.
- *Enhancing the likelihood of having a mentor or sponsor:* The complexity of planning encourages you to seek out an "influential other" to answer questions and provide guidance.
- *Examining possible motivations:* Aspiring administrators often focus solely on a narrow band of extrinsic inducements such as salary. Although relevant, these motivators do not address a fundamental question about job satisfaction: Will you be doing what you really want to do?
- *Reflecting on values:* An action plan causes you to look at what you value and believe about life and about work. Such mental activity further enhances your understanding of yourself and the types of jobs for which you are well suited (Lyon & Kirby, 2000).
- *Examining potential barriers to goal attainment:* Professions usually develop mechanisms that attempt to limit the number of recruits and aspirants (Spokane, 1991). These may range from admission standards for professional education to licensing requirements. In addition, entry into a profession may be blocked by conditions in society or the workplace—factors such

as outright discrimination. A career plan helps you evaluate the probability that you can overcome all types of potential obstacles.

- *Determining time parameters for action:* Goals in an action plan help you set time parameters for enhancing professional skills and for seeking career advancements.
- *Assessing performance and growth:* An action plan helps you determine if your original goals and objectives were realistic and whether adjustments are required. Because the process is continuous and lifelong, you are required to evaluate your progress periodically and to make necessary adjustments.
- *Preventing complacency:* Long-term goals remind you of what you intend to accomplish. This information makes it less likely that you will become complacent in an intermediate position.
- *Exploring human needs and wants:* Career planning prompts you to study developmental theories that provide additional insights into your behavior. For example, individuals typically move through three stages of career development: (1) a focus on job competencies and professional identity, (2) a focus on needs related to personal advancement, and (3) a focus on maintaining emergent status, gaining affirmations of success, and passing knowledge and experience to others (Arthur & Kram, 1989).

In the final analysis, an understanding of school administration is of limited value if you do not know yourself. Incomplete or distorted information increases the probability of poor career decisions.

Mismatches of individual abilities, needs, and aspirations on the one hand and job opportunities or requirements on the other, do occur in educational administration. When careers in education typically span periods of more than thirty years, it is tragic to discover how few give attention to or understand the rudiments of career planning. (Orlosky, McCleary, Shapiro, & Webb, 1984, p. 22)

Changing Attitudes and Assumptions

Career decisions are influenced by many things, not the least of which are attitudes and assumptions about employment, work, and career development. Clearly, values and beliefs play and important role in this regard. John Steele and Marilyn Morgan (1991) summarized three common defense mechanisms that are often articulated as rationalizations for avoiding personal career planning:

1. *The "I know what I want to be" defense:* Individuals claim that they do not need to plan because they have known since childhood what is "right" for them. For example, an aspiring principal says, "I've known since the fourth grade that I was destined to be a principal."

2. *The "let life decide" defense:* Individuals take a fatalistic attitude toward their careers. For example, an aspiring administrator says, "If I'm meant to be an administrator, the right opportunities will come my way."

3. *The "I'll pick something when I need to" defense:* Individuals claim that planning is unnecessary for two reasons: There are many opportunities awaiting them and they have the ability to be decisive at appropriate times. For example, an aspiring administrator says, "When I decide that I'm ready to move into administration, I'll pick the type of job that is best for me."

Although these interpretations provide temporary comfort to one's ego, they do nothing to enhance career development. For instance, knowing what you want to be is only one factor that needs to be weighed in making career decisions. Often, individuals never objectively consider whether their single aspiration is realistic. An unattainable career vision is merely an illusion.

Futurists frequently use trend analysis to make their predictions. This process entails comparisons of past and present data to monitor change. Trend analysis also is an important tool with regard to career planning. Four relevant trends are discussed next.

Determinants of Career Development

Have you ever looked at a highly successful administrator and asked yourself, "How did he get there?" In particular, you may question whether the person, the organizational setting, or simply blind luck is responsible for this person succeeding. Research conducted with business executives suggests that each factor plays some part, but their influence is not fixed. In other words, the actual weight of each is determined by situational variables (Bell & Staw, 1989).

Research findings on the effects of career planning in school administration also are mixed. Some studies have found luck to be a salient factor; however, there are ample reasons to treat such outcomes with caution. Many career development studies in education have been conducted with constraints, and most are descriptive reports generating data from limited population samples (Miklos, 1988). In addition, changing conditions in society and the profession alter the likelihood that you will get lucky with your career. For example, luck is more apt to be an important variable when employers are not well organized and when they have an inadequate supply of applicants.

Too often, individuals rely on luck because this decision does not require effort. If a person believes that relying on luck is as effective as career planning, then why would he or she take the time to build and maintain a plan? People who rely on luck often misinterpret opportunity as being luck. In truth, luck is when opportunity meets preparation. That is, what appears to be blind luck is often the convergence of opportunity and planning. Truly great people have prepared themselves for their careers (Buskirk, 1976); they were ready to deal with contingencies that presented opportunities—but they were always focused on their goals. A

greater realization that planning improves one's ability to take advantage of opportunity has led to the trend of *relying on planning instead of luck.*

Career Development Paths

Is there one best career path to becoming a principal or a superintendent? Career
patterns are described as regularities in the rise of people from position to position
in a profession (Miklos, 1988). Research on career paths in school administration
has led to several generalizations. For example, most principals began their administrative careers as assistant principals; women were most likely to enter administration as elementary school principals. Such information has often been used as a
guide for making career decisions.

In today's world of practice, however, there is less uniformity in career paths,
indicating that there are several ways that individuals can reach their career goals.
Often, contextual variables, such as the nature of the community and school district,
play an important part in determining which path may be most effective for you. In
rural areas, for example, administrators are more apt to bypass the assistant principal position, since these positions often do not exist in smaller schools. Or in times
when instructional improvement is a high priority, school boards may be willing to
employ a superintendent who has never been a principal, because he or she has
established a record of success as a curriculum director. Changes in contextual variables have created multiple paths to administrative positions; thus, the second trend
entails *believing that there are multiple paths to career goals rather than one dominant path.*

Career versus Life-Style

In many fields of endeavor, people have been led to believe that they should put
their careers above all else. This philosophy has often been visible in large corporations where executives have frequently endured the discomforts of being transferred as a means of gaining a promotion. Thus, personal job advancement took
precedent over family needs and wants. School administrators often found themselves in a similar situation. That is, they were able to advance their careers more
rapidly by being highly mobile.

In his study of school superintendents, Richard Carlson (1972) labeled administrators who were hired from outside an organization as "career bound." He noted
that most of them had accepted mobility as a means of advancing their careers.
For example, some principals in suburban school districts moved to rural districts
in order to become a superintendent despite the fact that their families did not
want to relocate. Career-bound administrators usually placed career advancement
above any other consideration in making job-related decisions. By comparison,
some administrators were "place bound." That is, in making career decisions,
location (community and school district) took precedent over personal advancement (Carlson, 1972). Within the profession, it was widely recognized that career-
bound individuals had a distinct advantage in reaching high-level positions

because they were willing to go to places where opportunities existed; thus, students preparing to be school administrators were often encouraged to be career bound.

The precept that career comes first, however, has been challenged in recent years. Today, there is more of a tendency to integrate work-related decisions with other considerations, such as family, leisure, and friends. Individuality makes it more difficult to predict the career decisions others will make (Borchard, Kelly, & Weaver, 1984). As a growing number of women enter the practice of school administration, the attitude of merging career with "whole life" has become even more prevalent. Historically, women have been more likely to face conflicts between work and family or work and personal life choices (Vondracek, Lerner, & Schulenberg, 1986). A study of married female superintendents conducted in the mid-1990s exemplifies this point. Many women, despite having had strong spousal support, said they would not relocate again to get a better job (Ramsey, 1997). Changing societal conditions and greater diversity in the profession contribute to the third trend—*believing that career is one of several important factors in determining life experiences rather than being the only factor.*

Determinants of Success

Symbols mean much in U.S. society. A person's clothes, house, and car are indicators of success because they are seen as manifestation of rewards for achievement. Historically, success in school administration also has been judged by salary and position (Carlson, 1972). For example, superintendents were generally considered more successful than principals, and the most successful superintendents were those who made the highest salaries. Thus, success could be assessed by upward mobility—that is, incrementally moving to higher-level and higher-paying jobs.

Today, success is apt to be defined more broadly. Philosophically, many individuals desire to set the terms of their work life (Manter & Benjamin, 1989). For them, being able to lead a certain life-style and to preserve values is at least as important as salary. Professionally, many practitioners now define success by performance in a position rather than by the nature of a position. Therefore, a contemporary practitioner can be "successful" even though he or she spends an entire career in a single position (e.g., principal or even assistant principal), and in some instances, even in the same school. The fourth trend entails a transition in the definition of success—*moving from defining success solely on the basis of salary and position to defining success on the basis of performance in a position.*

Building an Individual Plan

Career planning entails much more than just writing a resume and searching for jobs. It begins with self-awareness, encompasses life-style philosophy and career information, and includes specific and measurable goals. The process is examined with respect to knowledge, attributes, components, and potential pitfalls.

Required Knowledge

Individual career plans require both commitment and knowledge. With respect to the latter, five types of knowledge are essential: knowledge of self, knowledge of school administration, knowledge of contemporary conditions and trends, knowledge of career planning, and knowledge of goals and evaluation (see Figure 16.1).

Knowledge of self is produced by a personal inventory—a process that seeks to objectively determine abilities, interests, and attitudes. More specifically, the inventory should produce information about the following:

- *Personality:* For example, are you extroverted or introverted?
- *Values:* For example, how much emphasis do you place on life-style in making a career choice?
- *Attitudes:* For example, how do you feel about working in a public organization?
- *Ability:* For example, are you capable of completing the preparation required for a profession or occupation?
- *Achievement:* For example, does your academic record qualify you to enter a given profession or occupation?
- *Skills:* For example, what skills have you mastered?
- *Interests:* For example, what types of work activities are of greatest interest to you?

Knowledge Base	Common Factors
Self	Personality, abilities, attitudes, interests, values, achievement, skills
School administration	Nature of work, occupational opportunities, role expectations, common career paths
Contemporary conditions and trends	Changing nature of schools, supply and demand for school administrators, effects of school reform
Career planning	Personal planning, advantages of planning, structuring a plan, potential pitfalls
Goal setting and evaluation	Setting intermediate and long-term goals, assessing progress toward goals, making evaluative decisions, reformulating goals

FIGURE 16.1 *Knowledge Required for Personal Career Planning*

Knowledge about school administration is largely related to information presented earlier in the book. It includes vocational data (e.g., types of jobs, job availability, roles, and responsibilities) and it incorporates information regarding trends and changes affecting practice (e.g., collaborative decision making). It also includes information about employment practices, laws, contracts, and any other facts that are specific to being a practitioner of school administration.

To successfully plan your career, you also need to know what is occurring in the world around you. What is society expecting from schools? How are changes in social values and family structure affecting schools and the lives of school administrators? Does society provide the rewards to school administrators that meet your career expectations and needs? Two considerations are especially important for education directly and school administrators indirectly: movement to an information society and movement to a global economy.

The creation of an individual plan requires some information about careers and career planning. One of the primary purposes of this chapter is to provide this knowledge. Additional assistance for career planning is available from self-help books or from career-counseling specialists—both resources are available at virtually every university. Unfortunately, school administrators have not been prone to utilize these resources either in professional preparation or in continuing education.

Finally, career planning requires knowledge of goal setting and evaluation. An individual action plan is a living document; it requires continuous updating. To do this, you must be able to set measurable goals, assess the degree to which the goals have been met, and make evaluation decisions. These decisions will help you refine your goals.

Attributes of Effective Career Plans

Before reviewing the suggested components of career planning, a review of several desirable attributes is helpful:

- *A career plan should be continual.* No aspect of creating an individual plan for career development is more essential than the realization that the process is continual. Developing a plan is not something you do once and then put it away in a drawer. Properly managed plans are perceived as documents that have the potential of becoming stronger, more realistic, and increasingly effective. Each year of experience provides information necessary to fine-tune goals.
- *A career plan should be flexible.* Your career plan may span more than 30 years. During this period, you can expect many changes—some personal, some environmental, and some professional. A quality plan allows for goals to be adjusted periodically based on changes reflected in annual evaluations.
- *A career plan should be realistic.* No plan built on a foundation of unrealistic dreams is useful. This does mean that you should avoid lofty goals; rather, it implies that your goals are rooted in reality. Career objectives should be

predicated on a combination of facts about you and about the profession and society.

• *A career plan should be influential.* A plan is worthwhile if it actually affects behavior. For this to happen, you need to believe that the process and the product will produce meaningful results. With these conditions present, the plan constitutes a framework that you will use to make critical career decisions.

Individual Plan Components

Individual plans may vary in structure and specificity; however, several components are considered essential. They are illustrated in Figure 16.2. The first is a *vision of life.* This component seeks to answer the question, What kind of life do you want to have? Your vision of your life might focus on issues such as income, status, family, personal satisfaction, self-actualization, and leisure. Richard Buskirk (1976) developed a list of seven essential questions that are helpful in making quality-of-life decisions:

1. How much money do you really need to make to consider yourself successful?
2. What kind of work do you really want to do?
3. What type of environment do you want?

FIGURE 16.2   *Components of an Individual Career Plan*

4. What are the social needs of both yourself and your family?
5. What kind of family life do you want to lead?
6. How much prestige does your ego require?
7. How much security must you have? (pp. 16–20)

Self-assessment involves introspection—a process of bringing to the surface personal information that facilitates career planning. Components of this activity were identified earlier in relation to knowledge required for planning. Over the last few decades, a professional dimension to self-assessment has become available. Several national organizations serving administrators, such as the National Association of Secondary School Principals (NASSP), have created assessment centers that evaluate individual potential for dealing with administrative positions (Miklos, 1988). Although these centers have often been associated with merit-based selection decisions (i.e., assessment data may be used by employers to determine applicant capabilities), they also provide a source of objective data that can be used for individual career planning (McCleary & Ogawa, 1985). However, the construct and predictive validity of these assessment tools varies (Sirotnik & Durden, 1996); thus, information obtained from assessment centers should be weighed carefully against other information generated in a personal inventory.

Specific information that contributes to self-assessment includes details about your

- Interests, abilities, and skills
- Work values
- Accomplishments and disappointments
- Personal needs (psychological and physical)
- Aspirations
- Level of motivation
- Personality
- Strengths and weaknesses in relation to administrative work

The third component of an individual action plan is a *career needs statement.* This component identifies what you perceive to be your personal needs with regard to your work life. This might include statements about status, expected challenges, social interactions, opportunities for personal growth, and so forth. Career needs indicate how you anticipate that your work life will contribute to your vision of life.

A comprehensive career plan needs to include *intermediate and long-term goals.* This component provides job-related targets that guide decisions. As noted earlier, long-term goals should be flexible so that the ramification of unforeseen conditions can be infused into the planning document periodically. It is especially important that intermediate goals are measurable, because progress toward them provides the basis for adjusting long-term goals.

Your personal plan should also provide *goal attainment strategies.* These statements outline how you plan to achieve your objectives. Effective strategies reflect the integration of self-assessment career information. Often, plans include contingency strategies—alternatives for achieving a goal that depend on developments affecting you, the profession, and your work environment. Consider a high school social studies teacher in a suburban high school aspiring to become a principal in a large high school within seven years. She uses her knowledge of job opportunities to create two contingencies. The first is predicated on the intermediate objective of obtaining an assistant principalship in a larger school; the second is predicated on the intermediate objective of obtaining a principalship in a small high school. She believes that either strategy can lead to her primary goal (becoming a principal of a large high school in seven years). However, she cannot control job opportunities; and being amenable to making sacrifices to reach her goal, she sees both strategies as viable alternatives.

The nucleus of a good career plan is *assessment and evaluation*. This component allows you to determine three important matters:

1. The overall progress you are making toward your goals
2. The extent to which your initial needs, goals, and strategies were realistic
3. The extent to which components of your plan need to be adjusted

Evaluation should occur annually.

Potential Pitfalls

The development of an individual career plan is not without potential problems. Joseph and Lucille Hollis (1976) identified five of the most common pitfalls:

1. Often, the individual focuses solely on short-term goals. Given the overall purposes of the effort, goals should be projected to at least 10 to 15 years in the future.
2. The tendency to focus solely on one factor (e.g., only considering career) results in a form of tunnel vision; the individual ignores critical issues such as personal abilities and desired life-style.
3. Insufficient knowledge and information distort the quality of the plan. For example, the individual may not know enough about career development in school administration.
4. Plans can become too elaborate, causing the individual to lose site of purpose. Individual career plans should guide work-related decisions. If they are too complex, they may be more confusing than helpful.
5. The individual frequently sets career goals too high or too low. More important, the person fails to adjust original targets after several years of experience.

Other possible problems include failing to develop all key components in the plan, failing to engage in evaluation on a periodic basis, and expecting too much too soon.

Using a Career Portfolio

A *career portfolio* is a tool that you can use to maintain your individual action plan. This technique provides a tangible record of evidence with respect to your education, career goals, and work experiences (Pond, Burdick, & Yamamoto, 1998). Maintaining a portfolio increases the likelihood that your plan is sustained and that you remain proactive regarding your future. In addition, a portfolio provides organized evidence of work readiness and specific job skills that can be used in conjunction with job applications. However, the greatest benefits relate to evaluation and goal adjustment.

The portfolio's content is typically divided into sections based on the components of your plan. For example, material in the self-assessment section would include writing samples, evaluations of your performance as a teacher, records of performance on tests (e.g., your Graduate Record Examination scores and your scores on the state teacher licensing examination), and other performance data relevant to your career aspirations (e.g., videotapes of verbal presentations and results from an assessment center evaluation). Such evidence makes it more likely that the evaluation and goal adjustment components of your individual plan will be completed objectively. Discussing the use of portfolios by aspiring administrators, Genevieve Brown and Beverly Irby (1995) noted that the technique also facilitates reflection—a process that is integral to professional growth.

Implications for Practice

School administration is a diverse profession. Practitioners are faced with many important decisions, ranging from the type of positions they pursue to the type of schools in which they work. Far too often, teachers start academic study in school administration simply to create the potential for moving to a higher-paying position. Some school administration students, for example, admit that they simply want to be ready if opportunity knocks on their door. For them, the study of school administration is apt to be unexciting, basically irrelevant, and a waste of time and money. Thus, you should make every effort to determine your level of commitment to serving others in formal leadership and management roles before you move forward with your studies in this specialization.

Personal career planning, as discussed in this chapter, is one mechanism for understanding your true interests in administrative work. The process provides an integrative approach to controlling your life. In addition to detailing the purposes of career planning and the components of the process, this chapter examined changing attitudes and beliefs about the relationships between career and life-style.

As you continue your studies in school administration, you should reflect on your abilities, interests, and values and how they interface with the realities of being a practitioner in this profession. More specifically, you need to determine life-style goals and professional goals and to evaluate the extent to which the two are compatible. Most important, you should accept responsibility for directing your own life. Self-development is a synthesis of previous ideas that involves a constant transfer from experience to reflection and back again (Pedler, 1988). True professionals employ reflection as a method of growth. Each academic course and each day of work provide information and experience that serve to reshape how you look at the world, at your profession, and at your career.

For Further Discussion

1. What is a personal career plan? What purposes does it serve?

2. Students often enter the study of school administration with a narrow perspective of the ideal and real roles of practitioners in this specialization. How can a personal career plan serve to broaden this perspective?

3. Why do many individuals fail to develop career plans?

4. What is a career path? Why have some researchers studied the career paths of administrators?

5. Personal career plans were described in this chapter as continuous. What does this mean?

6. What services may be available to help you with your career planning?

7. Assessment centers provide data that can assist career planning. What is the purpose of these centers and what types of data do they provide?

8. What is self-assessment? Why is this process an essential element of career planning?

9. What factors should be included in a self-assessment?

10. What are alternative strategies or contingencies for reaching goals? What purpose do they serve?

11. What is a career portfolio? What is the advantage of using a portfolio in conjunction with a personal career plan?

12. What trends are affecting career planning in school administration?

Other Suggested Activities

1. Invite a professor who specializes in career counseling to meet with you or your class to discuss the development of individual career plans.

2. Women have entered the study of school administration in greater numbers in recent years. Discuss possible differences in ways that males and females tend to integrate life-style and career goals.

3. Draft an outline of the components you would include in your career plan. Identify the information you possess and the information you would need to obtain to complete your plan.

4. Discuss the value of creating a career plan at the early stages of your graduate work in this specialization.

5. One of the attributes of an effective career plan is flexibility. Discuss the meaning of this attribute and describe why it is cogent to evaluation and the reformulation of goals.

References

Arthur, M. B., Hall, D. T., & Lawrence, B. S. (1989). Generating new directions in career theory: The case for a transdisciplinary approach. In M. Arthur, D. Hall, & B. Lawrence (Eds.), *Handbook of career theory* (pp. 7–25). Cambridge: Cambridge University Press.

Arthur, M. B., & Kram, K. E. (1989). Reciprocity at work: The separate, yet inseparable possibilities for individual and organizational development. In M. Arthur, D. Hall, & B. Lawrence (Eds.), *Handbook of career theory* (pp. 292–312). Cambridge: Cambridge University Press.

Bell, N. E., & Staw, B. M. (1989). People as sculptors versus sculpture: The roles of personality and personal control in organizations. In M. Arthur, D. Hall, & B. Lawrence (Eds.), *Handbook of career theory* (pp. 232–251). Cambridge: Cambridge University Press.

Borchard, D. C., Kelly, J. J., & Weaver, N. P. (1984). *Your career* (3rd ed.). Dubuque, IA: Kendall/Hunt.

Brown, G., & Irby, B. J. (1995). The portfolio: Should it also be used by administrators? *NASSP Bulletin, 79*(570), 82–85.

Buskirk, R. H. (1976). *Your career: How to plan it, manage it, change it.* Boston: Cahners Books.

Carlson, R. O. (1972). *School superintendents: Careers and performance.* Columbus, OH: Charles E. Merrill.

Graen, G. B. (1989). *Unwritten rules for your career.* New York: John Wiley & Sons.

Hollis, J. W., & Hollis, L. U. (1976). *Career and life planning.* Muncie, IN: Accelerated Development.

Lyon, D. W., & Kirby, E. G. (2000). The career planning essay. *Journal of Management Education, 24*(2), 276–287.

Manter, M. A., & Benjamin, J. V. (1989). How to hold on to first careerists. *Personnel Administrator, 34*(9), 44–48.

McCleary, L. E., & Ogawa, R. T. (1985). Locating principals who are leaders: The assessment center concept. *Educational Horizons, 12*(3), 7–11.

Miklos, E. (1988). Administrator selection, career patterns, succession, and socialization. In N. Boyan (Ed.), *Handbook of research on educational administration* (pp. 53–76). New York: Longman.

Orlosky, D. E., McCleary, L. E., Shapiro, A., & Webb, L. D. (1984). *Educational administration today.* Columbus, OH: Charles E. Merrill.

Pedler, M. (1988). Applying self-development in organizations. *Industrial and Commercial Training, 20*(2), 19–22.

Pond, B. N., Burdick, S. E., & Yamamoto, J. K. (1998). Portfolios: Transitioning to the future. *Business Education Forum, 52*(4), 50–54.

Ramsey, K. (1997). Domestic relationships of the superintendency. *School Administrator, 54*(2), 34–36, 38, 40.

Sirotnik, K. A., & Durden, P. C. (1996). The validity of administrator performance assessment systems: The ADI as a case-in-point. *Educational Administration Quarterly, 32*(4), 539–564.

Spokane, A. R. (1991). *Career intervention.* Englewood Cliffs, NJ: Prentice-Hall.

Steele, J. E., & Morgan, M. S. (1991). *Career planning and development for college students and recent graduates.* Lincolnwood, IL: VGM Career Horizons.

Vondracek, F. W., Lerner, R. M., & Schulenberg, J. E. (1986). *Career development: A life-span development approach.* Hillsdale, NJ: Lawrence Erlbaum.

Zunker, V. G. (1990). *Career counseling: Applied concepts of life planning* (3rd ed.). Pacific Grove, CA: Brooks/Cole.

Author Index

Subject Index